To Derek,

With thanks for all your help, support and friendship over the years...

All best wishes

[signature]

11. 5. xvii

JOYCE'S DANTE

Joyce's engagement with Dante is a crucial component of all of his work. This title reconsiders the responses to Dante in Joyce's work from *A Portrait of the Artist as a Young Man* to *Finnegans Wake*. It presents that encounter as a historically complex and contextually determined interaction reflecting the contested development of Dante's reputation, readership and textuality throughout the nineteenth century. This process produced a 'Dante with a difference', a uniquely creative and unorthodox construction of the poet that informed Joyce's lifelong engagement with such works as the *Vita Nuova* and the *Commedia*. Tracing the movement through Joyce's writing on exile as a mode of alienation and charting his growing interest in ideas of community, *Joyce's Dante* shows how awareness of his changing reading of Dante can alter our understanding of one of the Irish writer's lasting thematic preoccupations.

JAMES ROBINSON is Leverhulme Early Career Fellow, Department of English Studies at Durham University.

JOYCE'S DANTE

Exile, Memory, and Community

JAMES ROBINSON

CAMBRIDGE
UNIVERSITY PRESS

One Liberty Plaza 20th Floor, New York NY 10006, USA

Cambridge University Press is part of the University of Cambridge.

It furthers the University's mission by disseminating knowledge in the pursuit of education, learning and research at the highest international levels of excellence.

www.cambridge.org
Information on this title: www.cambridge.org/9781107167414

© James Robinson 2016

This publication is in copyright. Subject to statutory exception and to the provisions of relevant collective licensing agreements, no reproduction of any part may take place without the written permission of Cambridge University Press.

First published 2016

Printed in the United Kingdom by Clays, St Ives plc

A catalogue record for this publication is available from the British Library.

Library of Congress Cataloging-in-Publication Data
Names: Robinson, James, 1984– author.
Title: Joyce's Dante : exile, memory, and community / James Robinson.
Description: New York : Cambridge University Press, 2016. |
Includes bibliographical references and index.
Identifiers: LCCN 2016021105 | ISBN 9781107167414 (hardback)
Subjects: LCSH: Joyce, James, 1882–1941–Criticism and interpretation. |
Dante Alighieri, 1265–1321–Influence. | Exiles in literature. |
Memory in literature. | Community in literature. |
BISAC: LITERARY CRITICISM / European / English, Irish, Scottish, Welsh.
Classification: LCC PR6019.O9 Z78484 2016 | DDC 823/.912–dc23
LC record available at https://lccn.loc.gov/2016021105

ISBN 978-1-107-16741-4 Hardback

Cambridge University Press has no responsibility for the persistence or accuracy of URLs for external or third-party Internet Web sites referred to in this publication and does not guarantee that any content on such Web sites is, or will remain, accurate or appropriate.

For Zoë and for Nick

Contents

Acknowledgements		*page* viii
Note on Texts and Editions		x
	Introduction	1
1	Uneasy Orthodoxy: Dante, the Jesuits and Joyce's First Reading	11
2	'Spiritual-heroic Refrigerating Apparatus': The Exiles of Dante in *A Portrait of the Artist as a Young Man* and *Exiles*	37
3	The Poetics of Infernal Metamorphosis: Stephen's Representation in 'Proteus' and 'Scylla and Charybdis'	81
4	The Mothering of Memory: 'Circe' and the Dantean Poetics of Re-membering	123
5	'The Flower that Stars the Day': Issy, Dantean Femininity and the Family as Community in *Finnegans Wake*	161
	Epilogue	206
Bibliography		211
Index		227

Acknowledgements

The Arts and Humanities Research Council supported the earliest stage of my research through the grant of a Doctoral Award, and the Leverhulme Trust have supported its completion through their award of an Early Career Fellowship.

I am very thankful for the help and encouragement of teachers, colleagues and friends at the Universities of York, East Anglia and Durham, most particularly John Nash, Tom Rutledge, Matt Taunton and Lawrence Rainey. And I have been assisted throughout by the helpful staff of Archbishop Marsh's Library, the National Library of Ireland, the Bodleian Library and the library of the Taylor Institution, Oxford.

My thanks are also due to my editor Ray Ryan, and to all the staff at Cambridge University Press for their help throughout production. I would also like to thank the anonymous readers for Cambridge University Press whose comments and criticisms helped me write a much better book.

My friends and family – particularly my parents – have been a constant source of support and encouragement throughout the many years spent on this project, and I am very thankful for all their kindness and understanding.

Piero Boitani, who examined my PhD thesis, has supported and encouraged my work for many years and has proved himself an unflagging writer of references.

Vicki Mahaffey co-supervised the earliest stages of this project, and without her encouragement and kindness to a medievalist 'lost in the bush' of Joyce Studies, I never would have found my way out again.

Derek Attridge took over co-supervision of my PhD at York, and has been unfailingly kind, perceptive and supportive of my work and career ever since. Without his advice, wisdom and continual encouragement I would not have written this book.

Acknowledgements

The debt of thanks that all who study Dante's 'modern afterlife' owe to Nick Havely is readily apparent from my bibliography, but my own debts are far greater. Ever since he met a lapsed archaeologist entering in on the 'cammino alto e silvestro', Nick has been an inexhaustible source of kindness, support, inspiration and help (not least in reading and commenting on the whole of the manuscript of this book). I am deeply thankful for his friendship, and hope that my dedication goes a small way towards acknowledging the depths of my gratitude. I am also very grateful for the unflagging support and encouragement of Cicely Palser Havely.

My final and deepest thanks are owed to my wife, Zoë Robinson, who – along with our 'pussens' Samwise – has been loving, understanding and patient over many years.

Note on Texts and Editions

The following abbreviations and editions have been used throughout the text:

D	James Joyce, *Dubliners*, ed. Hans Walter Gabler with Walter Heche (New York, 1993). References are to sequential number of story and line number.
E	James Joyce, *Exiles* (Harmondsworth, 1973). References are to page number.
FW	James Joyce, *Finnegans Wake* (London, 1968). References are to page and line number.
L	James Joyce, *Letters*, ed. Stuart Gilbert and Richard Ellmann, 3 vols. (New York, 1957–1966). References are to volume and page number.
OCPW	James Joyce, *Occasional, Critical, and Political Writing*, ed. Kevin Barry (Oxford, 2000). References are to page number.
P	James Joyce, *A Portrait of the Artist as a Young Man*, ed. Hans Walter Gabler with Walter Heche (New York, 1993). References are to chapter number and line number.
SH	James Joyce, *Stephen Hero*, ed. Theodore Spencer, John J. Slocum and Herbert Cahoon (London, 1977). References are to page number.
SL	James Joyce, *Selected Letters*, ed. Richard Ellmann (London, 1975). References are to page number.
U	James Joyce, *Ulysses: The Corrected Text*, ed. Hans Walter Gabler with Wolfhard Steppe and Claus Melchior (London, 1986). References are to episode and line number.
JJ	Richard Ellmann, *James Joyce*, revised edition (Oxford, 1982). References are to page number.
Conv.	Dante Alighieri, *Tutte le opere di Dante Alighieri*, ed. Edward Moore (Oxford, 1894), 235–338. English translations of *The Convivio* are taken from Dante Alighieri, *The Convivio*, trans. Richard Lansing, http://dante.ilt.columbia.edu/books/convivi. References are to book, chapter and sentence number.

Inf.   Dante Alighieri, *La Divina Commedia di Dante Alighieri con note tratte dai migliori commenti*, ed. Eugenio Camerini (Milan, 1904). English translations of the *Inferno* are taken from Dante Alighieri, *The Divine Comedy of Dante Alighieri, vol. 1, Inferno*, ed. and trans. Robert M. Durling (Oxford, 1996). References are to canto and line number.

Par.   Dante Alighieri, *La Divina Commedia di Dante Alighieri con note tratte dai migliori commenti*, ed. Eugenio Camerini (Milan, 1904). English translations of the *Paradiso* are taken from Dante Alighieri, *The Divine Comedy of Dante Alighieri, vol. 3, Paradiso*, ed. and trans. Robert M. Durling (Oxford, 2011). References are to canto and line number.

Purg.   Dante Alighieri, *La Divina Commedia di Dante Alighieri con note tratte dai migliori commenti*, ed. Eugenio Camerini (Milan, 1904). English translations of the *Purgatorio* are taken from Dante Alighieri, *The Divine Comedy of Dante Alighieri, vol. 2, Purgatorio*, ed. and trans. Robert M. Durling (Oxford, 2003). References are to canto and line number.

VN   Dante Alighieri, *La Vita Nova di Dante Alighieri illustrata dei quadri di Dante Gabriele Rossetti*. ed. Marco de Rubris (Turin: Società Tipografica-Editrice Nazionale, 1911). English translations of the *Vita Nuova* are taken from Dante Alighieri, *Vita Nuova*, trans. Mark Musa (Oxford, 1999). References are to chapter and sentence number.

All other quotations from Dante's works are taken from Dante Alighieri, *Tutte le opere di Dante Alighieri*, ed. Edward Moore (Oxford, 1894). Translations of poetry are taken from Dante Alighieri, *Dante's Lyric Poetry*, ed. and trans. Kenelm Foster and Patrick Boyde, 2 vols. (Oxford, 1967). References are to Moore's lyric and line numbering. Translations of letters are taken from Dante Alighieri, *Dantis Alagherii Epistolae: The Letters of Dante*, ed. and trans. Paget Toynbee (Oxford, 1920). References are to Moore's numbering of the letters and line number.

All further translations from Italian are my own, unless otherwise stated.

Introduction

Towards the end of the fourth chapter of *A Portrait of the Artist as a Young Man*, Stephen Dedalus is walking nervously by the sea. Waiting to hear about his entry to the University, he shuttles between two symbols of competing orthodoxies: '[f]rom the door of Byron's publichouse to the gate of Clontarf chapel, from the gate of Clontarf chapel to the door of Byron's publichouse' (*P* IV. 607–9). Unable to endure the wait any longer, Stephen walks out to the North Wall, from where he sees a young girl standing in the rivulet running down through the strand:

> She was alone and still, gazing out to sea; and when she felt his presence and the worship of his eyes her eyes turned to him in quiet sufferance of his gaze, without shame or wantonness. Long, long she suffered his gaze and then quietly withdrew her eyes from his and bent them towards the stream, gently stirring the water with her foot hither and thither. (*P* IV. 867–75)

In this moment of watching and reflection, another ethereal girl is turning, moving 'hither and thither' on the edge of a stream:

> Volsesi in su' vermigli ed in su' gialli
> Fioretti verso me, non altrimenti
> Che vergine, che gli occhi onesti avvalli:
> E fece i preghi miei esser contenti,
> Si appressando sè, che il dolce suono
> Veniva a me, co' suoi intendimenti.
> Tosto che fu là dove l'erbe sono
> Bagnate già dall'onde del bel fiume,
> Di levar gli occhi suoi mi fece dono.

> [so she turned on the crimson and yellow flowers toward me, not otherwise than a virgin who lowers her modest eyes, and she contented my prayers, drawing so near that the sweet sound reached me with its meanings. As soon as she was where the grass is already bathed by the lovely river, she made me the gift of raising her eyes.] (Purg. 28. 55–63)

The intertextual resonance between James Joyce's 'bird-girl' and the dancing figure of Matelda, whom the protagonist of the *Commedia* meets in the Earthly Paradise on the banks of the river Lethe, is one testament to Joyce's lifelong engagement with Dante. And in the imagery of religious life, liberation, secularism and Romantic poetry that surrounds the encounter, we find some of the contextual terms of competing orthodoxy, narrative trajectory and literary mediation that would characterise this relationship.

Joyce's interest in Dante began early, long before the *Portrait* was conceived of, or any of the other texts that attest to their relationship had been written. Indeed, such was the fervour with which Joyce proselytised his reading of Dante whilst attending University College Dublin that his peers christened him 'Dublin's Dante, a Dante with a difference'.[1] This witticism – which Richard Ellmann attributed to Oliver St John Gogarty (*JJ* 75, 131) – raises an interesting question: was there a 'difference' in Joyce's Dante? We're more used to seeing Dante as undifferentiated, a monolithic and overwhelmingly canonical presence; a medieval monument at the heart of Western literature, so much part of the scenery that it can be difficult to remember that he was ever built in the first place, let alone to trace the cultural processes of his construction.[2] The Dante who, to John Ruskin and the nineteenth century, was 'the central man of all the world' remains largely in-post today, and he has been the subject of literary, political, religious and cultural conversation (a conversation that has oftentimes descended into open argument) for nearly seven hundred years.[3] So which Dante did Joyce read and engage with throughout his career? Was it the medieval monument or the contested conversationalist?

For other modernist writers, Dante was certainly the monument man. To T.S. Eliot he was 'the most *universal* of poets in the modern languages', the bedrock on which European literature rested, and – in the *Commedia* – the author of a 'vast metaphor' that embraced all aspects of the intellectual and linguistic climate of a medieval Europe 'mentally

---

[1] W. K. Magee, 'The Beginnings of Joyce', 201.
[2] As Albert Ascoli has observed of Dante and the *Commedia*: 'No work is more central to the Western canon and the educational and cultural apparatus that still actively propounds it [...] no author possesses more "cultural capital"', *Dante and the Making of a Modern Author*, 1. For a superlative discussion of these processes of cultural construction within Dante's British readerships see Nick Havely, *Dante's British Public: Readers and Texts from the Fourteenth Century to the Present*.
[3] John Ruskin, *The Works of John Ruskin*, vol. 11, 187; for a discussion of Ruskin's engagement with Dante see Alison Milbank, *Dante and the Victorians*, 29–44. On the term 'conversation' as characterising ongoing reactions to Dante see Havely, *Dante's British Public*, xiv.

Introduction 3

more united than we can now conceive'.[4] As Seamus Heaney put it, for Eliot Dante 'walks in the aura of cultural history and representativeness'.[5] Equally, Ezra Pound's reaction to Dante was rooted in veneration and emulation in the shadow of the monolith, with *The Cantos* cast as the successor to the *Commedia* and the summation of Pound's lifelong wish to write a Dantean 'epic of judgement'.[6] For Pound, Dante was an overwhelming and institutional presence whose example was implicated in his plans for an 'American *risorgimento*' and national cultural renewal on the grandest scale.[7] And yet, before the poet could be drawn more fully into Pound's own poetic practice, he needed to reconfigure Dante into a more approachable form, a transfiguration achieved through the alternative canonicity Pound constructed around Guido Cavalcanti, that other *trecento* poet who was 'much more "modern" than his young friend Dante'.[8]

Yet it's long been acknowledged that Joyce's engagement with Dante differed significantly from these other modernists, that Joyce's Dante really was a 'Dante with a difference'.[9] One perennially popular explanation for this difference is the belief that Joyce could somehow enter straight into the heart of the Dantean monument. In the most lastingly influential statement of this position, Umberto Eco identified the 'presence of medieval patterns in the mental economy of our author'.[10] This sense that Joyce was in some way 'medievally minded' – that he possessed an innate 'medievalism' – is based on a structural parallel that Eco saw between Joyce's thought and an abstract model of the 'medieval': 'If you take away the transcendent God from the symbolic world of the Middle Ages, you have the world of Joyce.'[11] The move that Eco thus makes to put Joyce into direct contact with the 'medieval' can only be called radically subtractive: as

---

[4] T. S. Eliot, *Dante*, 9, 17,11. For discussion of Eliot's position in this essay of 1929 see Steve Ellis, *Dante and English Poetry: Shelley to T.S. Eliot*, 210–14; and Dominic Manganiello, *T.S. Eliot and Dante*, 11–16.
[5] Seamus Heaney, 'Envies and Identifications: Dante and the Modern Poet', 14.
[6] See Heaney, 'Envies and Identifications', 16; Reed W. Dasenbrock, *Imitating the Italians: Wyatt, Spenser, Synge, Pound, Joyce*, 212; Stephen Sicari, *Pound's Epic Ambition: Dante and the Modern World*, x–xii; and A. David Moody, *Ezra Pound: Poet*, vol. 1, *The Young Genius 1885–1920*, 46–9.
[7] See Moody, *Ezra Pound*, 130–3.
[8] Ezra Pound, *Literary Essays of Ezra Pound*, 149. On Pound's use of Cavalcanti see Maria L. Ardizzone, *Guido Cavalcanti: The Other Middle Ages*, 134–5; and James J. Wilhelm, *Dante and Pound: The Epic of Judgement*, 69–70. For a discussion of Pound's Dantean reading of Cavalcanti (and Cavalcantian reading of Dante) see Milbank, *Dante and the Victorians*, 233–6.
[9] On Joyce's difference see Lucia Boldrini, 'Introduction: Middayevil Joyce', 25–7; Dasenbrock, *Imitating the Italians*, 126; and Milbank, *Dante and the Victorians*, 238–9.
[10] Umberto Eco, *The Middle Ages of James Joyce: The Aesthetics of Chaosmos*, 7.
[11] Eco, *Middle Ages of James Joyce*, 7. For a range of resultant readings of Joyce's response to the medieval, see Lucia Boldrini (ed.), *Medieval Joyce*.

well as 'taking away' the notion of God, Eco effectively deletes the intervening six hundred years between the worlds of Joyce and Dante.

It is one aim of this study to put back those six hundred years, placing the slow, accretive and contested development of Dante's reputation, readership, personae and texts at the heart of our understanding of Joyce's relationship with the poet. Joyce's Dante *was* a 'Dante with a difference', most particularly because the terms of their first encounter in Joyce's youth were determinedly non-monumental. Indeed, as the first chapter will demonstrate, Dante's contestation by the prevailing orthodoxies of nineteenth-century Dublin was such that Joyce could not help but be acutely aware of the processes of erection – and thus the subsequent ease of deconstruction – of any Dantean monument. In resisting the urge to monumentalise, we can instead conceive of Joyce's engagement with Dante not as the meeting of medieval and modernist masters (or even 'modern' medieval or 'medieval' modernist), but as a historically complex and contextually determined interaction. The Dante who Joyce first read during his schooldays was a fundamentally nineteenth-century figure, and one who was subject to unusually intense political, religious and literary discourses that would determine the course of Joyce's lifelong engagement. However, this is not to claim that, for Joyce, Dante was not a medieval writer but rather to emphasise that when Joyce read Dante he was, crucially, always reading *through* the nineteenth century and the circumstances of their first encounter.[12] In this way, it will become clear that Joyce's Dante was not a monument to align with, or an authority to invoke, but rather a partner and 'collaborator' in a creative project.

In writing about Joyce's engagement with Dante, I am very much aware that I am walking a well-trodden path: ever since Samuel Beckett warned us that 'the danger is in the neatness of identifications', Joyce's readers have been discussing this relationship.[13] The intertextual presence of Dante has thus become something of an accepted premise in Joycean criticism, and has been the subject of many discussions, and included within the scope of many more.[14] This book benefits immeasurably from that wealth

---

[12] In this respect, my approach develops Lucia Boldrini's discussion of the role of Romantic and Victorian 'medievalisms' in determining Joyce's approach to the Middle Ages, see 'Introduction: Middayevil Joyce', 17–27.
[13] Samuel Beckett, 'Dante … Bruno. Vico … Joyce', 5. On Beckett's essay in relation to *Finnegans Wake* see Lucia Boldrini, *Joyce, Dante, and the Poetics of Literary Relations: Language and Meaning in 'Finnegans Wake'*, 15–25. For a discussion in the context of the modern reception of Dante's *De Vulgari Eloquentia* see Iman Javadi, 'The English Reception of Dante's *De Vulgari Eloquentia*', 301–3.
[14] Examples of readings that place Joyce within wider studies of Dante and Italian literary culture include Milbank, *Dante and the Victorians*, 238–9; and Dasenbrock, *Imitating the Italians*, 125–6, 209–19.

Introduction 5

of discussion, but two particular studies have proved invaluable. In what was the first full-length study of Joyce's relationship with Dante, Mary Reynolds revealed the wide scope of the engagement, uncovering a range of quotations and allusions to the *Vita Nuova* and the *Commedia* within works from *Stephen Hero* to *Finnegans Wake*. Reynolds advanced a number of comprehensive arguments for seeing Dante's texts as operating as structuring devices within Joyce's works, and emphasised his persistent interest in a number of Dantean themes. Indeed, Reynolds saw within Joyce's intertextual engagement 'a reasoned critical view of Dante's art, which he embodied in his fiction and did not otherwise express'.[15] Whilst today this kind of structural reading may seem a little problematic, Reynolds's study remains an important source that will be drawn on throughout our discussion. More recently, Lucia Boldrini has made a perceptive and stimulating study of the influence of Dante on the poetics of *Finnegans Wake*, in which she argues, not that 'the *Wake* was written according to a notion of poetics arrived at, practised or theorized by Dante and which Joyce adhered to, but that there is *a* poetics of *Finnegans Wake* [...] which is comparable to the poetics of Dante's work'.[16] In following this nuanced line of argument, Boldrini not only convincingly shows Dante's importance to the *Wake* but also offers intertextual readings with substantial implications for Joyce's other texts, particularly *Ulysses*.[17]

In its concern with contextualising Joyce's engagement and seeing his interaction with Dante taking place within a historical discourse, this study will take a different line from either Reynolds or Boldrini, and where the discussion does touch upon similar material to these earlier studies (such as in the poetics of *Ulysses*), it will view them from a different perspective. In this respect, this book is positioned to take advantage of a number of recent developments in scholarship and approach. One such development is the wealth of new manuscript material now available for the study of Joyce's writing; thanks to this expanding resource, we will for the first time be able to draw the documentary evidence of Joyce's first reading of Dante into a wider study of his Dantean engagements. This manuscript evidence of Joyce's early reading reflects the importance of relocating our view of his relationship with Dante within its textual context. Thus, every

---

[15] Mary Reynolds, *Joyce and Dante: The Shaping Imagination*, 3–4.
[16] Boldrini, *Joyce, Dante*, 13.
[17] Other notable studies of Joyce's relationship with Dante include Howard Helsinger, 'Joyce and Dante', 591–601; and Dominic Manganiello, *Joyce's Politics*, 190–202. Studies that parallel the canons of Joyce and Dante include Gian Balsamo, *Joyce's Messianism: Dante, Negative Existence and the Messianic Self*; Jennifer Fraser, *Rite of Passage in the Narratives of Dante and Joyce*; and Sam Slote, *The Silence in Progress of Dante, Mallarmé, and Joyce*.

quotation from Dante in this book will be drawn – in the case of the *Vita Nuova* and the *Commedia* – from the editions Joyce is known to have owned and used, or – in the case of the so-called *opere minori* – from Edward Moore's contemporary edition of he complete works (1894), and at points throughout we will engage closely with the material textuality of Joyce's Dantean texts. In contextualising and historicising Joyce's reading, this book joins a growing number of Joycean studies that are returning to the cultural and social contexts of Joyce's youth, and unearthing stimulating readings of his work through this historical discourse.[18] Finally, the discussion will take full advantage of the remarkable recent developments in the study of Dante. Such is Joyce's dominance in 'modern' literary studies that it's sometimes hard to see him as part of a larger 'conversation'; however, in recent years the study of Dante's 'modern afterlife' has intensified, and Dante's nineteenth-century appropriations and interpretations are being more fully understood and lucidly discussed than ever before.[19] Thus in re-contextualising Joyce's relationship with a 'nineteenth-century' Dante, this study will be seeking to further draw Joyce into the conversation around Dante, as well as drawing Dante more fully into a reading of Joyce.

With the benefit of these developments in scholarship and textual material, this book will seek to trace a trajectory through Joyce's reading of Dante. Whereas a study like Reynolds's positioned Dante as a structuring parallel for all of Joyce's work, I make no such comprehensive claims; the sheer breadth of Dantean material, and the lifelong nature of Joyce's engagement with the poet, offers ample reason to question any totalising reading of their relationship. Indeed, it is one hope of this study that, by re-visiting the presence of Dante within Joyce's work from a contextual perspective, it might stimulate further discussion and reappraisal of this central intertextual engagement. In this respect, the partiality of the term 'trajectory' commends itself: we will be taking one possible path through Joyce's Dantean engagement, of which there are many others equally traversable. However, as the first chapter shows, the trajectory of this study

---

[18] See Roy Gottfried, *Joyce's Misbelief* and Geert Lernout, '*Help My Unbelief': James Joyce & Religion* for two examples of contrasting, contextual readings of Joyce's attitude to religious faith.

[19] For examples of some of the most important work on Dante's nineteenth-century and 'modern' reception see Ellis, *Dante and English Poetry*, 3–139; Milbank, *Dante and the Victorians*; Julia Straub, *A Victorian Muse: The Afterlife of Dante's Beatrice in Nineteenth-Century Literature*; Havely, *Dante's British Public*, 128–259; Nick Havely (ed.), *Dante's Modern Afterlife: Reception and Response from Blake to Heaney*; Nick Havely (ed.), *Dante in the Nineteenth Century: Reception, Canonicity, Popularization*; Aida Audeh and Nick Havely (eds.), *Dante in the Long Nineteenth Century: Nationality, Identity and Appropriation*.

arises out of the circumstances of Joyce's first reading of Dante, and (as reflected in the subtitle to this book) traces a movement through Joyce's writing on a key thematic concern: his exploration of exile as a mode of alienation and his growing interest in ideas of community.

In discussing exile we will thus be considering a well-worn topic of Joyce criticism, most prominently addressed through Hélène Cixous's monumental study, but a subject that remains a continuing concern in scholarship today.[20] Previous critics have already paralleled Joyce's self-imposed 'exile' from Dublin with Dante's experience of politically inflicted exile from Florence; however, the path through Joyce's writing on exile and alienation that his Dantean reading will allow us to chart will come to condition and unsettle some of these earlier discussions.[21] By seeing Joyce's exilic discourse as unfolding throughout the course of his work in tandem with his developing conception of Dante, it will be possible to clarify Joyce's growing scepticism towards his early thoughts on exile, explore his discovery of a creative form of textual memory and chart the emerging co-implication of ideas of community and belonging within his exilic writing. In this respect, following an itinerary of exile and community through Joyce's Dantean engagement will reveal the potential for a re-contextualised sense of Joyce's reading to alter our understanding of this central literary relationship and of one of his lasting thematic and rhetorical preoccupations.

Contrary to the view that Dante's importance to Joyce diminished with time, or that his interest represented a 'Dante phase', Joyce's engagement with the poet was – as Boldrini and Reynolds have shown – truly life-long, and thus this study will offer substantial readings of works from *A Portrait of the Artist as a Young Man* to *Exiles*, *Ulysses* and *Finnegans Wake*.[22] Discussion of these works is not intended to offer a comprehensive survey of Joyce's oeuvre, but a particular itinerary through it, and one that originates in the terms of his earliest Dantean engagement. This particularity can easily account for the omission of *Dubliners* as a focus of discussion: whilst in stories like 'Eveline' and 'A Little Cloud' departure from Dublin figures prominently, there is no such explicit framing of these departures within the mode of 'exile' as we find in *A Portrait of the Artist*

---

[20] See Hélène Cixous, *Exile of James Joyce*; for more recent discussions of exile in Joyce's work see Joseph Kelly, 'Joyce's Exile: The Prodigal Son', 603–35; and Wim van Mierlo, 'The Greater Ireland Beyond the Sea: James Joyce, Exile, and Irish Emigration', 178–97.
[21] See Manganiello, *Joyce's Politics*, 190–202.
[22] On the 'waning' of Dante see Nino Frank, 'The Shadow That Had Lost Its Man', 80. On Joyce's supposed 'Dante phase' of 1903–6 see Cixous, *Exile of James Joyce*, 38.

as a Young Man.[23] However, the question of *Dubliners* and its relation to the trajectory of Joyce's Dantean engagement raises a further important methodological point.

The view that *Dubliners* is structured by an intertextual parallel with the *Inferno* – originating in Stanislaus Joyce's reading of 'Grace' – was significantly developed by Mary Reynolds, and has become a critical commonplace.[24] Recently, some readers have started to challenge Stanislaus's sense of the parodic structure of 'Grace', and whilst exploration of Dantean intertexts can continue to produce interesting readings, I would tend to share this scepticism.[25] For example, in reading the opening line of 'The Sisters': 'There was no hope for him this time: it was the third stroke' (*D* 1. 1), belief in the structural influence of the *Inferno* has led to seeing this sentence as a deliberate paralleling of the final lines inscribed above the Gates of Hell in the *Inferno*: ' "Lasciate ogni speranza, voi, ch' entrate!" ' ["Abandon every hope, you who enter!" '] (*Inf.* 3. 9). Quite apart from the apparent 'misalignment' of the opening of *Dubliners*' first story with the close of the incipit of the *Commedia*'s third canto, we must admit on reflection that in all grammatical aspects of the sentences there is no similarity, and in actuality only a single resonant word: 'hope' and 'speranza'.

My scepticism about the teleological formulation of Dantean readings of *Dubliners* raises the question of the forms of intertextuality considered in this study. The focus of discussion will be on an array of intertextual intersections and resonances with Dante's works. The idea of resonance, with its interconnected senses of sympathetic vibration, 'sounding again' and of a placement within a spectrum, is key to the model of intertextuality I will be utilising. This discussion of Joyce's engagement with Dante will not take the form of a source-study or model of influence, nor represent an attempt to advance new theories of the operation of Joycean modes of intertextuality. Sometimes the resonances we explore will be of such a strong 'frequency' that they can be characterised through a source or influence relation, but at other times they will represent a softer, illuminating rhythm. By contextualising Joyce's reading of Dante and following

---

[23] Although Katherine Mullin has shown how in 'Eveline' Joyce drew on the rhetoric of economic emigration figured as exile, see 'Don't Cry for Me, Argentina: "Eveline" and the Seductions of Emigration Propaganda', 172–200.
[24] See Reynolds, *Joyce and Dante*, 156–9, 236–47.
[25] See Lernout, '*Help My Unbelief*', 128; and Lucia Boldrini, 'The Artist Paring His Quotations: Aesthetic and Ethical Implications of the Dantean Intertext in *Dubliners*', 228–48.

an emergent trajectory through this engagement, we will both re-visit familiar intersections and uncover a range of new intertextual resonances of varying frequencies and significances.

Given the aims of this book to relocate Joyce's reading of Dante within a number of contexts, the structure of the discussion will be largely chronological.

Chapter 1 lays out the historical, cultural, educational and textual contexts in which Joyce first encountered Dante, and to which subsequent chapters will return. It explores the ways in which Dante's contestation by competing Catholic and secular orthodoxies within Joyce's Jesuit classroom established the liminal terms of his lifelong engagement with the poet.

Chapter 2 then follows the trajectory established by Joyce's early reading and considers his engagement with Dante's conceptions of exile and alienation. Drawing on both the nineteenth-century political and literary discourses of Dante as a figure of exile, and the manifestation of exile within such works as the *Vita Nuova*, the chapter shows how these Dantean traditions of 'heroic' and 'spiritual' exile determined the processes of self-fashioning alienation that Joyce explored within *A Portrait of the Artist as a Young Man* and *Exiles*.

Chapters 3 and 4 are concerned with the presence of Dante within the poetics of *Ulysses*. The first part of this discussion explores the ways in which Dante's process of 'Infernal metamorphosis' circumscribes the representation of Stephen Dedalus in the 'Proteus' and 'Scylla and Charybdis' chapters. Drawing on a range of intertextual resonances with Dante and other *trecento* authors, the third chapter shows how these Dantean poetics emphasise Joyce's growing scepticism towards exile, as expressed through Stephen's continual implication within a form of textual 'community'. Chapter 4 then considers the resonance between the poetics of 'Circe' and Dante's poetics of creative memory. Exploring the forms of textuality that Joyce encountered in the *Vita Nuova*, the chapter shows how Dante's memorative poetics can offer a reading of 'Circe' that reconceptualises the relation of the chapter to the rest of *Ulysses*, and alters our understanding of the operation of narrative and history throughout Joyce's novel.

Chapter 5 completes the trajectory of the study by further addressing the issues of interconnection and involvement raised in relation to *Ulysses*, through a discussion of the role of Issy in the family of *Finnegans Wake*. Exploring Issy's manifestation of a unique form of femininity intertextually conditioned by Joyce's reading of Dante's lyric poetry, this chapter demonstrates the *Wake*'s ultimate rejection of exile and withdrawal in favour of compromised participation and involvement in community.

Having thus arrived in the course of five chapters at a fuller sense of the contextual dynamics of Joyce's engagement with Dante, the Epilogue will address a final question. Did Joyce's Dante – this 'Dante with a difference' – have a life after Joyce?

CHAPTER I

Uneasy Orthodoxy
Dante, the Jesuits and Joyce's First Reading

Dante in the Classroom: Contextualising the First Encounter

The earliest documentary evidence for Joyce's reading of Dante comprises some twenty-eight notesheets now residing in the National Library of Ireland.[1] These notes, covering the first twenty-five cantos of *Inferno*, seem to record the reading of a schoolboy still grappling with the fundamentals of both the Italian language and Dantean exegesis. For instance, Joyce provides (often incorrect) English glosses on words such as 'pale' (which he gives as 'wings'), 'cappe' ['gown'] and 'cappuccio' ['hood'], and observes in his preparatory 'Notazioni' that the 'nomi venerabili' of God, Beatrice and Dante himself 'non si pronunziano nell'inferno' ['are not spoken in Hell'].[2] Accordingly, the notesheets have been dated by Dirk van Hulle to between 1897 and 1898, placing Joyce's first substantiated contact with Dante in his final two school years at Belvedere College, an encounter that had previously been firmly associated with Joyce's entrance into University College Dublin in 1899.[3] The NLI notesheets thus indicate the way in which re-contextualising Joyce's early engagement with Dante can reshape our understanding of their ongoing relationship. By reducing biographical reliance on the narrative of *Stephen Hero* and putting the encounter back in the classroom of Belvedere College, the NLI notes in turn emphasise the central importance of the Society of Jesus as an influence on Joyce's reading.

As a middle-class, Catholic schoolboy in late nineteenth-century Dublin, Joyce first read Dante within a range of complex historical,

---

[1] Dublin, National Library of Ireland, Joyce Papers 2002 MS 36,639/1, ff. 1r–28v.
[2] For Joyce's gloss on these words in *Inferno* 23 see NLI MS 36,639/1, f. 24r; for Joyce's 'Notazioni' see NLI MS 36,639/1, f. 1r.
[3] See Dirk van Hulle, *Joyce & Beckett: Discovering Dante*, 2. Mary Reynolds held that Joyce first read Dante immediately upon entering University College Dublin, leading to the view that Joyce's 'first serious interest in Dante' was sparked at University College Dublin in 1899, and that *Stephen Hero* (*SH* 152) represents a 'record' of this interest; see *Joyce and Dante*, 20–2.

spiritual and cultural contexts; contexts that were, in his case, largely dominated by the influence of the Jesuits. With the exception of a brief time with the Christian Brothers, all of the educational institutions that Joyce attended were, to a greater or lesser extent, controlled and run by the Society. From his first, affluent school of Clongowes Wood, to his later days at Belvedere College, and finally in his years at University College, the Jesuits were a constant, determining influence on Joyce's intellectual development, and one on which he would later look back with some gratitude.[4] Accordingly, the role the Jesuits played in Joyce's education has long been a subject of critical interest, and it now presents an important new avenue for considering his engagement with Dante.[5] For, whether Joyce first read Dante at school as we now suspect, or at university as was once thought, the importance of the Jesuits, not only as Joyce's educators but also as the mediators of his initial contact with Dante, seems clear. However, the form of this mediation was decidedly complex.

In briefly addressing the Jesuitical presentation of Dante and its potential impact upon Joyce, Mary Reynolds claimed that:

> Joyce's Dante, however, was not the Dante of his day, who had become something of an establishment figure. On one side were Joyce's Jesuit teachers: the Church had long since adopted the *Divine Comedy* as its own instrument in defense of a narrow orthodoxy. On the other side were the serious students of the *Divine Comedy* in England (in Dublin there was no counterpart of the Oxford Dante Society), where the work of Moore and Toynbee had brought explication a long way.[6]

Reynolds's perceptive sense of Dante as being under discussion by contrasting 'establishments' begins to open up a sense of the complexity of Dante's late nineteenth-century portrayal, suggesting the political, religious and literary-critical discourses that would all have intersected in the presentation of Dante within Joyce's Jesuit classroom. On one hand, Reynolds draws out the institutionalisation of Dante, both by the Roman Catholic Church and by the secular literary establishment of the Oxford Dante Society; whilst on the other she hints at an ongoing discourse of appropriation and reappropriation within his nineteenth-century presentation. This first chapter of our discussion will show the ways in which the experience

---

[4] In a letter to Valery Larbaud written in 1923, Joyce attributed his work ethic to the 'influence of *ad maiorem dei gloriam*, perhaps' (*L* III, 84), referring to the Jesuit motto.
[5] For overviews of Joyce's education by the Jesuits see Kevin Sullivan, *Joyce Among the Jesuits*; and Bruce Bradley, *James Joyce's Schooldays*.
[6] Reynolds, *Joyce and Dante*, 10–11.

of just such historical, social and critical discourses within Joyce's Jesuit education was crucial in establishing the character of his lasting, lifelong engagement with Dante. It will explore a range of historical, cultural, educational and textual contexts for Joyce's first reading of Dante, and locate Joyce within a wider discourse of orthodoxy and interpretation that characterised Dante's nineteenth-century personae. But, to start to contextualise Joyce's reading and the influence exerted on it by the Jesuits, we will necessarily have to travel a long way from late nineteenth-century Dublin.

'Indefatigable in Their Hostility': Dante and the Jesuits

The history of the Jesuit response to Dante is extremely long and complex, and stretches from the foundation of the Order in the sixteenth century, right up to the nationalising project of the Italian Risorgimento in the mid-nineteenth century and beyond, taking in issues of theology, philosophy, literary criticism and politics along the way. Indeed, the Jesuits' relation to Dante was instrumental in crystallising the so-called neo-Ghibelline and neo-Guelf schools of Dantean interpretation: the contrarily secularising and religious critical positions that helped create the two competing personae that were to define the poet's reputation throughout the nineteenth – and into the twentieth – century.[7] Therefore, whilst complicated, the history of the Jesuit attitude to Dante can't be ignored, if we wish to understand Dante's position within their classroom when Joyce encountered his work.

One of the earliest recorded examples of Jesuit interest in Dante comes from Reformation England, where Jesuits such as Robert Parsons were at the forefront of a rehabilitation project aimed at 'saving' Dante from his appropriation by Protestant polemicists, a project that established the character of ongoing attempts to 're-Catholicise' Dante.[8] However,

---

[7] The 'neo-Ghibelline' and 'neo-Guelf' interpretations of Dante were named by later Dante scholars using terms from the factional discord of Dante's Florence: the Ghibellines supported the Holy Roman Emperor and the Guelfs were (nominally) the pope's party. Dante himself belonged to the 'White' faction within the Guelfs, who, after their exile from Florence in 1302, sided with the Ghibellines in open opposition to the pope. Whilst the categorisation of secular readings of Dante as 'neo-Ghibelline' and religious (and particularly Catholic) readings as 'neo-Guelf' is somewhat reductive, these terms do serve to indicate the broad trends in late eighteenth-century and nineteenth-century Dante studies; see Michael Caesar, *Dante: The Critical Heritage: 1314(?)-1870*, 61–3; and Edoardo Crisafulli, *The Vision of Dante: Cary's Translation of 'The Divine Comedy'*, 268–9.

[8] For a detailed account of the Jesuits' role in countering the Protestant appropriation of Dante's *Monarchia* and *Paradiso* 29 see Nick Havely, ' "An Italian Writer Against the Pope"? Dante in Reformation England c. 1560–c. 1640', 127–49. For a wider account of sixteenth- and seventeenth-century polemical appropriations see Havely, *Dante's British Public*, 50–60, 62–4.

by the turn of the nineteenth century, this positive association between the Jesuits and the poet seems to have been largely forgotten; in the *Edinburgh Review* in 1818, Ugo Foscolo – the Italian novelist, poet and political exile – wrote that 'the Jesuits were indefatigable in their hostility to Dante'.[9] Even allowing for Foscolo's own 'neo-Ghibelline' critical predilections, his statement appears to indicate a striking *volte-face* in the perceived Jesuit attitude to the poet.[10] Was this apparent ambiguity in the Jesuit response to Dante reflected in the circumstances of Joyce's introduction to the poet? The answer is inevitably complex.

Arguably, the crux of the nineteenth-century discourse on the Society's attitude towards Dante can be found in the *Lettere Virgiliane*, a relatively obscure work of Italian literary criticism by the Jesuit Saverio Bettinelli published in Venice in 1757. Written in the persona of the Classical poet Virgil, the *Lettere* were satiric epistles on literary matters that Bettinelli used as the introduction to an anthology of some 'modern', eighteenth-century Italian poets. In the course of the *Lettere*, Bettinelli occasionally ridicules the supposed 'barbarism' of Dante in favour of a neo-classicist approach; a literary-critical stance not all that dissimilar from Petrarch and other early humanists.[11] Surprisingly, then, for a work intended primarily as a serious treatise on poetic style that tried to help 'aspiring poets [...] look for a more original, more modern source of inspiration' than Dante's medievalism, Bettinelli's *Lettere Virgiliane* caused considerable turbulence within the currents of Italian literary-critical discourse.[12]

Although the root of the critical response to the *Lettere* might be expected to be the apparent clash of Enlightenment and proto-Romantic paradigms, or the argument between poetic innovators and those championing 'la pietà delle tradizioni' ['the piety of tradition'], Franco Betti has convincingly shown that beneath these discourses lay a virulent prejudice against Bettinelli's religious order.[13] Jansenist sympathisers such as

---

[9] Ugo Foscolo, 'Article IX – Dante: with a new Italian Commentary', 463.
[10] Foscolo's writings on Dante have been the focus of a remarkable amount of recent critical attention. For examples see Nick Havely, '*Francesca franciosa*: Exile, Language and History in Foscolo's Articles on Dante', 55–74; Havely, *Dante's British Public*, 128–53; Joseph Luzzi, ' "Founders of Italian Literature": Dante, Petrarch, and National Identity in Ugo Foscolo', 13–29; and Andrea Ciccarelli, 'Dante and Italian Culture from the Risorgimento to World War I', 129–32.
[11] For Petrarch's reactions to Dante see Caesar, *Dante: The Critical Heritage*, 151–8; on the critical stance of the *Lettere Virgiliane* see Franco Betti, 'Dante, the Jansenists and the Jesuits in XVIII–XIX Century Italian Literary Criticism', 3–4.
[12] Betti, 'Dante, the Jansenists and the Jesuits', 4; see also Bruno Capaci, 'Attacco a Dante: Saverio Bettinelll'. *Dante oscuro e barbaro: commenti e dispute (secoli XVII e XVIII)*, 159–76.
[13] Mario Apollonio, 'Dante, Storia della *Commedia*', cited in Betti, 'Dante, the Jansenists and the Jesuits', 3.

Giovanni Lami, the publisher and 'fiero avversario dei gesuiti' ['fierce adversary of the Jesuits'], sought to move their theological dispute with the Society into the literary arena, and seized upon Bettinelli's mild criticisms of Dante as evidence of a Jesuit's lack of proper poetic sensibility.[14] Whilst this in itself would be an interesting critical overreaction, writers such as Lami represented the first voices in a new discourse in Italian letters that, building upon the increasing popularity of secular, anti-clerical and 'neo-Ghibelline' readings of Dante, would metamorphose Bettinelli's literary opinion into a 'manifestation of a particular hate nourished by the Society of Jesus as a whole against the Florentine poet'.[15]

In the articles that Ugo Foscolo wrote for the *Edinburgh Review*, this eighteenth-century myth of Jesuit hostility towards Dante entered both the nineteenth century and British literary circles. Written whilst in exile in England, Foscolo's articles sought to give an account of Italian literature tailored to the perspective of the nationalist Risorgimento project that aimed to unify the disparate states of Italy, and they focused upon furthering a secularised reading of Dante, a poet 'whose fame was rising again after a long eclipse'.[16] In the first of these articles for the *Edinburgh Review* Foscolo makes it clear where the blame for the waning of Dante's reputation lies:

> Towards 1550, the Jesuits possessed themselves of the education of Italy and they systematically decried a writer likely to produce effects on the opinions and on the character of youth so irreconcilable with their policy.[17]

Having thus established a sense of institutional antipathy towards Dante, Foscolo then provided a succinct précis and restatement of the earlier anti-Jesuit discourse, returning to its original Italian target in Bettinelli:

> The Jesuits were indefatigable in their hostility to Dante [...] Bettinelli in his Virgillian Letters, an ingenious but tasteless book, ridicules Dante as the most barbarous of poets.[18]

---

[14] Giulio Natali, *Il Settecento*, cited in Betti, 'Dante, the Jansenists and the Jesuits', 8.
[15] Betti, 'Dante, the Jansenists and the Jesuits', 11.
[16] Beatrice Corrigan, 'Foscolo's Articles on Dante in the *Edinburgh Review*: A Study in Collaboration', 213. On Foscolo in exile see Havely, *Dante's British Public*, 128–31; Havely, '*Francesca franciosa*', 55–8, 68; and Maurizio Isabella, 'Exile and Nationalism: The Case of the *Risorgimento*', 495–500.
[17] Foscolo, 'Article IX', 462. Whilst we have no way of knowing whether Joyce himself ever read Foscolo's articles (and I am very much inclined to doubt that he did), it is interesting to note that he was certainly aware of this sinister view of Jesuit educational policy. In *Stephen Hero* he writes that, in the context of the debate about the constitution of the Royal University, 'the Jesuits were accused of working the machine for their own ends without a just sense of impartiality' (*SH* 163).
[18] Foscolo, 'Article IX', 463.

However, in 1818 Foscolo faced an irreducible obstacle to this theory of institutionalised Jesuit antipathy with which earlier critics of Bettinelli had not had to contend: the Society's fall from grace and suppression by Pope Clement XIV in 1773.[19] Foscolo overcame this problem through an ingenious rhetorical device connecting the waning of Jesuit influence with the resurgence of interest in Dante:

> It was after the fall of the Jesuits that Lombardi, a Franciscan, incensed at their malignity and false taste, ventured to undertake his commentary on Dante. He was of the same order with Ganganelli, the pope who suppressed the Jesuits. But it was more easy to suppress than extinguish the literary and religious prejudices which they had established in Italy.[20]

This last move by Foscolo was an inspired attempt to reconcile the Jesuits' supposedly malign influence on Italian letters throughout the late eighteenth and early nineteenth centuries with their decline and suppression; indeed, the Jesuits had been restored as a religious order only four years before Foscolo wrote his articles, making his caveat about the difficulty of eradicating the Society's literary influence all the more telling.

Attempts to understand the critical stance of Foscolo's articles (beyond their clear adherence to a secularised reading of Dante) have often focused on the influence and silent co-authorship of leading Whig figures.[21] Yet, this view cannot explain Foscolo's continuation of the anti-Jesuit discourse started by Giovanni Lami fifty years earlier, and indeed even the 'neo-Ghibellinism' ascribed to Foscolo can't account for the focusing of his anti-clerical ire upon the Jesuits. As we have seen, the original context for Lami's criticism may well have been the Jesuit–Jansenist dispute, yet by the time of Foscolo's articles Jansenism was on the wane across Europe, and he makes no mention of it. It appears that by the nineteenth century – as we approach the time of Joyce's birth – the anti-Jesuit discourse within Dante studies had passed the limits of its initial context, and another explanation for it must be sought.

One rationale for the continuation of Lami's discourse can be found in the political situation of Italy during the Risorgimento.[22] Franco Betti sees Lami's attack on Bettinelli as 'a good example of the conservative

---

[19] See J. H. Pollen, 'Society of Jesus (Company of Jesus, Jesuits)', 99.
[20] Foscolo, 'Article IX', 463.
[21] Both Milbank (*Dante and the Victorians*, 14–16) and Corrigan ('Foscolo's Articles', 212–23) focus on this Whig influence on Foscolo's article, whilst Havely has traced the intricacies of the multilingual compositional process within this context, '*Francesca franciosa*', 59–65.
[22] For a good introduction to the Risorgimento see Harry Hearder, *Italy in the Age of the Risorgimento 1790–1870*.

academician ever ready to defend the centuries-old national tradition', and Dante's presence within an explicitly *national* tradition was crucial in determining Jesuit attitudes towards him in the nineteenth century.[23] As we saw, there is a long history of the appropriation of Dante as an 'anti-papal writer' by Protestant propagandists, and an equally long history of his reclamation by Catholic writers, often by Jesuits such as the sixteenth-century Cardinal Roberto Bellarmine.[24] However, within the context of a fractured nineteenth-century Italy, firmly in the grip of Risorgimento and the movement towards political unity, the scene had shifted; when the Jesuits re-emerged from suppression in 1814, they found the rules of the centuries-long game of appropriation and counter-appropriation had fundamentally changed. Dante's purported anti-papalism no longer took the form of a religious or ecclesiastical discourse that could be repudiated on its own terms. The problem wasn't that Dante had shown 'popes in Hell' or that, in the *Monarchia*, he had argued forcefully for the political independence of the Holy Roman Emperor; indeed, the content of Dante's work itself was no longer the issue.[25] Instead, thanks in part to his defence of the unity of the Italian language in *De Vulgari Eloquentia*, and his clear sense of Italy as a discrete geographic and cultural body, Dante had been co-opted as one of the cultural figureheads of the nationalising project of the Risorgimento, and as such posed a direct political threat to papal interests.[26]

The Risorgimento, a movement for which the creation of an Italian national myth was equally important as the formation of the nation state of Italy itself, also brought about considerable change for the Roman Catholic Church. This was the period that saw the transition of the role of the Church and the Papacy from that of a temporal and political potentate to a largely social and spiritual role, following the destruction of the independent Papal States in 1870.[27] In the context of the popular movement of the Risorgimento, when Dante's *Commedia* was paraded through the streets of a liberated Ravenna whilst its author was hailed as 'the ancient victor over priestly imposture', Dante was being used against papal

---

[23] Betti, 'Dante, the Jansenists, and the Jesuits', 10.
[24] See Havely, 'Dante in Reformation England', 140–6; and Caesar, *Dante: The Critical Heritage*, 34–7.
[25] See Stefano Jossa, 'Politics vs. Literature: The Myth of Dante and the Italian National Identity', 41–6.
[26] For more on Dante's appropriation by the Risorgimento see Ciccarelli, 'Dante and Italian Culture', 128–37; Isabella, 'Exile and Nationalism', 497–500; and Milbank, *Dante and the Victorians*, 58–82.
[27] See Lucy Riall, *Garibaldi: Invention of a Hero*, 352–5; Hearder, *Italy in the Age of the Risorgimento*, 283–93; and Christopher Duggan, *The Force of Destiny: A History of Italy since 1796*, 256–9.

interests in a far more politically concrete (and thus less easily redeemable) way than ever before.[28] Throughout this period, as the restored Jesuits realigned themselves with the Papacy, they moved inexorably into conflict with the Risorgimento presentation of Dante as 'father' of the nation and language, a persona for the poet that was now set implacably against the interests of the Vatican. Indeed, Dante represented one of the key cultural tools in the unification of Italy and the resultant diminution of the Papacy's temporal power.[29]

Therefore, in the heat of the Risorgimento, any Jesuit criticism of Dante – such as Bettinelli had offered in his *Lettere Virgiliane* – underwent a hostile reading by the nationalist movement; Bettinelli was not seen as attempting to further Enlightenment rationalism, but as a papal agent dishonouring the 'national poet'. In turn, the castigation of the Jesuits by Foscolo, despite the fact that it continued a discourse originating in the Jansenism of Lami, could now be seen as a blow struck against the power of the Papacy by the incipient Kingdom of Italy. Indeed, as Christopher Duggan has pointed out, the idea of a liberal, secular society was essential to the nationalist myth crafted by writers such as Giuseppe Mazzini during the Risorgimento, and which would result in the effective institutionalisation of Foscolo's brand of 'neo-Ghibelline' reading of Dante within the nascent Italian state.[30] It is small wonder that so heated a political climate bred the myth of an institutionalised Jesuit antipathy towards Dante.

'Perfect Submission': Jesuit Reappropriations

The potential difficulties in arriving at an understanding of the influence of the Jesuit attitude to Dante on the young James Joyce are already becoming clear. The political turmoil of the Risorgimento offers a plausible explanation as to why the Jesuits were painted so broadly as the poet's 'enemies', but in truth it is likely that some of the anti-papal content of Dante's writings did arouse suspicion on the part of the Society. By the time of the unification of Italy in 1870, the Jesuits had reassumed their position as close allies to the Papacy, and Dante's record with this

---

[28] Charles T. Davis, 'Dante and Italian Nationalism', 204.
[29] On the alignment of the Jesuits with papal interests see Hearder, *Italy in the Age of Risorgimento*, 291; on 'the employment of Dante as national icon' see Jossa, 'Politics vs. Literature', 36–41.
[30] See Duggan, *The Force of Destiny*, 292. For more on Dante's role in this national myth and his institutionalisation, see Ciccarelli, 'Dante and Italian Culture', 126–39. It is also worth noting that Mazzini helped ensure the primacy of Foscolo's reading of Dante by editing Foscolo's posthumous edition of the *Commedia* and commentary, see Havely, *Dante's British Public*, 151–3.

institution was undeniably spotty. Dante's treatise *Monarchia* suffered a rebuttal at the hands of a Dominican cleric in 1327, followed in turn by its ritual burning in 1329. Once the Vatican's Index of prohibited books had been established in 1554, *Monarchia* quickly earned a place on it (a Papal decision that, unsurprisingly, led to the speedy reprinting of Dante's treatise in a new Protestant edition in 1559).[31] In 1581 it was joined on the Index by some of the more controversial passages of the *Commedia*; indeed, the *Monarchia* remained on the Papal Index right up until 1881, the year before Joyce's birth.[32] That Dante was the author of a 'banned book' as well as a figurehead for the anti-papal nationalising movement in Italy would suggest that, whilst by the time Joyce entered Belvedere College in 1893 the Jesuit attitude to Dante was probably not the open hostility posited by Foscolo and his predecessors, it would surely not have been an uncomplicated veneration of a great 'Catholic poet'.

Yet there is compelling evidence elsewhere for just such a late nineteenth-century Jesuit veneration of Dante. In Mumbai, the Asiatic Society holds a late fourteenth-century manuscript of the *Commedia*, donated in the 1820s by Mountstuart Elphinstone; it appears that during the 1860s this manuscript acted as a quasi-shrine for Jesuits passing through India, who were drawn to Bombay to view it.[33] Whilst this example of Jesuit approval of Dante took place beyond the European context, there are many other indications of Dante's increasingly orthodox position within European Catholicism. Indeed, the distinctly 'neo-Guelf' literary critical discourse begun by the Jesuit Bellarmine was audible throughout the nineteenth and early twentieth centuries. Through this discourse, figures such as Cardinal Newman (who was to be an important writer in his own right for the young Joyce) sought to affirm Dante's doctrinal orthodoxy within the Catholic Church.[34]

Whilst not as vocal – or ultimately successful – as their Risorgimento counterparts, Italian 'neo-Guelfs' such as Gaetano Polidori and Bartolomeo Sorio, Luigi Ritelli and Lorenzo Felicetti (not to mention Pietro Del Poggetto, author of *Dante Alighieri poeta cattolico apostolico romano*), all

---

[31] On the *Monarchia*'s rebuttal by the Dominicans, the 1559 edition and the *Monarchia*'s inclusion on the Papal Index see Havely, *Dante's British Public*, 23–9, 52–3.
[32] Havely, *Dante's British Public*, 52, 70; Crisafulli, *The Vision of Dante*, 266.
[33] Letter from Sir George Birdwood, quoted in *The Times*, 25 October 1890. For the fascinating story of the Mumbai manuscript, its owners, their readings and its journey to India see Havely, *Dante's British Public*, 194–211.
[34] For details of the 'neo-Guelf' movement early in the nineteenth century see Crisafulli, *The Vision of Dante*, 267; for Cardinal Newman's relationship with Dante see Milbank, *Dante and the Victorians*, 164–6, 170–2.

placed themselves in direct opposition to the liberal, anti-clerical readings of the poet.[35] Attempting to politically neutralise Dante by reclaiming him to the Catholic fold, 'neo-Guelf' commentators rejected the Risorgimento appropriation of the poet as 'non pure inutile, ma fu estremamente dannosa alla vera intelligenza del divino poema' ['not only unhelpful, but extremely damaging to the true understanding of the divine poem'].[36] Even Anglican writers such as Gaetano Polidori (the grandfather of Dante Gabriel Rossetti, to whose importance to Joyce's engagement with Dante we will return) took issue with the Risorgimento distortion of Dante, and, in Polidori's case, levelled their criticisms at Foscolo directly: 'Fu scritto e pubblicato da Ugo Foscolo, coll' appoggio d' una falsa interpretazione [...] che San Pietro aveva ordinato Dante al sacerdozio' ['Ugo Foscolo has made the public assertion, based on a false interpretation [...] that Saint Peter had ordained Dante to the priesthood'].[37]

The most intriguing example of such 'neo-Guelf' readings for our present discussion is undoubtedly the Dante commentaries of Luigi Bennassuti. Whilst not a Jesuit himself, in works such as his *Commento Cattolico* and three-volume edition of the *Commedia*, Bennassuti advanced an unmistakably Jesuit reading.[38] His commentary, published in Verona in 1864 at the height of the Risorgimento and the campaign against Rome, was dedicated 'all'illustrissimo e reverendissimo Monsignor Luigi Marchese di Canossa' ['to the illustrious and most reverend Monsignor Luigi, Marquis of Canossa'], the Jesuit bishop of that city, and eventual Cardinal and elector of Pope Leo XIII.[39] Bennassuti's reading stressed that, 'checchè ne dicano in contrario molti moderni' ['whatever many modern commentators might say to the contrary'], the *Commedia* was 'un trattato sui generis della più alta perfezione cristiana, perchè tende a condur l'uomo dallo stato più profondo del peccato allo stato più sublime della grazia' ['a treatise *sui generis* of the highest Christian perfection, because it strives to bring back man from the state of lowest sin to the height of sublime grace'].[40] Indeed, as well as stressing

---

[35] I am indebted to Stefano Jossa for identifying this range of Catholic responses.
[36] Bartolomeo Sorio, *Lettere Dantesche dal P. Bart. Sorio P. D. O. di Verona scritte all' amico il Prof Francesco Longhena a Milano*, 3.
[37] Gaetano Polidori, *Dello Spirito Cattolico di Dante Alighieri: Opera di Carlo Lyell tradotta dall'originale Inglese*, v–vi.
[38] For a sparse biography of Bennassuti and details of critical reaction to the 'bizzarria metodo' of his commentary see Nicola Carducci, 'Bennassuti, Luigi', 589–90 cols. 2–1.
[39] Luigi Bennassuti, *La Divina Commedia di Dante Alighieri col Commento Cattolico di Luigi Bennassuti*, vol. 1, 5. For details on Luigi di Canossa's career see Pio Paschini, *La Enciclopedia Cattolica*, vol. 3, 610.
[40] Bennassuti, *Commento Cattolico*, 5.

the potency of the *Commedia* as an aid to the saving of souls – a reading that chimed well with the Jesuit militancy of his dedicatee – in a later edition of 1878, Bennassuti even went as far as to claim that, by depicting a three-step process of meditative salvation, Dante was 'il precursore del grande Lojola, che tiene lo stesso metodo' ['the forerunner of the great Loyola, for he took the same approach'].[41] Thus, to stand against the 'warrior-poet' of the Risorgimento, Bennassuti offered a version of Dante who shared the spiritual methods of Ignatius Loyola, and became, in effect, a posthumous Jesuit. This would hardly seem to qualify as 'indefatigable hostility'.

The terms of the 'neo-Guelf' rehabilitation established by readings such as Bennassuti's – that Dante was an exemplar of Catholic piety and that the *Commedia* represented a potent tool for conversion and salvation – quickly entered into the mainstream of Catholic orthodoxy. One example of the authorisation of such a view can be seen in the English-language *Catholic Encyclopedia*. Published between 1907 and 1914, the *Encyclopedia* presents itself as an authoritative reference work on Catholic constitution and dogma, and features an article on Dante by Edmund Gardner.[42] However, whilst attempting to follow the 'neo-Guelf' line and rehabilitate both Dante and his most contentious work, the *Monarchia*, Gardner's entry conveys a lingering sense of unease. Certainly, more time is spent detailing each of Dante's infractions against papal authority than in appreciating his poetry or thought; yet the fact of Dante's inclusion in this self-consciously central work of Catholic orthodoxy is significant.

Undoubtedly the clearest example of the 'neo-Guelf' desire to resituate Dante within orthodox Catholicism can be seen in two papal encyclicals from the late nineteenth and early twentieth centuries. The first of these, '*Auspicato Concessum*' – issued by Leo XIII (the pope whom Luigi di Canossa had helped elect) on 17 September 1882 – comprised a meditation upon St Francis of Assisi. Pope Leo considered the positive influence of St Francis upon Italy as a whole, contending that 'Dante even found in Francis matter for his grand and most sweet verse'; whilst this might not seem the most effusive endorsement of Dante or the *Commedia*, it is notable that, through the efforts of such writers as Bennassuti, within the

---

[41] Luigi Bennassuti, *La Divina Commedia di Dante Alighieri col Commento Medio tra il Grande ed il Piccolo di Bennassuti Luigi*, vol. 1, 1.
[42] Edmund G. Gardner, 'Dante', 628–33. Roy Gottfried has pointed out the relevance of the *Catholic Encyclopedia* to Joyce's education, see *Joyce's Misbelief*, 2–9.

space of a year (and in the year of Joyce's birth, no less), Dante, previously the author of a banned book, was having his name dropped in a papal encyclical.[43]

This papal rebranding of Dante was continued by Benedict XV and his '*In praeclara summorum*', given on 21 April 1921 and timed to coincide with the six-hundredth anniversary of Dante's death.[44] In what represents the zenith of the Catholic reappropriation of the poet, Dante was himself the subject of this particular encyclical, during which Benedict asserts that, for Dante,

> [t]he Roman Church is The Most Holy Mother, Bride of Him Crucified and to Peter, infallible judge of revealed truths, is owing perfect submission in matters of faith and morals. Hence, however much he may hold that the dignity of the Emperor is derived immediately from God, still he asserts that this truth 'must not be understood so strictly as to mean that the Roman Prince is not subject to the Roman Pontiff in anything, because this mortal happiness is subjected in certain measure to immortal happiness'. (*Mon.* III, 16)[45]

Here, then, is a pope who, only some fifty years after the capture of Rome and the completion of the Risorgimento project, is not only asserting Dante's 'perfect submission' to the Catholic Church but supporting his argument by correctly citing the *Monarchia*.

So it would appear that, by the end of the nineteenth century, the Jesuits had not really performed the *volte-face* on the poet suggested by the disparity between the polemical project of such sixteenth-century figures as Robert Parsons, and Foscolo's sense of their 'indefatigable hostility'. The long tradition of Dante's assimilation as an 'anti-papal' writer not only continued into Joyce's immediate historical context but had actually intensified through the agency of the Risorgimento; yet, equally, Dante was not solely defined by this secularised presentation, and nor was this politicised reading left unchallenged. In fact, the most apposite summary of Dante's presentation within a late nineteenth-century Jesuitical context would be to characterise him as occupying a place of uneasy orthodoxy, a position both simultaneously within and without the canon of Catholicism.

---

[43] '*Auspicato Concessum*: Encyclical of Pope Leo XIII on St Francis of Assisi'.
[44] The importance of '*In praeclara summorum*' in re-establishing Dante's position within Catholicism was first noted by Teodolinda Barolini, see *Dante and the Origins of Italian Literary Culture*, 7.
[45] '*In praeclara summorum*: Encyclical of Pope Benedict XV on Dante, to Professors and Students of Literature and Learning in the Catholic World'.

Yet, for Joyce, this uneasy orthodoxy could cut both ways; Klaus Reichert has perceptively questioned whether Dante would have appeared to Joyce as 'the greatest of Catholic poets' or occupied so central a position within Catholic orthodoxy as he appears to today. Indeed, Reichert feels that, in an example of a 'new' reading that probably originated in the opinions of Byron, Shelley and Carlyle, Joyce saw Dante as 'a "committed" writer, a political poet who is never cowed by authority'. However, as we now see, such a political and – to use Reichert's term – 'anti-Catholic' reading of Dante, far from being a 'uniquely modern' and liberated reading of the poet, represents instead an alignment with the competing orthodoxy of the Risorgimento.[46] Just as Dante's secular, political appropriation unsettled and simultaneously elicited his 'Catholicisation', so too did the 'neo-Guelf' position undermine and disrupt the Risorgimento reading. Thus, for Joyce, encountering Dante through an educational and textual context that, as we will see, emphasised and sustained these competing orthodoxies, to settle into an 'anti-Catholic' reading would have represented as reductive a transformation of the poet's personae as following the orthodox readings of figures such as Bennassuti. Indeed, there is clear evidence of Joyce's resistance to just such a 'neo-Ghibelline' orthodoxy in his 1903 review of Ibsen's *Catilina*, where he castigated the unthinking secular interpretation of Dante by writers of the previous generation who fancied themselves 'Dante without the unfortunate prejudices of Dante' (*OCPW* 73). As the details of Joyce's education and the text in which he first encountered the poet will clarify, it was the liminality of Dante's cultural position resultant from his claiming by fiercely opposed orthodoxies that would cement his lasting significance for Joyce.

Learning the Language: Dante and Joyce's Italian Education

In his lecture, 'L'Irlanda: isola dei santi e dei savi', delivered in Trieste in 1907, Joyce makes reference to 'Carey, traduttore classico della *Divina Commedia*' ['the classic translator of the *Divine Comedy*'], placing Henry Francis Cary amongst a list of 'i nomi dei tre più traduttori nella letteratura inglese' ['the names of the three greatest translators in English literature'] (*OCPW* 257). Joyce invokes these names to belie the view 'che l'irlandese sia veramente il cretino incapace' ['that the Irish are really the incapable cretins'] (*OCPW* 257), which they were made out to be in the

---

[46] Klaus Reichert, 'The European Background to Joyce's Writing', 56–7.

English tabloid press. Unfortunately, in claiming Cary – the Spanish-born, English clergyman and Regency translator of Dante – as an Irishman, Joyce seems to have muddled him up with the slightly earlier translator Henry Boyd, who, as well as being the producer of the first English version of the whole *Commedia*, was indeed Anglo-Irish.[47]

We can deduce from this slip on Joyce's part that he must have been aware of both of these translations of the *Commedia*, and indeed by the end of the nineteenth century both Cary's and Boyd's translations were well known within British literary circles. However, the weight of evidence – particularly the NLI notesheets with the limited knowledge of the *Commedia* that they display – would suggest that Joyce's reading of Dante was bound up with his learning of the Italian language. The history of Joyce's Italian instruction is sometimes hard to follow and has to be pieced together from his school records. Whilst the young James Joyce was an undeniably bright boy, he was not so obviously gestating his eventual genius that the records of his education were preserved with any great diligence and, consequently, those records that do survive are fragmentary and often confusing; however, all the available sources agree that Joyce's acquaintance with Italian began upon his entry into Belvedere College in 1893.[48]

His first Italian teacher was not a Jesuit himself, but appears to have been a layman named Mr Loup, who was employed only briefly by the College.[49] However, as Kevin Sullivan pointed out, the primary record for Loup (whose name 'may be anglicised as "error" or "trick"') is Herbert Gorman's early 'authorised' biography, in which Joyce himself was closely involved (and throughout which he displayed a fondness for seeding misinformation and misleading puns); thus the identity of Mr Loup may well have been invented.[50] Nevertheless, Bruce Bradley mentions that, in a reversal of Joyce's own academic trajectory, the mysterious Mr Loup transferred to the Jesuit college of Clongowes Wood in 1894, so his existence could have been more substantial than a Joycean pun.[51]

Joyce's second teacher of Italian, and the first for whom there is substantive documentary evidence, was Francis Ryan. Assigned to Belvedere

---

[47] On Cary and his translation of the *Commedia* see Crisafulli, *The Vision of Dante*. On Boyd's translation see Valeria Tinkler-Villani, *Visions of Dante in English Poetry*, 125–72.
[48] See Sullivan, *Joyce Among the Jesuits*, 91; Bradley, *James Joyce's Schooldays*, 106; Herbert S. Gorman, *James Joyce: A Definitive Biography*, 43; and *JJ* 47.
[49] Gorman, *James Joyce*, 43; Sullivan, *Joyce Among The Jesuits*, 91; Bradley, *James Joyce's Schooldays*, 106.
[50] Sullivan, *Joyce Among the Jesuits*, 91–2.
[51] Bradley, *James Joyce's Schooldays*, 106.

between 1894 and 1898, Mr Ryan was, like the possibly phantasmal Mr Loup, probably a layman at first, only later joining the Jesuit Order in 1897, whereupon he would have assumed the title of 'Father'. If this is the case, then it is likely that Ryan was the inspiration for the teacher in 'An Encounter':

> We revenged ourselves on Leo Dillon by saying what a funk he was and guessing how many he would get at three o'clock from Mr Ryan. (D 2. 116–18)

Although Ryan's existence is better attested than Mr Loup's (not least by this echo in Joyce's story), the exact nature of his function at Belvedere remains uncertain. Sullivan cites the *Catalogus* of the Society of Jesus for 1894 as evidence of Ryan's appointment as French and Italian teacher at Belvedere during Joyce's time there; however, having examined the Gorman papers, Bradley complicated this reading of the source to suggest that Ryan was the French teacher and only 'probably' the Italian tutor as well. Bradley also notes that Joyce did not remember Ryan 'kindly', an impression that might fit his association with corporal punishment in 'An Encounter'.[52]

Whilst many details of the personnel of Joyce's early Italian tuition thus remain uncertain, some of the texts on which he was eventually examined are known. Between his first Intermediate examination in 1894 and his departure from Belvedere in 1898, Joyce was examined on a range of Italian texts from De Amicis' *Cuore* to Metastasio's *Gioas Re di Giuda*; however, at no point did Dante appear upon the school examinations that he is known to have sat.[53] Yet this need not suggest an institutionalised suppression of Dante within Jesuit schools; reflecting on his schooldays, Joyce's friend J. F. Byrne (the inspiration for Cranly in *A Portrait of the Artist as a Young Man*) recalled an atmosphere of relatively 'liberal' literary appreciation at Belvedere.[54] The repercussions of this liberality were demonstrated on the occasion when – as Byrne relates it – a Jesuit master was harangued by an angry parent who had found her son reading *Ivanhoe*, apparently with his teacher's shocking encouragement.[55] Whilst more of a humorous anecdote than a serious testament to the school's attitude towards literature, Byrne's recollections in general suggest a sense

---

[52] See Sullivan, *Joyce Among the Jesuits*, 92; and Bradley, *James Joyce's Schooldays*, 112.
[53] Bradley, *James Joyce's Schooldays*, 108–17.
[54] John F. Byrne, *Silent Years: An Autobiography with Memoirs of James Joyce and Our Ireland*, 21–3.
[55] Byrne, *Silent Years*, 22–3.

of willingness on the part of the Jesuits at Belvedere College to allow, and even encourage, reading outside of the set examination texts.[56]

Indeed, although Belvedere was subject to the strict syllabus and controls of the Society's *Ratio Studiorum*, there is evidence that in the school year 1895–6 Joyce was, as a result of his success in previous examinations, allowed a good degree of academic freedom.[57] It is during this year that Joyce is known to have begun reading both widely and without supervision, and, whilst there is not much hope of exactly reconstructing the pattern of this reading, it does seem unlikely that, given the role Dante played in the history of the Italian language, Joyce would have ignored the poet completely in this period.[58] Certainly, the fact that he would not be examined on Dante would not have deterred him; Joyce's lack of interest in academic examination could already be seen in his woeful Euclid results.[59] Given that Dirk van Hulle has dated the NLI notesheets to c. 1897–8, it seems entirely possible that Joyce might have first opened the *Commedia* a year or so earlier, during his year of relative academic freedom.[60]

Hence, if we follow both the dating of the NLI notesheets and the conjectural evidence of Joyce's Italian education, it seems reasonable to conclude that Joyce probably did first read Dante towards the end of his career at Belvedere College, and that this encounter occurred outside of his regular syllabus.[61] If so, then the passage of *Stephen Hero* in which Joyce first makes an attempt to fictionalise his experience of reading Dante, and on which Mary Reynolds based her suggestion that Joyce first encountered Dante at university, can be read more clearly:

> The second year of Stephen's University life opened early in October [...] He chose Italian as his optional subject, partly from a desire to read Dante

---

[56] Certainly, Joyce's reading was not curtailed at home, as when a visitor to the Joyce house was shocked to see that the young man was reading Zola, he was told brusquely by Joyce's parents that 'Jim can read what he likes' (*JJ* 75).
[57] On Joyce's 'academic interlude' in 1895–6 see Sullivan, *Joyce Among the Jesuits*, 100.
[58] For Joyce's study of the history of Italian see Boldrini, *Joyce, Dante*, 4–5.
[59] See Bradley, *James Joyce's Schooldays*, 110–11, 116–17, 130–1, 140–1.
[60] See van Hulle, *Discovering Dante*, 2; although it should be noted that van Hulle gives no explicit reasoning for his dating, and the notes could well be even earlier than he is suggesting.
[61] This freedom, and the presumably positive memories it gave Joyce of his first reading of the *Commedia*, might go some way towards explaining the mystery as to why he would have preserved his early notes on the *Inferno*, carrying them across Europe throughout his peregrinations, and only finally abandoning them when forced to leave Paris after the onset of the Second World War. For more on the provenance of the Joyce Papers 2002 (of which the Dante notes are the earliest part) see Michael Groden, 'The National Library of Ireland's New Joyce Manuscripts: A Narrative and Document Summaries', 1–16.

seriously, and partly to escape the crush of French and German lectures. (*SH* 152)

The 'desire to read Dante seriously' that Joyce here ascribes to Stephen Daedalus, would obviously suggest that, prior to choosing Italian as a special subject, Stephen has *already* read Dante. Therefore, even if we were to follow Reynolds in reading *Stephen Hero* as a biographical source for Joyce, it must be concluded that Joyce was most probably familiar with Dante prior to 1899.[62] However, when he did finally enter the University, if Joyce shared Stephen's 'serious' desire, then University College Dublin certainly offered him the opportunity to satisfy it.

Joyce's 'Maestro' and Joyce's 'Autore': Charles Ghezzi and Eugenio Camerini

Joyce's days at University College could only have strengthened Dante's association with academic freedom that began in his 'spare' year at Belvedere. Firstly, the rigid syllabus of the *Ratio Studiorum* was replaced by the curriculum of University College's secular examining body, the Royal University of Ireland; and secondly, it was at University College that Joyce encountered his first real 'maestro' of Dante in the person of Fr Charles Ghezzi. In Joyce's novels, Ghezzi is a mercurial figure; he is evidently the inspiration for two characters who feature in *Stephen Hero, A Portrait of the Artist* and *Ulysses*. In the first and last of these works he appears under the name Almidano Artifoni, and in *Portrait* under his own; however, the differences in the presentation of Artifoni and the fictional 'Ghezzi' are striking. In *Stephen Hero*, Artifoni is described as 'an intelligent little *moro*, who came from Bergamo, a town in Lombardy' (*SH* 152), and he strikes a sympathetic figure, in contrast to many of the other portraits of Jesuits. Artifoni is willing to engage in wide-ranging discussions with Stephen Daedalus, just as Eugene Sheehy (who also attended Joyce's Italian tutorials) attests that the historical Ghezzi did with Joyce, and even seems to adopt an attitude of wry understanding towards his pupil:

> The teacher probably knew the doubtful reputation of his pupil but for this very reason he adopted a language of ingenuous piety, not that he was himself Jesuit enough to lack ingenuousness but that he was Italian enough to enjoy a game of belief and unbelief.[63] (*SH* 153)

---

[62] cf. Reynolds, *Joyce and Dante*, 20.
[63] Whilst Joyce took the name 'Almidano Artifoni' from the director of the Berlitz School in Pola (and later Trieste) (*JJ* 186–7), it is interesting to note an etymology that may have underlined its suitability for a character based on Ghezzi. Artifoni's name blends a sense of *artificio* ['artifice']

By the time Artifoni 'reappears' in the 'Wandering Rocks' episode of *Ulysses*, this willingness to engage in a teasing, sympathetic discourse with Stephen Daedalus has mellowed into an avuncular kindness; he greets Stephen Dedalus outside Trinity College with an attempt at real empathy:

> — *Anch'io ho avuto di queste idee, Almidano Artifoni said, quand' ero giovine come Lei. Eppoi mi sono convinto che il mondo è una bestia. È peccato. Perchè la sua voce ... sarebbe un cespite di rendita, via. Invece, Lei si sacrifica.*
>
> — *Sacrifizio incruento*, Stephen said smiling, swaying his ashplant in slow swingswong from its midpoint, lightly. (U 10. 344–9)

This exchange takes place nearly two years after Stephen has graduated from the University, and Artifoni's continued interest in his student represents a deepening of the sympathetic portrayal in *Stephen Hero*.

However, the brief appearance of a fictionalised Ghezzi in *A Portrait of the Artist as a Young Man* is a very different character. At the end of the novel, in the section taking the form of Stephen's diary, he records:

> Then went to college. Other wrangle with little roundhead rogue's eye Ghezzi. This time about Bruno the Nolan. Began in Italian and ended in pidgin English. He said Bruno was a terrible heretic. I said he was terribly burned. He agreed to this with some sorrow. (*P* V. 2648–52)

Here the character given Ghezzi's name lacks some of the intellectual and emotional sympathy with which Artifoni is portrayed. The scene described seems to be another version of the moment in *Stephen Hero* when Stephen and Artifoni also discuss Bruno, 'the author of *The Triumphant Beast*' (*SH* 153); yet, in *A Portrait*, Joyce chooses to place an emphasis upon the lack of understanding and communication between the two men, who are reduced by their failings in each other's languages to speaking 'pidgin' English, further developing the sense of alienation so crucial to Stephen's presentation in the novel.[64]

Whilst not wanting to succumb to the temptation to read Joyce's work as biography, the fact that a version of Ghezzi appears in three of Joyce's novels, and in each has undergone some new consideration

---

with an Italian echo of phonetics ['fonetica'], a Greek sound ('phono') and an English resonance of falsity ('phony') to create a sense of an artful or cunning speaker who might not believe what he says. Certainly, this reading of Artifoni's name would correspond well with the position his student Stephen takes in 'Scylla and Charybdis', where, having advanced an elaborate interpretation of *Hamlet*, he claims not to believe his own theory (*U* 9. 1064–7), perhaps proving himself a true 'artifono'. For a firsthand account of Joyce's tutorials with Ghezzi see Eugene Sheehy, 'My School Friend, James Joyce', 11.

[64] The historical Ghezzi could speak perfect English; see Sheehy, 'My School Friend, James Joyce', 11.

of character, does suggest that the historical Ghezzi, as the man who properly introduced Joyce to Dante, remained of some interest throughout Joyce's career. The details of Ghezzi's life are few but fairly well established: he was, as is suggested by *Stephen Hero*, an Italian Jesuit from Bergamo, and the *Catalogus* of 1902 records him as being 'on loan' from Venice, although Ellmann claimed that he had come to Ireland from a long residence in India.[65] Ghezzi taught Italian at University College in tutorials that seem to have quite closely resembled those that Joyce recreated, with the obvious exception that at least one other student (Eugene Sheehy) attended. Italian was certainly unpopular enough at the University to justify Gorman's exaggeration that, in the year of his graduation, Joyce was the only male student to sit the Italian exam in the whole of Ireland.[66]

One document related to Ghezzi that deserves mention as regards his relationship to Joyce is a manuscript notebook entitled 'The Academy of St Thomas Aquinas: Addresses of Members and Minutes of Meetings'.[67] The book records Ghezzi's presence, along with that of Joyce, at the inaugural meeting of this Aquinas society on 27 November 1901, further suggesting a shared intellectual sympathy (and interest in one of Dante's own shaping intellectual influences) between Joyce and his first Dante tutor.[68] Two unpublished letters to Joyce from Ghezzi also survive, both of which now reside in the Cornell Joyce Collection, and one of which may be referred to by Joyce in a letter to his mother from Paris in 1903, when he assures her that 'I answered Fr Ghezzi's letter' (*L* II, 38).[69] As this correspondence postdates Joyce's graduation, the letters suggest that – like Artifoni and Stephen in 'Wandering Rocks' – Ghezzi's interest in Joyce continued beyond his pastoral obligations.

The character of the historical Ghezzi was interestingly observed by Stanislaus Joyce, who determinedly placed the Jesuit tutor outside of the general Irish Catholicism of the time:

> Jim was in spite of that on good terms with this young Italian Jesuit who, coming from a Kultur-Stadt in the producer country of Catholicism, was

---

[65] Sullivan, *Joyce Among the Jesuits*, 155; Sheehy, 'My School Friend, James Joyce', 11; and *JJ* 60.
[66] Gorman, *James Joyce*, 59.
[67] See Sullivan, *Joyce Among the Jesuits*, 168.
[68] Ellmann discusses Joyce's attendance at the meeting in the context of his involvement with Catholicism during his time at University College Dublin, *JJ* 65.
[69] For details of the Cornell letters see Robert E. Scholes, *The Cornell Joyce Collection: A Catalogue*, 87–8. Ellmann suggests another letter may survive in Yale's collection but gives no details (*JJ* 764 n. 9).

not in full sympathy with the ignorant obedience mixed with Puritanism, which is the Irish blend.[70]

As well as a surprising example of praise from Stanislaus, this observation of Ghezzi also suggests that in Joyce's experience of studying Dante at University College Dublin, questions of Italian political and religious orthodoxy may have been bubbling below the surface. However, if Stanislaus saw Ghezzi as in some way out of step with his immediate Catholic context in Dublin, in *Stephen Hero* Joyce presents Artifoni as equally set apart from the nationalist context of Italian politics, stating that the tutor was 'unlike many of the citizens of the third Italy in his want of affection for the English' (*SH* 153).[71] It is tempting indeed to see this contextualisation of the figure of a Jesuit Dante teacher within the politics of the Risorgimento as evidence that Joyce was aware of the critical discourses that surrounded Dante earlier in the nineteenth century.[72] However, even if Ghezzi had nothing to say directly to his pupil about the Risorgimento or its version of Dante, the text that they were reading together certainly did.

If Charles Ghezzi was Joyce's Dante 'maestro', then Eugenio Camerini was his 'autore'. Camerini, the editor and annotator of the surviving copy of the *Commedia* that Joyce bought in Trieste c. 1907–14, is a figure of considerable importance in the history of Joyce's reception of Dante and one whose influence, following the discovery of the NLI notesheets, can now be more fully appreciated. Indeed, as we will see throughout this book, the apparatus of Camerini's edition of the *Commedia* played a highly significant role in shaping Joyce's reading of Dante.[73] Mary Reynolds briefly discusses this edition, speculating that Joyce may have bought a copy in Trieste because it was the same edition with which he had studied back in Dublin (and had presumably lost or sold during his European travels).[74]

---

[70] Stanislaus Joyce, *My Brother's Keeper*, 154. On the character of Irish Catholicism during Joyce's youth see Leernout, '*Help My Unbelief*', 41–51.

[71] For accounts of active British engagement with the Risorgimento and the 'third Italy' see Riall, *Garibaldi*, 142–4; Havely, *Dante's British Public*, 214–35, 265–6; and Anne Isba, *Gladstone and Dante: Victorian Statesman, Medieval Poet*, 43–4.

[72] Dominic Manganiello has noted Joyce's awareness of the politics of the Risorgimento and his connection of them with the Irish politics of his day, see *Joyce's Politics*, 43–4; see also Leernout, '*Help My Unbelief*', 31–2, 77–9.

[73] As the first documented Dante text that Joyce encountered, our focus in this chapter will be firmly on the *Commedia*; however, the context and Joyce's use of Marco de Rubris's edition of the *Vita Nuova* will be of central importance to Dante's presence in *A Portrait of the Artist as a Young Man*, see below, pp. 48–49.

[74] Reynolds, *Joyce and Dante*, 31. It is interesting to note that, given Reynolds's dating of Joyce's purchase, the years that Hélène Cixous called Joyce's 'Dante phase' (1903–6) were most likely the only years in his life when he did not own a copy of the *Commedia*; cf. Cixous, *Exile of James Joyce*, 38.

As Dirk van Hulle has outlined, this suspicion is fully borne out by the NLI notesheets, in which the vast majority of Joyce's notes are cribbed directly from Camerini's copious marginal annotations.[75] A clear example of Joyce's reliance on Camerini can be seen in one of his first notes on the first canto of *Inferno*:

> Il momento in cui comincia l'azione del
> poema è la notte precedente al Venerdi
> Santo, la notte del 24 Marzo 1300. Il
> Giorno in cui Dante esce dalla selva
> (il 15 Maggio 1300, V.S.) è il principio
> decimo
> del quarto secolo contando gli anni
> ab Incarnatione secondo l'uso fiorentino.
> (NLI MS 36,639/1 f. 2v)

This note by Joyce on the dating of the fictional journey in the 'selva oscura' that provides the *Commedia*'s narrative frame, is a crib of Camerini's more extensive note for the first line of the poem:

> Il momento in cui comincia l'azion del Poema, è la notte precedente al venerdi santo, cioè la notte del 24 al 25 marzo: il momento in cui termina, è l'ottava di Pasqua; cosicchè tutta l'azione dura dieci giorni. Questo 25 marzo del 1300 (stile commune a *Nativitate*), la cui mattina Dante, uscito dalla selva, si trova appiè del colle, è il primo giorno del nuovo secolo, cioè dell'anno 1301, contando gli anni *ab Incarnatione*, siccome usavano alcuni degli antichi, e fra essi i Fiorentini.[76]

[The moment at which the action of the poem begins is the night before Good Friday, that is the night of the 24th to the 25th of March; the time at which the poem ends is the eighth day of Easter; so all the action takes only ten days. This 25th March 1300 (common style, counting from the Nativity), the morning on which Dante left the wood at the foot of the hill, is the first day of the new century, that is of the year 1301, counting the years from the Incarnation, as some of the ancients, and amongst them the Florentines, used to do.]

In this way, the corroborating evidence of the NLI notesheets re-emphasises the importance of placing Joyce's reading of Dante within its textual context. Reynolds hinted at the importance of such an approach when she claimed that Joyce bought his later copy of the edition 'for the

---

[75] van Hulle, *Discovering Dante*, 2–4.
[76] Eugenio Camerini (ed.), *La Divina Commedia di Dante Alighieri con note tratte dai migliori commenti*, 27 n. 1.

sake of the notes'; more recently Jennifer Fraser has made brief use of Camerini's notes in her reading of *Purgatorio* 25 and its relation to *A Portrait of the Artist*.[77] However, as we can now appreciate, Dante was a much-contested figure in the nineteenth century, and this 'pugna tra i dantisti liberali [...] ed i dantisti cattolici' ['battle between the liberal Dantists [...] and the Catholic Dantists'] – as Luigi Bennassuti termed it – was fought on the pages of Dante editions as much as on the rhetorical battlefields of the Risorgimento.[78] In which case, as the textual context in which Joyce first encountered Dante, the background and character of Camerini's *Commedia* needs further consideration.

Mary Reynolds briefly discussed Eugenio Camerini, noting simply that he 'was not an academic scholar but an essayist and critic of the Mazzini era'.[79] Giuseppe Mazzini, along with Giuseppe Garibaldi, was arguably the most influential and totemic of all the Risorgimento revolutionaries and, in fact, Camerini himself seems to have been an active participant in the cultural wing of the Risorgimento. After being exiled from Florence, he moved to Turin, where 'si fu rapidamente inserito nell'ambiente politico-culturale torinese che faceva capo all'Azeglio' ['he was quickly assumed into the politico-cultural atmosphere of Turin, whose leader was d'Azeglio'].[80] Massimo d'Azeglio, the novelist, painter and eventual Italian statesman, whilst more moderate in his views than Mazzini, was certainly a proponent of the Risorgimento, and had even come into conflict with the Jesuits over the issue of their political influence in Piedmont; furthermore, Turin was, at the time Camerini lived there, 'the Risorgimento capital'.[81]

Unsurprisingly, given this background, Camerini's edition – both in the notes it supplies to the text, and in the emphasis that his long introductory essays on Dante's life and work place on the roles of Pope Boniface VIII in Dante's exile from Florence, and John XXII in the suppression of the *Monarchia* – was most certainly a Risorgimento edition.[82] What, then,

---

[77] See Fraser, *Rite of Passage*, 118; although it should be noted that Fraser's doubtful claim that Joyce bought his surviving copy of the edition in 1904 in order to use the notes as 'he knew the poem by heart' seems to be a misreading of Reynolds's earlier discussion of the copy as 'an undated reprinting of the 1904 edition', cf. *Rite of Passage*, 97–8, 105, and *Joyce and Dante*, 31.

[78] Bennassuti, *Commento Cattolico*, 9.

[79] Mary Reynolds, 'Joyce's Editions of Dante', 380.

[80] A. Palermo, 'Camerini, Salomone (Eugenio)', 187.

[81] Reynolds, 'Joyce's Editions of Dante', 380. For an account of d'Azeglio's Risorgimento activity see Hearder, *Italy in the Age of the Risorgimento*, 199–203, 213–15.

[82] For instance, Camerini's 'neo-Ghibelline' bent can be discerned in Joyce's note to *Inferno* 1. 45, where he interprets the allegorical figure of the she-wolf whom Dante-pilgrim encounters in the dark wood thusly: 'La Lupa – avarizia – potenza temporale dei papa' (NLI MS 36,639/1 f. 2v) ['the

was the significance of Joyce first encountering Dante in a Risorgimento *Commedia* within a Jesuit classroom? Having already characterised Dante as occupying a position of 'uneasy orthodoxy' within the Catholic culture of Joyce's education, Joyce's use of Camerini's 'neo-Ghibelline' edition would have introduced a further level of ambiguity into his early experience of the poem, in turn further strengthening the sense of Dante's liminality; the sense that he was neither wholly approved of by Joyce's teachers nor entirely condemned. This uneasy orthodoxy surrounding the poet, which had arisen out of Joyce's reading of Camerini's edition of the *Commedia* at Belvedere during a period of freedom from the rigours of the Jesuit syllabus, and was strengthened through contact with the liminal figure of Charles Ghezzi at University College, was to be crucial in determining the character of Joyce's interaction with Dante throughout his career.

The 'Inside Man': Dante as Collaborator

Having explored the historical, cultural, educational and textual contexts of their first encounter, we can see that Dante appeared to the young Joyce as a figure who, through the efforts of his 'neo-Guelf' readers, could be found within the sphere of Jesuitical Catholicism, but whose position within this sphere was subversive and unstable. The notion of an established literary authority being used to negotiate a heterodox space within a larger orthodoxy has been readily identified in Joyce's interest in other authors such as Giordano Bruno.[83] Roy Gottfried has argued that, in his attitude to orthodoxy, Joyce was not so much interested in formulating new heretical positions as he was in co-opting pre-existent, established ones.[84] Dante's uneasy orthodoxy, as encountered by Joyce during his Jesuit education, thus presented a uniquely powerful example of just such a position as, through this liminality – his contested position between heresy and veneration – Dante could remain permanently heterodox, circumscribed by – but never quite settling into – a religious, secular or literary orthodoxy.

Wolf – avarice – temporal power of the pope']. Camerini's introductory 'Vita di Dante' will be an important source for our later discussions of Joyce's reception of the narrative of Dante's exile, see below, pp. 67–68.

[83] See Gottfried, *Joyce's Misbelief*, 2–6. I have explored Dante's position as one of Joyce's heterodox authors in James C. Robinson, '*Purgatorio* in the *Portrait*: Dante, Heterodoxy, and the Education of James Joyce', 261–2.

[84] Gottfried, *Joyce's Misbelief*, 5.

This liminal aspect of Joyce's encounter with Dante found a strikingly physical expression in the locations of Joyce's reading; in order to move beyond the *Commedia* and encounter more relatively obscure works such as the *Convivio* or *De Vulgari Eloquentia*, Joyce was required to literally remove himself from a Catholic environment and enter either the Anglican setting of Archbishop Marsh's Library or else the determinedly secular environment of the National Library.[85] Thus, if we follow Ellmann in his belief that Dante was one of only a few authors whose work Joyce read in full, we can see the poet's essential liminality at the time of Joyce's early reading echoed through the peregrinations of the young writer across Dublin to seek out the so-called *opere minori*.[86] If this was the case, then by the time he took classes with Ghezzi at University College, Joyce could hardly have remained unaware of the *Monarchia*, Dante's most heterodox work (as of 1881 it was no longer technically heretical), and one that would have again emphasised Dante's potential as a subversive Catholic writer for the young Joyce.

This position of contested orthodoxy was certainly how Joyce came to portray Dante's situation within University College in *Stephen Hero*. Amongst many scenes alluding to or referencing Dante, one episode stands out, in which Stephen Daedalus is embroiled in a dispute with the President of the University over the reputation of Ibsen and Maeterlinck and the dangers and merits of modern literature. In their argument about the censoring of Stephen's paper for the literary society, Stephen argues that he should be allowed to discuss Ibsen, appealing for the artistic necessity of examining corruption. When told that this is work for men of politics and science, Stephen protests:

—Why not for the poet too? Dante surely examines and upbraids society.

—Ah, yes, said the President explanatorily, with a moral purpose in view: Dante was a great poet. (SH 85)

In this argument, we seem to find contested the personae of Dante constructed by the two competing traditions of nineteenth-century reading: Dante the Catholic poet with 'a moral purpose in view', and the 'modern', secular Dante whom Stephen has apparently read. The President (whose character was modelled on Fr William Delany S.J., the rector of

---

[85] On the Dante holdings in Marsh's library and the NLI see Boldrini, *Joyce, Dante*, 5; Joyce certainly portrays Stephen Daedalus as using Marsh's library in connection to Dante: 'Stephen went there a few times in the week to read old Italian books of the Trecento' (*SH* 159).

[86] Richard Ellmann, *Ulysses on the Liffey*, 12.

University College Dublin during Joyce's years there) puts forward a view that is close to the 'neo-Guelf' critical position.[87] Dante is to be read selectively, and those elements of his work that fit within the sphere of Catholic orthodoxy (his 'moral purpose') are to be accepted and the rest of him – such as his political dimension – is to be downplayed, ameliorated or ultimately ignored. By insisting on the whole of Dante – the man who examines corruption for its own sake – Stephen is presented, from one angle, as trying to break Dante free from this critical discourse; in effect trying to free Dante the political figure from his uneasy orthodoxy within Catholicism. However, in his attempt to assert this reading of Dante, Stephen subconsciously reinforces these established critical divisions. Indeed, as the President later acclaims Dante as 'the lofty upholder of beauty, the greatest of Italian poets' (*SH* 85), it becomes evident that their disagreement arises only because of Stephen's adherence to a critical position that is tellingly close to 'neo-Ghibellinism'. In effect, Joyce here stages the nineteenth-century discourse over the poet's interpretation, rehearsing both sides of the argument and thus escaping the urge to reduce his own view to an agreement with either: Dante remains permanently, tantalisingly, unorthodox.

The significance of Joyce's first reading of Dante, then, was not that it allowed a rebellious attempt to escape the poet's uneasy orthodoxy, as Stephen mounts in *Stephen Hero*, but rather that Joyce embraced the unique, febrile position that the liminal figure of Dante represented; a position that he would later exploit fully in the writing of *A Portrait of the Artist as a Young Man*. Stanislaus suggests that Joyce's discovery of Dante came at the end of reading a sequence of English authors, the last of whom was William Blake.[88] Blake is a figure who can helpfully remind us that Joyce was not alone in reading Dante in late nineteenth-century Dublin. In 1897, whilst Joyce was most likely making his notes on the *Inferno*, W.B. Yeats published an extensive article on Blake's illustrations to the *Commedia*, and the Dante of Yeats's essay serves to underline the unique nature of Joyce's reading.[89] To Yeats's Protestant ethos, the special power Dante accrued through his uneasy orthodoxy in Joyce's Jesuit context was meaningless; from a non-Catholic viewpoint, Dante's subversive potential could only ever be as a 'writer against the pope', he could only

---

[87] For an account of Fr Delany's interactions with Joyce at University College Dublin see Sullivan, *Joyce Among the Jesuits*, 153, 186, 194, 199.
[88] Stanislaus Joyce, 'James Joyce: A Memoir', 488.
[89] W. B. Yeats, *Essays and Introductions*, 116–45. For a brief account of Yeats's engagement with Dante see Ellis, *Dante and English Poetry*, 141–5.

act as an exterior assault upon Catholicism. And, by the end of the nineteenth century, with the shifting role of the Papacy and the establishment of the Kingdom of Italy, Dante's potency as such a figure was arguably fading.[90]

If, for earlier generations, Dante had famously been 'the central man of all the world', for Joyce first reading him within a Jesuit context, Dante was now his 'inside man', a figure at work within a potentially oppressive orthodoxy, helping the young artist to subvert, and ultimately elude, it. Indeed, it is worth remembering that at this point in his career Joyce was encompassed by a further oppressive orthodoxy. As Geert Lernout has noted, in late nineteenth-century Dublin, religious experimentation, anti-clericalism and atheistic refusal, far from being fringe positions, themselves represented a potent secular orthodoxy.[91] In facing the forces of both Catholic and secular orthodoxy, Dante represented a unique collaborator for Joyce – embraced by both wings of the argument, he was an equally unstable and potentially subversive presence within each. In this respect, the unique, doubled character of Dante that Joyce received from his Jesuit education would help him to occupy a similar position between these orthodox poles: circumscribed by both, but trammelled by neither.

Thus, Dante's uneasy orthodoxy within both Catholic and secular contexts – a contested position that was uniquely legible to the Jesuit-educated Joyce – set up a trajectory in Joyce's engagement with the poet that we will be following throughout the rest of this book. The compromised location of Dante between competing orthodoxies represented a liminal position of simultaneous inclusion and exclusion, which resonated with the polarities of alienation and involvement Joyce would come to explore through the notion of exile and the continued relation of the exiled individual to their lost community. In this respect, Joyce's discovery of his 'inside man' in the contested figure of Dante established an exilic trajectory that, through its resonance with the uneasy terms of their first encounter, would pattern both Joyce's lifelong engagement with the poet and significantly shape his own work. To the Protestant polemicists of three hundred years earlier, Dante had been a weapon with which to destroy the Catholic Church; for Joyce he was to be a potent, and lifelong, collaborator.

---

[90] See below, pp. 51–53.
[91] Lernout, *'Help My Unbelief'*, 60–1.

CHAPTER 2

'Spiritual-heroic Refrigerating Apparatus'
The Exiles of Dante in A Portrait of the Artist as a Young Man *and* Exiles

'I seem to have been'/'Is it not so?': Making the 'Exile'

Ever since he took ship with Nora Barnacle from the North Wall of Dublin Port on the evening of Saturday 8 October 1904, exile has been seen as the characteristic mode of alienation in the works of James Joyce. Whilst other, related models have been suggested, the persistence of exile as a path through Joyce's writing has been remarkable.[1] Exile has not only shaped the reading of alienation in Joyce's texts, it has also been repeatedly posited as a hermeneutic for reading the whole of his career, most famously through Hélène Cixous's notion of exile as Joyce's 'determining moment'.[2] Whilst exile has thus become a commonplace in both Joycean criticism and biography, the influence of Dante on Joyce's modes and conceptions of exile and alienation has yet to be fully discussed. It is this influence, its conditioning by the contextual circumstances of Joyce's first 'uneasy' reading of the poet, and the subsequent manifestation of forms of Dantean exile in both *A Portrait of the Artist as a Young Man* and the play *Exiles*, which will form the focus of this chapter.

Whilst the importance of exile to Joyce may be uncontroversial, it's a little more unusual to contend that his January 1904 essay 'A Portrait of the Artist' represents his first substantial 'exilic' text:

> Isolation, he had once written, is the first principle of artistic economy but traditional and individual revelations were at that time pressing their claims and self-communion had been but shyly welcomed. (*PSW*, 215)[3]

This passage inaugurates a discourse linking art, alienation, self-formation and compromised relations to community and tradition that, nine

---

[1] See, for instance, Jean-Michel Rabaté's reading of 'anarchistic "egoism" as a hidden backbone underpinning [Joyce's] personal and literary trajectory', *James Joyce and the Politics of Egoism*, 27.
[2] Cixous, *Exile of James Joyce*, xiv.
[3] James Joyce, *Poems and Shorter Writings*, 215 (all further references are to this edition).

months later, strengthened into Joyce's decision to leave Dublin for 'exile'. In turn, this discourse would provide the underpinning for Joyce's exploration of exile through the narrative of Stephen Dedalus when he returned to his 'Portrait' some three years later to begin *A Portrait of the Artist as a Young Man*.[4] The sense of dislocation both from and within a community that is captured in the adolescent essay reached its culmination in both Stephen's desire to 'fly by those nets' of 'nationality, language, religion' (*P* V. 1049–50) and his manifesto for this liberation:

> I will tell you what I will do and what I will not do. I will not serve that in which I no longer believe whether it call itself my home, my fatherland or my church: and I will try to express myself in some mode of life or art as freely as I can and as wholly as I can, using for my defence the only arms I allow myself to use, silence, exile and cunning. (*P* V. 2574–80)

Both Stephen's aim to 'fly by' entangling nets, and the arsenal he relies on, are deeply resonant with Dante's modes of exile and alienation, and rooted in specific moments of Dantean intertextuality. Indeed, 'silence, exile and cunning' will come to be seen as constitutive of the 'spiritual-heroic refrigerating apparatus, invented and patented in all countries by Dante Alighieri' (*P* V. 2764–5), the double terms of which concept shaped Joyce's Dantean understanding of exile.

Joyce's exile – or rather his fashioning of his departure from Dublin in 1904 into the mode of exile – has come to be seen as a 'determining moment'; however, the rhetorical shaping of this moment began some two years earlier, and is recorded in a 1902 letter to Lady Gregory, sent on the eve of Joyce's departure for an abortive sojourn as a medical student in Paris:

> I am leaving Dublin [...] I shall try myself against the powers of the world. All things are inconstant except the faith in the soul, which changes all things and fills their inconstancy with light. And though I seem to have been driven out of my country here as a misbeliever I have found no man yet with a faith like mine. (*SL* 8)

This letter represents the first instance of Joyce publicly shaping the narrative of his departures from Ireland into the inflicted terms of exile. The

---

[4] In tracing the persistence of a discourse of exile and alienation from 'A Portrait of the Artist' to *A Portrait of the Artist*, my engagement with *Stephen Hero* will be necessarily tangential. The reasons for this are twofold: firstly, Mary Reynolds has already discussed a range of possible Dantean intertexts within *Stephen Hero*, see *Joyce and Dante*, 20–6, 44–6, 181–3; and secondly, whilst concerned with alienation, the surviving text of *Stephen Hero* does not include any narrative of exile comparable to *Portrait*.

liminality inherent here in Joyce's rhetorical position of 'exile' – a position he would come to reoccupy after his 1904 departure – would later become an important aspect of Stephen Dedalus's own flight into 'exile' in *A Portrait of the Artist*.

Through the dual character of his nineteenth-century reception, Dante came to occupy a position of 'uneasy orthodoxy' within the cultural and religious contexts in which Joyce encountered him. This creatively compromised position of simultaneous inclusion and exclusion – both encompassed by and situated beyond prevailing orthodoxies – is echoed in the tensions of Joyce's fashioning of the narrative of his own 'rejection'. The ways in which both Joyce's and Stephen's rhetorically crafted exiles simultaneously signal their exclusion from, and affirm their involvement within, prevailing communities and systems of meaning represents a key example of the creative potential inherent in Dante's 'uneasy orthodoxy'. Indeed, through these resonant dynamics, Dante came to be the single strongest influence on Joyce's literary conception of exile, as explored in markedly Dantean forms within both *A Portrait of the Artist* and his only surviving dramatic work, *Exiles*.[5] In his engagement with Dante, Joyce modulated his earliest discourse of alienation (glimpsed in the 'Portrait' essay) through the significant form of 'exile', a form that would resonate with the possibilities and tensions, conflicts and contradictions within Dante's own discourses of exile.

Joyce's need to modulate and shape – to rhetorically fashion – his absence from Dublin, apparent already in the 1902 letter to Lady Gregory, persisted and intensified in his letters home after the 'determining moment' of October 1904. In February 1905 he wrote to Stanislaus from Pola: 'I have come to accept my present situation as a voluntary exile – is it not so?' (*SL* 56). The question is telling. Only some four months in, Joyce was already displaying a double perspective on his exilic identity rooted in an anxiety over its interpretation. It is a doubleness that seems to resonate with Dante's 'uneasy orthodoxy', anticipating as it does two diametrically opposed possibilities of interpretation, although, in the letter to Stanislaus, Joyce is clearly seeking to collapse – rather than sustain – the tension between them. The source of this anxiety is quite plain: what is the point in styling yourself 'exile' if no one in the community you are 'exiled' from sees you as such? In exploring Dante's influence on this double perspective in Joyce's identity and his generation of a similarly 'exilic'

---

[5] For discussion of Joyce's earlier dramatic works *A Brilliant Career* and the verse-play *Dream Stuff* see Claudia Corti, *'Esuli': Dramma, Psicodramma, Metadramma*, 7–11.

identity for Stephen Dedalus, it will thus be necessary to encroach onto questions of subjectivity and identity.

The nature and phenomenological experience of the self is a vast philosophical field, and the history of modernist literary responses to shifting conceptions of subjectivity and selfhood is almost as long and complicated.[6] In discussing the influence of Dantean modes of exile on discourses of alienation and self-formation in Joyce's work, I'm not seeking to make an intervention in this wider field, yet the forms of subjectivity that here arise within Dante's texts may support the position of those scholars who seek to challenge the division of the medieval from the continuum of self-identity, and the location of 'individuality' as an exclusively 'modern' phenomenon.[7] Drawing on both philosophical and psychoanalytic perspectives, identity can be seen as deriving from and subject to the fashioning action of narrative, and thus from an understanding of the self as fundamentally textual.[8] In this respect, the self appears as both linguistically constituted and conceivable as a text contingent on interrelated acts of writing and reading, acts that reveal identity to be hermeneutically derived.[9] As expressed by the 'double-aspect' theory of Thomas Nagel, this hermeneutic determination of the self is arrived at through a phenomenology of encounter:

> to possess the concept of a subject of consciousness an individual must be able in certain circumstances to identify himself and the states he is in without external observation. But these identifications must correspond by and large to those that can be made on the basis of external observation, both by others and by the individual himself.[10]

---

[6] For an intellectual history of subjectivity see Jerrold Seigel, *The Idea of the Self: Thought and Experience in Western Europe Since the Seventeenth Century*. For a summary of modernist responses see Finn Fordham, *I Do I Undo I Redo: The Textual Genesis of Modernist Selves in Hopkins, Yeats, Conrad, Forster, Joyce, and Woolf*, 19–26, 34–60.

[7] See Peter Haidu, *The Subject Medieval/Modern: Text and Governance in the Middle Ages*, 3–5, for his reading of the 'post-Althusserian theory of the subject' and contextualising of 'the contemporary discovery of subjectivity's fragility' within both medieval texts and forms of government. For Seigel's discussion of the 'inner experience' of medieval people see *The Idea of the Self*, 52–3. On Dante's place within this emergent discourse on periodicity and subjectivity see Ascoli, *Dante and the Making of a Modern Author*, 28–34.

[8] This view has been stated most baldly by Kim Worthington: 'human beings are to be understood as texts', see *Self as Narrative: Subjectivity and Community in Contemporary Fiction*, 25. On the self as 'delineated and embodied, primarily in narrative constructions or stories' see Anthony Kerby, *Narrative and the Self*, 1–14; and on the therapeutic praxis of embracing narrativity see Mark Freeman, *Rewriting the Self: History, Memory, Narrative*, 3–10, 50–3.

[9] On the subject as 'inscribed in language' and as arising as 'a function of language' see Jacques Derrida, *Margins of Philosophy*, 15. For Derrida's view of writing as 'constituting and dislocating [the subject] at the same time', see *Of Grammatology*, 67–9.

[10] Thomas Nagel, *The View from Nowhere*, 35.

In this respect, whilst subjectively initiated, 'the concept of the self is open to objective "completion"', and self-identity arises through a combination of encounter by that self, and by others – a process of self-formation that is 'completed' through recognition.[11]

Thus, we can conceive of the self as both narratively and linguistically constituted, and hermeneutically determined: a text that can be written by the self as subject, and read both by that self and by the other, and can in turn be rewritten through this reading. This fundamental contingency of the self (its ability to be hermeneutically fashioned and re-fashioned), and its essential plasticity through matrices of cultural signification that extend beyond verbal and textual modes, provides the basis of the understanding of subjectivity that will underpin this account of Dante's and Joyce's exiles.[12] This chapter will consider the associations between Dante's sense of exile as a mode of alienation through which to 'write' the self, and Joyce's exploration of such techniques and modes. Thus, the discourses of alienation and subjectivity that surround Stephen Dedalus in *A Portrait of the Artist* (and, to a lesser extent, Richard Rowan in *Exiles*) will be shown to derive from – and resonate with – the discourses of alienation and exile in the *Vita Nuova* and the *Commedia*.

The aim of this chapter will primarily be to explore the influence of Dante on the shaping of Joyce's conception of exile, and to demonstrate Joyce's use of this mode of alienation to craft the presentation of Stephen Dedalus in *A Portrait of the Artist* and the flight into 'exile' that it chronicles. Stephen's identity is fashioned through a series of resonant Dantean moments and postures, and through the inherent compromises that arise from this positioning he begins to be implicated in a significant form of community. Although focusing on *Portrait of the Artist*, in exploring the writing and rewriting of the self through exile, attention also needs to be given to *Exiles*. Whilst following an established pattern in seeing the latter as essentially Janus-faced, looking back to *Portrait* and forward to *Ulysses*, and thus able to clarify some of the tensions and problems in Stephen Dedalus's exilic position, we will also consider a resonant Dantean discourse within Joyce's play. Yet a reading of Joyce's engagement with Dante must be alive to the disconnections and the tensions between their discourses of alienation and exile, as well as to the alignments and

---

[11] Nagel, *The View from Nowhere*, 40.
[12] In emphasising the potential for all aspects of cultural signification to contribute to the 'writing' of the self, I am of course drawing on the seminal work of Stephen Greenblatt in his *Renaissance Self-Fashioning: From More to Shakespeare*. On the problem Dante's subjectivity poses to Greenblatt's 'Renaissance' periodicity see Ascoli, *Dante and the Making of a Modern Author*, 28–33.

correspondences. For example, whilst Joyce's exile from Dublin was rhetorically shaped, when Dante fled from Florence in fear of being burned alive, his exile was experienced in far more cut-and-dried terms.[13] This tension between the rhetorically embraced and externally inflicted forms of exile is a subject to be investigated later.[14]

A range of critics have discussed the parallels between narratives of Dante's and Joyce's exile.[15] Although Dominic Manganiello perceptively stressed some discontinuity between these narratives, the model of intertextual relation that arises from such paralleling can be both illuminating and deceptive: 'Joyce inherited from Dante the sense of moral and political intrepidity of the artist who, in rejecting all party affiliation, constitutes a party by himself.'[16] In thus conceiving of Joyce's reception of a 'heroic' mode of exile from Dante through the metaphor of heritage, Manganiello not only opens up an interesting issue but also risks erasing the multiple generations that lie between progenitor and inheritor. In directly paralleling the exile of Joyce with the exile of Dante, there is a real danger of re-enacting the problematic 'medievalism' that I criticised earlier in regard to Umberto Eco's approach to Joyce. Thus, Joyce's reception of Dantean modes of exile will again reveal the two authors as resonant poles, connected through the negotiating medium of history. To show how Dante became the pre-eminent figure of exile for Joyce, we will need to ask some further questions of the nineteenth-century personae of Dante.

Dante… Byron.. Rossetti. Risorgimento:
Joyce's Literary Tradition of Exile

Whilst there is a very long Irish tradition of rhetorically shaping acts of emigration into the inflicted alienation of 'exile', Joyce engaged with a different, far-longer tradition, and one that was implicated in his own rhetorical shifting: the literary tradition of exile.[17] This tradition was embodied in the nineteenth-century personae of Dante. There were certainly other literary figures whom Joyce might have associated with exile, chief

---

[13] This disparity between Dante's experience of exile and that of Joyce has been briefly discussed by Manganiello, see *Joyce's Politics*, 191.
[14] See below, pp. 77–80.
[15] See Manganiello, *Joyce's Politics*, 190–202. For Hélène Cixous's paralleling of Joyce and Dante within her wider reading of 'exile' in Joyce see *Exile of James Joyce*, 355, 639–40.
[16] Manganiello, *Joyce's Politics*, 232.
[17] For an overview of the historical Irish tradition of exile see Kerby Miller, *Emigrants and Exiles: Ireland and the Irish Exodus to North America*, 3–8, 11–25, 102–30.

amongst whom would be his early hero Henrik Ibsen. Indeed, writers such as Byron and Shelley were both prominent exponents of romanticised versions of exile in which the young Joyce took an interest.[18] However, it is exactly *through* the work of such figures as these Romantic poets and other, later nineteenth-century writers that Dante's pre-eminence as a figure of exile was established for Joyce. Byron and others were instrumental in transmitting a cultural construction of Dante as a figure of 'heroic' exile, a political reading that intersected with the subjective and 'spiritual' aspects of Dante's own discourses of alienation and exile. This intersection would harmonise with Joyce's 'uneasy' first reading of Dante's works to such an extent that the poet's importance would far outstrip any other literary figure in developing Joyce's ideas about exile.[19]

The story of Dante's exile, which was reconstituted into a nineteenth-century mythical form, was already quite complicated.[20] On 15 June 1300, Dante Alighieri was elected as one of the six priors of Florence, and for a term of two months he helped lead the newly formed 'White Guelf' administration of the city. During his tenure as prior Dante agreed to the exile of a number of political opponents, including his great friend, the poet Guido Cavalcanti. When, in October 1301, Florence sent a mission to Rome to negotiate a cooling of tensions with Pope Boniface VIII, it is likely that Dante was amongst their number. Certainly, he is not recorded as being in Florence in November 1301, when the 'Black Guelfs' (the pro-Papal splinter wing of the original Guelf party) returned from exile and seized power. On 27 January 1302, in the aftermath of the fall of the White government, Dante's name appears alongside three others in an indictment for political corruption, summoning them to appear before the *podestà* (the externally appointed head of the Florentine commune), imposing an extortionate fine and sentencing them to two years' exile from Tuscany. When Dante and the others failed to appear or pay the fine, on 10 March 1302 this sentence was commuted to lifelong exile, on pain of being burned alive if found within any of Florence's territories.

The political imposition of Dante's exile was the start of a long exile narrative. Whilst Dante's exact movements are sometimes uncertain,

---

[18] On Byron and Shelley within the discourses of separation and distance in *A Portrait of the Artist* see Vicki Mahaffey, *Reauthorizing Joyce*, 87–9.

[19] Indeed, as Manganiello has pointed out, one deficiency in the model of the exiled writer provided by Ibsen was his inability to provide the kind of 'reflections on politics centered on the city that had expelled him', which Joyce found in Dante, see *Joyce's Politics*, 191–2.

[20] I am drawing on Nick Havely's lucid, rigorous and readable narrative of Dante's exile throughout this summary; see *Dante*, 18–31.

he and the other exiled Whites lurked in neighbouring towns such as Siena and Arezzo for a while, making alliances with exiled Ghibellines and plotting possible political routes of return. Dante's participation in these plots is recorded for the first year or so, after which, in the spring of 1303, he temporarily distanced himself from his fellow exiles. However, by summer 1304 he had returned to the Whites at Arezzo, where he likely remained up until the disaster of their foolhardy attempt to force a return to Florence militarily, and their subsequent crushing by Florentine troops at La Lastra on 20 July. After this, Dante left the Whites and went into solitary exile, staying in a number of different Italian cities, harboured by different princely protectors (most famously by Cangrande della Scala in Verona), until his death in Ravenna in 1321. In distancing himself from the White Guelfs and withdrawing into political solitude, Dante affected an intensification of his exile that he would famously have his ancestor Cacciaguida praise in the *Paradiso*:

> Di sua bestialitate il suo processo
> Farà la prova, si che a te fia bello
> Averti fatta parte per te stesso.[21]

[Of their stupidity the outcome will provide the proof, so that for you it will be well to have become a party unto yourself.] (*Par*. 17. 67–9)

It was in the course of this period of individual exile that Dante wrote the *Convivio*, the *De Vulgari Eloquentia*, the *Monarchia* and the *Commedia*.[22] This historical narrative of Dante's inflicted exile from his city, and his self-willed separation from a community of exiles, provided the kernel from which the nineteenth-century personae of the poet were extruded. To understand how this mythical view of Dante was formed in circumstances that ensured its transmission to Joyce, we need to consider how the Risorgimento myth of exile helped define the perception of Dante within English literary circles.

The turbulence of Risorgimento politics had, by the start of the century, created no shortage of exiles, and figures such as Ugo Foscolo and Giuseppe Mazzini, along with those Risorgimento writers and politicians still living in Italy, set about crafting a role for themselves within the burgeoning nationalist discourse. In its simplest form, the Risorgimento

---

[21] Manganiello sees this passage as a crux in his paralleling of Dante's and Joyce's exiles, see *Joyce's Politics*, 198. Indeed, it can't have escaped Joyce's notice that his own year of self-imposed 'exile', 1904, was exactly six hundred years after Dante's.
[22] See Havely, *Dante*, 32–56.

myth of exile held that the birth of the unified Kingdom of Italy would be brought about through the agency of its exiled patriots, acting both as a source of international propaganda for the nationalist cause and as examples of moral fortitude for the peoples still languishing within the fractured lands of the peninsula.[23] This sense of exile as both a moral and political virtue echoed Ciceronian concepts of *patria* and the nobility of political exile; however, it was not to Cicero or other classical precedents that the Risorgimento exiles looked for their model of exile, but rather to Dante.[24]

The combination of Dante as political exile and poet made him singularly attractive to figures such as Foscolo and Mazzini. The medieval poet offered a strong precedent on which to model their own role as exiled writers, and also connected them back to the Middle Ages, a period that the Risorgimento intellectuals came to see as 'the great age of political freedom, independence and economic growth, in which Italian cities led European civilisation'.[25] This relationship between Dante and the Risorgimento exiles represented a reciprocal fashioning of identities: as much as Dante helped the Risorgimento writers to reclaim a sense of national identity in their exile, so their embroilment of the poet in the political discourse of the Risorgimento left a lasting mark on how subsequent generations would encounter him. Dante became synonymous throughout Europe with Italian nationalism; he came to be seen in effect as the 'national poet and the symbol of Italian cultural and political identity *par excellence*' and, just as his status as exile had legitimised the Risorgimento's national mythmaking, so now the exile of Foscolo, Mazzini and others began to fundamentally transform Dante's own cultural construction.[26]

The transmission of Dante's persona as 'heroic' exile into the realm of English literature was initiated by Ugo Foscolo, and the effects of Foscolo's and other Risorgimento intellectuals' intervention can be seen

---

[23] Isabella, 'Exile and Nationalism', 494–5.
[24] On the influence of Cicero see Isabella, 'Exile and Nationalism', 494. For more on Dante as the primary exilic exemplar of the Risorgimento see Andrea Ciccarelli, 'Dante and the Culture of Risorgimento: Literary, Political or Ideological Icon?', 77–8; Ciccarelli, 'Dante and Italian Culture', 125–39; and Rita Degl'Innocenti Pierini, 'Il Foscolo e la letteratura classica sull'esilio: appunti di lettura', 147–55.
[25] Isabella, 'Exile and Nationalism', 498; see also Adrian Lyttelton, 'Creating a National Past: History, Myth and Image in the Risorgimento', 27–74; and Jossa, 'Politics vs. Literature', 30–49. Interestingly, the Risorgimento writers tended to privilege the ethical virtues of their reading of Dante – his role as the pre-eminent example of 'Italian integrity' – rather than his poetic project, of which Manzoni was the only evident disciple, see Jossa, 'Politics vs. Literature', 41–6.
[26] Isabella, 'Exile and Nationalism', 497–8.

clearly in the work of a number of writers who were themselves substantial influences on Joyce.[27] Byron and Shelley both provided examples for Joyce not only of figures who had themselves undergone a form of 'heroic' exile, but also of poets who were profoundly inspired by and deeply engaged with the secularised, exilic presentation of Dante championed by the Risorgimento.[28] Shelley, for instance, was determined to use Dante to further his own liberal, atheistic project in what was, as Steve Ellis notes, 'an influential example of the recurrent modern practice of attending to Dante's "poetry" while neglecting or discounting his beliefs'; or, as Joyce put it earlier, fancying himself 'a Dante without the unfortunate prejudices' (*OCPW* 73).[29] However, among the Romantic poets, it was Byron who undoubtedly had the greatest influence on Joyce's reception of Dante as a figure of exile.

The scene in *A Portrait* in which Stephen takes a thrashing from his peers because he will not 'admit that Byron was no good' (*P* II. 783) – an incident supposedly repeated from Joyce's own schooldays (*JJ* 39–40) – hints at Byron's wider importance to Joyce. In linking Byron to Stephen's isolation through the perceived literary orthodoxy of his peers, this incident echoed a moment in the earlier *Stephen Hero* that cultivated an association between Byron and the nascent discourse of alienation in the even earlier essay 'A Portrait of the Artist':

> The burgher notion of the poet Byron in undress pouring out verses just as a city fountain pours out water seemed to him characteristic of most popular judgements on esthetic matters and he combated the notion at its root by saying solemnly to Maurice – Isolation is the first principle of artistic economy. (*SH* 34)

The discourse of alienation inaugurated by isolation as 'the first principle of artistic economy' (*PSW*, 215), underpins the alienated persona of Stephen Daedalus as transcending 'popular judgements', and is linked to the figure of Byron. That Dante effectively countersigns this exilic association

---

[27] Although Foscolo may have been one of the earliest figures to connect British literary and bibliographic circles with the political context of the Risorgimento, he was hardly the last, see Havely, *Dante's British Public*, 229–31, 265–6. The possibility of intertextual connections between Foscolo and Joyce has been considered by Alessandra Saturni, who compares Molly Bloom and Cassandra in *Dei Sepolcri*, although disappointingly Saturni finds no direct evidence that Joyce had read the poem, see 'La Parola al Femminile: Molly vs. Cassandra', 108–9.
[28] On Shelley and Byron's reactions to Dante see Ellis, *Dante and English Poetry*, 3–65; William Keach, 'The Shelleys and Dante's Matilda', 60–70; Michael O'Neill, '"Admirable for Conciseness and Vigour": Dante and English Romantic Poetry's Dealings with Epic', 16–19, 20–7; Havely, *Dante's British Public*, 149–51.
[29] Ellis, *Dante and English Poetry*, 3.

becomes clearer when we consider that, in a number of his verses, Byron forcefully restated the Risorgimento rhetoric of Dante as the pre-eminent figure of 'heroic' isolation and exile. In the 'Age of Bronze', for instance, it is 'Dante's exile sheltr'd by thy gate' (l. 421) that is hailed as Verona's highest civic achievement.[30] In 'The Prophecy of Dante', Byron comes yet more closely into line with the Risorgimento myth of Dante as national exile. Here, Byron's Dante-protagonist is voiced as both a Romantic self-determinist and the classic Risorgimento exile:

> For mine is not a nature to be bent
> By tyrannous faction, and the brawling crowd,
> And though the long, long conflict hath been spent
> In vain, – and never more, save when the cloud
> Which overhangs the Apennine my mind's eye
> Pierces to fancy Florence, once so proud
> Of me, can I return, though but to die,
> Unto my native soil, – they have not yet
> Quench'd the old exile's spirit, stern and high.
> ('The Prophecy of Dante', I. 31–42)

This image of resolute and implacable exile is typical of the bombast that Byron adopts throughout a poem whose 'furthest political ambition' is the unification of Italy.[31] Byron's view of Dante would have a lasting impact upon the nineteenth-century transmission of Dante in English literature, an influence arguably still felt today in the general preference for the *Inferno* over the other cantiche of the *Commedia*.[32]

Although dismissed by Mary Reynolds as being 'of all Dante's interpreters [...] the least likely to appeal to Joyce', the figure who was perhaps most instrumental in transmitting the Risorgimento myth of Dante's exile to Joyce was Dante Gabriel Rossetti.[33] This transmission took place through Rossetti's poetic work, his paintings and his shaping presence within Joyce's experience of a key Dantean text. It has long been

---

[30] George Gordon Byron, *Poetical Works*, 174 (all further references to Byron's works are to this edition).
[31] Ellis, *Dante and English Poetry*, 37.
[32] For Byron's infernal preferences see Ellis, *Dante and English Poetry*, 38. Interestingly, Byron's teasing condemnation of the *Commedia* to Shelley, in which he said (with a view to irritating his friend) that the poem was 'so obscure, tiresome, and insupportable that no one can read it for half an hour without yawning and going to sleep', was attributed by Corrado Zacchetti to Byron's reading of Bettinelli's *Lettere Virgiliane*; see *Shelley e Dante*, 140.
[33] Reynolds, *Joyce and Dante*, 178. As Vicki Mahaffey has pointed out, Rossetti's view of the *Vita Nuova* as the 'autobiography or autopsychology of Dante's youth', would in fact seem remarkably appealing to the author of *A Portrait*, see 'James Joyce in Transition: A Study of *A Portrait of the Artist as a Young Man, Giacomo Joyce, Exiles* and *Ulysses*', 155–6.

known that Joyce's surviving copy of the *Vita Nuova* (edited by Marco de Rubris, with introductory essays by Antonio Agresti and published in Turin in 1911), which he bought secondhand in Trieste in around 1912, was illustrated by a selection of Rossetti's paintings.[34] This edition of the *Vita Nuova*, designed by Rocco Carlucci, has been justly called 'a true example of Italian craftsmanship'.[35] It was lavishly produced in a beautiful vellum cover with gold incised title and green binding ribbons, with each page framed by Carlucci's foliate border in red ink, the rubrics within the *text* also highlighted in red, and eleven reproductions of Rossetti's Dantean paintings included. In this way, Rossetti's presence physically shaped Joyce's experience of the *Vita Nuova*, providing the Pre-Raphaelite aesthetic that governs the material textuality of the edition, and breaking up the flow of Dante's text by de Rubris's interspersal of his illustrations. However, as well as illustrating Dante's text and spatially shaping Joyce's reading of it, through the two extended essays by Antonio Agresti, Rossetti was also a substantial narrative presence within the edition.

Agresti's essays centre around three overlapping narratives: Rossetti's life and work, his engagement with the work of Dante, and the history of the Pre-Raphaelite Brotherhood as a whole.[36] In his reading of Rossetti's artistic style, Agresti formulated an interestingly anachronistic position:

> Mi sembra, talvolta, guardando il lavoro di lui, che esso non sia opera d'un moderno, ma sibbene d'un antico, contemporaneo di Giotto e dell'Orcagna per il sentimento.[37]
>
> [Sometimes, looking at his work, it seems to me that it is not the work of a modern but rather that of an antique, a contemporary in sentiment of Giotto or of Orcagna.]

Whilst this view of Rossetti as a contemporary of Giotto, building on the earlier assertion that really 'egli fu un italiano medioevale' ['he was a

---

[34] See Mahaffey, 'James Joyce in Transition', 155–6; and Reynolds, *Joyce and Dante*, 178–9. On the use of Rossetti's paintings in the de Rubris edition see Giuliana Pieri, 'Dante and the Pre-Raphaelites: British and Italian Responses', 115, n. 32.

[35] Carla M. Vaglio, '*Giacomo Joyce* or the *Vita Nuova*', 101. For how the material textuality of the de Rubris edition approximated a 'medieval' form, see below, pp. 147–48.

[36] Agresti was in a unique position to write these essays, as from 1892 until his death in 1926 he was the husband of Olivia Rossetti, Dante Gabriel's niece. In an intriguing connection that further blurs the permeable line between the Victorians and the modernists, Olivia Rossetti Agresti would go on to be a longtime friend and correspondent of Ezra Pound, with Dante being a frequent touchstone in their letters; see Leon Surette, 'Introduction' to Surette and Tryphonopoulos, *'I Cease Not to Yowl': Ezra Pound's Letters to Olivia Rossetti Agresti*, xvi.

[37] Antonio Agresti, 'Dell'arte di Dante Gabriele Rossetti', xviii.

medieval Italian'], is sufficiently naïve to have drawn Joyce's scepticism, Agresti's contextualising of Rossetti within the Risorgimento politics of exile was far more nuanced.[38] At the opening of his first essay, Agresti sets the scene for the young Rossetti's home life:

> A Londra, nella casa del padre suo – l'esule poeta Vastese – s'incontravano i profughi italiani, i fuggiti al capestro o alla galera del Borbone e dell'Austria, e chi sa quante volte correva e ricorreva su le labbra di quei forti, destinati a vivere nel paese umido e nebbioso, il nome della terra ricca di sole e di fiori! E chi sa quante volte sonò alle orecchie del giovine il nome di Dante, benedetto come quello di colui che, primo, aveva detto all'Italia la parola della sua libertà nazionale![39]

> [In London, in the house of his father – the exiled poet of Vasto – the Italian refugees met, those fugitives from the gallows and jails of the Bourbons and of Austria, and who knows how many times ran and recurred, on the lips of those strong ones destined to live in that wet and foggy country, the name of the rich land of sunshine and flowers? And who knows how many times in the ears of that young man sounded the name of Dante, blessed as he who had, for the first time, given to Italy the word of its national liberty!]

In this story of the young Rossetti overhearing the meetings of the Risorgimento exiles who gathered around his father, Gabriele, Joyce thus encountered a forceful – if histrionic – version of the myth of Dante as national hero and model for all of Italy's political exiles.[40] And, given its inclusion within Joyce's copy of the *Vita Nuova*, the intimate implication of Agresti's Risorgimento narrative within Joyce's developing conception of Dante as a figure of exile, is rivalled only by the narrative that, as we will see presently, was included in Eugenio Camerini's *Commedia*.

In this respect, de Rubris's edition of the *Vita Nuova* provided Joyce with a political narrative of Dante's heroic exile that would resonate strongly with his reading of Rossetti's poetic work. Joyce's familiarity

---

[38] Agresti, 'Dell'arte di Dante Gabriele Rossetti', xvii. It is also interesting to note that in this view of Rossetti as a 'medieval', Joyce would have encountered a crude formulation of just the kind of 'direct-inject' medievalism I questioned earlier.

[39] Agresti, 'Dell'arte di Dante Gabriele Rossetti', viii. The political implication of this passage is also discussed by Carla Vaglio, see '*Giacomo Joyce* or the *Vita Nuova*', 109.

[40] The source for Agresti's narrative was most likely his father-in-law, Rossetti's brother and the Pre-Raphaelite's self-appointed chronicler, William Michael Rossetti. Alison Milbank gives the best account of Gabriele Rossetti and his children in relation to the various, often conflicting, responses to Dante in the Rossetti household; see her *Dante and the Victorians*, 117–61. We should also note that, in its story of the young artist overhearing and absorbing political discussion that he cannot fully understand, there is a strong echo between Agresti's Rossetti narrative and the Christmas dinner scene in *A Portrait of the Artist*.

with the poetry of Rossetti has been somewhat overlooked, and in such works as 'Dante at Verona', he would have found a forceful deployment of the Risorgimento rhetoric learned at Gabriele's knee.[41] This poem, depicting Dante's life in exile at the court of Cangrande, echoes the line of Byron's 'Age of Bronze'; however, Rossetti's poem, drawing on Dante's hope that the *Commedia* might win him sufficient fame to allow his return to Florence in honour (*Par.* 25. 1–9), presents a more pessimistic scene than Byron's bombast allows, and one that hints at Dante's continuing exile:

> Alas! the Sacred Song whereto
>   Both heaven and earth had set their hand
> Not only at Fame's gate did stand
> Knocking to claim the passage through,
>   But toiled to ope that heavier door
>   Which Florence shut for evermore.[42]
>   ('Dante at Verona', ll. 25–30)

Rossetti's poem then builds upon the Risorgimento myth, affirming the unavoidable, self-perpetuating continuity of Dante's exile:

> So the day came, after a space,
>   When Dante felt assured that there
>   The sunshine must lie sicklier
> Even than in any other place,
>   Save only Florence. When that day
>   Had come, he rose and went his way.
>   (ll. 476–480)

In thus depicting Dante's departure from Verona and the perpetuation of his alienation, Rossetti emphasises the liminal reading of Dante's exile. In stressing the poet's restless motion and inability to settle into any form of community Rossetti manages to move the Risorgimento rhetoric closer to Dante's own texts on exile, such as Cacciaguida's invocation to self-exile (*Par.* 17. 61–9). So, first through the example of Byron, and then through the much more significant presence of Dante Gabriel Rossetti as mediated by Antonio Agresti, Joyce received an English literary version of the Risorgimento myth of Dante as 'heroic exile'.

Indeed, as well as reaching him through these English influences, this Risorgimento Dante was re-presented to Joyce within an Italian context.

---

[41] For examples of Joyce's engagement with Rossetti's poetry see below, pp. 173, 180, 187.
[42] Dante Gabriel Rossetti, *Collected Poetry and Prose*, 28 (all further references to Rossetti's works are to this edition).

Although not as explicit in invoking the figures of the Risorgimento as Agresti, the importance that Eugenio Camerini's edition of the *Commedia* placed on a Risorgimento reading of Dante's exile can be seen clearly in his 'Vita di Dante'. From tracing the various exiles of Dante's ancestors, to stressing the possible culpability of Boniface VIII in orchestrating Dante's banishment, Camerini relishes every aspect of Dante's unjust exile, a narrative emphasis epitomised in the drama with which he details its imposition:

> Cante de' Gabbrielli, allora podestà di Firenze, lo aveva citato in giudizio, come reo di baratterie e, sotto false cagioni, condannatolo in contumacia, il 24 gennaio 1302, alla multa di cinquemila lire di Fiorini piccoli. Dante nè comparve, nè pagò l'indebita ammenda.[43]

> [Cante de' Gabbrielli, then *podestà* of Florence, had pronounced sentence on him as being guilty of barratry, and under false pretence, condemned him in contumacy, on the 24th January 1302, to the fine of five thousand small Florins. Dante neither appeared there, nor paid the unwarranted fine.[44]]

This view of Dante as the noble man paying the unearned debt of a lifetime in exile resonates strongly with the myth of heroic exile that formed in the tumult of the Risorgimento and passed into English literature through such figures as Foscolo, Byron and Rossetti.

However, by the first decade of the twentieth century, in Italy the myth of Dante as exile that Joyce had received was coming under threat. As a new generation of writers and intellectuals grew up in a unified country, they sought to kick out against the establishing myths of the Risorgimento, which were no longer the rhetoric of rebellion but an institutionalised status quo. Prominent amongst the myths to be debunked was that of Dante and the Risorgimento exiles.[45] Indeed, whilst most often conceived of as a reaction to the national myth, this new irreverent attitude towards the poet was arguably inherent in his Risorgimento construction: as Stefano Jossa has cogently argued, in separating out Dante the exile from Dante the poet – in effect using Dante '*against* literature' – the Risorgimento established a dialectic pendulum that inevitably swung back the other

---

[43] Eugenio Camerini, 'Vita di Dante', 9. For the previous discussion of Camerini and his edition see above, pp. 30–33.
[44] Modern scholarship gives the date as 27 January 1302; see Havely, *Dante*, 21.
[45] For an account of the post-Risorgimento transition in Italian literary culture see Ciccarelli, 'Dante and Italian Culture', 135–40.

way, and came close to knocking down the patriotic statue of the poet in the process.[46]

One group within this new twentieth-century generation of writers were commonly known as the *vociani* through their association with the influential Florentine literary magazine *La Voce*. The *vociani* sought to consciously affect the 'modernisation' of Italian culture through its liberation from 'the cult of the past [...] encouraged by the traditional scholarly and academic centres'.[47] A cultural struggle over Dante was inevitable as they thus attempted to rest attention away from the 'heroic exile' and back onto Dante the poet and his poetry. However, as Scipio Slataper (one of the most prominent *vociani*) pointed out in 1909, there was one area of the Italian peninsula where the Risorgimento had failed to achieve its political – if not its cultural – aims. This was the last region of 'Italy' where, as Slataper noted with the unmistakable frustration of a native, it wasn't yet fashionable 'a ridere di Dante precursore di Mazzini' ['to laugh at the idea of Dante as precursor to Mazzini']: the so-called unredeemed territories of Trento and Trieste.[48] Thus, when Joyce moved to Trieste in 1904/5, he not only embarked on the first stage of his own experience of 'exile' but entered into a city that, in many ways, could still be considered a microcosm of the Risorgimento. Still dominated by a foreign power in the form of the Austro-Hungarian Empire, still racked with rebellion and irredentism, Trieste was a place where the political potency of Dante as a figure of exile and patriotism was undimmed. In this respect, through the efforts of *vociani* writers such as Slataper to resist irredentist nationalism by embracing the multicultural diversity of Trieste, Dante (and the historiography of the Middle Ages as a whole) became a key battleground.

For the irredentists of Trieste, Dante remained the icon of the Risorgimento, and the poet's importance was actively promoted within the city by the Triestine branch of the *Società Dante Alighieri* founded by Luigi Guelpa.[49] Thus, for the *vociani* and others who sought to oppose the stifling cultural orthodoxy of irredentist nationalism, the reconfiguration

---

[46] On Dante as being misread against supposedly 'decadent' Italian literature see Jossa, 'Politics vs. Literature', 41–6.
[47] Ciccarelli, 'Dante and Italian Culture', 138.
[48] Scipio Slataper, 'I figli di Segantini', quoted in Ciccarelli, 'Dante and Italian Culture', 140.
[49] The Dante Society of Trieste was sufficiently vocal in its advocacy of the poet that in 1921 it drew the attention of the Turkish writer Cevad Gültekin in his article 'Avrupa'da: Dante Aligieri' ['In Europe: Dante Alighieri'], see Cüneyd Okay, 'The Reception of Dante in Turkey through the Long Nineteenth Century', 347. The Trieste branch continues its activities to this day: www.dantealighieritrieste.it/comitato.html (accessed 23 June 2015).

and cultural deconstruction of Dante offered an easy line of resistance. In this way, the poet came to be claimed by two opposing – if unequal – cultural and political movements in the city.[50] As John McCourt has shown, during his time in Trieste, Joyce was able to move between these camps with relative ease and frequency, making friends and contacts amongst both the irridentists and a range of 'opposition' groups, including both the Futurists and the *vociani*.[51] In entering such a febrile atmosphere, clouded over by opposing cultural orthodoxies, Joyce must have felt strangely at home. Indeed, he was soon bending Roberto Prezioso's ear about the 'similarity between irredentism and the Irish independence movement', a political paralleling of Dublin and Trieste to which the newspaper editor quickly acquiesced.[52]

Given the way in which Joyce negotiated the cultural orthodoxies that surrounded Dante in Dublin, we might suspect his sympathies within Trieste to have lain with the more 'moderate' and multicultural *vociani* position. However, Manganiello records that in furthering his socialist interests Joyce purchased and read approvingly *Saggio su la rivoluzione* by Carlo Pisacane.[53] Although pursuing it from a slightly different angle than the earlier Risorgimento intellectuals, Pisacane's book is unequivocal in its historiography of national unity:

> Gli Italiani siamo unitari; tali furono gli antichi, ed una aspirazione fra i moderni comincia da Dante. L'idea che nel 1814 ha cominciato a farsi popolare, che ha progredito sempre, che s'è mostrata dominante in tutti gl'istanti di vita vissuti dal popolo italiano, è l'unità; ma gli ostacoli per attuarla son più che moltissimi.[54]
>
> [We Italians are unitary; just as the ancients were, and the moderns aspire to be, beginning with Dante. The idea that began to be popular in 1814, which has progressed ever since, and which predominates in every moment of the life lived by the Italian people, is unity; but the obstacles to its achievement abound.]

---

[50] On Trieste as a 'continuation' of the Risorgimento culture and Dante as 'still the strongest vehicle for communication of any message related to the unsettled issues of Risorgimento' see Ciccarelli, 'Dante and Italian Culture', 139–42.

[51] On Joyce's relation to irredentist elements in Trieste, most directly through his lectures at the Università Popolare in 1907 and 1912, as well as his 'shared thematic concerns' with Slataper and other *vociani*, see John McCourt, *The Years of Bloom: James Joyce in Trieste 1904–1920*, 8–13, 99–102, 169–70; and John McCourt, 'Trieste', 232–5. On the wider political contexts Joyce encountered in Trieste see Manganiello, *Joyce's Politics*, 43–58.

[52] Manganiello, *Joyce's Politics*, 43–4.

[53] Manganiello, *Joyce's Politics*, 45.

[54] Carlo Pisacane, *Saggio su la rivoluzione*, 99.

Through Pisacane, Joyce thus encountered another forceful statement of the political-heroic myth communicated to him by Byron, Rossetti, Agresti and Camerini. In this respect, Joyce's political paralleling of Dublin and Trieste resonated on a deep level with the cultural situation of Dante in both cities. As within Dublin, where Dante had been subject to the competing pressures and tensions of the orthodoxies of secular and Catholic readings, so within Trieste he cut a similarly contentious figure. This time Dante was pulled not only between the familiar Dublin polarities, but also came under the new influence of the political rhetoric of the *vociani*, keen to move away from the historiography of the Risorgimento, whilst equally striving to maintain a secular cultural identity and to refuse the centripetal tug of Catholic orthodoxy. In entering into exile in Trieste, Joyce entered a cultural climate that both countersigned and began to problematise the myth of Dante's heroic exile, an unmistakable resonance with the terms of the 'uneasy orthodoxy' of his first reading of Dante. In Trieste, Joyce found his 'inside man' was still very much public property.

By the time he was living in Trieste, Joyce had thus received the forceful myth of Dante as 'heroic' exile from a number of interconnected sources, and this myth was implicated in turn in a discourse of orthodoxy and resistance that resonated strongly with the contexts of Joyce's earlier reading of the poet in Dublin. However, we shouldn't overlook the place of Dante's own texts within this discourse; despite the nineteenth-century mediations and distortions that determined the mode in which Joyce encountered it, there remains an important and substantial medieval tradition of exile inscribed in Dante's writings. Exile in medieval Italy was indeed an overwhelmingly political experience, as the Risorgimento was keen to stress. Yet the legalised exclusion of a citizen from his community – the fate that Dante suffered in January 1302 – was also personally devastating, a tragedy that resonated on a deeper subjective and spiritual level than quotidian politics.[55]

Within medieval thought (infused as it was by Aristotle's *Politics*) exile from the community had a severe ontological effect:

> E però dice lo Filosofo, che 'l'uomo naturalmente è compagnevole animale.' E siccome un uomo a sua sufficienza richiede compagnia domestica di famiglia; così una casa a sua sufficienza richiede una vicinanza, altrimenti molti diffetti sosterrebbe, che sarebbono impedimento di felicità. E

---

[55] See Havely, *Dante*, 23–4; Randolph Starn, *Contrary Commonwealth: The Theme of Exile in Medieval and Renaissance Italy*, 1–85, 121–38; and Lauro Martines, *Power and Imagination: City-States in Renaissance Italy*, 150.

perocchè una vicinanza non può a sè in tutto satisfare, conviene a satsifacimento di quella essere la città.

[Therefore the Philosopher says that man is by nature a social animal. And just as for his well-being an individual requires the domestic companionship provided by family, so for its well-being a household requires a community, for otherwise it would suffer many defects that would hinder happiness. And since a community could not provide for its own well-being completely by itself, it is necessary for this well-being that there be a city.] (*Conv.* 4. 4. 2)

In the *Convivio*, Dante thus captures the way in which the alienation of the citizen through exile affected a rupturing in the social nature of his being. Within a Christian context, this subjective significance of exile as a form of alienation came to be theologically associated with the formation of identity through the trope of the *homo viator*.

Originating in the thought of the Early Church, the concept of the *homo viator* came to occupy a central position within medieval spirituality. The trope posited life as, in essence, a form of spiritual exile in which man acts as a 'terrestrial wayfarer struggling to regain the peace of his celestial home'.[56] Underlying the position of the *homo viator* was the complementary concept of the *alienus*: a figure such as Lucifer who has become hopelessly and eternally separated from God. The distinction between the *alienus* and the *viator* hinged on the salvific action of Christ, whose Resurrection transformed humanity from one to the other, able now to journey back from exile towards the original, pre-Edenic relation with the divine.[57] The emphasis that the trope of *homo viator* placed upon separation and transition associated the eschatological journey of the Christian soul with the contemporary social and religious phenomenon of *peregrinatio* or pilgrimage. In turn, man came to style himself as *peregrinus*, the pilgrim who is simply passing through the 'temporal comfort on this earth' on his way back to the heavenly home from which he was exiled.[58]

In this way, the spiritual centrality of the trope of the *homo viator* not only positioned exile at the heart of medieval self-conceptions, but

---

[56] George A. Trone, 'Exile', 363. The best single overview of this vast and important topic in medieval intellectual life remains Gerhart B. Ladner, 'Homo Viator', 233–59, and I am indebted to Ladner's work throughout this discussion.

[57] Ladner, 'Homo Viator', 234–8. In connection to the role of Eden in the story of *homo viator*, note Adam's reference in the *Paradiso* to life after expulsion from Eden as 'tanto essilio' (*Par.* 26. 116) ['so long an exile'].

[58] Ladner, 'Homo Viator', 235–7.

also allowed exile – and the eschatological virtue of redemption that it offered – to pattern other forms of alienation, even those experienced within a community. And so in the *Commedia*, written in the years of Dante's lonely exile after 1304, he explores the potential of the exilic journey of the *homo viator* to act as a kind of meta-narrative through which a range of complex spiritual, psychological and poetic concerns could be encountered.[59] However, even in the *Vita Nuova* – completed some ten years before Dante's exile – the Christian tradition of the *homo viator* and the attendant fashioning of subjectivity through exilic narrative, patterns an extensive discourse of alienation. It is arguably the continuum that the *homo viator* forms between these two discourses of alienation that allowed Dante, through the *Commedia*, to encounter and figuratively redeem the harsh, inflicted form of alienation in his political exile. In other words, it is the extrapolation of the subjective framework laid down by the discourses of alienation within the *Vita Nuova*, which provide the figurative and symbolic structures by which Dante can find meaning within – and thus poetically transcend through the writing of the *Commedia* – his tragic personal circumstances. An earlier attempt to thus rhetorically fashion the political affliction of exile into a form of 'positive' alienation through which to write subjective identity can be seen in Dante's *canzone* 'Tre donne intorno al cor mi son venute':

> Ed io che ascolto nel parlar divino
> Consolarsi e dolersi
> Così alti dispersi,
> L' esilio, che m' è dato, onor mi tegno;

> [And I who listen to such noble exiles taking comfort and telling their grief in divine speech, I count as an honour the exile imposed on me;]
> (*Canzoniere* XX. 73–6)

Written between the *Vita Nuova* and the *Commedia*, this poem represents Dante's first explorations of the potential for poetry to rewrite identity, and through such subjective fashioning to surmount inflicted political exile; a redemptive spiritual-subjective discourse that, as we will see, would reach its peak in *Paradiso* 25.

Dante thus came to represent the paramount figure of exile for Joyce, shaping his conception of the scope and importance of exile as a mode of alienation, as through Dante, Joyce in effect received two competing exilic traditions. On one hand, there was the political-heroic myth of the

---

[59] On the *Commedia* as *peregrinatio* see Giuseppe Mazzotta, *Dante, Poet of the Desert*, 107–46.

Risorgimento Dante, and on the other there was the subjective-spiritual discourse, rooted in medieval theology and written into Dante's own writings on exile. This latter tradition, whilst perhaps not as prevalent within other nineteenth and early twentieth-century versions of Dante, was one to which Joyce – with his Jesuit background and thus his exposure to a climate of 'neo-Guelf' Catholicisation of the poet – was uniquely receptive. Joyce received – within the nineteenth-century construction of Dante's competing personae – a view of exile as simultaneously a form of heroic individuation and political resistance, as well as a complex, personal mode of alienation that could be used to negotiate separation both from within and without a community. In this respect, the doubled terms of Dante's 'uneasy orthodoxy' were echoed in the double perspective on exile that arose as Joyce continued to read the poet's works through his personae. In *A Portrait of the Artist as a Young Man* (and then in *Exiles*) Joyce would engage with –and begin to reconcile – the competing demands of these spiritual and heroic traditions of Dantean exile.

Silence and Separation: A 'Portrait of the Artist' as a 'Vita Nuova'

In *A Portrait of the Artist as a Young Man*, Joyce explores the unique double-perspective conception of exile that he received from the nineteenth-century personae of Dante, crafting Stephen Dedalus's self-fashioning persona through alignment with Dantean moments of both 'heroic' and 'spiritual' exile. Joycean criticism has sometimes tried to parallel the canons of Joyce and Dante, comparing the respective positions and retrospective relationships of the *Vita Nuova* and the *Commedia*, and of *A Portrait of the Artist* and *Ulysses*.[60] Such a paralleling view necessitates a distortion of both writers' oeuvre, ignoring, for instance, the important mediating presences of such works as the *Convivio*, the *Monarchia*, *De Vulgari Eloquentia*, *Giacomo Joyce* and *Exiles*. However, despite the danger of simply reading *A Portrait of the Artist* as Joyce's '*Vita Nuova*', there is undoubtedly a substantial resonance between the two works.[61] One aspect of this resonance is the intertextual echoing of Dante's exilic discourse

---

[60] See Reynolds, *Joyce and Dante*, 178–80.
[61] Whilst there is no documentary evidence for Joyce's early engagement with the *Vita Nuova* comparable to the NLI *Commedia* notesheets, a letter from Samuel Beckett to David Hayman (22 July 1955) establishes Joyce's early familiarity with the book. Beckett (who discussed Dante at length with Joyce during their early meetings in Paris) writes that 'one can well imagine the effect on Joyce, when he read it in Dublin as a very young man, of the Vita Nuova and its systematic trivalence'; see Samuel Beckett, *The Letters of Samuel Beckett*, vol. 2, 537.

within the presentation of Stephen, particularly in the latter sections of his *Portrait*.

Throughout the *Vita Nuova*, Dante presents a complex discourse of alienation patterned through silence, self-fashioning separation, and the narratives of spiritual exile. Reflected in both the social and subjective portrayal of the 'Dante' protagonist, this discourse ultimately results in the crafting of a dual-perspective subjectivity. Within the *Vita Nuova*, the idea of a self which is forged through the phenomenology of encounter is apparent from the famous first meeting with Beatrice, which turns the protagonist's focus inwards, to where the approach of a 'ruling' figure of love is signalled:

> In quel punto dico veracemente che lo spirito della vita, lo quale dimora nella segretissima camera del cuore, cominciò a tremare sì fortemente, che apparia nelli menomi polsi orribilmente; e tremando disse queste parole: Ecce Deus fortior me, qui veniens dominabitur mihi. [...] D'allora innanzi dico ch'Amore signoreggiò l'anima mia.
>
> [At that moment, and what I say is true, the vital spirit, the one that dwells in the most secret chamber of the heart, began to tremble so violently that even the least pulses of my body were strangely affected; and trembling, it spoke these words: 'Here is a god stronger than I, who shall come to rule over me.' [...] Let me say that from that time on Love governed my soul.]
> (*VN* 2.4–7)

This idea of a 'God of Love', whilst an established trope within lyric poetry in the thirteenth century, introduces an interesting element of duality within the experience of subjectivity at the opening of the *Vita Nuova*, as it seems to overwhelm and isolate 'Dante' from his own will and agency.[62] The voice of the Dante-protagonist's overwhelmed 'spirito de la vita' speaks in Latin, the contemporary tongue of spiritual and literary orthodoxy; that he should do so within the context of a vernacular work, when announcing his subjugation by the higher power of Love, only heightens the interplay of dislocations, alienations and otherings within the passage.

From this initial encounter with Beatrice onwards, the 'Dante' of the *Vita Nuova* repeatedly suffers from the various emotional and spiritual alienations brought about by his love, and uses these separations to fashion his identity. For instance, his desire to keep his love for Beatrice secret leads to a significant form of social and subjective isolation as, after having

---

[62] On the personification of Love in the Middle Ages see C. S. Lewis, *The Allegory of Love*, 1–23.

composed and distributed a sonnet in which he related a vision wherein Beatrice ate his heart (*VN* 3. 10–12), 'Dante' is shown in conversation with his friends and rivals, all of whom are eager to learn the name of the lady who has inspired the poem:

> E quando mi domandavano: Per cui t'ha così distrutto questo Amore? ed io sorridendo li guardava, e nulla dicea loro.
>
> [And when people would ask, 'For whom has Love so undone you?' I, smiling, would look at them and say nothing.] (*VN* 4. 3)

This 'smiling' refusal to speak fashions the Dante-protagonist's subjectivity through a doubled process of encounter: on the one hand he performs his silence and refusal to himself, affirming his identity as secret lover, and on the other he countersigns this identity through its recognition by his 'audience'. In this respect, the silence of 'Dante' in the *Vita Nuova* comes to represent a kind of 'legible silence', an exilic alienation from spoken discourse through which he both writes his identity, and opens up that subjectivity to the reading of others. The silence of 'Dante' will come to be a key aspect of Joyce's use of exilic alienation in crafting the presentation of Stephen Dedalus.

Another strategy of separation through which subjectivity is moulded in the *Vita Nuova* centres on the figure of the 'screen-lady'. Attending a church service, 'Dante' gazes across the nave at Beatrice; however, between them sits an unsuspecting 'gentile donna di molto piacevole aspetto' ['worthy lady of very pleasing aspect'] (*VN* 5. 1). In the course of the service, the congregation mistakenly interpret the lovelorn looks of 'Dante' as aimed at this intermediate lady, a misreading that is quickly taken advantage of:

> ed inmantanente pensai di fare di questa gentile donna ischermo della veritade; e tanto ne mostrai in poco di tempo, che il mio segreto fu creduto sapere dalle più persone che di me ragionavano.
>
> [At once I thought of making this good lady a screen for the truth, and so well did I play my part that in a short time my secret was believed known by most of those who talked about me.] (*VN* 5. 3)

This construction of an 'ischermo della veritade' works to further separate 'Dante' from social congress and community. For through the rhetorical alienation introduced by the 'screen-lady', the Florentine public's misreading of the culturally fashioned visible signature of the Dante-protagonist – and subsequently the texts of the love poetry he writes – opens up a widening discrepancy between the 'truth' of his self-identity, and its interpretation within the community. In this way, the *Vita Nuova* experiments with the creative potential of the tension between the writing and reading of self-fashioned identity, and the hermeneutic 'exile' within a community that can be generated by such rhetorical misreading of autographical posturing.

That these forms of alienation and separation within the *Vita Nuova* are discursively patterned by the *homo viator* and the medieval tradition of spiritual exile is clarified by Dante's exploration of physical separation and isolation within his narrative. Having set up a rhetorical dissonance between the origin of his love for Beatrice and its deflection onto the 'screen-lady', 'Dante' inevitably falls foul of his own trickery. As a scandal over his apparent mistreatment of the 'screen-lady' escalates, the outraged Beatrice refuses to greet him in the street (*VN* 10. 2), a scene in the narrative prominently illustrated in Joyce's copy by Rossetti's famous painting, *Beatrice nega il saluto a Dante*. The result of Beatrice's refusal is further alienation and withdrawal:

> poi che la mia beatitudine mi fu negata, mi giunse tanto dolore, che partitomi dalle genti, in solinga parte andai a bagnare la terra d'amarissime lagrime: e poi che alquanto mi fu sollevato questo lagrimare, misimi nella mia camera là dove io potea lamentarmi senza essere udito.
>
> [after my blessed joy was denied me, I was so grief-stricken that withdrawing from all company, I went to a solitary place and bathed the earth with bitter tears. After my sobbing had subsided somewhat, I closed myself in my room where I could lament without being heard.] (*VN* 12. 1–2)

In this post-refusal scene of 'Dante' in self-imposed isolation, with its emphasis on his separation from other people and on his tears and lamentation, Dante has moved the discourse of alienation tellingly close to the kind of fraught exilic imagery usually associated with the *homo viator*.

Given Dante's use of the imagery and spatial dynamics of a figurative exile to encounter and negotiate a subjective alienation experienced within the city of Florence, there would seem to be an obvious resonance with Stephen's discourse of alienation in the Dublin of *A Portrait of the Artist as a Young Man*. Joyce's *Portrait* shows the development of the self-conscious identity of an artist-protagonist through the mechanism of subjective, spiritual and artistic 'exile', an alienation drawn in terms equally explicit as in the *Vita Nuova*. When Stephen first attempts to establish some form of cosmological and social context for his existence – to consciously locate himself within a community – he does so in a manner that spatially emphasises his isolation:

A 'Portrait of the Artist' as a 'Vita Nuova'   61

He turned to the flyleaf of the geography and read what he had written there: himself, his name and where he was.

> Stephen Dedalus
> Class of Elements
> Clongowes Wood College
> Sallins
> County Kildare
> Ireland
> Europe
> The World
> The Universe
> (P I. 298–308)

In locating his own person at the opposite polarity of this juvenile text to the totalising, communal notion of 'the Universe', Stephen begins a process of writing his identity through alienation that continues throughout the novel. At the far end of the *Portrait*, having undergone the revelatory Dantean experience of seeing the 'bird-girl' on the seashore at Clontarf, Stephen's process of fashioning a self reaches its height, with Joyce demonstrating how the sharpening of Stephen's sense of alienation into the terms of his eventual 'exile' acts as a catalyst for the formation of his new persona as 'artist'.

In the fifth chapter, Stephen's long, peripatetic discourse with Lynch on the subjects of aesthetics and nationalism is arrested by their arrival at the National Library and his companion's teasing announcement, '—Your beloved is here' (P V. 1484).[63] This shift in Lynch's register, whilst consistent with his playful, mocking tone, marks the start of what emerges as a remarkable intertextual moment in the *Portrait*, and one that establishes Dante's 'legible silence' as a key aspect of Stephen's strategies of 'exile'. There is a clear similarity between Stephen and Lynch on the library steps and the chapter of the *Vita Nuova* in which 'Dante' is taken by a friend to an unexpected meeting with Beatrice:

> alla qual parte io fui condotto per amica persona, credendosi fare a me gran piacere in quanto mi menava là dove tante donne mostravano le loro bellezze [...] Allora dico che io poggiai la mia persona simulatamente ad una pintura, la quale circondava questa magione; e temendo non altri si fosse accorto del mio tremare, levai gli occhi, e mirando le donne, vidi tra loro la gentilissima Beatrice. Allora furono sì distrutti li miei spiriti per la

---

[63] The identity of Stephen's beloved in *A Portrait* is deliberately obscure; whereas in *Stephen Hero* she is identified frequently as Emma Clery (*SH* 51, 63–4, 168–70), in the *Portrait* she is referred to as simply 'E— C—' (P II. 362) or 'Emma' (P III. 506).

forza che Amore prese veggendosi in tanta propinquitade alla gentilissima donna, che non ne rimase in vita più che gli spiriti del viso;

> [I was taken to this place by a friend who believed he was giving me great delight by taking me to such a place where many ladies displayed their beauty [...] Then, so as not to attract attention, I leaned against a painting that ran along the walls of that house, and fearing that people might have become aware of my trembling, I raised my eyes and, gazing at the ladies, I saw among them the most gracious Beatrice. Then my spirits were so disrupted by the strength that Love acquired when he saw himself so close to the most gracious lady, that none remained alive except the spirits of sight;] (*VN* 14. 1–5)

This scene haunts the encounter in *Portrait*, and Lynch's teasing, coupled with the impact of seeing his 'beloved' on the library steps, triggers Stephen's ongoing fashioning of an alienated, 'artistic' persona through the same strategies of separation that we saw in the *Vita Nuova*:

> Stephen took his place silently on the step below the group of students, heedless of the rain which fell fast, turning his eyes towards her from time to time. (*P* V. 1485–7)

In this moment, Joyce draws Stephen into a discourse of alienation and exilic separation that is crafted through Dante's 'legible silence' before the poets of Florence (*VN* 4. 3). All aspects of Stephen's presentation in this scene work to signal his alienated identity: from his physical separation from his peers through his positioning on a lower step, to his pointed refusal to engage in the other students' discussions. But it is this silence that forms the most potent tool for shaping Stephen's identity as 'exiled' among his friends, allowing him to 'write' his alienation and have this contingent identity confirmed through his 'reading' by an audience. In turn, this act of 'legible silence' causes Stephen to encounter his erstwhile community as a taxonomy within which he is no longer included: 'He heard the students talking among themselves' (*P* V. 1492), an exiling of himself that is both initiated and consummated by his continuing silence throughout the rest of the scene.

In her reading of the parallel positions of the *Vita Nuova* and *A Portrait of the Artist* within the respective oeuvres of Dante and Joyce, Mary Reynolds perceptively identified the writing of love poetry as one thematic concern that binds these two shorter works together.[64] However, for Reynolds, the connection between the *Portrait* and the *Vita Nuova* is

---

[64] Reynolds, *Joyce and Dante*, 178–80.

made by their shared depiction of the creation of love poetry, in the famous 'villanelle scene' (*P* V. 1523–767), and the prose passages proceeding each of the thirty-one poems included in the *Vita Nuova*. Yet at no place in the *Vita Nuova* does Dante depict the writing of love poetry. Rather, the prose passages that accompany the poems, whether in the form of narrative accounts of visions or incidents that 'inspire' the following poem, or the subsequent interpretations of the verse, are all written from an exegetical perspective. In this respect, the act of composition is clearly marked off from a narrative ('e feci *poi* questa ballata' ['And *later on* I composed this ballad'; my emphasis] *VN* 12. 9), which thus stands in the relation of a fictional pre-text to the accompanying poem: a 'source' of material to be transmuted. Indeed, many, if not all, of the poems included within the *Vita Nuova* were written (and circulated) before the prose narrative of their supposed 'inspiration'.[65]

Whilst the forms of the narrative surrounding the appearance of love poems within *A Portrait of the Artist* and the *Vita Nuova* are importantly distinct – with Joyce's narrative focusing not on the exegesis of the resultant text but on the phenomenology of inspiration and composition – there is a distinct resonance between the isolating, exilic mechanisms that 'poetic' narratives introduce into both texts. The visions, which from the exegetical perspective of Dante's text provide the 'stimulus' for many poems in the *Vita Nuova*, almost always occur in a liminal setting, whether in the protagonist's self-imposed seclusion or during either Beatrice's or the Dante-protagonist's absence from Florence. As when, having briefly left on a trip, 'Dante' has a vision on the road of the figure of Love dressed 'in abito legger di peregrino' ['in pilgrim's rags'] (*VN* 9. 9), which Dante as author then interprets as the subject of the chapter's concluding sonnet, 'Cavalcando l'altr'ier per un camino'. This liminal vision of a pilgrim-Love stresses the importance of exile to the exegesis of the poem: firstly, in leaving Florence 'Dante' temporarily adopts the persona of the exile, whereupon he forms in his imagination the vision of Love as a pilgrim, a figure that was an aspect of the archetypal medieval trope of exile, the *homo viator*.[66] In this respect, the exegetical narrative surrounding 'Cavalcando l'altr'ier per un camino' reaffirms the importance of exile as a narrative mode in mediating Dante's discourse

---

[65] For a concise discussion of the composition and form of the *Vita Nuova*, see Michelangelo Picone, 'Songbook and Lyric Genres in the *Vita Nuova*', 874–7. For more on the considerations of authority, originality and retrospection that arise from the exegetical and compilation traditions of the *Vita Nuova* see below.
[66] Ladner, 'Homo Viator', 233.

of alienation within the *Vita Nuova*, and also moves the poem into an explicitly Christian exegetical sphere, altering the interpretation of what appears at first as a simple love lyric and highlighting the poem's deeper theological resonances.

In considering Dante's presence in the narrative framing the villanelle in *A Portrait*, we're not breaking new ground; in addition to Reynolds's reading of the *Vita Nuova*, Hélène Cixous has explored the way in which the villanelle scene engages – through the 'form of parodies' – with the *Commedia*. Ultimately, the significant link Cixous claims between the red roses of Stephen's wallpaper and the white rose of the *Paradiso* seems questionable, founded as it is on the notion that 'at the heart of [Stephen's] rose is the offer of exile'.[67] This view requires such a distortion of the white rose as the archetypal Dantean image of community as to question the extent to which the notion of 'parody' can be extrapolated to connect dissimilar states and images. Thus, instead of Cixous's 'metaphorical analogy' with the *Commedia* our focus remains the resonance with the *Vita Nuova*.

The villanelle scene in *A Portrait of the Artist* proceeds immediately from the meeting of Stephen with the 'beloved' on the steps of the National Library and, just as the figure of the *peregrino* broadened the exegetical potential of Dante's sonnet in the *Vita Nuova*, so the figure of the *alienus* works in Stephen's villanelle to expand and elaborate the earlier exilic alienation fashioned by his 'legible silence'. The exilic dynamics of the encounter at the library are certainly furthered by the physical setting of the villanelle, and echo the unexpected encounter with Beatrice in the *Vita Nuova*, after which 'Dante' 'ritornai nella camera delle lagrime [...] E in questo pianto stando, proposi di dire parole, nelle quali, a lei parlando' ['returned to my room of tears [...] And in the midst of my tears, I decided to write a few words addressed to her'] (*VN* 14. 9–10). However, the switch of the narrative of *A Portrait* from the library steps to Stephen's bedroom is a little more ambiguous than this clear withdrawal in the *Vita Nuova*; after all, Stephen has, in some respects, returned to a form of 'home-life', with the connectedness and sense of community this might imply. This is where the medieval idea of the *alienus* can strengthen the exilic associations of the villanelle scene and locate it within the wider context of Stephen's on-going process of self-fashioning separation and 'exile'.

---

[67] Cixous, *Exile of James Joyce*, 639–40.

As noted earlier, the first and foremost medieval example of the *alienus* was Lucifer, a figure with a strong presence in both Stephen's villanelle and his narrative as a whole:

> *Are you not weary of ardent ways,*
> *Lure of the fallen seraphim?*
> *Tell no more of enchanted days.*[68]
> (*P* V. 1552–4)

Through the Luciferian significance of the 'fallen seraphim', the villanelle reveals itself as a small ode to alienation, solidifying the significance of the composition of this trite, derivative poem within Stephen's strategies of separation and his on-going self-fashioning. In an echo of the effect that the pilgrim figure had in Dante's poem, the Eucharistic imagery that occurs later in the villanelle ('the smoke of praise', 'sacrificing hands upraise/the chalice flowing to the brim', 'eucharistic hymn', *P* V. 1755–62) evokes the theological solutions to the Christian understanding of exile. Yet here Joyce's phenomenological approach is substantially different from Dante's exegetical one: whereas Dante's poem is presented after the fact of its composition (and in a setting encouraging allegorical interpretation), Joyce never lets us forget that Stephen's villanelle is rooted in the isolating and immature experience of his emotions. Whilst Stephen is composing the villanelle he is focused upon both polarities of his encountered subjectivity. He interprets his memories of the 'beloved' and his desires in relation to their effect upon his own emotional state, using them to further fashion his sense of self. And yet he cannot help also imagining the isolating effect that his verses might have upon the object of his affection, and how his 'written' identity might shape her reactions: 'even if he sent her the verses she would not show them to others. No, no: she could not' (*P* V. 1724–5).

Through this dual focus in his sense of self, Stephen's subjective position resonates strongly with the dynamics of exile: comported both towards his own isolation and suffering, and also towards the object from which he is isolated. It is a focus that, in his weepings and sighings and imaginings of Beatrice, 'Dante' in the *Vita Nuova* shares; but from which, in the strong Christian imagery of the poetry, Dante as author suggests a possible escape. However, there is an interesting similarity between the effects that both Dante and Joyce imagine the poetic voices of their protagonists

---

[68] On Lucifer in *A Portrait of the Artist* see Mahaffey, *Reauthorizing Joyce*, 15–16.

as having upon the objects of their desire. 'Dante' is told by the figure of Love that, once he surrenders the diversion of the 'screen-lady', he must erect a rhetorical proxy between himself and Beatrice:

> Queste parole fa che sieno quasi uno mezzo, sì che tu non parli a lei immediatamente, chè non è degno.
>
> [Let these words be as it were an intermediary so that you do not speak directly to her; for it is not fitting that you should.] (*VN* 12. 8)

In this instruction, there is a clear implication of the potential for direct engagement with poetry to act as a violation, a 'rewriting' of identity through poetic congress that could 'injure' the recipient and possibly, in the case of Beatrice, compromise her virtue. Similarly, in Stephen's construction of an imagined 'beloved' responding to his villanelle, Joyce also draws out the potential for poetic re-writing of identities to harm her:

> He began to feel that he had wronged her. A sense of her innocence moved him almost to pity her, an innocence he had never understood till he had come to the knowledge of it through sin, an innocence which she too had not understood while she was innocent or before the strange humiliation of her nature had first come upon her. (*P* V. 1726–31)

And so an extended resonance with the *Vita Nuova* – a resonance of such a strong intertextual 'frequency' that it can surely be characterised as a source – helps shape the dynamics of Stephen's self-fashioning separations both within the villanelle scene and throughout *A Portrait of the Artist*. This process of posturing alienation, allowing Stephen to 'write' his exilic identity – and most significantly to have it 'read' by his community – through strategies of separation and withdrawal, poetic construction and 'legible silence', represents a resonant doubling of the medieval discourse of figurative exile and subjective alienation that Joyce encountered within the *Vita Nuova*. In this respect, the 'silence' of the tri-partite toolbox with which Stephen aims to liberate himself by the end of the novel ('silence, exile and cunning'), is revealed to be significantly modelled on the silence of Dante in the *Vita Nuova*. Given the emphasis that Joyce places on the performative aspect of Stephen's alienation through this silence, we might suspect that the 'exile' of his arsenal will not only resonate with the subjective-spiritual alienations of the *Vita Nuova*, but also embrace the 'heroic' mode of Dantean exile as well.

Rewriting the 'Exile': Reading Dante's Problem of Return in *Exiles*

The self-fashioning discourses of alienation in the *Vita Nuova* and *A Portrait of the Artist* give rise to a textual model of identity, in which the sense of self is contingent on the processes of writing and reading inherent in such techniques as 'legible silence'. Does this autographic model persist in Dante's and Joyce's considerations of the more concrete, political aspects of exile? Or is it an artefact of the 'spiritual' side of the equation, effective in crafting the experience of alienation within a community, but not in shaping an exile from without? There is a resonance between Dante's and Joyce's explorations of just such questions through the ways in which both the *Commedia* and *Exiles* envision the problems posed to the 'written' exilic identity by the loss of physical separation from the city as community engendered by the act of return.[69]

The political, worldly experience of exile for both Dante and Joyce was defined respectively by the loss of Florence and Dublin, the cities of their births. Yet this alienation from a hugely significant form of community was, in its historical aspect at least, arguably more fluid than their identities as 'exiles' would suggest. Although legalistically circumscribed and underwritten by the threat of a particularly grisly death, Dante's position as 'Florentinus et exul immeritus' ['a Florentine undeservedly in exile'] (*Epistolae* V. 1) was not fixed. As Joyce knew the story, following the election of a new *podestà* in 1316, there was a concerted attempt to return Dante to Florence:

> Il 16 dicembre del medesimo anno fecero uno stanziamento in virtù del quale quasi tutti i banditi potevano ripatriare, sì veramente che pagassero una certa somma, e, stati alcun tempo in prigione, nella festa di San Giovanni andassero processionalmente con mitera in capo e coi ceri nelle mani ad offerire al santo; modo di grazia serbato ai malfattori ed esteso allora ai condannati politici. Dante rifiutò.[70]

> [On 16th December of that same year [the *podestà*] made a provision under which almost all of the banished could return home, provided they pay a certain fine, spent some time in prison and, on the feast of St John, went mitred in procession, with candles in hand, to make an offering to the

---

[69] Dominic Manganiello also briefly considers a resonance between Joyce's and Dante's writings on return, see *Joyce's Politics*, 201.
[70] Camerini, 'Vita di Dante', 11.

saint; a traditional mode of pardon for criminals that was now extended to political offenders. Dante refused.]

In Eugenio Camerini's narrative of the Florentine amnesty there is, as ever, the distinct presence of the Risorgimento myth of Dante's 'heroic' exile, conveyed through his now familiarly dramatic style: 'Dante rifiutò'. The crux of this perhaps otherwise puzzling refusal – after all, Dante had claimed that Florence was where 'desidero con tutto il cuore di riposare l' animo stanco, e terminare il tempo che mi è dato' ['I desire with all my heart to rest my weary mind and to complete the span of time that is given to me'] (*Conv* I. 3. 4) – is clarified in what Joyce would have known as Dante's ninth epistle, '*In litteris vestris*'.[71]

> Absit a viro philosophiae domestico temeraria terreni cordis humilitas, ut more cuiusdam Cioli et aliorum infamium quasi victus, ipse se patiatur offerri!
>
> [Far be from a familiar of philosophy such a senseless act of abasement as to submit himself to be presented at the oblation, like a felon in bonds, as one Ciolo and other infamous wretches have done!] (*Epistolae* IX. 3)

Dante's refusal of the amnesty hinged on the act of *oblatio*, the ritual contrition required of him. Later in his letter, the 'exul immeritus' presents himself as 'viro praedicante iustitiam' (*Epistolae* IX. 3); however, within Florence the established symbolic potency of the public ritual of the *oblatio* would have effectively obliterated this self-fashioned persona as 'a man speaking justice'. Were Dante to submit himself to the *oblatio*, then he would also be submitting himself to a conventional 'reading' by the Florentine citizenry; he would cease to be the 'heroic exile' and become just another in a long line of pardoned civic sinners.

However, when rejecting the amnesty, Dante did hold out the hope that some other route of return might be found for him, one 'quae famae Dantis atque honori non deroget' ['which would not derogate the fame and honour of Dante'] (*Epistolae* IX. 4). The imagined form of this alternate route further emphasises his resistance to relinquishing an autographical position:

> Se mai continga che il poema sacro,
> Al quale ha posto mano e cielo e terra,
> Sì che m'ha fatto per più anni macro,
> Vinca la crudeltà, che fuor mi serra

---

[71] In modern editions, '*In litteris vestris*' is numbered twelfth.

Rewriting the 'Exile': Problems of Return in Exiles 69

Del bello ovile, ov'io dormii agnello
Nimico ai lupi, che gli danno guerra;
Con altra voce omai, con altro vello
Ritornerò poeta, ed in sul fonte
Del mio battesmo prenderò il cappello;

[If it ever happen that the sacred poem, to which both Heaven and earth have set their hand, so that for many years it has made me lean, vanquish the cruelty that locks me out of the lovely sheepfold where I slept as a lamb, an enemy of the wolves that make war on it, with other voice by then, with other fleece I shall return as poet, and at the font of my baptism I shall accept the wreath;] (*Par.* 25. 1–9)

In this passage of the *Paradiso* (which Rossetti drew on in 'Dante at Verona') Dante presents the *Commedia* itself – the 'poema sacro' – as the way by which he might return to Florence. In the scenario envisaged by the Florentine amnesty, Dante would necessarily have had to surrender his autographic position as exile and, in a reversal of the poetic project that began with his shaping of the discourse of alienation in the *Vita Nuova* into the self-fashioning of the *canzoni* of exile, allow the city and its ritual to effectively rewrite his identity. Through poetry, Dante hopes to overcome the 'cruelty' of his exile, returning to Florence not only with the honour inherent in the act of taking the laurel wreath but also with his self-fashioned identity intact. To return through the 'altra voce' – the changed voice acquired through the years of his poetic development in exile – would be to return and yet somehow remain the poet of exile. *Paradiso* 25 thus presents a vision of return to the city on Dante's own terms, one in which he retains control over how the act of his return will be read, what effect it will have upon his self-created persona and how, through the influence of his great poem, the text of his exile will be written into the history and civic landscape of Florence.

Dante's steadfast and principled refusal of the opportunity of return obviously complicates the parallel between the exiles of Dante and Joyce.[72] Far from the mortally impelled, inflicted and lifelong separation from his city that Dante underwent, Joyce returned to Dublin twice in 1909 and then once again in 1912.[73] Indeed, the prospect of return was one that never really faded, and in 1920 Joyce memorably contemplated returning from 'exile' to purchase some new trousers (*SL* 253). Thus, Joyce could

---
[72] cf. Manganiello, *Joyce's Politics*, 191–2.
[73] See *JJ* 276–91, 301–8, 322–38.

not but have been keenly aware of the difference between the rhetorical shaping of Dante's experience of exile into the transcendent poetic voice of the *Commedia*, and the rhetorical ontology of his own self-willed position. However, dipping his toe back into 'the black pool of Dublin' (*JJ* 275) would also have sharpened Joyce's own awareness of the difficulty of sustaining an 'exiled' identity upon returning to the 'lost' community, and the ability which that community had to fatally 'misread' and rewrite him. It was just such problems that Joyce explored in *Exiles*, where he chronicles the return of Richard Rowan and his lover Bertha from a continental 'exile'.

Given the attention paid to every scrap of Joyce's writing in recent years, there is a relative paucity of criticism on *Exiles*, and the play remains the only one of Joyce's works to lack an adequate critical edition. There are, of course, notable exceptions, and interestingly two such studies of the play have been made within the context of Joyce's relationship with Dante: firstly in Mary Reynolds's extended reading of the presence of *Purgatorio* 31 in the relationship of Richard Rowan and Beatrice Justice, and then in Vicki Mahaffey's discussion of Dantean numerology in the play.[74] Also, whilst Anglo-American Joyce criticism might tend to overlook *Exiles*, the play has been something of a focus of study for Italian critics, most notably Carla de Petris and Claudia Corti, the latter of whom has written the only monograph on the work of which I'm currently aware.[75] In discussing the play, we'll be following de Petris's active resistance to biographical readings and her observation that '*Exiles* is not a play about adultery, it is a play about identity.'[76]

The nature of this discourse of identity is clarified by Joyce's discussion of the play's title with Italo Svevo. Picking up on a question Joyce himself asked in his notes for the play ('Why the title *Exiles*?', *E* 149), in a lecture he gave in Milan in 1927 Svevo offered a very different answer:

> Esiliati? [...] Esiliati coloro che ritornano in patria? E il Joyce mi disse: Ma Lei non ricorda come il figliol prodigo fu ricevuto dal fratello nella casa

---

[74] See Mary Reynolds, 'Dante in Joyce's *Exiles*', 35–44; Reynolds, *Joyce and Dante*, 166–74; and Vicki Mahaffey, 'Joyce's Shorter Works', 204–5.
[75] Corti, '*Esuli*'. For examples of de Petris's work on *Exiles* see her '*Exiles*, or the Necessity of Theatre', 65–75; and 'Léon Blum's *Du Mariage* and James Joyce's *Exiles*: "Yet there is method in't"', 31–42. Other Italian discussions of the play include Giuseppina Restivo, 'L'*Otello* di James Joyce: nota sulla vicenda di *Esuli*', 101–20; and Achille Mango, 'Gli *Esuli* di Joyce', 169–80.
[76] de Petris, 'Léon Blum's *Du Mariage* and James Joyce's *Exiles*', 36. For examples of psychosexual and biographical approaches see Ruth Bauerle, 'Bertha's Role in *Exiles*', 108–31; Cixous, *Exile of James Joyce*, 527–35; Sheldon R. Brivic, 'Structure and Meaning in Joyce's *Exiles*', 29–52.

paterna? È pericoloso abbandonare la propria patria, ma anche più pericoloso ritornarci perché allora i vostri compatrioti se possono vi cacciano il coltello nel cuore.[77]

['*Exiles?* [...]Exiles are those who return to their own city?' And Joyce said to me: 'But don't you remember how the prodigal son was received by his brother in his parent's house? It's perilous to leave your own city, but yet more perilous to return there, because then your compatriots, if they can, will stick a knife in your heart.']

Whilst drawing on the same Biblical narrative as his more well-known notes on Robert Hand (*E* 149), Joyce's evocation here of the parable of the Prodigal Son – particularly in the focus he places upon the reaction of the brother – makes clear *Exiles*' concern with the threat posed to the 'exiled' identity by a return home. Whilst certainly not strong enough to suggest a simple source-relationship, the sense of violent threat to the self posed by the image of 'il coltello nel cuore' does resonate with the existential and rhetorical danger of Dante's posited political return, the narratives of which Joyce would have encountered not only obliquely through the *Commedia* but explicitly through Camerini's 'Vita'.

As Vicki Mahaffey has pointed out, the structure of *Exiles* consists of a procession of dialogues between all possible combinations of the characters; it is through the shifting positions adopted by the speakers in these dialogues that the discussion of identity – its writing, reading and rewriting – takes place.[78] Just as Dante's persona as 'exul immeritus' was contingent upon a semiotic matrix of inscriptive, self-fashioning acts and their readings, so the identities of Richard Rowan, Bertha, Beatrice Justice and Robert Hand represent rhetorically woven texts. In a manner reminiscent of the 'legible silence' of the *Vita Nuova*, the personae of the characters of *Exiles* emerge from an interplay of self-performance and encountered interpretation.

This dialectic of imprinting and evasion – of the resistance of the self to being both read and then rewritten by the other – is a repeated element of Joyce's drama, such as in Robert's attempts to force Bertha to see herself as a conventional adulterous lover (*E* 40). However, in highlighting the resonances between this discourse of the reading and writing of identity, and Dante's awareness of the rhetorical dangers of political return, we need to focus on the arch-exile himself, Richard Rowan. Throughout the play, Richard is shown to be resistant to a rewriting of the narrative of his

[77] Italo Svevo, *Scritti su Joyce*, 47.
[78] Mahaffey, 'Joyce's Shorter Works', 200.

now-lapsed 'exile' from Dublin, through which he has fashioned his sense of self. Richard's exilic identity is thus contingent on the number of separations that pattern this narrative: from Robert and Bertha in youth; from Ireland in the scandalous manner of his leaving; and, most interestingly, from his mother. In his encounters with Beatrice Justice, Richard aggressively narrates this latter relationship:

> She drove me away. On account of her I lived years in exile and poverty too, or near it. [...] I waited too, not for her death but for some understanding of me, her own son, her own flesh and blood; that never came. (*E* 24)

Richard thus aligns his identity as exile both with his mother's hostile attitude towards him, and his subsequent writing of himself as being perpetually misunderstood. In this respect, Richard's relationship with his mother is positioned as the central thread of the double-perspective text of his exilic identity. Richard's resistance to having this thread rewoven, and the threat that such rewriting would pose to his contingent identity, is clarified when Beatrice tries to read his relationship with his parents in a new light:

> They are both gone now, Mr Rowan. They both loved you, believe me. Their last thoughts were of you. (*E* 25)

Beatrice here attempts not only to reinterpret the central narrative of Richard's self-identity but also, through her 'writing' of the unknowable contents of his parents' 'last thoughts', to force Richard to reread the narrative of his exile. It is a hermeneutic imposition that Richard is simply unable to accept: 'while she lived she turned aside from me and from mine. That is certain' (*E* 23). Trapped in the suburban wilderness on the edge of Dublin, a returnee unwilling to take the final steps towards the community symbolised by the possibility of a University chair arranged for him by Robert (*E* 139–40), Richard cannot afford to allow the founding tenet of his exile to be rewritten. If he accepts Beatrice's reading of the situation, then Richard must in turn rewrite his exile narrative as not a creative martyrdom but an act of cowardice before the conventional morality of his city: a flight into 'exile' due to the fact that he was having sex with – but not marrying – Bertha.[79]

---

[79] In this respect my reading of *Exiles* as charting Joyce's growing awareness of narrative contingency, differs greatly from Hélène Cixous's view of the play as recording the 'determining moment' of Joyce's career, a 'crystallisation' in which 'life becomes a kind of "history" defined by its own laws, with a structural system', see *Exile of James Joyce*, xii.

It is just this hermeneutic concern that Bertha herself highlights in the second act of the play, when she too attempts to rewrite Richard's identity, challenging his reading of her past actions, including her decision to follow him into exile:

> I am simply a tool for you. You have no respect for me. You never had because I did what I did. (*E* 94)

Indeed, in an earlier dialogue in which Bertha tries to rewrite Richard's relationship with Beatrice Justice as an erotic obsession, Richard expresses his central defence against the perils of return, and his best method of perpetuating his self-fashioned identity as 'exile':

> *[Calmly.]* You are trying to put that idea into my head, but I warn you that I don't take my ideas from other people. (*E* 67)

The 'heroic' individuation of this stance resonates not only with Cacciaguida's advice to Dante-pilgrim in *Paradiso* 17, 'che a te fia bello/ averti fatta parte per te stesso' (*Par.* 17. 68–9) ['that for you it will be well to have become a party unto yourself'], but also with the Dantean myth of the Risorgimento, and centres separation and alienation once more in Richard's self-fashioned identity. Now that he has apparently reversed his physical exile and returned to Dublin, it is of paramount importance that Richard maintain the 'heroism' of his subjective exile. Indeed, much has been made of Richard's perceived masochism in the play, particularly the 'rough and tumble' (*E* 157) of his relationship with Robert Hand. Given the resistance he displays to the attempts of Beatrice and Bertha to re-fashion his exilic identity, perhaps Richard's perplexing desire for Robert to commit adultery with Bertha, his longing to be 'passionately and ignobly [...] dishonoured for ever in love and in lust' (*E* 88) by him, represents the sublimated desire to lose his own reading of the narrative of his exile, and so to allow himself to be finally and fatally 'rewritten'.

Thus, just as the Florentine amnesty had forced Dante to recognise the threat that the possibility of political return posed to his poetic identity as 'exul immeritus', so too, in *Exiles*, Joyce reveals the precariousness of the exilic identity in the face of renewed participation in the lost community. For such failed and aspiring 'exiles' as Richard Rowan and, as we will see presently, Stephen Dedalus, the city holds the potential to continually short-circuit the signifying systems of their self-fashioned identity. Passing into actual physical separation from the community as Richard (and, indeed, Joyce himself) did simply raises the stakes of the game of 'alienation as exile'. As Dante knew, the ever-present geographical potential for return leaves the written identity – both in its new 'political-heroic', or earlier 'subjective-spiritual' modes – open to cataclysmic rewriting by the overwhelming semiotic significance of the act of return, and the attendant realignment with and within the community through this 'coming home'. The difficulty of thus sustaining the narrative self of the 'exile' highlighted in *Exiles* will be an important focus in discussing the Dantean poetics of Stephen in *Ulysses*. But, as Stephen Dedalus contemplated the transition from his subjective mode of alienation within the city towards the more straightforward 'exile' of his departure, the narrative concerns apparent in *Exiles* were already starting to unsettle the discourse of exile in *A Portrait of the Artist as a Young Man*.

'Spiritual-heroic Refrigerating Apparatus': the 'In-determining' Moment

Let's return to Stephen where we left him, 'pouring out verses' in an exilic alienation fashioned through his use of such Dantean techniques as 'legible silence'. The model of identity that arises from such autographic separations proves problematic in the face of actual physical exile, with its accompanying 'threat' of return. Given this threat, how does the self-writing persona negotiate the movement between the spiritual-subjective aspect of Dantean exile, and the political-heroic? Does the movement between these modes reflect a shift in the Dantean patterning of Stephen's presentation, and what might such a shift suggest about Joyce's engagement with Dante ahead of the writing of *Ulysses*? In addressing this transition in Stephen's alienation, Hélène Cixous saw the movement towards 'heroic' exile as charting his liberation from a 'passive feeling of being in exile into the decision to take up a deliberate physical exile' through the 'determining moment' of departure.[80] The discourse of actively fashioned alienation in *A Portrait of the Artist*, resonating with the tradition of subjective exile within the *Vita Nuova*, already questions Stephen's supposed passivity, and, as *A Portrait* reaches its end, Dante's presence further disrupts Cixous's 'liberation' model. Whilst the terms of Stephen's alienation become ever more concretely exilic – seeming to shift his rhetorical position more into resonance with the Risorgimento myth of Dante's 'heroic' exile – significant moments of Dantean intertextuality work to undermine

---

[80] Cixous, *Exile of James Joyce*, 438.

and complicate both this 'liberating' departure and his earlier alienated discourse.

The terms through which the prospect of actual departure emerges within Stephen's exilic narrative are highly significant:

> When the soul of a man is born in this country there are nets flung at it to hold it back from flight. You talk to me of nationality, language, religion. I shall try to fly by those nets. (*P* V. 1047–50)

Stephen's first broaching of 'flight' grows out of the idea of a 'soul-birth', setting up a trajectory that will harden the notion of avoiding the restraint of subjective expression into the necessity for physical departure. His famous formulation for these individuating aims ('I shall try to fly by those nets') – aims that he clarifies later will be achieved through his use of the Dantean tools of 'silence, exile and cunning' (*P* V. 2580) – reveals an important intertextual moment in this crucial passage of the *Portrait*:

> Non ti dovea gravar le penne in giuso,
> Ad aspettar più colpi, o pargoletta,
> O altra vanità con sì breve uso.
> Nuovo augelletto due o tre aspetta:
> Ma dinanzi dagli occhi de' pennuti
> Rete si spiega indarno o si saetta.

> ['Your wings should not have been weighted down, to await more blows, by either a young girl or some other new thing of such short duration. A young bird waits for two or three, but before the eyes of one full-fledged, nets are spread and arrows shot in vain.'] (*Purg.* 31. 58–63)

Whilst *Purgatorio* 31 was a focus of Mary Reynolds's reading of Joyce's engagement with Dante, this particular moment in Beatrice's dialogue has gone unremarked.[81]

The significance of the intertextual resonance with *Purgatorio* 31 is clear: Joyce gestures to Beatrice's pinpointing of the moment within the narrative frame of the *Commedia* in which Dante-pilgrim got caught in worldly 'nets', and that only the poetic transformation of his exile into the 'pilgrimage' of the 'poema sacro' will now allow him to 'fly by'. Thus, Stephen's declaration of his 'heroic' individuation resonates strongly with the very moment in the *Commedia* that recalls Dante's failure. This

---

[81] cf. Reynolds, *Joyce and Dante*, 166–74. I am indebted to Nick Havely for pointing out this intertextual resonance. The biblical source that Dante draws on for his bird imagery (and of which Joyce, given his Jesuit education, would likely also have been aware) was Psalms 24. 7; for an account of this biblical tradition see B. G. Koonce, 'Satan the Fowler', 176–84.

failure would in turn necessitate Dante's conditioning and expansion of the 'spiritual-subjective' discourse of the *Vita Nuova* into the new poetic form that (in the complex retrospection of the *Commedia*) would now facilitate – and so had already achieved – the 'redemption' of his inflicted exile. In this respect, the resonance of Stephen's 'nets' with Dante's 'rete', introduces a decidedly ironic perspective into this crucial moment in the *Portrait*: what Stephen presents as a figure of liberation – flying by the nets – is underwritten by Dante as a figure of entanglement and entrapment. Thus, the 'heroic' statement that generates the movement in Stephen's thought, setting up his launching from 'exilic' alienation into the prospect of actual departure from Dublin, can be seen through its resonance with Dante's text, to also underscore ideas of compromise, failure and ineluctable connection.

So it seems clearer than ever that the first two terms of Stephen's toolbox of liberation – 'silence, exile and cunning' (*P* V. 2580) – are fundamentally determined by Dante. Indeed, the third term also has a Dantean resonance:

> Per correr miglior acqua alza le vele
> Omai la navicella del mio ingegno
> Che lascia dietro a sè mar sì crudele.

[To run through better waters the little ship of my wit now hoists its sails, leaving behind it a sea so cruel.] (*Purg.* I. 1–3)

As a faculty launching his flight past the nets and into exile, Stephen's 'cunning' resonates strongly with the voyaging 'ingegno' that opens the *Purgatorio*. This resonance will be important when discussing the poetics of Stephen's intellect in the next chapter, but for now we can simply note the way in which this alignment serves to further emphasise an important transition.[82] In presenting 'silence, exile and cunning' as the arsenal of Stephen's liberation, Joyce emphasises Dante's continuing presence in the *Portrait*, underscoring the movement from a subjective alienation drawn from the *Vita Nuova*, towards the 'heroic' mode of Stephen's posited departure into an exile from where, in what represents a restatement of the Risorgimento myth of exile Joyce found in Agresti and Pisacane, he will 'forge [...] the uncreated conscience of my race' (*P* V. 2789–90).

In closing the *Portrait*, Joyce re-emphasises these doubled terms of Stephen's Dantean identity through an encounter that not only introduces

[82] See below, pp. 95–109.

Dante as a named presence within the novel, but also resonates once again with the scenes of encounter in the *Vita Nuova*:

> *15 April*: Met her today pointblank in Grafton Street. The crowd brought us together. We both stopped. She asked me why I never came, said she had heard all sorts of stories about me. This was only to gain time. Asked me was I writing poems. About whom? I asked her. This confused her more and I felt sorry and mean. Turned off that valve at once and opened the spiritual-heroic refrigerating apparatus, invented and patented in all countries by Dante Alighieri. Talked rapidly of myself and my plans. In the midst of it unluckily I made a sudden gesture of revolutionary nature [...] People began to look at us. She shook hands a moment after and, in going away, said she hoped I would do what I said. (*P* V. 2758–70)

This presumed re-encounter with the 'beloved' of the library steps represents the culmination of many of the issues we have been discussing: from Stephen's concern with his public interpretation ('she had heard all sorts of stories about me'), to his anxiety over the address of poetry ('I felt sorry and mean'), and even the internationalism of Dante's personae ('invented and patented in all countries'). I've argued elsewhere that the transformation of the word 'Dante' from its appearance as the colloquial name of Mrs Riordan in the first chapter, into the name of the poet Dante Alighieri in this passage, underscores the persistent, 'subterranean' presence of Dante in the *Portrait*.[83] But for the present purpose, it's time to finally unpack the 'spiritual-heroic refrigerating apparatus'.

Having explored the contextual construction of Dante's nineteenth-century personae, and his own complex discourse of exile and alienation, we can now fully appreciate Stephen's mechanised formulation of the 'refrigerating apparatus'. Evident in this wonderful image of Dante as poetic fridge is the idea of a self-preserving separation, enacted through a conscious switch in mode of alienation.[84] The expression of this modality in turn emphasises the doubled terms of Joyce's reception of Dantean exile: the medieval, subjective-spiritual discourse of the *homo viator* is brought into combination with the Risorgimento's political-heroic myth of Dante as the 'noble exile'. In this respect, Stephen's idea of Dante as the inventor of a mode of alienation which operates through both a 'spiritual' and 'heroic' aspect, stands as a further reiteration of the precariously balanced double terms of the 'uneasy orthodoxy' that characterised Joyce's

---

[83] Robinson, '*Purgatorio* in the *Portrait*', 271–5.
[84] We might note here that Stephen's Dantean arms of 'silence, exile and cunning' are also envisioned as preservatives to be used in 'defence' (*P* V. 2579)

first reading. Although this spiritual-heroic combination could be seen as suggesting a cogent synthesis of the two traditions of Dante's exile, there is an important difference between this Dantean moment in *A Portrait* and other earlier examples.

When Stephen offers Dante's 'spiritual-heroic refrigerating apparatus' as a model for his self-preserving, exilic mode of emotional alienation, we're not being presented with the familiar representation of Stephen as a character 'writing' his identity through self-fashioning acts. Rather, through the fiction that the final pages of *A Portrait of the Artist* are Stephen's own diary entries, the reader is encountering him actually writing. This switch in 'authorial' position is hugely important, pointing back towards the ever-present question of ironic distance in the *Portrait*.[85] Derek Attridge has argued persuasively that, in his diary entries, Stephen displays a growing sense of literary self-awareness otherwise absent from the novel, a self-awareness that would seem to be typified by the sudden 'name-dropping' of Dante Alighieri.[86] So, in his conception of the 'spiritual-heroic refrigerating apparatus', is Stephen signalling his awareness of the Dantean postures he has been striking throughout the book? Is he now aware that he has been modelling the personae of Dante in his 'legible silence', his self-fashioning separations and his recent desire for 'heroic' flight? Or is Joyce using this final evocation of Dante's presence in the *Portrait* to introduce a final ironic perspective on Stephen's 'development'?

The tensions between these competing perspectives on Stephen are febrile and stimulating. If Stephen is aware of himself as a Dantean figure, then the shift in the mode of his alienation into a consciously 'heroic' form of exile represents a development of the earlier discourse and would thus seem to align the *Portrait* with the Risorgimento myth. From this perspective, Stephen's Dantean exile represents a truly liberating act: the 'determining moment' that Cixous argues the departure of October 1904 remained for Joyce himself.[87] However, the presence of the mature Joyce as the 'principio e cagion' ['origin and cause'] (*Inf.* I. 78) of Stephen's words in the fictional 'diary', and thus of the Dantean posture he strikes, complicates this reading. The Joyce who completed *A Portrait of the Artist as a Young Man* in 1914 after ten years of living abroad was not the same figure who wrote the baldly rhetorical letter to Lady Gregory in 1902, or even

---

[85] The most cogent expression of the case for reading Stephen as ironised remains Hugh Kenner's, see *Dublin's Joyce*, 109–33.
[86] Derek Attridge, *Joyce Effects: On Language, Theory, and History*, 74–7.
[87] Cixous, *Exile of James Joyce*, xiv, 437–9.

the young teacher writing home in 1905, keen to check his departure from Ireland was being read as the 'exile' he wanted.

The language of Stephen's diary entry is central to unravelling the ironic conundrum that thus surrounds Dante's final appearance in the *Portrait*. The key consideration in the 'spiritual-heroic refrigerating apparatus, invented and patented in all countries by Dante Alighieri' (*PV*. 2764–5) is arguably the word 'apparatus'. Stephen's positing of Dantean exile as a mechanical mode seems to underscore an important oversight in his 'heroic' posture. He presents Dante as originating a mode of alienation that can be instrumentally applied in order to achieve a desired result: a liberating separation into the 'self-communion' that, if 'but shyly welcomed' in the 1904 'Portrait of the Artist' essay (*PSW* 215), now seems to be wholly embraced. But in extrapolating his earlier spiritual-subjective alienation into the heroic mode of exile in this mechanistic way, Stephen ignores both the complex contextual construction of the two competing traditions of Dantean exile, and also their continuum with Dante's own discourse. The discourse of alienation that Dante explored in the *Vita Nuova* provided the necessary groundwork through which he could seek to arrive at the 'other way' of the *Commedia*, and try to poetically redeem the otherwise intractable fact of his exile. It was Dante's earlier spiritual conception of alienation as deriving significance through a figural relation to the exile of the *homo viator* that allowed him to heroically render the 'poema sacro' out of the pain of his exile, and achieve some form (however partial) of poetic 'return' and resolution. Thus, in his 'spiritual-heroic refrigerating apparatus', Stephen is positing a redemptive process as a generative one: what for Dante functioned as a way to 'overcome' the circumstances of an inflicted disaster, is positioned by Stephen as a mode to get started on a self-fashioning, heroic 'exile'.

Stephen's position appears as a striking reduction of what Joyce received as a complex, historically constructed and contextually conditioned discourse of exile. This figuring of Dante's traditions of exile as a unitary 'apparatus' must surely question readings such as Cixous's that posit the rhetorically fashioned 1904 'exile' as Joyce's own 'determining moment'. Rather, it would seem that, as his engagement with Dante went on, Joyce became increasingly alive to the discongruities with Dante as well as the alignments. Indeed, if we were to look for a turning point in Joyce's career, I would follow Jean-Michel Rabaté in seeing this as 1907, the year in which he began the final version of *A Portrait of the Artist as a Young Man*, the book in which he first arrived at the realisation of the difference between his exile and Dante's.[88] Unlike Stephen Dedalus, the Joyce who

---

[88] Rabaté, *James Joyce and the Politics of Egoism*, 19–20.

wrote the *Portrait* no longer saw himself as 'driven out' of Ireland; Dante was impelled to leave his home, he was not. Rather, Joyce's alignment now seems to have been with the poet who consciously resists the invitation of return and, through that chosen position, comes to craft his poetic voice and identity as a writer. In this respect, by putting the two traditions of Dante's exile into Stephen's 'refrigerating apparatus', Joyce neatly expresses his scepticism of them both; instead of the subjective alienation of Stephen's self-fashioning separations or his flight into 'heroic' exile with its wholesale endorsement of the Risorgimento myth, Joyce's epiphany seems to be a realisation of the uselessness of just such epiphanic thinking, and his arrival at the freedom of an 'in-determining' moment.

In thus opening up what appears as a deconstructive aspect in Stephen's exilic discourse – the way in which his urge to embrace the instrumental utility of Dante's traditions of exile serves to counter the validity of his self-claimed 'heroic' position – a latent tension is emphasised within the trajectory we are following. Through the increasing contingency of the personae of the exile (whether Stephen, Richard, Dante or Joyce himself) on its writing through encounter and interpretation by the community from which it seeks to signal its difference, an inherent implication is revealed in the 'polarities' of alienation and participation, separation and belonging, exile and community. This 'contradictory' implication is clarified when we consider that, throughout this reading of the *Portrait*, we've seen Stephen embodying 'the giddy sense that personal identity is totally independent of everything else', by fashioning a self-separated identity through an *alignment* with the figure and works of Dante.[89] In this way, whether he is consciously 'playing' Dante, or simply being represented in Dantean terms, Stephen's 'exile' in *A Portrait of the Artist* actually serves to affirm his involvement in a significant form of intertextual 'community'.

---

[89] Nagel, *The View from Nowhere*, 42.

CHAPTER 3

The Poetics of Infernal Metamorphosis
Stephen's Representation in 'Proteus' and 'Scylla and Charybdis'

'Playing Dante', or Joyce in the Dark Wood

In December 1918, James Joyce was absorbed by two activities. One was the composition of *Ulysses* (which by this point had reached the 'Scylla and Charybdis' episode), and the other was the romantic pursuit of a young girl whom he had seen using the toilet.[1] From his flat on Universitätstrasse in Zurich, the myopic Joyce had caught a glimpse of a young, dark-haired woman in a flat across the road, rising from the toilet seat and pulling the lavatory chain.[2] From this point on, until February 1919, when their relationship dissolved amongst the comedy of a bungled seduction and an art-show-cum-black-mass, Joyce was infatuated with the young Marthe Fleischmann, and wrote her a number of remarkable letters.[3] In the first of these letters, apparently written a few days after they had met each other, one particular statement stands out:

> Moi, je suis vieux – et je me sens plus vieux encore.
> Peutêtre ai-je trop vécu.
> J'ai 35 ans. C'est l'âge que Shakespeare a eu quand il a conçu sa douleureuse passion pour la 'dame noire'. C'est l'âge que le Dante a eu quand il est entré dans la nuit de son être.
>
> [As for me, I am old – and feel even older than I am.
> Perhaps I have lived too long.
> I am 35. It is the age at which Shakespeare conceived his dolorous passion for the 'dark lady'. It is the age at which Dante entered the night of his being.] (*SL* 233)

---

[1] On Joyce writing 'Scylla' in this period see *JJ* 452; however, Joyce's friend Frank Budgen remembered him as 'composing the *Sirens* episode' at this time, see *Myselves When Young*, 187.
[2] See Budgen, *Myselves When Young*, 191; however, Brenda Maddox has pointed out that the two buildings 'are not positioned directly opposite one another', and Joyce's voyeurism would have necessitated better eyesight than he had by 1918, see *Nora: A Biography of Nora Joyce*, 216.
[3] For details see Budgen, *Myselves When Young*, 192–4; Maddox, *Nora*, 216–18; and *JJ* 450–1.

It is small wonder that, in December 1918, Joyce felt 'plus vieux encore', being in fact thirty-six, and very nearly two years older than the 'romantic computation' he gave Fleischmann.[4] However, Joyce's fudging of his age was clearly motivated by a desire to strengthen the resonance of his self-fashioned biography with that of Shakespeare, and that of Dante. The reasons to invoke Shakespeare in the first of a sequence of increasingly romantic letters to a dark-haired young woman are self-evident.[5] And yet, whilst the Shakespearean allusion has dominated the three major narratives of Joyce's relationship with Fleischmann, there is no further reference to Shakespeare or his works in the correspondence.[6] In contrast, Joyce's reference to Dante inaugurates a remarkable sequence of self-fashionings.[7]

The language of the letters through which Joyce performed his romantic persona to Fleischmann is replete with the kind of Beatricean and Dantean motifs and imagery that characterised Stephen Dedalus's presentation in *A Portrait of the Artist*. Joyce repeatedly draws on Dantean images of watching and observing, and of the giving and receiving of signs and signals:

> quand je vous ai reconnue à la fenêtre je vous regardais dans une espèce de fascination dont je ne peux me libérer.
>
> [when I recognised you at the window, I watched you with a kind of fascination from which I cannot free myself.] (*SL* 233)

He then adds that when 'hier soir vous m'avez fait un signe [...] mon coeur a sauté de joie' ['yesterday evening you gave me a sign [...] my heart leapt for joy'] (*SL* 233). Indeed, at the opening of his second letter, Joyce clearly evokes the incident in the *Vita Nuova* in which Beatrice denies Dante her 'dolcissimo salutare' (*VN* 10. 2), her most sweet greeting; a moment which was illustrated in Joyce's edition by Rossetti's famous

---

[4] On the disparity in Joyce's ages here, see *SL* 233 n. 1.
[5] As Budgen put it, 'literary gentlemen's adventures with dark ladies are usually worth the fringe benefit of a sonnet or two', see *Myselves When Young*, 188.
[6] These narratives, by Budgen, Ellmann and Maddox, all make much of the easy assonance between Shakespeare's 'dark lady' and Joyce's imagined identity for Marthe as 'une juive' ['a Jewess'] (*SL* 233); see Budgen, *Myselves When Young*, 188–97; *JJ* 449–51; and Maddox, *Nora*, 217.
[7] The only critic to have acknowledged the importance of Dante in this letter is Hélène Cixous, who briefly – if somewhat puzzlingly – notes that 'at thirty-seven [Joyce] saw himself as Shakespeare or Dante – or rather both of them at once, with Dante providing him the passionate and ecstatic images which Shakespeare lacks', see *Exile of James of Joyce*, 569.

painting, and which would seem to underlie the dramatic form of Joyce's address to Fleischmann: 'Qu'y-a-t-il? Vous ne m'avez pas salué!' ['What is the matter? You gave me no sign of greeting!'] (*SL* 235).[8]

In his third letter, Joyce sketches Fleischmann a portrait of himself that seems to be consciously drawn from another passage of the *Vita Nuova*:

> Chaque matin j'ouvrais, j'ouvrais le journal et j'avais peur de lire votre nom parmi les annonces des morts! Je l'ouvrais toujours avec angoisse, très, très lentement.
>
> Je pensais: elle s'en ira – elle qui m'a regardé avec pitié– peutêtre avec tendresse.
>
> [Every morning I opened, opened the paper and was afraid I might read your name in the death announcements! I would open it always in anguish, very, *very* slowly.
>
> I thought: she will go away – she who has looked at me with pity – perhaps with tenderness.] (*SL* 236)

In this scene of the dawning mortality of his beloved, Joyce echoes an identical moment in the *Vita Nuova*:

> Onde sospirando forte, fra me medesimo dicea: Di necessità conviene che la gentilissima Beatrice alcuna volta si muoia. E però mi giunse uno sì forte smarrimento, ch'io chiusi gli occhi, e cominciai a travagliare come farnetica persona.
>
> [Then sighing loudly, I said to myself: 'Some day the most gracious Beatrice will surely have to die.' I went so out of my head that I closed my eyes and became convulsed as one in a delirium.] (*VN* 23. 3–4)

Whilst Joyce stops short of claiming the kind of visionary experience that Dante's realisation triggers, his emphasis on the action of Fleischmann's pitying eyes recalls the moment of their meeting as evoked in the first of his letters. The terms in which he narrates this first encounter also bear markedly Dantean characteristics:

> Je me figure un soir brumeux. J'attends – et je vous vois vous approcher de moi, vêtue de noir, jeune, étrange et douce. Je vous regarde dans les yeux et mes yeux vous disent que je suis un pauvre chercheur dans ce monde, que je ne comprends rien de ma destinée ni de celle des autres, que j'ai vécu et péché et crée, que je m'en irai, un jour, n'ayant rien compris, dans l'obscurité qui nous a enfantés tous.

---

[8] On Rossetti's presence in Joyce's edition of the *Vita Nuova* and his influence on Joyce's reading of Dante in general see above, pp. 47–50.

84   The Poetics of Infernal Metamorphosis

[I imagine a misty evening to myself. I am waiting – and I see you coming towards me, dressed in black, young, strange and gentle. I look into your eyes, and my eyes tell you that I am a poor seeker in this world, that I understand nothing of my destiny, nor of the destinies of others, that I have lived and sinned and created, and that one day I shall leave, having understood nothing in the darkness that gave birth to both of us.] (*SL* 233–4)

This exchange of vision, the legibility of the eyes and gaze, and the connection of these phenomena with destiny, mortality and understanding, can't fail to put us in mind both of the Beatrice of the *Vita Nuova*, and of the more mystical, salutary encounters with her in the *Purgatorio* and the *Paradiso*.[9] Indeed, the association between Fleischmann and Beatrice in this passage of the letter, echoes and extends the Dantean resonances that surrounded the object of Joyce's affection from their first meeting. According to the interview she gave Heinrich Straumann in 1941, when Marthe Fleischmann first met James Joyce, he had stopped in the street with a look of 'grösstem Erstaunen' ['greatest astonishment'], and informed her that 'Sie erinnern mich an ein Mädchen, das ich einmal in meinem Heimatland am Strand stehen sah' ['You remind me of a girl I once saw standing on a beach in my homeland'].[10] Thus, from the very beginning of their relationship, Fleischmann was clearly associated for Joyce with the figure of the girl who became the 'bird-girl' of *A Portrait of the Artist*, and whose resonances with such Dantean women as Beatrice and Matelda I have discussed at length elsewhere.[11]

And so, through his use of Dantean motifs and imagery, Joyce significantly strengthened his initial self-fashioning identification with Dante, the poet whose pilgrim persona was entering 'la nuit de son être' ['the dark night of his being'] (*SL* 233) as he ventured into the 'dark wood' at Easter 1300.[12] In the first letter, Joyce presents himself as the Dante-pilgrim of the *Commedia* embarking on his pilgrimage through the otherworld towards

[9] The emphasis that Joyce places on vision and light throughout the Fleischmann correspondence would also seem to further suggest the mediating presence of D. G. Rossetti in Joyce's 'playing Dante'; for more on Rossetti's influence and the importance of light and vision see below, pp. 173–74.
[10] Heinrich Straumann, 'Four Letters to Martha Fleischmann', 428.
[11] See above, pp. 1–2, and Robinson, '*Purgatorio* in the *Portrait*', 268–71. In his account of the interview with Fleischmann, Straumann is quick to point out after this reference to the 'bird-girl' that 'I at once asked Fräulein Fleischmann whether she had read any books by Joyce and she admitted in a slightly embarrassed way that, not knowing any English, she had not' (*L* II, 428). Whether Fleischmann's denial of familiarity with *A Portrait* verifies or complicates her account, or suggests a Joycean 'fudging' on Straumann's part, remains open to speculation.
[12] On Joyce's careful notes from Camerini's edition on the dating of the *Commedia* (NLI MS 36, 639/ 1 f. 2v), see above, p. 31.

salvation, but for the rest of the correspondence he postures as the lover figure of the *Vita Nuova*, setting off on the path that will ultimately lead to the despair and darkness of the 'selva selvaggia'. Through this seemingly inimical combination of personae, Joyce emphasises the importance of transition and transformation to his interest in Dante at this point in his career. Understandably, given that he was in mid-flow with *Ulysses*, the Joyce of the Fleischmann correspondence, presenting himself as 'un pauvre chercheur dans ce monde' ['a poor seeker in this world'], would seem to identify more with the pilgrim entering on the 'cammino alto e silvestro' – with the poet whose work is 'in progress' – rather than with the 'maestro' and 'autore', the great figure of Dante who has already achieved the masterpiece of the *Commedia*.

This interest in incipience and transition around the figure of Dante might go some way towards explaining the otherwise perplexing incoherence in Joyce's position. Particularly given the hints of ironic self-perception that surrounded Stephen's attitude towards it at the close of *A Portrait of the Artist*, we might wonder what exactly the author of *Ulysses* is doing experimenting with the Dantean machinery of the 'spiritual-heroic refrigerating apparatus' of *A Portrait of the Artist as a Young Man*. In his letters to Fleischmann, Joyce would seem to be indulging in a piece of simple self-fashioning: aligning his own presentation with that of 'Dante' in the *Vita Nuova*, and from a romantic standpoint this strategy seems to make some sense. Did Joyce simply hope that, by evoking Rossetti's so-called cult of Beatrice, and pushing her towards the role of Dantean love object, he would flatter Fleischmann into submission? This certainly seems a plausible, if (given what Richard Ellmann tells us of Fleischmann's literary tastes) potentially incomprehensible and ineffective strategy.[13] Or perhaps, as he pursued his doomed romance with Fleischmann, the reason that the *Vita Nuova* and Stephen Dedalus's Dantean posturing – with its exilic separations and self-fashionings – were uppermost in Joyce's mind was that, in his representation of Stephen in *Ulysses*, he was currently exploring their utter failure and exhaustion.

This chapter will again follow the thread of exile and separation – and its interweaving with notions of self-fashioning presentation – to explore how, in his portrayal of Stephen in *Ulysses*, Joyce marks a significant

---

[13] 'Marthe did not work; she spent her days smoking, reading romantic novels, and primping' (*JJ* 449); however, whilst taking care in her appearance and having a taste for romance novels need not preclude a knowledge of Dante (or even D. G. Rossetti's 'Dantism'), it seems unlikely that Fleischmann would have been alive to the allusions Joyce was sending her way.

development in his reading of Dante. Whereas in *Portrait*, Dante was used to help craft Stephen's self-imposed 'exilic' identity and to begin – towards the end of the novel – to unsettle just such an identity, in *Ulysses* the poet's presence is fundamental to Joyce's exploration of the shortcomings and failures of this earlier stance. In *Ulysses*, Joyce's reading of Dante remains bounded by the parameters of his initial encounter and the double terms of Dante's uneasy orthodoxy. The figure who was on one hand presented to Joyce as the poet of exile and heterodoxy continues to evolve into a poet who helps him critique Stephen's easy adherence to just such positions, and who will also ultimately underpin Joyce's attitude towards the difficulties and significances of living within a community. Indeed, whilst the trajectory arising from Joyce's early reading remains, the focus moves away from mediated and contextualised readings of Dante, and towards an exploration of his presence within the complex poetics of *Ulysses*.

By declaring himself as a Dante figure in his letters to Fleischmann, entering 'die Nacht der Bitterkeit meiner Seele' ['the night of the bitterness of my soul'] (*SL* 237), Joyce engages in a simple self-fashioning presentation. However, the impetus for Joyce's letters to Fleischmann was to condition and extend a connection that he had first made between them in person. Thus, the presentation of himself that Joyce offered Fleischmann in the letters – his 'acting as Dante-Shakespeare', as Cixous puts it – is importantly a re-presentation, a corrective offered to the initial impression that his look of 'grösstem Erstaunen' ['greatest astonishment'] had made.[14] In which case, his Dantean posturing needs to be viewed not simply as self-fashioning but as a re-fashioning of the self. This distinction – between fashioning and re-fashioning, presentation and re-presentation (or 're-presentation') – will underpin much of our discussion of Joyce's poetics.

Indeed, in exploring the tension between how Stephen 'signs' his identity within *Ulysses* – telegraphing a continuation of his status as alienated 'exile' – and how this signature is read or represented within the wider discourse of his poetics, I am drawing on an anxiety that Joyce himself expressed. In the initial letters to Fleischmann, the letters in which his attempt to 'play Dante' is at its height (and the letters in which he is continually concerned with signs and signals: 'hier soir vous m'avez fait un signe', *SL* 233), he refuses to sign his own name.[15] Only in the later letters,

---

[14] Cixous, *Exile of James Joyce*, 638.
[15] As will be evident throughout, my sense of the potentially deconstructive tensions between 'signing' and 'reading' – presentation and re-presentation – that forms the basis of the model for the

when the game is over and their relationship is crumbling, does Joyce contravene his early 'signing' of himself as Dante (or Shakespeare) and apply a terse and literal signature: 'J' (*SL* 237).[16] These poetics of presentation and re-presentation – of the tension between signing and reading – as they surround Stephen in *Ulysses*, can be explicated through the interplay of stasis and motion within Dante's notion of punitive, Infernal metamorphosis.[17]

It would seem sensible, therefore, to focus attention here on the figure of Stephen and those episodes of *Ulysses* that offer the best view of him. Stephen is a character who would benefit from more often being viewed within a poetic – as opposed to philosophical or theoretical – discourse. The focus of this chapter is thus squarely on the influence of Dante on the poetics of Stephen's narrative in *Ulysses*; on the tensions that Dante's presence in Joyce's text highlights between Stephen's presentation and representation. In *Ulysses*, Joyce gives us, as it were, our 'second look' at Stephen, and this doubled perspective both clarifies and metamorphoses aspects of his earlier portrayal in *A Portrait of the Artist*. Accordingly, the earlier chapters of *Ulysses* will be foregrounded, particularly the 'Proteus' episode, and then 'Scylla and Charybdis'. Between them, 'Proteus' and 'Scylla' offer the most sustained view of Stephen in the book; however, these chapters also offer perspectives with an unusually strong Dantean resonance, featuring some of the most significant, extensive and sustained quotation from the *Commedia* in any of Joyce's works.

Interestingly the points in Dante's poem to which Joyce gestures through quotation in *Ulysses* are often places where the poet is himself engaged in the active presentation or re-presentation of such literary figures as Aristotle and Brunetto Latini. Indeed, the 'Proteus' and 'Scylla and Charybdis' chapters of *Ulysses* feature an extended discourse of shaping

---

discourse of Stephen's poetics, draws on Jacques Derrida's influential discussion of the 'signature'; see his *Acts of Literature*, 362–4.
[16] There is a further – more practical – level of anxiety surrounding the issue of Joyce's signature within the Fleischmann correspondence. The fallout from the discovery of Joyce's infatuation by Fleischmann's lover Vortmund, was all too predictable: '[She gave] him all my correspondence. Violent gestures towards me' (*SL* 239). By signing his initial to the last letters, Joyce thus not only contravened the game of 'playing Dante' but also opened himself up to physical threat through identification, a development that can't fail to recall 'Henry Flower' and his predicament with Martha Clifford in *Ulysses* (*U* 15. 757–67).
[17] It is worth stressing at this point that the 'signing' action that we will discuss throughout this chapter refers to Stephen's acts within both the fictional and textual discourses of *Ulysses*. Thus, the audience presupposed by this signing may be delimited as the characters who surround him, his own consciousness, the textual perspective of the reader or – more commonly – an inextricable interplay of all of these positions.

and reshaping presentations of the figures and texts of medieval Italian writers, a discourse that revolves around the presence of Dante. In exploring Dante's influence on the poetics of Stephen's narrative, we will also observe the ways in which Dante implicates *Ulysses* within a textual community made up of 'ghostly' *duecento* and *trecento* voices.

The Cunningly Silent Exile or Stephen Back in Dublin

When readers of *A Portrait of the Artist as a Young Man* re-encounter Stephen Dedalus atop the Martello Tower in the opening pages of *Ulysses*, it quickly becomes apparent just what a poor job he has made of his 'heroic' exile. When judged against the criteria set out in his diary – even with the often-overlooked hint of irony in his going to 'encounter for the *millionth* time the reality of experience' (*P* V. 2788–9; my emphasis) – Stephen's continental 'exile' has been a 'ridiculous failure'.[18] As Hans Walter Gabler astutely observed, not only has Stephen's time in Paris failed to help him 'fly by' the nets of 'nationality, language [and] religion' (*P* V. 1049), this failure of exile, and his consciousness of it as a narrative now that he is back in Dublin, 'should itself be recognised as a trapping net'.[19] Indeed, the absurdity of his situation manages to register with Stephen himself:

> My Latin quarter hat. God, we simply must dress the character [...] Just say in the most natural tone: when I was in Paris, *boul' Mich'*, I used to. (*U* 3. 174–9)

However, this awareness of dress and its connection to character suggests that Stephen is still very much interested in issues of self-fashioning; and, as will become apparent, his self-fashioned persona as the Dantean 'exile' persists into *Ulysses*. Indeed, despite the irony surrounding Stephen's 'spiritual-heroic refrigerating apparatus, invented and patented in all countries by Dante Alighieri' (*P* V. 2759–60), he remains desperately dependent on his Dantean toolbox of 'silence, exile and cunning' (*P* V. 2579–80). If there is a strong Dantean resonance in Stephen's idea of eluding nets, then his continued use of such tools must surely suggest that, despite his 'heroic' departure, he has not yet shown himself 'pennuti' ['full-fledged'] (*Purg.* 31. 62).[20] And so, our discussion of the poetics of Stephen will begin by exploring the ways in which these Dantean tools start to fail him, and

---

[18] Charles H. Peake, *James Joyce: The Citizen and the Artist*, 133.
[19] Hans W. Gabler, 'Narrative Rereadings: Some Remarks on "Proteus", "Circe" and Penelope"', 62.
[20] On the Dantean intertext of Stephen's 'nets' in *A Portrait of the Artist* see above, p. 75.

will consider how a tension between Stephen's self-fashioning presentation and his re-presentation to the reader is underscored by this failure.

In the opening chapters of *Ulysses*, Stephen is clearly engaged in a series of self-consciously hermeneutic acts:

> Signatures of all things I am here to read, seaspawn and seawrack, the nearing tide, that rusty boot. Snotgreen, bluesilver, rust: coloured signs. (*U* 3. 2–4)

Through the kind of radical legibility posited by the notion of reading 'all things', Stephen effectively marks himself off as the authoritative reader of a world that he both renders as a perceptual 'text' and subjects to a hermeneutic process rooted in separation. Dante was a strong influence on Joyce's presentation of such a distanced hermeneutic; after all, the *Commedia* is a poem deeply concerned with reading, and draws upon various forms of separation and difference in many of its representations of the process. For instance, the numerous apostrophes that stud the text call for the reader to take a step back from the subject matter of the poem whilst foregrounding the hermeneutical act:

> O voi, che avete gl'intelletti sani,
> Mirate la dottrina che s'asconde
> Sotto il velame degli versi strani.
>
> [O you who have sound intellects, gaze on the teaching that is hidden beneath the veil of the strange verses.] (*Inf.* 9. 61–3)

The hermeneutic strategy of Dante-pilgrim on his journey through the otherworld seems to be predicated upon just such a repeatedly emphasised separation between the protagonist as 'reader' and the assemblage of characters, symbols and localities that he interprets as a form of eschatological 'text'.[21] As has often been observed, the City of Dis (which comprises the lower four circles of Hell) is closely modelled upon the civic landscape of Florence, an association that establishes an important distance between Dante-pilgrim and the locale through which he travels.[22] Through Dis's similarity to Florence, Dante-pilgrim finds himself within both a familiar cityscape and a strange Infernal context, a liminal dislocation that

---

[21] For a study of Dante's theory of history and modern ontological and phenomenological thought see William Franke, *Dante's Interpretive Journey*. On how these kinds of hermeneutical processes and distinctions underpin Dante's use of allegory and the structure of the *Commedia* see Mazzotta, *Dante, Poet of the Desert*, 227–30.

[22] See Catherine Keen, *Dante and the City*, 123–4; and Nick Havely, 'The Self-Consuming City: Florence as Body Politic in Dante's *Commedia*', 100–1.

underpins his hermeneutic position. Furthermore, encounters with figures like Charon (*Inf.* 3. 82–96) repeatedly emphasise both the pilgrim's existential separation from the souls suffering in Hell and his further eschatological separation:

> E tu che se' costì, anima viva,
> Pàrtiti da cotesti che son morti.
> Ma poi ch' ei vide ch' io non mi partiva,
> Disse: Per altra via, per altri porti
> Verrai a piaggia, non qui, per passare:
> Più lieve legno convien che ti porti.

['And you who are over there, living soul, separate yourself from these here, who are dead.' But when he saw that I did not leave, he said: 'By another way, through other ports will you come to shore, not by crossing here: a lighter vessel must carry you.'] (*Inf.* 3. 88–93)

In a position clearly patterned by the trope of the *homo viator*, although travelling through Hell, the pilgrim is not subject to the damnation under which all of the other characters (including even Virgil) have fallen. It is this eschatological difference between Dante-pilgrim and the souls of the *Inferno* that allows the allegorical hermeneutic of the *contrapasso* to explicate theological and cosmological meanings through the phenomena of suffering souls.

Whilst this aspect of separation and distance is markedly present in the hermeneutics of the *Inferno*, as Dante-pilgrim moves through the other two realms of the otherworld, its prominence and importance arguably start to lessen. In a process inaugurated by the encounter with an angel at the gates of Purgatory who inscribes seven letters on his forehead and thus turns him into a bodily text (*Purg.* 9. 112–15), Dante-pilgrim's position as separated 'reader' of the otherworld is an increasingly unsettled one. Whilst the pilgrim's existential and eschatological distance from the souls of the *Purgatorio* and the *Paradiso* remains, by the time he reaches the spheres of heaven his hermeneutical strategy has started to fail. This process of hermeneutic frustration accelerates in the *Paradiso*, beginning with an early discussion of the insufficiency of the poet's mental faculties (*Par.* 1. 5–6) and a direct warning to readers about the poem's difficulty (*Par.* 2. 1–6). Indeed, the *Paradiso* and the *Commedia* as a whole reaches its climax in the famous evocations of ineffability in the final canto (*Par.* 33. 142–4), where Dante as poet finds himself unable to provide the necessary images to make sense of the experience the Pilgrim is undergoing, ending the poem at a point of shared, hermeneutical inadequacy. However, with a seemingly unconscious irony, it is with the earlier Infernal hermeneutic that Stephen Dedalus aligns himself in *Ulysses*.

Nevertheless, if Dante's Infernal hermeneutic is rooted in distance and alienation — in the Pilgrim's difference and separation from the world through which he moves — then at first it might not seem all that useful for characterising Stephen's position at the start of *Ulysses*. For, whilst Dante-pilgrim's alienation is repeatedly signalled to him by the figures he encounters, Stephen is hardly marked off or kept at a distance by the people he meets. From the opening pages of the novel, characters such as Mulligan, Haines, Deasy, Uncle Richie, Almidano Artifoni, Lynch and, most prominently, Mr Bloom, all try to engage or connect with him in one way or another. Of course, Dante-pilgrim's alienation is also far from complete, even in the *Inferno* where a figure like Brunetto Latini (*Inf.* 15. 22–4) greets his presence in Hell with disbelief and sympathy ('Qual meraviglia?').[23] But, rather than suggesting that there is a comprehensive structural alignment between the position of Dante-pilgrim in the *Inferno* and Stephen Dedalus in *Ulysses*, this apparent disparity highlights the first tension between how Stephen 'signs' himself through his processes of self-fashioning alienation and how he is represented to the reader.

Despite clear indications of his inclusion within the life of the city around him, at the opening of *Ulysses* Stephen presents himself as an 'exile' moving through a city to which he once belonged, but from which he is now intractably severed.[24] In thus deploying a 'schema of alienation and defensive withdrawal' that both evokes Richard Rowan's obstinacy in *Exiles* and represents a significant extension of Stephen's 'spiritual-subjective' exile in *A Portrait*, Stephen signals his occupation of a liminal position that strongly resonates with that of Dante-pilgrim in the *Inferno*.[25] Indeed, Joyce seems to indicate this resonance with the protagonist of the *Commedia* through his description of 'Stephen Dedalus, displeased and sleepy' (*U* 1. 13), walking into *Ulysses* through remarkably similar language to Dante-pilgrim wandering into the Dark Wood 'pien di sonno' ['full of sleep'] (*Inf.* 1. 11).[26] Therefore, regardless of how the

---

[23] It's interesting to note that Camerini's edition would have stressed this sympathy to Joyce through the use of a question mark ('Qual meraviglia?') in place of the exclamation mark common to all modern editions of the *Commedia*.
[24] One of the most influential statements of this view of Stephen as distanced and separated at the start of *Ulysses* was made by Richard Ellmann; see *Ulysses on the Liffey*, 8–20. Declan Kiberd more recently restated this position, see, *'Ulysses' and Us: The Art of Everyday Living*, 41–76, 318.
[25] Cixous, *Exile of James Joyce*, 350.
[26] I am grateful to Nick Havely for pointing out this echo of the somnambulistic Dante-pilgrim in the sleepy Dedalus.

reader may perceive his position in Dublin, self-conscious alienation from his community still forms the bedrock of Stephen's self-fashioned identity, a 'signed' identity that – like Richard's – is now under more or less continual threat. The 'exile' that in the pages of *Portrait of the Artist* had been experienced only in rhetorical, self-fashioning forms has, in *Ulysses*, been transmuted into the physical reality of a failed move to Paris, the narrative of which has become a source of frustration and regret:

> You were going to do wonders, what? Missionary to Europe after fiery Columbanus. (*U* 3. 192–3)

In this respect, through the disappointment engendered by the failure of his grand project of artistic separation – and the banality of his return home – Stephen has, in effect, become alienated from his fantasies of 'heroic' exile. This leaves him at the start of *Ulysses* in the uncomfortable position of being a kind of 'über-exile', alienated from his own postures of alienation.

By the opening of *Ulysses* the physical manifestation of Stephen's 'exile' has thus been lost to a narrative of failure and frustration. Given the loss of his heroic posture, the most potent tool remaining to sustain Stephen's 'exilic' or separated identity would seem to be his 'silence'. Stephen's silence within *A Portrait* – modelled as it was on the *Vita Nuova* – represented an effective mode of alienation, becoming a kind of 'legible silence' capable of fashioning his presentation to an audience. And it is this kind of silence that seems to be enacted in the first chapter of *Ulysses*, where there is a striking contrast between the verbose, merrily mocking figure of Mulligan, blessing 'gravely thrice the tower, the surrounding land and the awaking mountains (*U* 1. 10–11), and the sullen, silent Stephen. However, Stephen's somnolent witness at Mulligan's mock mass – where he is determinedly unwilling to engage in the joke – represents both a reprise of the 'signing' silence of the *Portrait*, and the attendant failure of this strategy. Eventually, as Mulligan's japery continues, Stephen surrenders this tool as well and allows Mulligan's jibing, and his own concerns over Haines, to move him to speak:

> —Tell me, Mulligan, Stephen said quietly.
> —Yes, my love?
> —How long is Haines going to stay in this tower? (*U* 1. 47–9)

This brief question is enough for Mulligan to break Stephen's silence and pull him into a conversation whose reverberations and reiterations, particularly in the discussion of his mother's death (*U* 1. 179–222), will resound throughout the novel.

The Cunningly Silent Exile or Stephen Back in Dublin 93

Indeed, in *Ulysses*, the Dantean legible silence of *A Portrait of the Artist* has arguably become a vocative silence, underpinned by the presence of a commenting, hermeneutic voice in the form of the interior monologue.[27] This development in Stephen's silence is perhaps an inevitable consequence of his apparent alignment with an Infernal, distanced hermeneutic, a compromised position that is clarified during 'Telemachus' when the old milk woman arrives at the Martello Tower. In an echo of Dante-pilgrim explicating cosmological truths from the suffering he sees, Stephen's monologue makes an initial allegorical link between the old woman delivering their morning milk and Ireland as a nation, reading her as

> A wandering crone, lowly form of an immortal serving her conqueror and her gay betrayer, their common cuckquean, a messenger from the secret morning. (*U* 1. 404–6)

In a very simple sense, the hermeneutic with which Stephen makes this allegorical reading is defined by distance, reaching beyond the immediate context of the scene in the tower to draw down a well-worn Irish rhetorical trope and apply it to the old woman. Stephen's hermeneutical position thus systematically transforms Mulligan and Haines as well, reducing them to symbols within an ironic nationalist discourse. Yet Stephen's allegorical over-reading of the scene does not end with a simple semiotic decoding; to put things within more medieval terms, he then seems to extend the process to an almost anagogical level, in which the old lady's perceived attitudes become symbolic of Ireland's attitude towards himself as its most misunderstood, exiled son.[28] Observing the old woman's deference to Mulligan, Stephen bitterly muses:

> She bows her old head to a voice that speaks to her loudly, her bonesetter, her medicine man: me she slights. (*U* 1. 418–19)

Following him in reading the old lady as Ireland, Haines as imperial oppressor and Mulligan as craven appeaser, then inevitably we must see Stephen as the symbolic proxy for all of Ireland's exiles. Stephen's 'signing' of his symbolic role as 'exile' within his own semiotic system is clarified by his applying this manipulative hermeneutic from a position of a further distance enacted through his silence, dumbly watching the

---

[27] On the role of the interior monologue as underlining the striking shift between *Portrait* and *Ulysses* see Attridge, *Joyce Effects*, 77.
[28] For a lucid explanation of Dante's theories of allegory and anagogy as expressed in the *Convivio* (*Conv.* 2. 1. 1–7), and their relation to Dante's poetics and theories of textual exegesis, see Mazzotta, *Dante, Poet of the Desert*, 227–37.

interaction of Mulligan and Haines with the old woman. And thus Joyce seems to underscore the inevitable failure of Stephen's distanced, Infernal hermeneutic as a strategy for sustaining his 'exilic' identity. Since – despite beginning from a Dantean position of liminality – by including himself within the allegorical system he constructs, Stephen effectively emphasises his interconnection and integration with the other figures, and short-circuits the claim to alienation from which he began.

The efficacy of Stephen's vocative silence as a tool to maintain his distanced hermeneutic position, and thus sustain his Dantean self-fashioned identity as 'exile', is highly questionable. For one thing, unlike Dante-pilgrim, Stephen's separation from the 'text' he reads is not eschatologically guaranteed, and thus his inclusion within his own hermeneutic and semiotic systems leaves him open to a fluid dynamic between text and reader. Indeed, whereas Dante-pilgrim's journey through Hell is assured and fundamentally underwritten – or 'signed' – by the transcendent will of God ('Vuolsi così cola dove si puote/Ciò che si vuole' ['this is willed where what is willed can be done'] *Inf.* 3. 95–6), Stephen's return to Dublin and his movement through the city are ultimately motivated by the receipt of a textually corrupt telegram: '—Nother dying come home father' (*U* 3. 199). However, there also seems a distinct possibility that the basic technique of his hermeneutic distance – the interior monologue – is itself fatally compromised.

Paola Pugliatti has usefully clarified the difficulty of using interior monologue – or vocative silence – to sustain hermeneutic distance. In a rigorous structural-linguistic study of Joyce's monologic techniques in *Ulysses*, Pugliatti concludes that 'the textual organisation of "interior monologue" is continuously and more or less explicitly "disturbed" by an interference which at times becomes "interaction"'.[29] Thus, on a linguistic level, through its hermeneutic reaction to external stimuli, Stephen's interior monologue actually reaffirms his interaction and interconnection with the world around him. This aspect of his double-bound hermeneutic problem is succinctly summarised by Pugliatti when she considers the function of nomenclature within the monologue: 'the act of naming something is a "response" to innumerable other acts of naming the same thing, and any word uttered results in an interaction with somebody else's

---

[29] Paola Pugliatti, 'The Ulyssean Challenge: Time, Monologue, Discourse, "Arranger"', 168.

word and semantic (let alone ideological) orientation.'[30] Thus, Stephen's silence in *Ulysses* – underpinned as it now is by a hermeneutic voice in the form of interior monologue – cannot work in the same way that his Dantean legible silence did to craft an 'exilic' identity in *A Portrait of the Artist*. The distanced hermeneutic position that Stephen adopts in *Ulysses*, resonating though it does with the place of Dante-pilgrim in the *Inferno*, ultimately works to affirm his interconnection with and encompassment by the world and his community. In this way, both Stephen's 'exile' and his 'silence' are now blunted tools in his Dantean box, unable to sustain his self-fashioned identity, and the distance between how he tries to 'sign' himself and how he is represented widens. The only tool that would seem to remain to Stephen at this point is his 'cunning' or *ingegno*: his thoughts and intellect.

'Maestro di color che sanno' or Stephen on the Seashore

It has long been an open question as to just how seriously readers should take the thoughts of Stephen Dedalus. The language of 'Proteus', particularly the dense cluster of quotation and abstruse allusion with which it opens, can often dazzle us into believing that Stephen is, in his walk along Sandymount strand, silently expounding an important philosophical position – the blueprint for a kind of 'Dedalian semiotics': 'Signatures of all things I am here to read, seaspawn and seawrack, the nearing tide, that rusty boot' (*U* 3. 2–3). Joycean scholarship has often sought to trace and delineate the vagaries of this Dedalian position, with critics quick to discuss the possible influences of such figures as Aristotle, Berkeley, Newman and Aquinas on what Ernesto Livorni has characterised as the thorough development of 'Stephen Dedalus's aesthetic conception'.[31] However, ever since Hugh Kenner's intervention into the question of irony in *A Portrait of the Artist*, the intellectual veneration implicit in such treatments of Stephen has bred a concomitant iconoclasm amongst some of Joyce's readers.[32] As Declan Kiberd has put it of 'Proteus':

---

[30] Pugliatti, 'The Ulyssean Challenge', 169. Pugliatti notes elsewhere that the connective action of the reader's mind when deciphering the interior monologue provides another substantial interactive element in Joyce's textual discourse, see 'Isotopia e monologo interiore', 10–11.

[31] Ernesto Livorni, '"Ineluctable modality of the visible": Diaphane in the "Proteus" Episode', 127. For an example of a detailed, philosophic reading of Stephen see Pierre Vitoux, 'Aristotle, Berkeley, and Newman in "Proteus" and *Finnegans Wake*', 161–9.

[32] Kenner, *Dublin's Joyce*, 109–33.

> Many readers drop *Ulysses* at this point, finding themselves unable to keep up with Stephen's remorseless and obscure pedantry: but the truth is that Joyce is laughing at the pitiful pretentiousness of the youth he once was. *Nobody* could understand all that Stephen says or thinks. *Nobody* could take all his ideas with utter seriousness.[33]

Whilst this view of Stephen as suffering 'the lethal after-effects of a recent university degree [...] weighed down rather than illuminated by his knowledge', and full of 'learned quotations' which are 'impressing nobody but himself', is refreshingly irreverent, perhaps we needn't go quite that far. Nor, however, can Stephen be comfortably seen as a nascent philosopher, and to do so would be to align our reading of him entirely with how he 'signs' himself. Rather, I would agree with Umberto Eco's more sober assessment that, in his treatment of intellectual matters, Joyce 'approaches ideas, shows connections, plays on references but does not make philosophy'.[34] Thus, the philosophical, phenomenological and semiotic systems that make up Stephen's thought in 'Proteus' – his 'cunning' or *ingegno* – need to be viewed, first of all, within the frame of his poetic representation.

The commingling of the poetic and the philosophic is immediately apparent in the famous opening lines of 'Proteus':

> Ineluctable modality of the visible: at least that if no more, thought through my eyes. Signatures of all things I am here to read, seaspawn and seawrack, the nearing tide, that rusty boot. Snotgreen, bluesilver, rust: coloured signs. Limits of the diaphane. But he adds: in bodies. Then he was aware of them bodies before of them coloured. How? By knocking his sconce against them, sure. Go easy. Bald he was and a millionaire, *maestro di color che sanno*. Limit of the diaphane in. Why in? Diaphane, adiaphane. If you can put your five fingers through it it is a gate, if not a door. Shut your eyes and see. (*U* 3. 1–9)

In this passage, Joyce interweaves Stephen's thoughts on Aristotelian perceptual theory and Dr Johnson's famous experimental method with his awareness of Dante. The poet's presence is signalled by the quotation of the description of Aristotle in Limbo: 'Vidi il Maestro di color che sanno' ['I saw the master of those who know'] (*Inferno* 4. 131): the first such direct, untranslated quotation from Dante in Joyce's fiction.[35]

---

[33] Kiberd, *'Ulysses' and Us*, 65.
[34] Eco, *Middle Ages of James Joyce*, 50.
[35] Interestingly, this line from *Inferno* 4 is also the first quotation of Dante to feature in any of Joyce's public work (in distinction to his school or university notes), closing his 3 September 1903 *Daily Express* review of John Burnet's *Aristotle on Education*: 'when the scientific specialists and the whole cohort of Materialists are cheapening the good name of philosophy, it is very useful to give heed to

The interconnection of Dante and Aristotle made in this opening passage has formed the focus of the only substantial consideration of Dante's presence throughout 'Proteus'. Ernesto Livorni has traced what he sees as Dante's mediation of Thomas Aquinas's reception of Aristotelian perceptual theory, arguing that the position Stephen adopts in 'Proteus' has been importantly conditioned by Dante's *Convivio*.[36] Whilst there may be some reservations over the necessity of Dante's mediation (given that Joyce is known to have studied both relevant Aristotelian texts, *De Sensu et Sensibili* and *De Anima*), his essay not only breaks the relative stranglehold of glosses of Bishop Berkeley as the way in to the intellectual world of 'Proteus', but also succeeds in establishing the poet as a vital presence in the episode.

However, such work – helpful and interesting though it is – could be usefully set within the context of Joyce's poetic frame; before we can start to engage with the content of Stephen's thought (if we should wish to do so), we need to fully acknowledge that its most immediate effect is in the representation of Stephen as character. This poetic consideration is underscored by the structure of Stephen's thought at the opening of 'Proteus':

> Then he was aware of them bodies before of them coloured. How? By knocking his sconce against them, sure. Go easy. Bald he was and a millionaire, *maestro di color che sanno*. (*U* 3. 4–7)

Looking more closely at this passage, it is apparent that the element within the thought that establishes Aristotle as Stephen's subject – both clarifying the earlier 'limits of the diaphane' and associating them with the 'he' who was aware of them – is not any thought of Aristotle himself, but rather of Dante's representation of Aristotle in *Inferno* 4:

> Poi che innalzai un poco più le ciglia,
> Vidi il Maestro di color che sanno,
> Seder tra filosofica famiglia.
> Tutti l'ammiran, tutti onor gli fanno.
> Quivi vid'io Socrate e Platone,
> Che innanzi agli altri più presso gli stanno.

---

one who has been wisely named "maestro di color che sauno"' (*OCPW* 80). Whether this misquotation of the pertinent verb 'sanno' was a misprint, an error on the part of the twenty-one-year-old Joyce, or a particularly 'knowing' joke is delightfully uncertain. However, given the context of the quotation within a criticism of 'materialism', Joyce's review does provide fascinating evidence that the interrelation of Dante, Aristotle and the discussion of idealist philosophies was brewing in his mind for more than ten years before 'Proteus'.

[36] Livorni, ' "Ineluctable modality of the visible" ', 128–37.

[When I lifted my brow a little higher, I saw the master of those who know, sitting among a philosophical company. All gaze at him, all do him honor: there I saw Socrates and Plato, standing closer to him, in front of the others.] (*Inf.* 4. 130–5)

Thus, Stephen's concept of 'Aristotle' the 'bald millionaire' is not so much as the pre-Christian philosopher, but as the fictional head of Dante's 'filosofica famiglia': a category error in Stephen's thinking that has a key and repeated function in his poetic representation throughout the episode. In which case, if Aristotle – as critics have comprehensively shown – is to be a presence within 'Proteus', Joyce's opening passage makes it plain that it is not Aristotle himself but rather Dante's fashioning of Aristotle that is encountered within the text. In light of which observation, we might suspect that all of the philosophical aspects of Stephen's discourse are not being so much intellectually mediated by Dante as poetically conditioned. This is not to entirely dismiss the intellectual content of Stephen's thought, but rather to acknowledge its context: if in 'Proteus' we encounter 'thought through my eyes' (*U* 3. 2), then the encounter firstly takes place not on an epistemological level, but through the poetic structures surrounding Stephen.

Following the presence of a Dantean poetics within 'Proteus' also moves us away from a recent trend in criticism that has privileged the philological aspect of the episode.[37] Instead of concentrating on philology as the 'scienza' assigned to 'Proteus' by the Linati schema, we will turn instead to the last 'simbolo': 'metamorfosi'. To consider 'Proteus' through metamorphoses is also to return to the position Joyce himself took on the episode when discussing it with Budgen: 'It's the struggle with Proteus. Change is the theme. Everything changes – sea, sky, man, animals. The words change, too.'[38] In thus embracing mutability and transition, 'Proteus' 'takes us to the centre of *Ulysses* and provides the basis of a world dominated by metamorphoses'.[39] Indeed, obvious though it may seem, it is also worth remembering the totemic position of the Homeric figure of Proteus, the shape-shifting sea god who lends his name to the episode's informal title.[40] Given this Homeric association, discussions of metamorphosis in Joyce's work tend to be patterned by Classical (and

---

[37] For an example of this philological trend see G. M. Downing, 'Richard Chenevix Trench and Joyce's Historical Study of Words', 37–68.
[38] Frank Budgen, *James Joyce and the Making of "Ulysses" and Other Writings*, 49.
[39] Eco, *Middle Ages of James Joyce*, 46.
[40] For Proteus's fight with Menelaus and his metamorphoses see Book IV of *The Odyssey*; as I will discuss later, Joyce was also aware of the presentation of Proteus in Virgil's *Georgics* (4. 387–444).

particularly Ovidian) conceptions; however, I'm not the first reader to suggest a Dantean influence in this area.[41] In her study of *Finnegans Wake*, Lucia Boldrini advances a convincing argument for seeing Joyce's 'thieving' intertextual practice as deriving from Dante's discourse of metamorphosis and literary contest in *Inferno 25*.[42]

However, in the preceding canto, *Inferno* 24, Dante presents a form of metamorphosis that most closely resonates with the poetics of 'Proteus', offering a new perspective on the representation of Stephen. Whilst, as Eco notes, the overarching form of the *terza rima* will not allow the *Commedia* to accommodate the sort of formal shifting that we see in *Ulysses*, the theme of metamorphosis is present within every semantic level of *Inferno* 24.[43] In the canto's opening extended simile, Dante characterises a visual confusion between hoarfrost and snow through a kind of metamorphosis in which the frost mimics the snow by taking on its image:

> Quando la brina in su la terra assempra
> L'imagine di sua sorella bianca,
> Ma poco dura alla sua penna tempra
>
> [when on the ground the frost copies the image of her white sister, but her pen retains its temper only briefly.]
>
> (*Inf.* 24. 4–6)

This idea of metamorphosis as the duplicitous assumption of another's form is of obvious significance to the sin of thievery that provides the moral theme of the canto. In the seventh *bolgia* of the eighth circle of Hell, the mechanism of the *contrapasso* traps the sinners in a constant cycle of infernal repetition of their earthly sin: their act of thievery manifesting itself as a repeated bodily metamorphosis. Bitten by a snake, a thief changes before Dante-pilgrim's eyes:

> Ed ecco ad un, ch'era da nostra proda,
> S'avventò un serpente, che il trafisse
> Là dove il collo alle spalle s'annoda.
> Né O sì tosto mai, né I si scrisse,
> Com'ei s'accese ed arse, e cener tutto
> Convenne che cascando divenisse:
> E poi che fu a terra sì distrutto,

---

[41] A recent example of an exploration of the Classical and biblical resonances of metamorphosis in Joyce's work is Franca Ruggieri's introduction to a volume of *Joyce Studies in Italy: James Joyce Metamorphosis and Re-writing*; see Ruggieri, 'Foreword', 9.
[42] Boldrini, *Joyce, Dante*, 2.
[43] Eco, *Middle Ages of James Joyce*, 36.

> La cener si raccolse per sè stessa,
> E in quel medesmo ritornò di butto:
> Così per li gran savi si confessa,
> Che la Fenice muore e poi rinasce,
> Quanto al cinquecentesimo anno appressa.

[And behold, a serpent hurled itself at one near our bank and transfixed him where the neck is knotted to the shoulders. Neither *O* nor *I* has ever been written so fast as he caught fire and burned and was all consumed, falling to ashes; and when he was on the ground, destroyed, the dust gathered together by itself and instantly became the same one again. Thus the great sages profess that the Phoenix dies and is reborn, when it approaches its five hundredth year.] (*Inf.* 24. 97–108)

This punitive metamorphosis of the thief contains within it many other examples of metamorphoses: the assumption by the sinner of the allegorical relation to a Phoenix (*Inf.* 24. 107), the transformation in the sinner's awareness of his surroundings later in the canto (*Inf.* 24. 112–18), and not least the action of the poet's similes themselves, which transform that which is unlike into that which is like. However, the key to this Dantean process lies in the actual moment of the sinner's metamorphosing combustion. The snake transfixes the sinner (*Inf.* 24. 98), providing a point of stillness after the rapid motion of its strike and preceding the movement of the consuming fire and falling ash. Indeed, the whole busy matter of the metamorphosis is bookended by moments of physical stasis, with the dust and ash re-gathering to leave the sinner in the same form in which he started (*Inf.* 24. 103–5). Through an allusive connection between Dante's line depicting this second moment of stasis, 'E in quel medesmo ritornò di butto' ['and instantly became the same one again'] (*Inf.* 24. 105) and Virgil's description of Proteus's defeat by Aristaeus in the *Georgics*, 'victus in ses redit' ['vanquished he returns to himself'] (*Georgics* 4. 444), there is a significant link between the metamorphosis and return to stasis of *Inferno* 24 and the shape-shifting figure of Proteus.[44]

Nevertheless, there is an important distinction between Dante's Infernal metamorphosis and that of either Virgil's or Homer's Proteus: these latter forms are predicated upon the persistence of a static, essential self that is identified with the physical form. When wrestled by Menelaus in the

---

[44] For more on this allusion see Ronald L. Martinez and Robert M. Durling, 'Notes to Canto 24', 376. Disappointingly, Camerini did not note this allusion in his edition of the *Commedia*; however, Joyce was familiar with the *Georgics* and associated them with both Stephen and the 'Proteus' episode, as we can see from his reference to Virgil and allusion to *Georgics* 3.271–7 in 'Oxen of the Sun' (*U* 14. 241–5).

Odyssey or Aristaeus in the *Georgics*, Proteus ultimately returns to a form isomorphic with his initial appearance, and a form within which his 'true' self rests: the self that holds the information desired by his assailants. However, in *Inferno* 24 there is no such completed teleological progression, and if there is a moment of ultimate rest for the thief, an actual endpoint to his metamorphosis, it is not in the physical return to the 'original' form, but in the poetic image of the phoenix, an image that figures in turn an unending, ever-repeating cycle of destruction and creation. Thus, Dante presents a view of metamorphosis within this context as a truly hopeless, infernal process; it represents the assumption of a stolen form that will always result in a return to the momentary stasis of the original, physical self and a subsequent cyclical, never-ending metamorphosis. In this sense, Dante's Infernal metamorphosis locates the identity of its subject in flux: offering circles and cycles and never-ending processes as the markers of identity, as opposed to the revelation of a fixed, essential self. In doing so, Dante emphasises the ultimate futility of this flux as a form of motion that will never lead anywhere, a transformation with no endpoint, and a 'change' that will just keep happening. Thus, in the process of Infernal metamorphosis as encountered in *Inferno* 24, the distinction between stasis and kinesis effectively collapses, and motion and transformation become simply another expression of persistence and stillness.

As seen earlier, through the initial quotation of his representation of Aristotle, Joyce established Dante as a key figure in the poetics of the 'Proteus' episode, that chapter in which 'everything changes'. This idea of a kinetic-static structure of Infernal metamorphosis, with its emphasis on ceaseless shaping and reshaping, fashioning and re-fashioning, thus offers a striking Dantean model for these Protean poetics of change. Of course, the metamorphosis of *Inferno* 24 is not the only Dantean model of the process; indeed, as Boldrini has noted, in the *Paradiso* metamorphosis assumes a far more positive – if less physically realised – aspect. These Paradisal metamorphoses involve not only 'the object observed, but also [...] the observing subject', and form a 'two-way movement that leaves neither side untouched', a formulation that – Boldrini argues – has substantial resonance for the poetics of figures such as ALP in *Finnegans Wake*.[45] Indeed, with their emphasis on the perceptual act, the metamorphoses of *Paradiso* in which figures only *appear* to change form ('e fecemi sembiante/che fosse ad altro volta' ['and it seemed to me she turned to

---

[45] Boldrini, *Joyce, Dante*, 184–5.

something else'] *Par.* 9. 64–5) would seem to have a strong relevance to the issues of sight and perception in 'Proteus'. However, in his struggle to reconcile the perceptual and the physical, Stephen overlooks this Paradisal form of subjectively conditioned metamorphosis. Stephen's approach reveals a preference for the more concrete phenomenal changes of the *Inferno* rather than the simple appearance of transformation, relying instead on his ability to read 'all things' and thus render them as transmutable signs: 'Signatures of all things I am here to read' (*U* 3. 2). After all, 'Proteus' is the chapter, as Joyce told Budgen, in which 'everything changes', not in which everything *seems* to change.

Thus, in failing to observe the phenomenal distinction brought out between the earlier and later discourses of metamorphosis in the *Commedia*, Stephen's attempts to control and metamorphose the world around him through his semiotic 'reading' – just as with his 'Infernal' hermeneutic of distance – succeed in obliviously aligning him with a structure of punishment and damnation. In this way, the circumscription of Stephen's determination to 'sign' his fixed self-fashioned identity as 'exile' by an Infernal poetics of metamorphosis introduces an unexpectedly tragic aspect into his representation. The Infernal poetics of 'Proteus' also serve to remind us that, whilst engagement with the intellectual content of Stephen's thoughts can prove fascinating, they are fundamentally nested within a poetic structure of futility and insubstantiality, and one that repeatedly emphasises the ineluctable mutability of form over the settled substance of conclusion.

The punitive stasis manifested as change and motion that is embodied in Dante's Infernal metamorphosis certainly seems to underpin much of the representation of Stephen in 'Proteus'. A recurrent subject of Stephen's thoughts throughout *Ulysses* is the persistence of the self, a paradox first expressed when he remembers his schooldays at Clongowes and observes: 'I am another now and yet the same' (*U* 1. 311–12). This notion of a change that, once undergone, leaves one the same – resonating as it does with the kinetic-static structure of Infernal metamorphosis – also patterns Stephen's experience of the persistence of self-fashioning narratives in 'Proteus'. As Gabler's discussion of 'narrative rereading' has shown, Stephen's self-fashioning narrative of 'exile' is continuously defused in 'Proteus' by the promptings of his memory and his growing awareness of failure: 'You were going to do wonders, what?' (*U* 3. 192–3).[46] The

[46] See Gabler, 'Narrative Rereadings', 62.

dilemma Stephen is struggling with here is hopelessly recursive, with his identity tied up in a 'flight' that led to an embarrassing return home, and that has in turn led to a different, more introspective form of escape.[47] The recursive pattern of this narrative predicament resonates strongly with the poetics of Infernal metamorphosis: a cycle of change that returns to stasis and then enacts further, fruitless change until the motion of the process itself becomes the trapping stasis. In which case, the signs of growing self-awareness on Stephen's part in 'Proteus' – the glimmer of understanding that his 'Latin quarter hat' is, within the present context, faintly ridiculous – are disastrously illusory. In a repetition of the problem surrounding his 'heroic' departure in *Portrait*, this 'development' in how Stephen thinks of himself doesn't so much suggest a progression or an epiphanic arrival as exemplify his failure to realise that the new 'epiphany' reached is simply part of the ceaseless pattern of fashioning and re-fashioning – of presentation and re-presentation – in which his identity is now intractably stuck.

This trapping cycle of failure and frustration also characterises Stephen's attempts to liberate himself by reducing the world around him to a field of infinitely extensible signs and signatures. As we saw, Stephen's hermeneutic position in *Ulysses* resonates strongly with the liminal position of Dante-pilgrim, and his semiotic strategies in 'Proteus' work to further present himself as an alienated figure to whom the city and its environs have become uniquely legible. Thus, when Stephen catches sight of the distant power station known locally as the 'Pigeonhouse' (*U* 3.158–73), he quickly 'reads' within this sign both the memory of his time in Paris and a quotation from Léo Taxil's *La Vie de Jésus* ('*C'est le pigeon, Joseph*'. *U* 3. 161). This hermeneutic act is rooted in the semiotic transformation of the visible 'signature' of a power station into a text from which he can read a reference to the Holy Spirit, and from which he in turn can extract the memory of his encounters with Fenian figures in Paris (*U* 3. 159–73). Initially, Stephen's 'reading' seems to be a simple and relatively effective way to retreat into the sustaining memory of his exile. And yet – in an echo of the linguistic operation of the interior monologue – the sequence of shifting thoughts that this act initiates ultimately serves to lead Stephen back to his current situation of failure and return:

---

[47] I am using the idea of 'recursion' to draw attention to the way in which the terms of Stephen's narrative of exile, failure and return effectively self-replicate, each generating the subsequent term in the never-ending cycle of the classic 'recursive loop'; for more on recursion in relation to Joyce's reading of Dante see below, pp. 194–95.

> Rich booty you brought back; *Le Tutu*, five tattered numbers of *Pantalon Blanc et Culotte Rouge*; a blue French telegram, curiosity to show:
> —Nother dying come home father.
> The aunt thinks you killed your mother. That's why she won't. (*U* 3. 196–200)

Earlier Stephen attempted to dismiss Mulligan through the allegorical metamorphosis of him into Ireland's 'gay betrayer' (*U* 1. 405), and yet here (and throughout 'Proteus') his mind returns again and again to his erstwhile friend and rival. Thus, despite his distanced posturing in 'reading' the Pigeonhouse, the connection with Mulligan persists, as does Stephen's concern with his recently deceased mother: the emotional impact that these two figures have had on him is too pronounced for Stephen to effectively separate himself from them simply by reducing them to symbols in his mind.

The sense in which Stephen's attempts to construct a distancing semiotic structure are continually defused by his circumscription by a poetics of Infernal metamorphosis is further clarified by his various attempts to fashion his presentation in 'Proteus', to 'sign' himself within his system. In his continuing thoughts of Mulligan there is evidence not only of the difficult, compromised nature of Stephen's self-fashioning, but also one of the 'ghostly' *trecento* voices that surround Dante's presence in his narrative:

> He saved men from drowning and you shake at a cur's yelping. But the courtiers who mocked Guido in Or san Michele were in their own house. House of … We don't want any of your medieval abstrusiosities. (*U* 3. 317–20)

Whilst at this point in 'Proteus' the reader probably *doesn't* want any more 'medieval abstrusiosities', the complex weave of the allusion to 'Guido' is well worth unpicking. On one hand, Stephen seems to be engaging in another relatively simple act of self-fashioning, redeeming his sense of his own failings in courage by aligning his presentation with that of the poet (and famous exile) Guido Cavalcanti.[48] However, whereas in *A Portrait of the Artist* Stephen may 'recall the dark humour of Guido Cavalcanti' (*P* V. 84–5) directly, the reference here to 'Or san Michele' reveals an important mediation. At this moment in 'Proteus', Stephen is not drawing so much on a knowledge of Cavalcanti himself as on the representation of Cavalcanti within Giovanni Boccaccio's *Decameron*.[49]

---

[48] On Dante's role in exiling Cavalcanti see above, p. 43.
[49] At this point, I would strongly echo Lucia Boldrini's call for greater study of the influence of Boccaccio on Joyce. Given the complexity of Boccaccio's narrative strategies, his juxtapositions and explorations of genre and form, and his prominent place within medieval literary traditions

'Maestro di color che sanno' or Stephen on the Seashore   105

The ninth novella of the sixth day of the *Decameron* recounts the story of one Brunetto Brunelleschi's attempts to convince Cavalcanti to join his group of Florentine 'bright young things', who throw lavish, socially exclusive parties (*Decameron* 6. 9. 4–5).[50] In the course of the story, Boccaccio states that Cavalcanti had a reputation as 'un de' miglior loici che avesse il mondo e ottimo filosofo naturale' ['one of the finest logicians in the world and an expert natural philosopher'] (*Decameron* 6. 9. 8, translation modified).[51] These were virtues, Boccaccio observes, for which 'poco la brigata curava' [Brunelleschi's 'company cared little'] (*Decameron* 6. 9. 8, translation modified). We'll return to the resonance between the view of Cavalcanti as 'un de' miglior loici' and the intellectually self-regarding figure that Stephen cuts in 'Proteus'; however, the most significant resonance between Stephen and Boccaccio's romanticised representation of the imperious and isolated Cavalcanti comes in the description of the poet's relation to Brunelleschi's 'glitterati' and his fellow citizens:

> Ma a messer Betto non era mai potuto venir fatto d'averlo, e credeva egli co' suoi compagni che ciò avvenisse per ciò che Guido alcuna volta speculando molto abstratto dagli uomini divenia;
>
> [However, Messer Betto had never succeeded in winning him over, and he and his companions thought this was because of his passion for speculative reasoning, which occasionally made him appear somewhat remote from his fellow beings.] (*Decameron* 6. 9. 9)

A young intellectual whose 'speculative reasoning' renders him 'molto abstratto' is a description tailor-made for the self-fashioning Stephen of 'Proteus'. In fact, so closely does the description of Cavalcanti fit Stephen that Boccaccio's story seems a more important source both for the young Dedalus's self-image and for Joyce's presentation of him than has been adequately acknowledged before. Indeed, that Joyce was consciously

---

with which Joyce was demonstrably interested (not to mention the fact that Joyce once lived on a road named after him), it seems a shame that Joyceans have shown so little interest in 'Boccuccia's Enameron' (*FW* 561. 24). See Boldrini, 'Introduction: Middayevil Joyce', 29 n. 28. On Joyce's residence at 1 via di Giovanni Boccaccio see Terence Matthews, 'A Significant Trieste Address', 18–20.

[50] In a piece of wordplay that Joyce must surely have appreciated, Boccaccio's story hinges on the juxtaposition between the lone figure of Cavalcanti, and the plural past tense verb 'cavalcavano' (*Decameron* 6. 9. 6) that describes Brunelleschi's gang riding together through the city; see Giovanni Boccaccio, *Decameron*, ed. Vittore Branca, 537 (all further references to the *Decameron* are to this edition). All translations from the *Decameron* are taken from G. H. McWilliam's version, with alterations noted.

[51] In his characterisation of Cavalcanti as an aloof intellectual, Boccaccio is drawing upon the biographical tradition initiated by Dante and Cavalcanti's contemporary Dino Compagni; for further details see Havely, *Dante*, 118.

drawing on Boccaccio's story for this particular passage of 'Proteus' is, for once, surprisingly certain. In an entry on Cavalcanti in his 'Trieste notebook' made sometime between 1907 and 1909, Joyce recorded the basic details of the story of Cavalcanti's persecution (although he slightly misattributed it: 'Bocc. 6.viii'):

> Betto Brunelleschi and his brigade railed at him one day as he was coming in from Orsanmichele. He (being in/near a burial ground) said to them: *Signori, voi mi potete dire a casa vostra ciò che vi piace.*[52]

Thus, Stephen's thought that 'the courtiers who mocked Guido in Or san Michele were in their own house. House of ...' evokes this comic crux in Boccaccio's story: 'Signori, voi mi potete dire a casa vostra ciò che vi piace' ['Gentleman, in your own house you may say whatever you like to me'] (*Decameron* 6. 9. 12). In this respect, by aligning Stephen with Boccaccio's Cavalcanti moving through the 'house of the dead', Joyce significantly thickens his intertextual web, and the dim shade of Dante seems to fall across Sandymount strand. As Mary Reynolds notes, the first part of the 'Trieste notebook' entry on Cavalcanti – before the details of Boccaccio's story – is a reference to Dante:

> *Calvacanti* (Guido)
>   His father Cavalcante Cavalcanti asks Dante where he is (Inf. cant X). Dante hesitates before he replies.[53]

Joyce's note refers to the passage of *Inferno* 10 in which Dante-pilgrim encounters Cavalcante di Cavalcanti and meditates on the subsequent death of Guido, his close friend (*Inf.* 10. 52–72).[54] In this respect, the note demonstrates Joyce's association of Boccaccio's representation of Cavalcanti with Dante's earlier shadowy representation in the *Commedia*, an association that thus haunts the presence of Boccaccio's Cavalcanti and the 'house of the dead' on Sandymount strand.[55] Indeed, the whole

---

[52] Robert Scholes and Richard Kain (eds.), *The Workshop of Daedalus: James Joyce and the Raw Materials for 'A Portrait of the Artist as a Young Man'*, 94.

[53] Scholes and Kain, *The Workshop of Daedalus*, 94. For Reynolds's brief discussion of the notebook entry and Boccaccio's story within the context of her reading of the wider significance of *Inferno* 10 in *Ulysses* see *Joyce and Dante*, 56–7.

[54] As Teodolinda Barolini has characterised it, Cavalcanti is a shadowy presence 'encoded' throughout the *Commedia* and with whom Dante can be seen to be in continual dialogue and disagreement; see *Dante's Poets: Textuality and Truth in the 'Comedy'*, 136, 142–8. On Dante's relation with Cavalcanti generally see also Havely, *Dante*, 118–21.

[55] As Scholes and Kain have already noted, Boccaccio's notion of a socialising group who are already unwittingly moving in the world of the dead, would seem to provide a clear precedent for the central motif of Joyce's own story 'The Dead', a further example of Joyce's engagement with Boccaccio in need of greater attention, see *The Workshop of Daedalus*, 94.

of Joyce's note on '*Calvacanti* (Guido)' is comprised of references to the works of Dante and Boccaccio, and within it – through an import 'error' in Joyce's spelling – the poet Guido Cavalcanti makes no appearance.

Having unpicked this web around Cavalcanti's presence on Sandymount strand, Stephen's thought about Mulligan, and his apparent self-fashioning alignment with the alienated and 'heroically' exilic figure of Guido Cavalcanti, start to look significantly more complex than it might first appear. Whereas Joyce's note (mis)recorded the derivation of the Cavalcanti story from the *Decameron* ('Bocc. 6. viii'), Stephen demonstrates no such awareness that his self-fashioning identification has not been with the actual figure of Cavalcanti but rather with his fictional re-presentation by Boccaccio. Stephen's thought is thus decidedly compromised: he tries to present himself as someone who can easily bring to mind such 'medieval abstrusiosities' as Cavalcanti, and through alignment with them 'sign' his self-fashioned identity as an alienated and 'exiled' figure. But in unwittingly aligning with a fiction of Cavalcanti-as-outsider, Stephen's signing instead draws attention to the flickering intertextual mirrors that Joyce sets up around the thought.[56] Echoing the way in which Dante's fiction mediates the presence of Aristotle in 'Proteus', these mirrors reflect not a substantive connection with Cavalcanti or his work as poet and philosopher, but rather an identification with a fashioned pattern of representation: with an inherently fictive form. Thus, Stephen's attempt to define himself through identification with one of the 'miglior loici', and so by connection to 'sign' himself within his semiotic system as an equally misunderstood and overlooked philosopher, emphasises instead the misunderstandings and oversights in his own reading. In this respect, through a poetics of Infernal metamorphosis within which he mistakes the flux of re-presentation surrounding 'Calvacanti (Guido)' for the static authority of Guido Cavalcanti, Stephen's alignment with knowledge actually serves to highlight his reliance on narrative. His attempt to shore up

---

[56] The extent of Joyce's own knowledge of Cavalcanti and his work is uncertain. Ellmann briefly mentions Joyce as talking about Cavalcanti during his time studying with Father Ghezzi, but mentions no source for this anecdote (*JJ* 59). Mary Reynolds and Corinna del Greco Lobner also both mention Cavalcanti in connection with Joyce's university education, but again give no supporting documentation, see *Joyce and Dante*, 21, and *James Joyce's Italian Connection: The Poetics of the Word*, 8. In the correspondence between Joyce and Ezra Pound, there are several mentions and quotations of 'noster Guido', although interestingly these all come from Pound's end, often within the context of trying to prove his learned credentials to Joyce. Indeed, when Pound wrote to Joyce in 1927 to ask for help interpreting a reference to 'natural dimostramento' in Cavalcanti's 'Donna mi prega', Joyce's response was simply to note that neither of his editions of Aquinas mentioned the term (*L* III, 166), see Forrest Read (ed.), *Pound/Joyce: The Letters of Ezra Pound to James Joyce*, 95, 230–1.

his fixed 'exilic' identity opens Stephen to an ongoing discourse of metamorphic reshaping and re-presentation.

The metamorphic circularities that thus surround Stephen in 'Proteus', fostering the impression that he has got himself caught in an infernal loop, are also reflected in the cyclical form of the episode itself. Towards the end of the chapter, as Stephen's twin urges to write poetry and urinate are strengthening, his thoughts start to run in familiar tracks:

> Who ever anywhere will read these written words? Signs on a white field [...] veil of space with coloured emblems hatched on its field. Hold hard. Coloured on a flat: yes, that's right. Flat I see, then think distance, near, far, flat I see, east, back. Ah, see now! (*U* 3. 414–19)

As Stephen thinks again of Aristotle and his perceptual theory, the language of the famous opening passage also starts to resurface: 'Now where the blue hell am I bringing her beyond the veil? Into the ineluctable modality of the ineluctable visuality' (*U* 3. 424–6). This retrenchment of the opening thought – with its faintly mocking, double dose of ineluctability – serves to create the impression that, at the end of 'Proteus', we are very much returning to the beginning.[57] In this respect, Stephen's peregrinations undercut his assumed identity as 'pilgrim': the intellectual motions he has moved through in 'Proteus' have not only led him nowhere but also returned him to the ineluctable terms of his starting point, and thus themselves become yet another trapping net, a stifling form of stasis masquerading as transformation.

The resonance between the structure of Infernal metamorphosis and the poetics through which we read the nebulous forms of Stephen's thoughts in 'Proteus' underlines again that the primary impact of Stephen's intellectual presentation in the episode is not in the creation of philosophical or epistemological structures, but rather in the conditioning of his poetic representation. The nesting of his thought within a poetics of futility and stasis suggests that, just as with his 'silence' and his 'exile', his 'cunning' or *ingegno* – the final tool in his Dantean inventory – has been blunted. In the light of such failure in 'Proteus', the self-fashioned identity that Stephen crafted in *A Portrait of the Artist* crumbles away to be replaced by the structure of an Infernal poetics of endless fashioning and re-presentation. This paradox perhaps underpins Joyce's decision to

---

[57] In this way, the circular structure of 'Proteus' resonates strongly with the structure of *Inferno* 24, which, in its final images of 'torbidi nuvoli' ['roiling clouds'] (*Inf.* 24. 146), returns to the figurative weather imagery of its beginning.

move *Ulysses* away from Stephen: '[he] no longer interests me to the same extent. He has a shape that can't be changed'; Dante's notions of punitive metamorphosis reveal that this fixity on Stephen's part is, in a sense, the result of his infinite plasticity.[58]

The apparent Dantean paradox in Stephen's protean poetics – the way in which he continually attempts to 'sign' his fixed identity through a process that repeatedly emphasises the potential for this 'signature' to be rewritten and re-presented – warrants further consideration.[59] Do the poetics of Infernal metamorphosis only characterise Stephen in 'Proteus' and the earlier chapters, or do they apply in other passages of *Ulysses*? Can these Dantean poetics continue to condition the way in which his character can be read not through his welter of intellectual 'abstrusiosities' but through the representational effect of this abstruseness? And does the presence of Dante in Stephen's narrative continue to implicate *Ulysses* in a 'ghostly' community of mediated *trecento* texts?

'Playing Aristotle' or Dante in the Library

After walking 'into eternity along Sandymount strand' (*U* 3. 18–19), and making a brief pit-stop at the newspaper offices of 'Aeolus', Stephen next emerges as the focus of *Ulysses* in 'Scylla and Charybdis'. This ninth chapter features the most extensive quotations from the *Commedia* of any part of *Ulysses* other than 'Aeolus', and Dante is also interestingly present within the setting of the episode. From its opening in 1890, the glazing scheme of the National Library of Ireland included a sequence of windows depicting literary figures, and in the front hall of the library, located between windows featuring Virgil and John Milton, there is a roundel image of Dante.[60] This inclusion of Dante within the 'infernal' pantheon of the secular literary orthodoxy of the National Library could not have failed to register with the young James Joyce during his regular visits; and, indeed, the physical proximity of Dante and Milton would underscore Joyce's treatment of these writers when he wove them into the fictional library of 'Scylla and Charybdis'. And so, the final section of this chapter will explore the action and significance of Joyce's Dantean quotations, and

---

[58] Budgen, *James Joyce and the Making of 'Ulysses'*, 107.
[59] For more on the contravention of the signature see Derrida, *Acts of Literature*, 362–3.
[60] On the history of the fabric of the NLI see Justin Furlong, 'A Magnificent Pile! A Brief Architectural Tour of the Main Library Building'. For photographs of the Virgil, Dante and Milton windows see www.nli.ie/en/gal/gallery-main.aspx?page=3&image=cc91d842-518e-42c1-95ee-c582579e104e (accessed 09 July 2015).

thereby try to find out just exactly what Dante is doing in the National Library of Ireland.

The first quotation from the *Commedia* in 'Scylla', following the model of the NLI's glazing scheme, draws together Dante and Milton, and would also seem to demonstrate the persistence of Stephen's Infernal poetics. Having been lightly ribbed by John Eglinton over his poetic aspirations ('—Have you found those six brave medicals [...] to write *Paradise Lost* at your dictation?' *U* 9. 18–19), Stephen reacts to George Russell's ('AE') interjection on mystical numerology:

> Glittereyed his rufous skull close to his greencapped desklamp sought the face bearded amid darkgreener shadow, an ollav, holyeyed. He laughed low: a sizar's laugh of Trinity: unanswered.
>
> *Orchestral Satan, weeping many a rood*
> *Tears such as angels weep.*
> *Ed egli avea del cul fatto trombetta.* (*U* 9. 29–34)

Stephen's hermeneutic position once again embodies the hopeless dichotomy of separation and involvement. He marks himself off from the discourse around him through his snide, would-be penetrative observations, but his paraphrase of Milton's *Paradise Lost* (1. 196, 1. 619–20) only serves to underscore the validity of Pugliatti's reading of interior monologue as inextricably implicated in the surrounding discourse from which it seeks to signal its difference.[61] This compromised hermeneutic also seems to underpin Stephen's closing quotation of the final line of *Inferno* 21:

> Per l'argine sinistro volta dienno;
> Ma prima avea ciascun la lingua stretta
> Coi denti, verso lor duca per cenno,
> Ed egli avea del cul fatto trombetta.
>
> [They made left face on the bank; but first each bit his tongue toward their leader, as a salute, and he of his ass had made a trumpet.] (*Inf.* 21. 136–9)

There is an obvious satiric intention in Stephen's linking the speech of Russell and Eglinton with Calcabrina and the other Malebranche (the devils who patrol the fifth *bolgia*) breaking wind. However, whilst the juxtaposition of Milton's 'Orchestral Satan' with Dante's farting devils is undeniably funny, the action of the quote within the representation of Stephen follows a familiar pattern. On one hand, he seeks to dismiss George Russell's earlier, cliquish name-dropping of Yeats ('The shining

---

[61] Pugliatti, 'The Ulyssean Challenge', 168–9.

seven WB calls them', *U* 9. 28), and in doing so, through an allusion to Dante, tries to reassure himself of his own literary knowledge and self-worth.[62] And yet, in contrast to how he 'signs' himself, Stephen's thought again underwrites his hopeless 'medieval' abstrusiosity: he has to formulate his thoughts through a reference to Dante even when he thinks someone is talking out of their arse.[63]

So this first appearance of Dante in the National Library fits the pattern of compromised self-fashioning and discordant representation that indicate the operation of the poetics of Infernal metamorphosis. Certainly, throughout 'Scylla and Charybdis' Stephen is continually engaging in the kinds of 'exilic' presentations and separations that failed in 'Proteus'. This process is perhaps best exemplified by his consciously playing the role of 'Plato's schoolboy' (*U* 9. 57) Aristotle in the middle of a Platonic dialogue: 'Unsheathe your dagger definitions. Horseness is the whatness of allhorse' (*U* 9. 84–5).[64] And the struggle that the persistence of the self poses in the flux of Infernal metamorphosis is never far from his mind: 'Wait. Five months. Molecules all change. I am other I now. Other I got pound' (*U* 9. 205–6). However, the humour of these thoughts – the pleasing rhythm of the recurrence of 'horse', and the notion of using the all-too-profound existential and metaphysical question of bodily regeneration as a way to default on a small debt – raises again the question of irony surrounding Stephen's representation. These elements were not so prominent in Stephen's thoughts in 'Proteus', but in 'Scylla' there seems a slight narrowing of the distance between how he fashions and 'signs' himself, and how he is read and re-presented to the reader.

This sense of a growing awareness and alignment between Stephen's self-presentation and his poetic representation strengthens a little later in the chapter, interestingly at the very point at which Stephen is beginning his own act of re-presentation through his 'biography' of Shakespeare. The lynchpin of Stephen's biographical reading of Shakespeare is his logically fallacious interpretation of the theme of forgiveness and healing in such late plays as *The Winter's Tale*. He expresses this central tenet of what

---

[62] If, as Margot Norris has argued, the object of Stephen's discourse in 'Scylla' is to 'display his intellectual and critical merit and earn him the reward of admiration and support from a group of well-respected Irish editors, authors and intellectuals', then he seems to be off to a particularly poor start; see 'The Stakes of Stephen's Gambit in "Scylla and Charybdis"', 3.
[63] For a discussion of the literary discourse of flatulence in 'Scylla' see Enrico Terrinoni, *Leggere, tradurre, interpretare: percorsi letterari possibili d'Inghilterra e Irlanda*, 59–70.
[64] On Stephen's 'alliance' here with 'Aquinas and in particular Aristotle' see Cixous, *Exile of James Joyce*, 569.

Cixous calls a 'brilliant analysis' in a striking formulation: 'Where there is a reconciliation [...] there must first have been a sundering' (*U* 9. 334–5), and again, in logically reversed terms: 'There can be no reconciliation [...] if there has not been a sundering' (*U* 9. 397–8).[65] Whilst from a logical standpoint Stephen's position might seem a teleological fallacy, his interest in a possible aetiological relationship between separation and re-aggregation – between alienation and belonging – suggests a sense in which he is becoming aware of both the possibility of affecting his own reconciliation, and the growing impetus to do so.[66] In this way, Stephen's conscious performance of a re-presentation of Shakespeare's biography allows his thoughts to align more closely with his own representation as a failed exile. Called upon to refashion a view of Shakespeare for his audience, Stephen seems to momentarily lose the animus to keep signing himself as circumscribed by 'silence, exile, and cunning'. Indeed, through his re-presentation of Shakespeare, Stephen arguably starts to align himself with the trajectory of Joyce's own engagement with Dante, between the nodes of exile and community.

However, any conclusion that Stephen's conscious performance of the interrelation of reconciliation and sundering might represent a genuine transition in his representation, and thus a surmounting of the poetics of Infernal metamorphosis, is challenged by a subsequent intertextual moment. Shortly after first stating his sundering-reconciliation fallacy, Stephen makes an intriguing reference to another of the medieval Italian literary voices that – as with Boccaccio and Cavalcanti – seem to haunt Dante's presence throughout Stephen's narrative in *Ulysses*:

> Stephen withstood the bane of miscreant eyes glinting stern under wrinkled brows. A basilisk. *E quando vede l'uomo l'attosca*. Messer Brunetto, I thank thee for the word. (*U* 9. 373–5)

There is a complex of easily overlooked metamorphoses in Stephen's observation of John Eglinton here, the presence of which is most clearly indicated by the source of his Italian quotation. This description of the sight of a basilisk as poisonous to the beholder comes from Brunetto Latini's *Les Livres dou Tresor*, a French-language encyclopedic work written

---

[65] For Cixous's charitable reading of Stephen's 'critical biography' of Shakespeare see *Exile of James Joyce*, xi.
[66] It is in this moment in 'Scylla' that Stephen seems to come closest to embodying Cixous's lyrical formulation of his exile: 'he wills his exile for the sake of the hope of return (or despair of return) it involves – like Dante', although, as I argued in the previous chapter, this view of exile as 'willed' is not really all that much 'like Dante', Cixous, *Exile of James Joyce*, 355.

'Playing Aristotle' or Dante in the Library

by Latini during his exile from Florence between 1260 and 1267, and completed shortly after his return to the city.[67] As a *duecento* text written by a returned Florentine exile, the *Tresor*'s relevance to Stephen's Dantean position and predicament in *Ulysses* is readily apparent; however, the line that Stephen actually misquotes is taken from the *Tesoro*, the Italian translation of the *Tresor* – which, as noted in Camerini's edition of the *Commedia*, is traditionally ascribed to Bono Giamboni.[68]

> Basilischio si è una generazione di serpenti: ed è lo re dei serpenti. E sì pieno di veleno, che ne riluce tutto di fuori: eziandio, nonchè solo il veleno, ma il puzzo avvelena da presso e da lungi, perchè egli corrompe l' aria e guasta gli arbori, e il suo odore uccide gli uccelli per l' aria volando, e col suo vedere attosca l' uomo quando lo vede: tutto che gli uomini anziani dicono, che non nuoce a chi lo vede in prima.[69] (*Tesoro* V. 3. 1)

> [The basilisk: a species of snake and the king of the serpents. It is so full of venom, that it gleams outwardly with it. Indeed, not only its venom but its stench can poison from near or far, for it corrupts the air and blasts the trees, and its stink kills birds on the wing, and its glance poisons the man who sees it. But, as all the old men say, it cannot harm those who see it first.]

Thus, when Stephen deploys the *Tesoro* (in distinction to the *Tresor*) as another abstruse text through which to 'sign' his role as rarefied scholar, he draws upon a 'static' authority that has itself, through the act of translation (and its garbling by his memory), undergone an unsettling process of metamorphosis.[70] Joyce draws attention to the implicit oversight in Stephen's reading by having him ascribe 'the word' of his authority to 'Messer Brunetto'; who, whilst perhaps the originator of the idea here,

---

[67] Peter Armour, 'Brunetto Latini', 127. For more on Latini's life see, Bianca Ceva, *Brunetto Latini: l'uomo e l'opera*.

[68] Although this attribution of the translation of the *Tresor* is now widely disputed – with many scholars arguing that Latini himself carried it out – Joyce's copy of the *Commedia* confidently asserts: '*Li livres dou Tresor*, scritto da lui in francese, fatto Italiano da B. Giamboni' ['*Les Livres dou Tresor*, written by him [i.e. Brunetto] in French, translated into Italian by B. Giamboni'], see Camerini, *La Divina Commedia*, 86 nn. 119, 120. At the time of the writing of *Ulysses*, the standard edition of the *Tesoro* reaffirmed this attribution, see Brunetto Latini, *Il Tesoro di Brunetto Latini volgarizzato da Bono Giamboni*.

[69] Latini, *Il Tesoro di Brunetto Latini*, vol. 2, 137–8.

[70] In this respect, I would draw a strong distinction with Mary Reynolds's reading of this moment. Although Reynolds acknowledges that Stephen's phrasing is 'actually a paraphrase' of the *Tresor* (not, as is the case, the *Tesoro*), her view that Brunetto is 'brought back to life in twentieth century Dublin' by a Stephen who can 'call spirits from the deep' would seem to directly oppose the dynamics of translation and metamorphosis at work in the passage, and overlook an important irony I will discuss presently; see *Joyce and Dante*, 53–4.

was – as far as was known at the time – certainly not the author of the words that gave it form.

The uncertainty created by Stephen's desire to position a text as an authority whose translated nature he completely overlooks, also seems to wash over onto the subsequent chain of self-fashioning associations that he fastens to it. By thanking 'Messer Brunetto' as the source and transmitter of his thought, Stephen implicitly positions himself as a student of Brunetto. In doing so, he not only claims a literary filiation with Brunetto as his 'author', but also locates himself in relation to the 'ghostly' presence of Latini's most famous intellectual 'son', Dante. The anxiety around Dante's relation to Brunetto, and his evocation of this relationship with his old teacher in *Inferno* 15, has long been one of the more talked-about aspects of the *Commedia*.[71] However, the portrait Joyce encountered in Camerini's 'Vita di Dante' was unequivocal about their filial dynamic: 'Il padre suo Alighieri perdé nella sua puerizia [...] nondimanco, confortato da' propinqui e da Brunetto Latini' ['Alighieri lost his father in his childhood [...] nonetheless he was comforted by his neighbours and by Brunetto Latini'].[72] This view of Brunetto as becoming Dante's proxy-father through grief would certainly seem to add some concrete support to the kinds of uneasy paternal-filial relations that Mary Reynolds has read within the encounter between Stephen Daedalus and Wells, the young priest-to-be in *Stephen Hero*.[73] However, within *Ulysses*, Stephen's implicit claim of fraternity with Dante as co-student of 'Messer Brunetto' draws once again on a metamorphosed source. Stephen's claim of a pedagogical filiation with Brunetto, can be seen in essence – to employ Boldrini's useful term – as an attempt to 'thieve' Brunetto's greeting to Dante-pilgrim in *Inferno* 15:

> E quegli: O figliuol mio, non ti dispaccia;
> Se Brunetto Latini un poco teco
> Ritorna indietro, e lascia andar la traccia.

---

[71] Whilst, as Peter Armour acknowledged, the exact nature of Dante's 'debt' to Latini is uncertain, the importance of their relationship has never been doubted, see 'Brunetto Latini', 128. For some modern discussions of Dante and Brunetto see Lillian M. Bisson, 'Brunetto Latini as a Failed Mentor', 1–15; Charles T. Davis, 'Brunetto Latini and Dante', 421–50; Nick Havely, 'Brunetto and Palinurus', 29–38; and Eugene Vance, *Mervelous Signals: Poetics and Sign Theory in the Middle Ages*, 230–55.

[72] Camerini, 'Vita di Dante', 8.

[73] See Reynolds, *Joyce and Dante*, 46–8.

[And he: 'O my son, let it not displease you if Brunetto Latini turns back with you a little and lets his troop run on.'] (*Inf.* 15. 31–3)

By presenting himself as the receiver of 'Messer Brunetto''s 'word', and thus equally worthy as Dante-pilgrim of the title of 'figliuol', Stephen repeats his earlier error with Boccaccio and Cavalcanti in 'Proteus', fashioning himself this time on the double re-presentation of the poetic figures of Brunetto and Dante-pilgrim, rather than on the historical personae of Dante and Latini. Joyce draws attention to the inherent danger in such 'category errors' in Stephen's fashioning through the phrasing of his thought: 'Messer Brunetto, I thank thee for the word. (*U* 9. 375)'. The gratitude for Brunetto's 'word' that Stephen expresses cannot fail to make us think of the most famous discussion of Latini's words – of the text, indeed, of the *Tesoro* that Stephen is misquoting:

> Sieti raccomandato il mio Tesoro
> Nel quale io vivo ancora: e più non chieggio.

[Let my *Treasure* be commended to you, in which I live still, and I ask no more.] (*Inf.* 15. 119–20)

Brunetto's hope that he will 'live still' after his death – be literally 're-presented' – by the presentation of his words in the form of the *Tesoro* (or indeed its original in the *Tresor*) is, of course, famously – if ambiguously – frustrated. For the vast majority of the literate world, their only encounter with Brunetto Latini or his 'treasure' comes not through his work or historical persona, but through his poetic representation by Dante in the *Inferno*.[74]

In this respect, Stephen is again planting his stake into watery ground: he tries to fashion himself by association with a static 'authority' in the form of the 'medieval abstrusiosities' of Brunetto and his *Tesoro*, only to find that both text and author are unexpectedly subject to the flux of metamorphosis at the hands of Dante. In the same way that Brunetto's hope is displaced by Dante's word, Stephen's intellectual 'signing' of himself is ultimately rewritten by the re-presentation of him as misreading and misunderstanding his sources, a readerly refashioning that his very abstruseness has invited. Thus, following Stephen's quotations and thoughts through to their end, for all their telegraphed significance

---

[74] See Barolini, *Dante's Poets*, 229. For a contrasting view that the *Tresor* and the *Tesoro* may be said to 'live within the *Commedia*', see Havely, 'Brunetto and Palinurus', 34.

they are still patterned by the stasis of Infernal metamorphosis. This rich intertextual example of the errors and circularities that mark the poetics of Stephen, coming so soon as it does after the 'epiphany' about sundering and reconciliation, must surely question whether that earlier moment really eluded the nets of Infernal metamorphosis. Joyce, indeed, seems to juxtapose the apparent narrowing of the ironic gap between Stephen's presentation and representation with the complex interweaving of representations around Brunetto Latini. In doing so, he stresses once again that Stephen's insights – even when they appear to be changing in character – remain fundamentally nested within his earlier poetics. Indeed, we could (somewhat cautiously) note that the passage of the *Tesoro* that Stephen calls to mind concerns the 'king of the serpents', the basilisk. As well as evoking the tradition of transfiguration through the serpent's gaze, the context that Brunetto (with his inextricable link to Dante) provides leads back ineluctably to the serpents as figures of punitive metamorphosis in *Inferno* 24 and 25.

The flux of presentation and representation, fashioning and refashioning, which masks the apparently static authority of Brunetto Latini, also flows through Dante's final appearance on the stage of the Library:

> If you hold that he, a greying man with two marriageable daughters, with thirtyfive years of life, *nel mezzo del cammin di nostra vita*, with fifty of experience, is the beardless undergraduate from Wittenberg then you must hold that his seventyyear old mother is the lustful queen. No. The corpse of John Shakespeare does not walk the night. From hour to hour it rots and rots. He rests, disarmed of fatherhood, having devised that mystical estate upon his son. Boccaccio's Calandrino was the first and last man who felt himself with child. (*U* 9. 829–37)

It's interestingly unclear whether this quotation of the opening line of the *Commedia* (*Inferno* 1.1) is spoken by Stephen (thus operating as a sign within both the diegetic and textual discourses of *Ulysses*), or is a silent, automatic association with the age of thirty-five (and we should remember here Joyce's letter to Marthe Fleischmann). Either way, whilst making his re-presentation of the life of Shakespeare, Stephen's mind is clearly drawn to the autobiographical frame for the fiction of the *Commedia*:

> Nel mezzo del cammin di nostra vita
> Mi ritrovai per una selva oscura,
> Chè la diritta via era smarrita.
>
> [In the middle of the journey of our life, I came to myself in a dark wood, for the straight way was lost.] (*Inf.* 1. 1–3)

As shown earlier, in the notes he made from Camerini's edition, Joyce paid careful attention to the details of Dante's biography and their reshaping into the fiction of the *Commedia*, as laid out in the first canto.[75] Thus, in fashioning his fiction of Shakespeare, Stephen seems to be drawing on a conscious awareness of the precedent of Dante, who fashioned his own life into the teleological journey of 'Dante-pilgrim'. In this respect, whether his listeners heard him speak in Italian or not, in his dialogue in the Library, Stephen not only re-presents the life of Shakespeare but, in doing so, also 'signs' himself as consciously repeating Dante's earlier process of fictive re-presentation.

The self-fashioning association that thus emerges from the tangle of the 'dark wood' of Stephen's Dantean representations resonates for once not with the figure of Dante-pilgrim but with Dante the poet himself. In this, Stephen would seem to be echoing Joyce's own growing engagement with the poetics of the *Commedia*. And indeed, this resonance between Stephen and Dante is underwritten by the apparent discongruity of the subject of their fashioning acts. Whereas the fiction of Dante's fictionalising is that he is himself his own subject ('mi ritrovai' ['I came to myself']), Stephen is obviously not Shakespeare, thus the subject of his fashioning is self-evidently other to himself. However, in the same way that Dante's fictionalising act problematises and distorts the identification between himself and the 'Pilgrim' as the figure found in the wood – an act of self-fashioning that renders the self that fashions ineluctably 'other' – Stephen's repeated associations with the figure of Hamlet throughout *Ulysses*, and Hamlet's implication in the discourse of Shakespeare's identity he is currently decrying, complicate the divisions between his self and Shakespeare as the subject of his fiction. However, whilst the watery relations surging around Stephen's self-fashioning may ultimately never resolve, the natural inclination to see the development of an alignment with 'Dante as poet' as a liberation from the poetics of Infernal metamorphosis – to see Stephen as, for once, stepping onto firmer epistemological ground – is complicated by the reference to 'Boccaccio's Calandrino' (*U* 9. 836).

As seen earlier, Boccaccio is a figure who haunts Dante's presence in the narrative of Stephen in *Ulysses*, and here Joyce brings the two *trecento* authors into direct intercourse. By so closely associating Boccaccio with the quotation of *Inferno* 1, Stephen introduces a now-familiar

---

[75] See above, p. 31.

deconstructive aspect into his discourse. In his re-presenting of Shakespeare's life, Stephen seems to be consciously modelling himself on the example of Dante as biographical shaper. However, Boccaccio stands at the wellspring of the biographical tradition for Dante: his *Vita di Dante* and commentaries on the *Commedia* determined how all subsequent readers encountered and presented Dante's life, and made connections between this biographical narrative and his poetic and theoretical works.[76] Joyce would have been well aware of Boccaccio's mediating role: the *Vita di Dante* was present in the National Library of Ireland in both Francesco Macrì-Leone's edition and within Gaetano Milanesi and A. M. Salvini's edition of Boccaccio's critical writing on Dante, and Eugenio Camerini made frequent use of these works throughout his edition of the *Commedia*.[77] Thus, Stephen's mentioning Boccaccio so quickly after he has invoked the self-fashioning of the *Commedia* as a representational model would seem to underscore Boccaccio's potentially compromising presence as mediator of this model. The Dante-figure whom Stephen aligns with – the historical Dante who re-presented his life in fictional form in the *Commedia* – is in fact a figure to whom neither Stephen nor any reader can ever have unmediated access. Thus, the Dante whose poetic processes of self-fashioning and representation in the *Commedia* underwrite Stephen's discourse is himself fundamentally Boccaccio's fictive re-presentation. Just as with his earlier thoughts of Cavalcanti, Stephen seems to have 'signed' his own identity through alignment with an identity that is subject to continual rewriting, catching him in the flux of Infernal metamorphosis. Indeed, through the persistence of these Dantean poetics, there is a growing resonance between the watery flow of 'Proteus' and the whirlpool of the schematic associations of 'Scylla and Charybdis'.

---

[76] On Boccaccio's role in Dante studies see Jason M. Houston, *Building a Monument to Dante: Boccaccio as 'Dantista'*, 52–90. However, Guyda Armstrong has recently argued that Boccaccio's pre-eminence as a writer on Dante was partly the creation of nineteenth-century engagements (or lack thereof) with his own work; see her 'Nineteenth-Century Translations and the Invention of Boccaccio-*dantista*', 201–20.

[77] See, for instance, Camerini's account of Dante's involvement in a scene redolent of 'Scylla and Charybdis': 'Vuolsi pure che dalla Lunigiana movesse alla volta di Parigi, ove, secondo il Boccaccio, sostenne in quella celebre Università una disputa *de quolibet*' ['He [Dante] also decided to set out from Lunigiana for Paris, where, according to Boccaccio, he took part at that famous University in a *de quolibet* disputation'], Camerini, 'Vita di Dante', 10. The editions of Boccaccio's *Dantista* writings that were the principal sources for Camerini's notes are both present in the NLI: in Boccaccio, *Il comento di Giovanni Boccacci sopra La Commedia con le annotazioni di A. M. Salvini*; and Boccaccio, *La vita di Dante*.

A final affirmation of the poetics of Infernal metamorphosis that underwrite Stephen's representation in *Ulysses* can be inferred from the detail of the story of 'Boccaccio's Calandrino'. The woebegone and rather gullible hero of four of Boccaccio's stories, in *Decameron* 9. 3 the painter Calandrino is the subject of an elaborate joke by his fellow artists Bruno, Buffalmacco and Nello. In a convoluted attempt to extract a recent inheritance from him, they convince Calandrino that he is ill, and then call on their mutual friend, the doctor 'maestro Simone', to diagnose him with a startling condition:

> 'Vedi, Calandrino, a parlarti come a amico, tu non hai altro male se non che tu se' pregno.'
>
> ['Look here, Calandrino, speaking now as your friend, I'd say that the only thing wrong with you is that you are pregnant.] (*Decameron* 9. 3. 20)

This rather unexpected pregnancy is, Calandrino quickly decides, the fault of his wife Tessa: 'Oimè! Tessa, questo m'hai fatto tu, che non vuogli stare altro che di sopra: io il ti diceva bene!' ['Ah, Tessa, this is your doing! You always insist on lying on top. I told you all along what would happen!'] (*Decameron* 9. 3. 21). Luckily for Calandrino, 'maestro Simone' is able to supply him with 'una certa bevanda stillata molto buona e molto piacevole a bere, che in tre mattine risolverà ogni cosa' ['a certain draught, well brewed and pleasant to drink, that in three days heals everything'] (*Decameron* 9. 3. 28; translation modified). Happy to be spared the seemingly insoluble dilemma of birth ('come partorirò io questo figliuolo?' ['How am I to produce this son?'] *Decameron* 9. 3. 23), Calandrino blithely pays over his inheritance to 'maestro Simone', gulps down the placebo and, unlike the far more canny Tessa, remains oblivious to the trick his friends have played.

The relevance of nearly every aspect of Boccaccio's story to *Ulysses* is remarkable: from the resonance of the loving, fractious marriage of Calandrino and Tessa with that of Mr Bloom and Molly, to their shared experiences of sexual dysfunction; from the similarities of the mocking Buffalmacco and the scurrilous doctor Simone to Mulligan and his band of medicals, to the echo of Mr Bloom's touchingly impossible desire to give birth to a child (*U* 15. 1821–2). Indeed, *Decameron* 9.3 further suggests that Boccaccio represents an important and largely overlooked part of Joyce's reading. Whilst the need for more study of Joyce's engagement with the *Decameron* looks ever more pressing, at this point we can only note that Calandrino's pregnancy – which gestates but doesn't come to term – seems to stand as a perfect figure for Stephen's theory of Shakespeare:

—You are a delusion, said roundly John Eglinton to Stephen. You have brought us all this way to show us a French triangle. Do you believe your own theory?
—No, Stephen said promptly.
—Are you going to write it? Mr Best asked. You ought to make it a dialogue, don't you know, like the Platonic dialogues Wilde wrote. (*U* 9. 1064–9)

By thus dismissing the theory he has spent pages and pages of the book outlining, Stephen aligns himself with Calandrino's personal experience of pregnancy. Whilst the reader of the *Decameron* is perfectly aware that Calandrino's pregnancy is a fiction and never took place, to Calandrino it was a substantive process whose issue was simply prevented from appearing by Simone's 'medicine'. In the same way, Stephen's dismissal of his theory is not an ontological denial: he does indeed have an 'idea of Hamlet', as Haines asks him back in 'Telemachus'(*U* 1. 545), but it is one that, whilst he is prepared to gestate and rehearse, he will not allow to be epistemologically 'born'. Indeed, in his unwitting question of whether Stephen is 'going to write it', Mr Best hints at the way in which the presentation of Stephen's theory has already been 'written': displaced by its representation as a dialogue in the text of *Ulysses* by Joyce, who thus – from a metafictional perspective – denies Stephen the opportunity to escape his poetic trap through an act of self-representation. In this respect, then, both Calandrino's pregnancy and Stephen's re-presentation of Shakespeare are bound by a poetics of Infernal metamorphosis, exhibiting and undergoing, but never surmounting, a perpetual process of becoming.

From this perspective, it is apparent that the Stephen of the Library is as circumscribed as ever by the poetics of stasis which held him in perpetual, pointless motion on Sandymount strand. In this way, Stephen's re-presentative discourse on Shakespeare can be seen to embody the destructive, stultifying metamorphosis of *Inferno* 24 in its dislocation and privileging of form over substance, and in the ultimate stasis of its intellectual movement. That the Infernal poetics swirling around Stephen in 'Proteus' should be further clarified when he takes the stage again in 'Scylla and Charybdis' is perhaps not that surprising given the theatrical context of this later episode. After all, 'Scylla' is a chapter of such dramatic potential that towards its end it momentarily erupts into the form of a playtext (*U* 9. 893–934); and thus its highlighting of the disparity between presentation and representation in the poetics of Stephen – between the roles we see him consciously adopting, and the part we watch him playing – seems wholly appropriate.

Indeed, in 'Scylla and Charybdis', Joyce brings the dynamics of the poetics of Infernal metamorphosis out onto the stage directly, figuring them through the way in which, by consciously playing the role of Aristotle and thus aligning himself with intellectual 'substance', Stephen actually succeeds in demonstrating his miscasting as Plato and his resonance with the mutability of form. In this way, the final demonstrative act of Stephen's Infernal poetics is, of course, his rejection of Bloom's offer of hospitality in 'Ithaca':

> Was the proposal of asylum accepted?
>
> Promptly, inexplicably, with amicability, gratefully it was declined.
> (*U* 17. 954–5)

As has long been observed, Stephen's 'inexplicable' decision to become the 'centrifugal departer', in contrast to Bloom's 'centripetal remainder' (*U* 17. 1214), would seem to interrupt and interestingly frustrate the patterns of motion established throughout the wider poetics of *Ulysses*, undermining the sense of *nostos* that surrounds Mr Bloom.[78] However, having seen the way in which Dante's ideas of Infernal metamorphosis pattern his poetics, Stephen's movement into continuing motion is now only 'inexplicable' to Bloom. Rather than representing another 'heroic' departure into 'exile', Stephen's decision to leave 7 Eccles Street further exhibits the perpetuation of the kinetic stasis that has characterised his representation throughout the book. In leaving, Stephen is unlikely – contrary to what he promises Bloom – to 'inaugurate a series of static, semistatic and peripatetic intellectual dialogues' (*U* 17. 964–5) between them, for the simple reason that, being wholly circumscribed as he is by the 'semistatic' poetics of Infernal metamorphosis, true motion and peripatesis is seemingly beyond him. He has, time and again throughout *Ulysses*, attempted to 'sign' a static form of identity through a process whose essential and unconsidered flux leaves him open to perpetual rereading and rewriting. Thus, when as Stephen's readers we seek to explore the glittering avenues and fascinating dead-ends of his thoughts, the Dantean poetics of his representation helps us keep in mind that he is – in a very significant sense – just going through the motions.

---

[78] Derek Attridge captures the compromised but pleasurable nature of this frustration when he observes that 'the moment the narrative had seemed to be leading towards, the bonding of its Telemachus and its Odysseus, doesn't arrive; but there has been a union of sorts, and the older man's kindness registers strongly on the reader and, we must assume, Stephen', see *How to Read Joyce*, 76.

At this point, it seems appropriate to acknowledge the changes that have taken place in the trajectory of Joyce's engagement with Dante. At the start of this chapter, through his 'playing Dante' to Marthe Fleischmann, Joyce's interest in the processes of Dantean self-fashioning that characterised the poet's influence on Stephen's presentation in *A Portrait of the Artist* continued into the timeframe of *Ulysses*. But, as we have seen, Dante's presence within Stephen's narrative in such episodes as 'Proteus' and 'Scylla and Charybdis' serves to further emphasise the deconstructive aspects of this earlier use of the poet, washing an uncertainty back onto the self-fashioning discourses of *Portrait*. In this respect, the exilic personae of Dante that patterned that earlier book's engagement with the poet (and that Joyce began to question by its end) through *Ulysses* are shown to be similarly subject to the flux of re-presentation. However, the uneasy orthodoxy of the young Joyce's reading of Dante meant that the potential for such a disruption – for movement between the polarities of that first encounter – was arguably latent within his engagement.

Nevertheless, the fundamental role that Dante's conception of Infernal metamorphosis plays in the poetics of Stephen's narrative in *Ulysses* – and the resultant unsettling of the last vestiges of his earlier 'heroic' mode – represents a marked shift in Joyce's attitude towards Dante. The poet, whom he had received as a figure of 'spiritual' and 'heroic' exile, was now supplying Joyce with a poetics through which to critique and ultimately transcend his earlier concern with modes of self-fashioning alienation. Indeed, in the 'haunting' of Dante's presence by the texts and figures of such other *duecento* and *trecento* figures as Brunetto Latini, Guido Cavalcanti and Giovanni Boccaccio, Dante continued to implicate Stephen – and, through him, *Ulysses* itself – in an important intertextual community.

CHAPTER 4

The Mothering of Memory
'Circe' and the Dantean Poetics of Re-membering

Encountering 'Circe': Memories of Difference

Even by the standards of so playful and peculiar a book, the fifteenth chapter of *Ulysses* is wonderfully weird. The sheer oddness of 'Circe' stands out against the background of the increasing strangeness and experimentalism of such chapters as 'Sirens' and 'Cyclops', and is inscribed most clearly in the typographical form of the chapter.[1] Turning the final page of 'Oxen of the Sun', the close, square and interminable block of type is finally broken, and laid out before us is the promising archipelago of space and text that constitutes the play-form of 'Circe'. As we embark on this new chapter, 'we soon realize that this break in the form is representative of a radical change' in the book itself, an impression reinforced by the initial stage direction.[2] Derek Attridge has brilliantly captured the 'peculiar intensity' of this experience:

> This moment was stranger than all the strange moments I'd encountered [...] There were the completely unexpected, verbless stage directions, announcing the scene [...] There was the enticing notion of nighttown itself, a whole town dedicated to the night and its secret doings, made even stranger by Joyce's hyphenless spelling. There was the odd sense that this was and wasn't a theatre – as if a whole street had become a stage. And there was the garish hyperreality of the descriptive method [...].[3]

In this reflective memory of his first reading, Attridge draws out the way in which the subtlety of effect in 'Circe' produces the 'sheer bewildering potency' of a new reading experience.[4] This experience, and the mode of reading that it elicits, is characterised by an immediacy of presentation and

---

[1] On the typography of 'Circe' see Daniel Ferrer, 'Circe, Regret and Regression', 127–8.
[2] Ferrer, 'Circe, Regret and Regression', 128; see also Jean-Michel Rabaté, *James Joyce, Authorized Reader*, 76–7.
[3] Derek Attridge, 'Pararealism in "Circe"', 119.
[4] Attridge, 'Pararealism in "Circe"', 119.

involvement that, as Hélène Cixous shows, familiarity need not diminish: 'Sing the *Introit*, you are Stephen, you enter the quarter of tolerance walking stick raised and the carnival begins. Totter, fall seven times: you are Bloom on the verge of being Booloohoom and Company'.[5]

The initial strangeness underlying the reading experience of 'Circe' strengthens as we read on; firstly, we must contend with the sheer length of the chapter. Over twice as long as the preceding 'Oxen of the Sun' and three or four times that of the opening episodes of *Ulysses*, 'Circe' keeps on unfolding without a break in its playtext form, and what began as a startling encounter with an unexpected stage soon becomes the reassuring textual lattice embounding the increasingly disturbing, riotous events of nighttown.[6] Equally, it doesn't take long to realise that these events, the happenings on the impossible stage of 'Circe', are unlike any others in the novel: 'persons decompose, partial objects are personalized; hoary voices resound; everything becomes detached and stands in suspension; sudden apparitions enter things into the general dislocation'.[7] And yet we come to recognise that the outlandish apparitions and irruptions of 'Circe' – the 'general dislocation' – in fact represents a 'recapitulation' of the entire novel, a stage on which events, characters and elements of earlier chapters reappear and on which Joyce effectively 'replays all parts of *Ulysses* in one scene'.[8]

The disconcerting experience of 'Circe', and its strange recapitulation of Joyce's book, establishes a mode of reading in which the fundamental 'otherness' of the episode is continually encountered. This 'otherness', rooted in the sense of breaking and shifting in the chapter's opening, once led critics to see 'Circe' as in many ways significantly separate from the rest of *Ulysses*, to hold that 'this strange chapter [was] indeed a stranger to the novel'.[9] In the thirty-plus years since Daniel Ferrer's seminal essay was published, this view of the chapter's 'alienation' has largely faded; indeed, there has been an increasing critical focus on the interrelation of 'Circe' to the whole of *Ulysses*, and in turn the episode has come to occupy an ever more central position in the study of the novel. However, as we read and reread the chapter, the initial 'otherness' encoded in its typography and fundamental to the unique reading experience that 'Circe' offers, never

---

[5] Hélène Cixous, 'At Circe's, or the Self-Opener', 389.
[6] On the levelling effect of the 'typography and tone' of 'Circe' see Attridge, 'Pararealism in "Circe"', 123–4.
[7] Cixous, 'At Circe's', 387.
[8] Cixous, 'At Circe's', 387; see also Richard Brown, '"Everything" in "Circe"', 232–4.
[9] Ferrer, 'Circe, Regret and Regression', 128.

Encountering 'Circe': Memories of Difference

fully dissipates, and this persistent oddity could easily strengthen into the sense of aberration that Ferrer identified. Indeed, there is a clear resonance between the position of the fifteenth chapter in a reading of *Ulysses*, and the historical view of nighttown as 'a marginal space [within Dublin], its activities sanctioned by official authority, and yet marked off from the rest of the city'.[10] In this respect, 'Circe' too stands in a simultaneously central and tangential relation to the whole, and the notion of the chapter as being 'marked off' – differed and yet 'sanctioned' or authorised through its referential relationships to the rest of *Ulysses* – proves a very fruitful way of reading the episode.

This liminality of 'Circe' – it's 'marking off' within the book – might seem to lead us back to the dominant mode of exile in Joyce's reading. The liminal space of 'Circe' in which Mr Bloom, pursued by a 'beast' '*walks on towards hellsgates*' (*U* 15. 577–8), could easily be configured to represent a Dantean 'otherworld' within *Ulysses*. Certainly, this is how the episode's earliest readers saw it: writing to Joyce on 21 May 1921, T. S. Eliot complimented him on the achievement of his 'Descent into Hell', and for Ezra Pound the Circean 'otherworld' represented 'a new Inferno in full sail'.[11] Thus, the first recuperative strategy developed for encountering the 'otherness' of 'Circe' was to construct an intertextual association with the *Commedia*. However, the poetics of Infernal metamorphosis which circumscribe Stephen in *Ulysses* would seem to suggest Joyce's growing scepticism towards just such exilic and Infernal modes. Indeed, if 'Circe' is a 'new Inferno', then its Dantean character as 'otherworld' would in fact stress its interconnection and inclusion within the wider 'community' of the novel; for in Dante's cosmology, the three realms of the otherworld are as inextricably linked through the operation of divine justice as the *Inferno*, *Purgatorio* and *Paradiso* are through the tripartite structure of the *Commedia*, or the lines of the verse through the pattern of the *terza rima*. Indeed, Dante's poem stands not simply as an account of the realities of a Christian afterlife, but as a lesson on the fundamental interconnectedness of all aspects of worldly and otherworldly existence.[12] Dante's continuing presence within the poetics of *Ulysses* indicates the developing trajectory

---

[10] Liam Lanigan, ' "A Necessary Evil": Anti-Spatial Behaviour in "Circe" ', 100.
[11] T. S. Eliot, *The Letters of T. S. Eliot*, vol. 1, *1898–1922*, 561; Read, *Pound/Joyce*, 189. Subsequent critical perspectives that developed this view of 'Circe' as an 'otherworld' (both Dantean and Homeric) include: Thomas McGreevy, 'The Catholic Element in *Work in Progress*', 123; Stuart Gilbert, *James Joyce's 'Ulysses'*, 314–19; and John Paul Riquelme, *Teller and Tale in Joyce's Fiction: Oscillating Perspectives*, 142–51.
[12] See Alison Morgan, *Dante and the Medieval Other World*, 11–84.

of Joyce's Dantean reading, and his growing interest in ideas of community and interconnection over modes of exile and alienation.

So far, in discussing exile, we've been used to seeing memory acting as a mechanism for supporting static identities, from Richard Rowan's memories of his life in Dublin and his unsuccessful continental exile, to Stephen's memories of Paris and the failure of his earlier ambitions ('You were going to do wonders, what?', *U* 3. 192). In 'Circe' Joyce was to employ a far more creative and poetically febrile form of memory than this recollective – and ultimately restrictive – mode, a reconceptualisation that flowed out of his continued reading of Dante. In thus suggesting Dantean forms of memory as a possible recuperative strategy for encountering the 'strangeness' of 'Circe', and for explicating its unique form of textuality, it will be immediately apparent that this chapter differs significantly from earlier chapters of this book.

The central resonance to be explored here is that between Dante's poetics and the poetics and textuality of 'Circe'.[13] However, turning our attention wholly to Dante's and Joyce's resonant poetics is not a rejection of the contextualising of Joyce's reading that has so far underpinned our discussion. Whilst exploring Joyce's engagement with forms of memory, textuality and authority that have their earliest expression within the medieval poetics underscoring Dante's work, I am not suggesting that in writing 'Circe' Joyce suddenly acquired a 'medieval mind'. Instead, we will see how Joyce's awareness of these 'medieval' poetics resulted from his continued reading of Dante within the pattern established by his education, and encouraged by the textual context of this reading within the editions of Eugenio Camerini and Marco de Rubris.

The chapter begins by considering the ways in which critical accounts of the so-called technic of Circe have influenced attitudes towards the poetics of the episode, and argues that Dante's formulation of the epistemology of memory and imagination can intervene in this discourse and helpfully condition our reading of the fantastical or 'hallucinatory' aspects of Joyce's text. It then shows how Dante's interrelation of conceptions of creative memory with theories of medieval textuality and composition can provide an effective hermeneutical position from which to engage with

---

[13] For examples of intertextual intersections between 'Circe' and the *Commedia* see: Reynolds, *Joyce and Dante*, 66–76; Keith M. Booker, 'From the Sublime to the Ridiculous: Dante's Beatrice and Joyce's Bella Cohen', 357–68; Ellmann, *Ulysses on the Liffey*, 147–9; and Peter Kuon, *'Lo mio maestro e 'l mio autore': die produktive Rezeption der 'Divina Commedia' in der Erzählliteratur der Moderne*, 69–82.

the textual and epistemological questions posed by the apparent recapitulation of *Ulysses* within 'Circe'. The resultant Dantean hermeneutic can thus fundamentally condition our view not only of the relation of 'Circe' to the rest of *Ulysses* but of the operation of narrative and its relationship to history throughout Joyce's novel.

Hallucination, Memory, 'Visione': Reconsidering the 'Technic' of 'Circe'

In the famous schema that Joyce allowed Stuart Gilbert to publish in 1931, the 'technic' of 'Circe' is given as 'hallucination'.[14] Accordingly, in addressing the combination of the prevailing mode of textuality and the mode of reading that this elicits – a mixture of representation and hermeneutic that seems to underpin Joyce's idiosyncratic use of the term 'technic' – discussion has traditionally focused on issues of psychology, realism and fantasy. The development of the 'hallucinatory' technic into the common view of 'Circe' as a psychological phantasmagoria was inaugurated by E. M. Forster, who claimed that 'the Night Town scene does not come off except as a superfetation of fantasies, a monstrous coupling of reminiscences'.[15] Ever since Forster's influential reading of 'Circe' as the phantasmagoric accretion of fantasies, there has been a strong tendency to see the chapter through the lens of externalised psychology.[16] This psychologised approach seems reasonable; after all, with its litany of accusing fathers, disappointed mothers, irrepressible sexuality and nightmarish scenes of excess, 'Circe' presents a semiotic field of unmistakable Freudian potency.[17] However, as Richard Brown points out, such is the riotous, unbounded mixing of different types of experience encountered in 'Circe' that Forster's initial unitary identification of the mode of the chapter as fantasy 'barely fits', and even 'Joyce's own label for the technique, "hallucination", barely serves to contain' the scope of nighttown.[18] Put simply, if we wish to read 'Circe' as the manifestation of psychological fantasies and hallucinations, then who exactly is hallucinating?

---

[14] For full versions of both the Gilbert and Linati schemas see Ellmann, *Ulysses on the Liffey*, 188–9.
[15] E. M. Forster, *Aspects of the Novel*, 127.
[16] For examples see Andrew Gibson, 'Introduction', 9–15; Gilbert, *James Joyce's 'Ulysses'*, 317–18; and Mark Schechner, *Joyce in Nighttown: A Psychoanalytic Inquiry into 'Ulysses'*, 100–52.
[17] See Budgen, *James Joyce and the Making of 'Ulysses'*, 238–45. For Ferrer's engagement with the later psychoanalytic theories of Melanie Klein and what he terms 'the multitudinous mother' see 'Circe, Regret and Regression', 138–42.
[18] Brown, '"Everything" in "Circe"', 227.

In the encounter between Stephen and the ghostly form of his mother, 'the hallucination may be explained as an attempt to expel into the outer world the persecutor who is threatening the subject from the inside'.[19] And yet none of the hallucinations can be 'fully understood as the fantasies of either Stephen or Bloom (or any other character)', and to attempt to do so would risk conflating the difference between the mode of the episode and what Udaya Kumar helpfully identified as its 'character subjectivities'.[20] Indeed, beyond the problem of locating the hallucinations or fantasies of 'Circe' within a character perspective, there are a number of underlying contradictions in this approach to the chapter's mode. Hugh Kenner posited a realist frame for 'Circe' into which hallucinatory episodes are interpolated, and from which the origin of each of these fantasies can be traced through the idea of 'triggering'. However, in thus splitting 'Circe' into two epistemological realities – an 'outer' and an 'inner' world – with each hallucinatory event ascribed an 'outer-world' trigger within a realist narrative, Kenner's reading both contravened the formal unity of the chapter, and overlooked Joyce's ironising of just such a hermeneutic of persistent realism when he has Bloom tell a talking hand-fan that 'every phenomenon has a natural cause' (*U* 15. 2795–6).[21] Furthermore, such notions of triggered hallucination violate the terms of the realism on which they are predicated; as Derek Attridge has pointed out, in 'Circe' 'there's no reason to suppose that Bloom has been imbibing a hallucinogen, or that he suffers from an occasionally surfacing psychotic condition'.[22] Thus, within the realist frame of the 'stimulus–response' dynamic, there is no reason for Bloom to hallucinate or fantasise in such a vivid manner; indeed, in 'Eumaeus', Joyce emphasises that Bloom 'was in complete possession of his faculties, never more so, in fact disgustingly sober' (*U* 16. 61–2). If 'stimulus–response' fails in regard to Bloom, then it ultimately fails as a recuperative strategy for 'Circe' as a whole.

Even where a more measured approach to the hallucinatory or 'fantastic' technic of 'Circe' has been taken, insuperable problems remain. For

---

[19] Ferrer, 'Circe, Regret and Regression', 138; although note that here Ferrer appears to contradict his earlier statement that 'there is no difference [...] between the apparition of the mother and the actions of Stephen and the other characters in Circe: they are all set on the same level of reality – or unreality', 132.

[20] Brown, '"Everything" in "Circe"', 232. Udaya Kumar, *The Joycean Labyrinth: Repetition, Time, and Tradition in 'Ulysses'*, 19.

[21] See Hugh Kenner, 'Circe', 345–62. Gabler has argued that realistic 'triggering' is insufficient in explaining the action of thought even within such relatively 'simple' chapters as 'Proteus'; see 'Narrative Rereadings', 59.

[22] Attridge, 'Pararealism in "Circe"', 123.

instance, Ferrer argued that, when grappling with the chapter, 'it takes time to accustom ourselves to the idea that the hallucination is not being represented: it is a mode of representation. It is not a question of content, but of writing – and of reading.' And yet to maintain that when reading 'Circe' the experience is one of 'whirling dizzily' is to again collapse the productive tension between the formal sobriety of the Circean playtext and the strangeness of its content.[23] Critics have thus attempted to find alternative conceptions that offer more sustainable, or creatively productive, ways of understanding the mode of 'Circe'. In this respect, Circean criticism is following a line suggested by Joyce himself, who noted that 'the hallucinations in *Ulysses* are made up out of elements from the past, which the reader will recognise if he has read the book, five, ten or twenty times'.[24] Thus, it's possible that these 'elements of the past', the recurring features that reappear on the Circean stage, may offer a key to understanding the chapter's mode of representation and – given Joyce's injunction to reread the book – its mode of reading.[25]

The recurring elements within 'Circe' include narratives, objects, events and – most prominently – characters from earlier chapters in the book. These latter crop up on nearly every page of 'Circe' and include both major characters such as Gerty MacDowell from 'Nausicaa' and the Citizen from 'Cyclops', as well as more relatively minor characters like Cissy Caffrey or Sweny the chemist. However, these recurring persons are not drawn solely from the earlier chapters of *Ulysses*, and figures from Joyce's other works, such as Mrs Riordan – the first 'Dante' of *Portrait* – also reappear on the streets of nighttown (*U* 15. 1715). Given these repetitions, memory has become an increasingly popular way through which to interpret both the episode's recapitulation of *Ulysses* and its technic or mode. Certainly, ideas of memory would seem to present an attractive, elegant approach to the initial strangeness of 'Circe': when Bridie Kelly is encountered in her 'den' amidst the ruined landscape of nighttown (*U* 15. 361–8), it requires only a short interpretive step to see, within her otherwise incongruous appearance in a brothel district, the external manifestation of Bloom's memory of his first sexual encounter, a memory already encountered in more conventional form: 'Bridie! Bridie Kelly! He will never forget the name, ever remember the night: first night, the bridenight' (*U* 14. 1067–9). And

---

[23] Ferrer, 'Circe, Regret and Regression', 132–3.
[24] Jacques Mercanton, 'The Hours of James Joyce', 207.
[25] Criticism of 'Circe' seems to be still determined by Forster's initial response, having now shifted from his first characterization of the chapter to his second: 'a monstrous coupling of reminiscences', *Aspects of the Novel*, 127.

yet this apparently commonsense position proves just as problematic as ascribing the events of 'Circe' to a form of triggered fantasy, particularly in its blurring of 'character subjectivities' and the modes of representation and reading. For, whilst Bloom's personal, subjective memory may account in some degree for the presence of Bridie Kelly, it can't explain the sheer range and variety of the other recurring characters, events and objects encountered in 'Circe'.

One possible way in which notions of recurrence and memory might be brought more fully into alignment with the mode of 'Circe' is suggested by Colin MacCabe's observation that 'in "Circe" *the whole text is taken up and repeated*'.[26] This raises the prospect that there might be 'nothing in "Circe" that is not a recapitulation of something occurring in the earlier parts of the book [...] that there is nothing in the earlier parts of the book that does not get, in some way, re-cycled or re-cannibalised here'.[27] We could thus conceive of 'Circe' as a site in which, through the action of memory, the entire novel re-presents itself, and so locate the act of memory that underpins the strange events and inhabitants of nighttown not within the limited psychological perspective of any of the characters, but within the textuality of the episode. It is this notion of 'textual memory' that underpins Hans Walter Gabler's concept of narrative rereading. Gabler argues that, through his rereading of earlier parts of *Ulysses* whilst composing 'Circe', Joyce established a relationship between the narrative of the later episode and the 'pre-narrative' of the preceding chapters that is analogous to that between empirical reality and fiction.[28] In this respect, 'Circe' appears as a fundamentally memorial text, one whose writing is predicated on an act of rereading, and whose reading inevitably elicits recognition of the 'pre-narrative' encoded within it. Thus, memory offers itself as an important model for the hermeneutical experience of 'Circe', and the strangeness of the chapter can be seen to align with the strangeness of re-encountering the recurrent textual elements.

Memory is certainly a strong presence within the drama of 'Circe'. In a moment that recalls the kind of re-encounters that characterise some of Dante-pilgrim's meetings in the *Commedia*, Mr Bloom is brought face to face with his paternal grandfather, who *chutes rapidly down through the chimneyflue and struts two steps to the left on gawky pink stilts* (*U* 15. 2304–6) out into Bella Cohen's brothel:

[26] Colin MacCabe, *James Joyce and the Revolution of the Word*, 128.
[27] Brown, ' "Everything" in "Circe" ', 233.
[28] Gabler, 'Narrative Rereadings', 65–6.

VIRAG

(heels together, bows) My name is Virag Lipoti, of Szombathely. *(he coughs thoughtfully, drily)* Promiscuous nakedness is much in evidence hereabouts, eh? [...]

BLOOM

Granpapchi. But ... (*U* 15. 2311–18)

The memorial frame of this encounter is clear – the re-encounter with familial history – but in the course of their conversation, Virag issues his grandson with a significant instruction: 'exercise your mnemotechnic' (*U* 15. 2385–6).[29] In this moment, Joyce offers a new form of technic for the chapter, a memorial technic in contrast to the hallucinatory technic of the Gilbert schema. Yet if memory thus comprises the mode of representation and the hermeneutic elicited by 'Circe', the 'mnemotechnic' would need to account not simply for the recurrence of elements from the 'prenarrative' of the earlier chapters of *Ulysses*, but also for their transfiguration on the Circean stage. For, whilst *Ulysses* may be recapitulated within 'Circe', there is barely a recurrent element that does not seem to have undergone some significant change, and a change not wholly explicable simply by its appearance within a different setting.

One instance of this form of Circean transfiguration is the unexpected presence of the Citizen on the streets of nighttown. In the pageant of the 'New Bloomusalem', the Citizen's enthusiastic endorsement of King Leopold stands in stark contrast to his final act of violence towards Bloom in the 'Cyclops' chapter (*U* 12. 1853–7):

THE CITIZEN

(choked with emotion, brushes aside a tear in his emerald muffler) May the good God bless him! (*U* 15. 1616–18)

In this instance of a recurring element in 'Circe', psychologically expressive fantasy would appear to be the more immediately satisfying explanation for the Citizen's new attitude to Bloom: here is how Bloom *wishes* the Citizen had treated him. And yet, within this fantasy version of the

---

[29] In his study of memory throughout *Ulysses*, John Rickard only discusses 'Circe' in passing, see *Joyce's Book of Memory: The Mnemotechnic of 'Ulysses'*, 123, 153–4. For Mary Reynolds's reading of the Virag encounter as structured by the meeting with Cacciaguida (*Par.* 15–17) see *Joyce and Dante*, 66–76. However, given that Virag (as an immediate family member) is a well-known figure for Bloom, and Cacciaguida was a distant ancestor of Dante's, there might be a stronger resonance with the re-encounter with Dante's 'other' father, Brunetto Latini (*Inf.* 15).

Citizen, there are preserved several clear aspects of his earlier, unpleasant representation, most prominently his tendency for overblown, emotive rhetoric and the tellingly nationalistic detail of his 'emerald muffler'. Within this recurrent element, there seems to be a significant mixing of fantasy and imaginative change with memory, suggesting that the 'mnemotechnic' of 'Circe' will represent a distinctly alloyed mode.

This mixing of memory and imagination – the alloying of the 'mnemotechnic' – has been posited in differing formulations by two previous readers of 'Circe'. Udaya Kumar, in his study of repetition throughout Joyce's oeuvre, views 'Circe' as 'an elaborate repetition machine' in which 'there is a systematic repetition of earlier events of the day in the form of fantasy'.[30] Drawing on Forster's initial characterisation, Kumar sees the term 'fantasy' as in some degree synonymous with 'hallucination' (in terms of an apparition) and imagination (in terms of a mental act of creation), further clarifying the possibility that the 'hallucinations' of nighttown are equally explicable as apparitions – manifested images – of memory. This epistemological similarity between memory and fantasy is explicitly developed by Vicki Mahaffey in her remarkable essay on 'Joyce and Gender'. Mahaffey defines fantasy more rigorously as both a 'making visible' and, through its connection to desire, 'a future-directed model of virtual experience' analogous to the action of memory as 'a fiction based on historical reality but not isomorphic with it'.[31] Developing Stephen's definition of history in 'Nestor' as 'fabled by the daughters of memory' (*U* 2. 7), Mahaffey sees memory and fantasy within 'Circe' as twin fictionalising, creative processes whose shared production of 'fabled' narratives further closes the epistemological distance between them.[32] In interconnecting memory and fantasy within the 'technic' of 'Circe', both Kumar and Mahaffey ultimately return to the terms laid down by Joyce:

> The hallucinations in *Ulysses* are made up out of elements from the past, which the reader will recognise if he has read the book, five, ten or twenty times. Here is the unknown. There is no past, no future; everything flows in an eternal present.[33]

In this observation, Joyce clearly presents the possibility that the apparitions, events and characters of 'Circe' may represent an imaginative manifestation not only of psychologised memory but of the kind of textual memory that both Kumar and Gabler posit. Joyce also clarifies the

---

[30] Kumar, *The Joycean Labyrinth*, 19, 24.
[31] Vicki Mahaffey, 'Joyce and Gender', 122–3.
[32] Mahaffey, 'Joyce and Gender', 125.
[33] Mercanton, 'The Hours of James Joyce', 207.

importance of memory to the act of reading 'Circe', indicating that his text is one predicated on rereading, a mode that intimately involves the reader's memory of what has gone before. Thus Joyce's own characterisation of the operation of 'Circe' stresses the importance of reconciling the imaginative-fantastic aspect of the chapter with its fundamentally memorial nature. In her notion of fantasy as a literal 'making things seen', Mahaffey points towards a way this might be done.

Whilst the Gilbert schema tends to dominate structural discussions of *Ulysses*, in the earlier Linati schema Joyce offered a different and altogether more intriguing 'technic' for 'Circe': 'visione animata fino allo scoppio' ['vision animated to bursting point'].[34] This gnomic phrase positions the visual aspect of 'Circe' as a potentially unifying medium for the interconnected but often conflicting and compromised conceptions of memory and fantasy within the chapter. Indeed, Joyce's claim that in 'Circe' 'there is no past, no future: everything flows in an eternal present' would seem to suggest that within this 'visione' we will find a similarly balanced representative and hermeneutic mode, combining both imagination and memory into a unified, visionary position. In the work of Dante and the poet's interconnection of the action of memory and imagination, Joyce found just such a model for the mode of representation and reading – for the 'technic' – of 'Circe'.

Joyce's 'Visione' and Dante's Poetics of Memory

Today we're used to thinking of memory as a mechanism of recall and reproduction, and whilst this classical model of a heuristic mnemonic was certainly current in the Middle Ages, it perhaps obscures the most unusual and important aspect of medieval conceptions of memory.[35] In the Middle Ages it was memory (*memoria*), and not imagination (*fantasia*), which was venerated as the supreme faculty of artistic genius.[36] Indeed medieval thought observed no significant epistemological distinction between memory and imagination, or fantasy, conceiving of both the *fantasia* and the *memoria* as mental faculties engaged in a unified process of 'imagination': the creation, storage and formation of associative connections between mental images, or *phantasms*.[37] Indeed, such was

---

[34] On the Linati schema see *JJ* 519. For discussions of the 'visionary' over the hallucinatory/fantastic technic see Brown, '"Everything in "Circe"', 227; and Rabaté, *Authorized Reader*, 82–4.

[35] For an overview of modern models of memory see Alan Baddeley, *Human Memory: Theory and Practice*, 1–26, 133–42, 211–27, 351–72.

[36] Mary Carruthers, *The Book of Memory: A Study of Memory in Medieval Culture*, 1–2.

[37] This discussion of medieval memory and perceptual theory necessarily adumbrates a complex and often contradictory discourse. The notion that there is a single, coherent 'medieval' understanding

the co-identification between these faculties that, in his commentary on Aristotle's *De Memoria et Reminiscentia*, Thomas Aquinas went so far as to assert that, 'memory then, of itself, is a kind of imaginative appearance'.[38] The *fantasia* – as the faculty that creates mental images from sensory experience – and its relation to memory thus 'costituisce il fondamento del conoscere' ['constitute the foundation of thought'], as according to Aristotle it was through an internal perception of these images, enabled by the action of the *memoria*, that cognition took place.[39] To put the discourse into more easily explicable modern terms: when we create a new idea or thought – when we 'imagine' something – we do so by a process that combines together previously created images and ideas through the action of memory; in this respect, from a 'medieval' perspective, anything 'imagined' is, in fact, 'remembered'.

This unusual form of memory, rooted in the Aristotelian image-based model of cognition, with its interconnection of *memoria* and *fantasia*, formed the background to Dante's conceptions of memory and imagination. Whilst to Dante – just as it was to Aristotle, Augustine and Aquinas – the *fantasia* was the faculty of image formation, his treatment of the subject displays a vital interest in the bodily limitations of the faculty and, consequently, the bodily limitations of the imagination:

> [...] dico che il nostro intelletto, per difetto della virtù della quale trae quello ch' el vede (che è virtù organica), cioè la fantasia, non puote a certe cose salire, peròcche la fantasia, nol puote aiutare, chè non ha il di che; siccome sono le Sustanze partite da materia;
>
> [...] I say that our intellect, by defect of that faculty from which it draws what it perceives, which is an organic power, namely the fantasy, cannot rise to certain things (because the fantasy cannot assist it, since it lacks the means), such as the substances separate from matter.] (*Conv.* 3. 4. 9)[40]

---

of memory is not a proposition I would wish to seriously defend; however, for our purposes, it is essential to understand some of the basic aspects of the medieval process. For more details on the operation of medieval memory and imagination from a range of medieval perspectives see Carruthers, *The Book of Memory*, 18–19, 24–37, 56–7. Other accounts can be found in: Frances A. Yates, *The Art of Memory*, 50–104; V. A. Kolve, *Chaucer and the Imagery of Narrative: The First Five Canterbury Tales*, 9–58; Alistair J. Minnis, 'Literary Imagination and Memory', 239–74.

[38] Thomas Aquinas, *Selected Philosophical Writings*, 142.
[39] Michele Rak, 'Fantasia', 793; Alfonso Maierù, 'Memoria', 889. This development of an internal vision was first advanced by Augustine, see *Confessions*, 185–7. For a discussion of Augustinian, medieval perceptual theory see Jean-Claude Schmitt, *Ghosts in the Middle Ages: The Living and the Dead in Medieval Society*, 22–4.
[40] On Dante's place within the medieval tradition of memory see Spencer Pearce, 'Dante and the Art of Memory', 20–61; see also Rak, 'Fantasia', 7932–3; Sally Mussetter, 'Fantasy', 370; Paul A. Dumol, 'Imagination', 505–6; Maierù, 'Memoria', 888–92; Paul A. Dumol, 'Memory', 605–6.

In his poetic work, Dante presents the 'alta fantasia' ['the high fantasy'] of the *Commedia* as capable of divine inspiration (*Purg.* 17. 13–35) and yet, due to its organic nature, also ultimately unable to grasp the transcendent reality of heaven and the beatific vision (*Par.* 33. 142–5).[41] Dante's awareness of the failings of a fantasy-based imagination would thus seem to echo the fallibility of modern notions of hallucination and psychological fantasy in explicating the technic of 'Circe', underscoring for Joyce the potential of interconnecting fantasy and imagination within the action of memory.

However, just like *fantasia*, Dante also presents *memoria* as a flawed and failing mental faculty. The opening canto of the *Paradiso* clarifies the problem that the pilgrim's heavenly journey presents an earthly poet:

> Nel ciel che più della sua luce prende
> Fu' io, e vidi cose che ridire
> Né sa, né può qual di lassù discende;
> Perché, appressando sè al suo disire,
> Nostro intelletto si profonda tanto,
> Che retro la memoria non può ire.

[In the heaven that receives the most of his light have I been, and I have seen things that one who comes down from there cannot remember and cannot utter, for as it draws near to its desire, our intellect goes so deep that the memory cannot follow it.] (*Par.* 1. 4–8)

Just as the *fantasia* buckled in the face of the 'Sustanze partite da materia' – the immaterial substances encountered through divine experience – so too does the memory fall short, unable to follow the subject matter of the pilgrim's narrative and furnish the necessary mental images. And yet, whilst acknowledging its contingency, Dante privileged *memoria* (or 'mente') above the other faculties, positioning it as the frame for the whole of the *Commedia*. At the opening of *Inferno* 2, as Dante-pilgrim undertakes his journey, the muses, the traditional patrons of imagination, are appealed to as figures of poetical inspiration, but it is their mother, Mnemosyne, who is presented as the instrument of composition:

> O Muse, o alto ingegno, or m'aiutate:
> O mente, che scrivesti ciò ch' io vidi,
> Qui si parrà la tua nobilitate.

---

[41] See Pearce, 'Dante and the Art of Memory', 31–5; and Patrick Boyde, *Perception and Passion in Dante's 'Comedy'*, 120–1.

> [O muses, O high wit, now help me; O memory that wrote down what I saw, here will your nobility appear.] (*Inf.* 2. 7–9)

In this invocation, Dante fundamentally aligns his poetics with the epistemological and cognitive theory of his day; just as imagination was understood as essentially an act of memory, so Dante establishes a memorial frame for his poetic project: the fictive narrative of the otherworldly journey is validated through the pilgrim's claim to have 'seen' what the poet relates.[42] Thus, there is an inherent resonance between the levelled epistemology of the interconnected *fantasia* and *memoria* and Dante's memorial poetics, with the *Commedia* being presented as the imaginative product of a creative form of memory, the memory that supplied the poet with the images to write down 'what he saw'.

This co-identification of memory and imagination within Dante's poetics establishes a unique, visionary mode of reading for the *Commedia*: as the poem is positioned as a product of a creative form of memory, all elements of the poet's vision are similarly epistemologically levelled. The kind of binary distinctions that underpin realist approaches to modern texts (what is *really* going on in Bella Cohen's brothel?) simply have no relevance in reading the *Commedia*, the visionary mode of which will not sustain subdivision into separate spheres of the 'real' and the 'imagined'. To illustrate this point more clearly, we might compare Dante-pilgrim's encounter with Cavalcante de' Cavalcanti in *Inferno* 10 with his meeting with the hybrid monster Geryon in *Inferno* 17. The presentation of Cavalcante, a historical figure and a personal acquaintance of Dante, would thus, in modern terms, be considered as deriving from Dante's memory. Whereas the obviously unhistorical, mythical figure of Geryon would be seen as a product of his imagination; however, from Dante's perspective, such an epistemological distinction is fundamentally false.[43] The mental images of Cavalcante and the mental images of Geryon that enabled Dante to write their respective sections of the *Commedia* were both produced by the combining process of the

---

[42] On the authorising effect of Dante's claims of witness in the *Commedia* and their association with memory see Boyde, *Perception and Passion*, 119; Keen, *Dante and the City*, 8.

[43] Of course, we must remember that Dante did not invent Geryon *ex nihilo*, but rather created his own presentation of a pre-existing mythical figure mentioned by Virgil in the *Aeneid* (6. 289, 8. 202). This process of mythical elaboration and development clarifies the manner in which, from Dante's perspective, the substance of what we would call imagination is consistently drawn from the past and thus a product of memory. For a discussion of Geryon within the poetics of the *Commedia* see Teodolinda Barolini, *The Undivine Comedy: Detheologizing Dante*, 58–73.

memoria; they are both fundamentally 'memories'. This epistemological in-distinction is clearly manifested in Dante's text; whilst the figure of Cavalcante is historically resonant, and Geryon's hybridity carries clear allegorical meaning, both are presented to the reader with equal vividness.[44] In the visionary mode of the *Commedia*, there is no difference in representation signalled between Cavalcante's anxious visage – fearing when he meets the pilgrim that his son has also passed into Hell and so trying 'veder s'altri era meco' ['to see whether another were with me'] (*Inf.* 10. 56) – and Geryon's misleading 'faccia d'uom giusto' ['face of a just man'] (*Inf.* 17. 10), both are equally present to Dante-pilgrim, and to the reader.

The visionary mode of reading established by the epistemology of the *Commedia* would seem to resonate with Joyce's identification of the technic of 'Circe' as being 'visione animata fino allo scoppio' ['vision animated to bursting point']. With its imaginative form of memory, blending the modern actions of 'imagining' and 'remembering', the *Commedia* encodes a poetics that significantly widens conventional models of realism; as Teodolinda Barolini has observed, Dante's poetics is 'a poetics of realism, with its concomitant surrealism, not a poetics of naturalism'.[45] This Dantean poetics, blending realism and the otherworldly and rejecting the notion of simple isomorphism with everyday experience, presents a strong model for characterising the mode of representation and the mode of reading within 'Circe'. If we remove the epistemological distinction between those things that are imagined and those that are remembered, then the transfiguration of the recurrent elements within 'Circe' comes into clearer focus.

To ask whether Bridie Kelly, or the Citizen, or Virag, is 'really there' in nighttown or whether they are the manifestation of a memory (or hallucination, or fantasy) is to cling to a fundamentally flawed conception of 'realism' that struggles to account for the unruly fecundity of Joyce's text. Equally, to conceive of 'Circe' as undergoing a series of modal shifts in which conventional realism is switched on and off like a flashlight would seem to negate the careful formal unity that Joyce constructed. Dante's elision of the difference between memory

---

[44] On allegorical approaches to Geryon see Antonio Lanza, 'L'allegoria della corda nel canto XVI dell'*Inferno*', 97–100; John B. Friedman, 'Antichrist and the Iconography of Dante's Geryon', 108–22.
[45] Barolini, *The Undivine Comedy*, 59–60.

and imagination, between myth and history, provided Joyce with the model of a piece of literature that avoided these reductive, 'technical' problems. As perceptive readers such as Attridge have shown, in 'Circe' Joyce presents a text that, as with the *Commedia*, profits less from vertiginous shifts in interpretive approach, oscillating between equally compromised forms of conventional realism, than it does from being approached from a broad, unitary and anti-realist position.[46] In the visionary mode of the *Commedia* we must accept the fundamental premise that Dante 'saw' the things he writes about, and in approaching 'Circe' we must start by accepting that 'everything that is said to happen *does* happen, that everything present as speech is spoken'.[47] Once having accepted this visionary mode, having accepted, in Attridge's terms, the seamless blending of the 'real' and the 'parareal', both the *Commedia* and 'Circe' open into a rich field of literary signification. Joyce found within Dante's poetics of memory, the possibility of bringing the otherworldly and the everyday into creative connection, revealing the presence of the one within the other through the fundamentally imaginative character of memory.

Thus, the visionary mode of the *Commedia* and Dante's poetics of memory can provide a rich intertextual heritage for Joyce's identification of the technic of 'Circe' as 'visione animata fino allo scoppio', the 'bursting point' being the moment in which significant distinction between the 'real' and the 'unreal' – between 'memory' and 'fantasy' – collapses and the reader encounters the worldly and the otherworldly on the same epistemological stage.[48] And yet the resonance between Dante's poetics and 'Circe' extends beyond this modal consideration, and Dante's theories of memory and medieval attitudes to composition, rhetoric and hermeneutics exerted a strong influence upon the unique form of textuality encountered in the chapter. Returning to Dante's notion that memory 'wrote down' 'ch' io vidi' ['what I saw'] will uncover a fundamental resonance between medieval processes of textual production and a hermeneutical position encoded within 'Circe'. What then is the action of memory within Dante's poetics? What kind of writing does Dante's 'mente' engage in, what form of textuality does it produce, and can this provide a model for reading 'Circe'?

---

[46] For Attridge's criticism of a 'recuperative strategy' in which we 'assume that from one sentence to the next we shift radically out of a realistic mode' see his 'Pararealism in "Circe"', 123.
[47] Attridge, 'Pararealism in "Circe"', 125.
[48] cf. Rabaté, *Authorized Reader*, 82.

Copying Dante's Book of Memory: Medieval Processes of Textuality and Authority

In the *Commedia*, Dante positions memory as the author of his work, but it is the famous incipit of the *Vita Nuova* that supplies the clearest discussion of this process. This passage needs careful and attentive reading, for in it we can find the paradigmatic expression of a form of medieval textuality that resonates significantly with the poetics of 'Circe'. In the Middle Ages, memory and not imagination was conceived of as the principle of artistic production and textual generation, and in the opening of the *Vita Nuova* Dante demonstrates how memory both composes and authorises texts. This is how the passage appeared to Joyce in Marco de Rubris's edition:

> [I]n quella parte del libro della mia memoria, dinanzi alla quale poco si potrebbe leggere, si truova una rubrica, la quale dice:
>
> INCIPIT VITA NOVA.
>
> Sotto la quale rubrica io truovo scritte le parole, le quali è mio intendimento d'assemprare in questo libello; e se non tutte, almeno la loro sentenzia.
>
> [In that part of the book of my memory before which there would be little to read is found a chapter heading that says: 'Here begins a new life'. It is my intention to copy into this little book the words I find written under that heading – if not all of them, at least their significance.] (*VN* I. 1–2)

In this narrative of the writing of the *Vita Nuova*, Dante figures himself as copying down a pre-existent text, a text constituting his 'book of memory'. The key to unravelling the complex form of textual generation and the accompanying form of authority – the conception of the role of the author and his relation to his text – that is written into this passage lies in grasping the full meaning of the verb 'assemprare', to copy. What form of textuality and what form of memory are present in this act of copying, and what influence did Dante's medieval textuality have on Joyce's modernist practice?

The initial meaning of 'assemprare' is captured clearly in Musa's elegant translation: Dante presents the writing of the *Vita Nuova* as a process of copying out a pre-existent source. In this respect, 'assemprare' would seem to embody the simple, hierarchical structure of original-copy that underpins modern notions of reproduction, and that provides the familiar heuristic model of memory as a mechanism for recalling the past. However, in a post-Benjaminian age, the mechanical implications of reproduction can obscure the nuanced, medieval character of the act of copying that is so central to Dante's poetics and to the textuality of the *Vita Nuova*. In order to recover this medieval reading of copying, it is necessary to carefully explicate both the etymology and the material-cultural context of 'assemprare'.

As a variant form of the more common 'assemplare', which tends to be preferred in modern editions of the *Vita Nuova*, 'assemprare' derives etymologically from the Latin verb *exemplare*, from which the noun *exemplum* or 'example' in turn derives.[49] In which case, the root meaning of 'assemprare' can be most fully given as 'to copy from an example'. Given this etymology, it quickly becomes apparent that Dante's lexis in the opening passage of the *Vita Nuova* draws on the language of manuscript production: 'libro' [book], 'rubrica' ['rubric'], 'assemprare' ['to copy']. Dante's narrative of composition, and the act of copying, at its heart is, as Vincenzo Laria has observed, framed 'nel linguaggio notarile del Duecento', in the scribal discourse of the thirteenth century.[50] Thus, to grasp what is truly at stake in Dante's copying out the book of his memory, we need to locate this action within the context of medieval manuscript – and textual – production.

The view of copying that arises from the thirteenth-century scriptorium is not one of the isomorphic reproduction of a single source-text, but rather of a process of textual arrangement and assembly. The material context of Dante's image of himself as a scribe copying out his text, would thus seem to underpin Laria's etymological reading of 'assembrare' (another variant form of 'assemprare' preferred by such influential nineteenth-century textual critics as Luciani, Fraticelli and Casini) as carrying the 'significato di *radunare, riunire*' ['the meanings of "to gather", "to assemble"'].[51] This view of copying as a process of assembling a text, curious though it may seem to a modern perspective, is exactly what was enacted through the so-called pecia system of scriptoria in thirteenth-century universities:

> Texts were divided into pecia that allowed as many as seven or eight scribes to copy an exemplar at the same time. As each scribe finished copying his own portion, his text too might be copied, so that copies proliferated ad

---

[49] For more on the meanings and etymology of 'assemprare' see Giorgio B. Squarotti *et al.* (eds.), *Grande Dizionario Della Lingua Italiana*, vol. 1, 757, col. 1.

[50] Vincenzo Laria, 'Assemprare (ASSEMPLARE)', 419, col. 1; see also Jesse M. Gellrich, *The Idea of the Book in the Middle Ages: Language Theory, Mythology, and Fiction*, 139–66.

[51] Laria, 'Assemprare', 419, col. 1; Vincenzo Laria, 'Assembrare', 419, col. 1. For more on the textual work of Tommaso Casini, see below pp. 168–69.

infinitum. Upon completion the manuscript was submitted to the university for inspection and correction; then it was bound by a stationer.[52]

The production of a copy of a manuscript – the process of 'copying' – involved numerous acts of compilation and gathering together, both of textual elements and of scribal effort, all of which culminated in the gathering of the 'pecia' or manuscript quires made by the university stationer.[53] In this respect, the sense of 'copying' as the unitary, isomorphic process of reproducing a source is wholly misleading; instead, to copy from an *exemplum* – to copy in the fullest sense of 'assemprare' – was a process of textual production predicated on acts of gathering and assembly. Given Dante's bureaucratic, diplomatic and poetic careers (all of which necessitated the production of numerous copies of scribal documents) this system of accretive material textuality would have supplied the most immediate imaginative context for his narrative of composition of the *Vita Nuova* as an act of 'copying'.[54]

If the 'pecia system' supplies a material model of 'copying' that usefully unsettles any modern associations with reproduction, are there other ways in which Dante's writing of the *Vita Nuova* could be conceived of as an act of copying and assembly?[55] Guglielmo Gorni succinctly characterised the *Vita Nuova* as 'una raccolta di trentuno liriche giovanili di Dante in vario metro, saldate insieme da [...] prosa', a view that positions the whole book as a gathering of earlier texts, welded ('saldate insieme') into a new form by the accompanying prose passages and glosses.[56] Gorni's position echoes Michelangelo Picone's discussion of the place of the *Vita Nuova* within the twelfth- and thirteenth-century tradition of the *canzoniere*, the artfully arranged songbook. In his arrangement of pre-written poems

---

[52] Laurel Amtower, *Engaging Words: The Culture of Reading in the Later Middle Ages*, 19; see also G. Pollard, 'The Pecia System in Medieval Universities', 145–61.

[53] See Malcolm B. Parkes, 'The Influence of the Concepts of *Ordinatio* and *Compilatio* on the Development of the Book', 115–41.

[54] Indeed, in the *Convivio* Dante presented an unusual description of an 'auctore' or 'author' as 'quanto legare parole' (4. 4. 3) ['one who binds words together']; on this etymology within Dante's own discourse of authority see Ascoli, *Dante and the Making of a Modern Author*, 16, 117–20, 301. On Stephen Dedalus's possible awareness of this passage of the *Convivio* in 'Scylla and Charybdis' (*U* 9. 213) see Boldrini, *Joyce, Dante*, 160–1; and Rabaté, *Authorized Reader*, 160–2.

[55] As Mazzotta has noted, the opening of the *Vita Nuova* describes a dual act: 'to copy and edit into a little book the essential meaning [...] of the larger book of memory'. The assembling nature of the act of copying resonates strongly with this secondary editing process, see Dante, *Poet of the Desert*, 262.

[56] Guglielmo Gorni, 'La Vita Nuova di Dante Alighieri', 153. On the compiling of the lyrics of the *Vita Nuova* see also Picone, '*Vita Nuova*', 874; Barolini, *Dante's Poets*, 15; and Ascoli, *Dante and the Making of a Modern Author*, 176.

and their interrelation with exegetical prose, Dante establishes a literary sequence that encodes narrative and poetic meaning through the relations of the text, resulting in 'an exemplary story [...] of the poetic and spiritual formation of the protagonist'.[57] Thus, the *Vita Nuova* embodies a process of textual generation whereby the 'new' text is produced by the arrangement and interrelation of 'old' ones.[58]

In this respect, the textuality of the *Vita Nuova* echoes the epistemological action of the faculty of the *memoria*, whereby new thoughts and ideas are generated by the memorial perception and rearrangement of pre-existent images or *phantasms*. Dante's conceit at the opening of the *Vita Nuova* – that his work represents a 'copying' or arrangement of the contents of his memory – thus reveals a substantial connection between his poetics and the conception of a generative form of memory, a memory that doesn't so much recall a fixed source as shape and arrange it in an act of 're-membering'.[59] This re-membering process not only underpins and explicates the textuality of the *Vita Nuova*, but also enabled Dante's later reworking of this work, along with the rest of his oeuvre, into the form of the *Commedia*; in an important sense, the *Commedia* can be seen as a generative memory of all which has gone before it.

This reminder of the medieval co-identification of memory and imagination within Dante's poetics also emphasises another important aspect of Dantean textuality. Dante's texts, along with those of all medieval authors, were products of 'memorative composition'.[60] Drawing upon the thought of such figures as Quintilian, Augustine, Avicenna and Aquinas, the tradition of medieval rhetoric understood the composition of texts as a process of (largely mental) assembly through the action of the memory. The medieval view of 'memorative composition' was complex and often contradictory, but a brief outline can be given in five stages. First the author engaged in *cogitatio*, the stage in which thoughts and ideas were assembled in the mind through the action of the *memoria* and the arrangement of *phantasms*. Next came the process of *inventio*, which medieval pedagogy – in a

---

[57] Picone, 'Songbook and Lyric Genres in the *Vita Nuova*', 159, 164; see also Dino De Robertis, *Il Libro Della 'Vita Nuova'*, 18–24.

[58] Dante's practice in the *Vita Nuova* can thus be seen to embody medieval attitudes towards chronology and authority in which 'to be old was to be good', see Alistair Minnis, *Medieval Theory of Authorship: Scholastic Literary Attitudes in the Later Middle Ages*, 9.

[59] My conception of memory as a creative process of 're-membering', and awareness of the connection between the actions of remembering and dismembering, derives from the perceptive observations of Vicki Mahaffey, see 'Joyce and Gender', 122.

[60] Carruthers, *The Book of Memory*, 240; This discussion of the medieval composition process will draw on Carruthers's account throughout, see *The Book of Memory*, 240–57.

marked contrast to modern notions of 'invention' – considered 'a wholly mental process of searching one's inventory', of accessing and arranging texts and rhetorical formations already stored in the memory.[61] By arranging the materials compiled by the act of *inventio*, the medieval author arrived at the *res* of his own text, the basic substance of his composition arranged in a state analogous to a very rough draft. The *res* was then given a rough rhetorical shape through a process of *compositio*, which resulted in the *dictamens*, the first draft of the finished composition, a draft that would sometimes be written down and other times remain mentally composed. Finally, the *dictamens* was copied down and subjected to further rhetorical shaping to arrive at the written version of the text, the *exemplum*.

This process of textual composition reveals the intrinsic interrelation of rhetoric and hermeneutic within medieval textuality; the key compositional process of *inventio* was conceived of as an arrangement and assembly of memorial sources, in effect a kind of memorial reading governed by the hermeneutical connections between these mental 'texts'.[62] Within any medieval act of composition, there was encoded a hermeneutical process that – at the level of the *inventio* – dictated the form of the rhetoric, and thus from which form the hermeneutical process should, in theory, be discernible. This interrelation is played out in the narrative image of Dante copying the *Vita Nuova* from his book of memory, with Dante's process of 'assemprare' involving both the 'reading' of the text of his memory – a text in a compositional state roughly analogous to the *dictamens* – and then copying this down and shaping it into the *exemplum* of the finished text. And yet, within Dante's rhetorical tradition, this *exemplum* was not considered an authoritative, finished text; as Carruthers argues, 'a medieval text was not presumed to be *perfectus*, "finished", even though it had been *scriptus*, "written"'.[63] The *exemplum* – the text Dante copied down from his book of memory – was conceived of as always being contingent upon correction and alteration, whether by a scribe or by the composer themselves. In this way, medieval textuality undercuts the modern notion of an 'original' or 'authorised' – as in deriving from the author – text in a way that will be important to our reading of 'Circe'.

---

[61] Carruthers, *The Book of Memory*, 241.
[62] Rita Copeland's authoritative study remains the standard work on medieval rhetoric and hermeneutics, in which she draws on theoretical models deriving from Gadamer, Heidegger and Derrida to explore 'the range of interpretive mechanics and assumptions that are brought to bear upon textual production', see *Rhetoric, Hermeneutics, and Translation in the Middle Ages: Academic Traditions and Vernacular Texts*, 3–62.
[63] Carruthers, *The Book of Memory*, 243.

Authority – the status of being an *auctor* or originator – in the Middle Ages derived from the treatment of a text, not from the identity of its writer.[64] In order to become an *auctoritas*, a text needed to generate responsive texts, either through its incorporation into the 'memorative composition' of adaptive texts, becoming one of the sources of *inventio* (in a process akin to what might now be called intertextual appropriation), or in accruing textual descendants in the form of glosses, commentaries and exegeses. Thus, as Carruthers points out, for the medieval reader an 'author' is 'simply one whose writings are full of authorities': texts capable of generating a rhetorical response tradition.[65] In which case, the *auctoritas* is 'authorised' not by the rhetorical-hermeneutical process of its writing, but by its generating a similar rhetorical-hermeneutical process for subsidiary texts. Thus, within the composition narrative of the *Vita Nuova*, Dante presents himself as 'copista, breviatore ed esegeta della propria opera', the scribe, arranger and exegete of his own work.[66]

In this respect, by both assembling and authorising his text through the hermeneutical perspective of the prosimetrum commentary, Dante effectively mimicked Scholastic forms of textual exegesis and so appropriated 'the normative canons of cultural *auctoritas*'.[67] This 'self-authorising' action thus used relatively 'conservative' means to achieve a radical poetic aim, as Dante's texts were – through their vernacular language – denied 'the intrinsic *auctoritas* of high Latin culture', and as products of a living figure they 'could not hope to claim [the] depersonalised *auctoritas* [of] Biblical and classical *auctores*'. However, through the mimesis of the commentary tradition within the *Vita Nuova*, Dante effectively achieved the 'transgressive desire' of bestowing just such prohibited *auctoritas* upon his text.[68] There is a striking contrast between this form of responsive and hermeneutical authorisation and the more conventional kind of intertextual authorisation presented in the *Inferno*, where, in calling Virgil 'mio maestro e il mio autore' ['my master and my author'] (*Inf.* 1. 85),

---

[64] For a general discussion of medieval theories of *auctoritas* drawing on a range of writers and examples see Carruthers, *The Book of Memory*, 233–7; and Minnis, *Medieval Theory of Authorship*, 10–13, 165–7. For a discussion of Dante's authorising by a commentary tradition see Ascoli, *Dante and the Making of a Modern Author*, 9, 42–3, 176–8.

[65] Carruthers, *The Book of Memory*, 236; Minnis, *Medieval Theory of Authorship*, 10. For Ascoli's cogent – if not wholly convincing – criticism of Carruthers' 'depersonalised' sense of medieval authority and authorship see *Dante and the Making of a Modern Author*, 36–7.

[66] Gorni, 'La Vita Nuova di Dante Alighieri', 154.

[67] Ascoli, *Dante and the Making of a Modern Author*, 176; see also Minnis, *Medieval Theory of Authorship*, 165–6.

[68] Ascoli, *Dante and the Making of a Modern Author*, 9, 20–1.

the pilgrim foregrounds the way in which, through its appropriation of Virgil's poem, the *Commedia* authorises the *Aeneid*. In the *Vita Nuova* we instead encounter an effectively self-authorising text, supplying both the *exemplum* in the form of the lyrics, and generating its own authorising response tradition through both the exegetical passages and the adapted narratives of each poem's 'composition'.[69]

In this form of self-authorising, memoratively assembled textuality that underwrites Dante's poetics, there is a creatively productive tension. Gianfranco Contini, discussing the involvement of memory in any reading of Dante, argued that 'la vera sede della *Commedia* stia nella memoria e non nel libro' ['the true seat of the *Commedia* is in the memory, and not in the book'].[70] According to Contini, in producing copies of the *Commedia* 'gli scribi copiavano ma, come faremmo noi stessi, con la memoria oberata di ricordi', ['the scribes copied as we would ourselves, burdened by the memory of memories'].[71] Thus, such is the implication of the memory of the transmitter of the *Commedia* on a textual level – be they scribe, speaker, singer or Dante himself – that there is in effect no possibility of their being an 'original' text of the poem, a text deriving from a single originary point.

Instead, as Contini's observations emphasise, any version of the text that we receive – whether written or spoken – is effectively a product of what Carruthers called 'memorative composition', a process of creative re-membering. Considering Contini's notions of 'textual memory' within the wider context of medieval textuality raises the prospect of there being no fixed version of a text able to be authorised into the status of an *auctoritas* – a textually generative originary point. As the *auctoritas* – the authorised text – is subject to the same transformations and rearrangements – the same re-membering – as govern the creation of the reception texts that cement its originary status.[72] Thus, for a text to become an

---

[69] In objecting to Carruthers' reading of a 'depersonalised' form of medieval *auctoritas*, Ascoli thus seems to overlook the textual locus of the self-authorising process of such works as the *Vita Nuova* (and the similarly structured *Convivio*): the way in which the text provides within itself all of the conditions necessary for its authorisation. Ascoli instead displaces this process onto a static 'historical' persona of the 'author', an anticipation of the Renaissance 'god-Author' structure that, he contends, Dante effectively originated; cf. Ascoli, *Dante and the Making of a Modern Author*, 33–7, 398–9.
[70] Gianfranco Contini, *Varianti e Altra Linguistica: una raccolta di saggi (1938–1968)*, 372.
[71] Contini, *Varianti e Altra Linguistica*, 372.
[72] In preferring the term 'originary' – the condition of making a claim of origination – over the ontologically assured 'originating', I am following Rita Copeland's lead in drawing on the thought of Derrida and Heidegger as a framework through which to encounter the issue of textual generation in the Middle Ages, see *Rhetoric, Hermeneutics, and Translation*, 230 n. 2. For Heidegger's influential discussion of origination see his 'The Origin of the Work of Art', 143–212. For Derrida's

authority – the origin point and generator of other texts – it must make itself available as a source for hermeneutical arrangement in the act of rhetorical composition; yet it is itself, according to Contini, continually undergoing an act of hermeneutical rearrangement and compositional re-membering. Therefore, the claim of any text to stand in a truly originary relation to its authorising tradition breaks down, as it is subject to perpetual transformation and rearrangement, not least through the hermeneutical action of the authorising tradition.

These observations can be grounded in the form of textuality discussed within the *Vita Nuova*. Thus, on one hand we can see that the 'libro della mia memoria' is authorised by its transformation and rearrangement – its 'copying' – into the text of the *Vita Nuova*, yet on the other, the book of memory is subject to the same process of hermeneutical re-membering as the text that it generates. In this respect, the *Vita Nuova* presents a conception of memory that stresses the contradiction of the recollecting or reproducing model of heuristic memory: there is no static, fixed originary point to recover, and thus any act of memory is fundamentally a creative act of re-membering. By conceiving of memory as a text authorised by its rearrangement into 'copies', and yet subject itself to the same processes of 'copying', then, in a significant sense, we must acknowledge that there is no 'original', only many copies.

A case in point is the arguable crux of the narrative of the *Commedia*: the meeting of Dante-pilgrim and Beatrice in the Terrestrial Paradise. *Purgatorio* 30 and 31 present a version of the Dante–Beatrice relationship that re-members their historical interaction (or, more immediately, the re-membered version of this interaction as written in the *Vita Nuova*) into a redemptive narrative. This re-membered narrative in the *Purgatorio* thus both authorises the historical and the earlier textual narratives and, by pointing up the similar processes of memorial shaping that re-membered these earlier narratives, authorises itself. In this respect, the relationship between the historical narrative of Dante's interactions with Beatrice and the *Commedia*'s redemptive, poetic narrative is not analogous to that between an original and copy, or between a 'true' narrative and a 'false' one, or between a recalled narrative and an imagined one. The historical narrative, the narrative of the *Vita Nuova* and the culminating narrative of

criticisms of 'originary claims' see *Of Grammatology*, ix, 87–94. For Alistair Minnis's contrasting and problematic call for a 'medieval' literary theory through which to discuss medieval texts, see *Medieval Theory of Authorship*, 1–2.

the *Commedia* can be seen to be equally real or equally fictional, as all are equally re-membered.

The form of memorial textuality that arises from Dante's writings is creatively complex: rooted in the notion of a gathering, shaping act of memorial writing – of re-membering – that rhetorically inscribes within it the bases of its own hermeneutic, Dante's memorial poetics significantly deconstructs the claims of authority and textual generation with which it engages. This view of Dantean textuality arises, Albert Ascoli has argued, from a reading of the poet's oeuvre that places a teleological weight on the *Commedia* that is untenable within the parameters of 'an internal history of Dante's evolving relationship to the "culture of authority"'.[73] Whilst Ascoli's criticism of the 'depersonalised' reading of medieval textuality as anachronistic is not wholly sustainable, his own historicist method emphasises an important contextual question. Was there any aspect of the pattern of Joyce's own evolving reading of Dante that would have encouraged his sense of this Dantean poetics and textuality, or are we slipping into an anachronistic reading of a 'medieval' Joyce? The answer is refreshingly simple.

Joyce's acquaintance with Dante began with the *Commedia*, thus establishing a pattern of reading that would have strengthened his sense of the poem as the summation of such earlier works as the *Vita Nuova* and the *Convivio*. In turn this reading pattern left him particularly receptive to the re-membering and authorising movements between the narrative of this 'first' work and those subsequent encounters.[74] Equally, whilst its uncertain how much Joyce himself knew about the physical processes of medieval textuality, as Gabler has shown, in the composition of *Ulysses*, Joyce grew increasingly familiar with the destabilising and 're-memberative' aspects of the scribal process.[75] Furthermore, the textual context in which Joyce encountered the process of 'assemprare' and creative re-membering – Marco de Rubris's edition of the *Vita Nuova* – strove for a 'medieval' character in all aspects of its material textuality, from its

---

[73] Ascoli, *Dante and the Making of a Modern Author*, 274, see also 59–60.
[74] This *Commedia*-centric reading pattern was far from unique to Joyce: in his 1929 essay T. S. Eliot warned of the dangers of 'Pre-Raphaelite quaintness' if starting chronologically with the *Vita Nuova*; see *Dante*, 55, 62–3.
[75] On Joyce as 'both scribe and author' of *Ulysses* see Gabler's comments in James Joyce, *Ulysses: A Critical and Synoptic Edition*, vol. 3, 1864. Indeed, such is the extent to which *Ulysses* can be read as a scribal text, that it has even been used as an experimental subject in studying medieval scribal process, see Aidan Conti, 'Scribes as Authors, Transmission as Composition: Towards a Science of Copying', 280–5.

vellum cover, full-page illustrations and illuminated initials, to its floriated borders and literal rubricking in red ink.[76]

Whilst the synthetic works of scholarship on which our discussions of 'memorative composition' and the creative aspect of medieval memory were based were not available to Joyce, their medieval epistemology and rhetorical theory derived from authors with whom Joyce was directly acquainted: Aristotle, Augustine, Aquinas.[77] Indeed it is surprisingly certain that Joyce would have read Dante's act of 'assemprare' in the *Vita Nuova* along similarly accretive lines. In *Inferno* 2, Dante presented the notion of memory as 'writing' the *Commedia*: 'O mente, che scrivesti ciò ch' io vidi' (*Inf.* 2. 8), and in his gloss to this poetic crux Eugenio Camerini provided Joyce with an explicit statement of the assembling, creative action of 'memorative composition': '8–9. *Che scrivesti*, in te raccogliesti' [*'What you wrote*, you gathered from within']. Camerini's reading of memorative writing as a gathering or assembly, thus introduced Joyce to Dante's concept of creative re-membering, prior to his reading the process of 'assemprare' in the *Vita Nuova*. So the pattern and contexts of Joyce's early reading would have worked to strengthen his awareness of the processes of imaginative memory and textual re-membering within Dante's poetics.

The relevance of the form of textuality that arises from such Dantean poetics to a reading of 'Circe' – the mode of which, as already noted, resonates with Dantean notions of visionary memory – is substantial, and quickly apparent. Dantean textuality, with its resistance to originary claims, allows us to expand significantly upon previous critical approaches to 'Circe'. In her perceptive essay on the chapter, Vicki Mahaffey argued that 'we have limited access to the past through memory, which fictively rearranges and re-members it'.[78] Dantean textuality and poetics both reaffirm Mahaffey's insight into the action of memory and usefully question her tacit conception of the past as a kind of static, pre-existent and originary text to be faultily accessed. Equally Dante's textuality provides an

---

[76] For a discussion of the visual presentation of de Rubris's edition of the *Vita Nuova* and the visual textuality of *Giacomo Joyce*, see Vaglio, '*Giacomo Joyce* or the *Vita Nuova*', 101–6. For a complementary discussion of the material textuality of modernist deluxe editions see Lawrence Rainey, 'The Cultural Economy of Modernism', 43–4.

[77] Joyce's familiarity with Augustine was such that, according to Jan Parandowski, whilst writing the final episodes of *Ulysses*, Joyce was able to recite long passages of Augustine from memory in conversation. Interestingly, Parandowski noted that later he was unable to locate the passage Joyce recited, raising the intriguing possibility that in his talk Joyce was actively engaged in a medieval form of creative re-membering, see 'Meeting with Joyce', 159.

[78] Mahaffey, 'Joyce and Gender', 122.

important way to build upon and extend Gabler's discussion of 'Circe', whilst reconsidering the static model of textual relation that underpins his notions of 'narrative rereading'.

'Harking Back in a Retrospective Arrangement': The Dantean Textuality of 'Circe'

We can begin by considering the Dantean idea of memory as a creative, rearranging process. Whilst this process of re-membering presents a possible hermeneutic for reading all of the recurrent elements within 'Circe', the transformative model that underpinned Dante's act of 'copying' in the *Vita Nuova* informs the two most explicit discussions of memory in Joyce's chapter. The first of these occurs early in 'Circe' when, encountering Mrs Breen, Bloom asks her to recall the distant time they attended a party together:

> How time flies by! Do you remember, harking back in a retrospective arrangement, Old Christmas night, Georgina Simpson's housewarming while they were playing the Irving Bishop game, finding the pin blindfold and thoughtreading? (*U* 15. 442–5)

Bloom's notion of 'retrospective arrangement' offers a model of memory that foregrounds the action of Dante's shaping, rearranging form of creative re-membering, and acknowledges the fallibility of seeing memory as a mechanism to recall a scene isomorphic with the 'original' event. Whilst Bloom's 'harking back' is perhaps the most pithily quotable expression of the Dantean form of creative memory in 'Circe', later in the chapter there is a sustained example of this process of 'retrospective arrangement' in action.

During their remarkable re-encounter, Virag Lipoti enjoined his grandson Bloom to 'exercise your mnemotechnic' (*U* 15. 2384–5); however, prior to this, Virag makes another, more complex demand on Bloom's memory:

VIRAG

> (*arches his eyebrows*) Contact with a goldring, they say. Argumentum ad feminam, as we said in old Rome and ancient Greece in the consulship of Diplodocus and Ichthyosauros. For the rest Eve's sovereign remedy. Not for sale. Hire only. Huguenot. (*he twitches*) It is a funny sound. (*he coughs encouragingly*) But possibly it is only a wart. I presume you shall have remembered what I will have taught you on that head? Wheatenmeal with honey and nutmeg. (*U* 15.2370–7)

Virag's engagingly garbled view of the past in which dinosaurs are elected as Roman consuls, arguably demonstrates a kind of Dantean re-membering of history; however, it is the complex form of temporality in Virag's question that points most clearly towards the rearranging action of memory. In his confusing question ('I presume you shall have remembered what I will have taught you on that head?'), Virag seems to approach the ambiguous temporality that Joyce associated with 'Circe': 'here is the unknown. There is no past, no future; everything flows in an eternal present.'[79] The answer Bloom offers is an example of the kind of accretive re-membering that underpinned Dante's memorative textuality:

BLOOM

(reflecting) Wheatenmeal with lycopodium and syllabax. This searching ordeal. It has been an unusually fatiguing day, a chapter of accidents. Wait. I mean, wartsblood spreads warts, you said … (U 15. 2378–2381)

Bloom's effort of memory is cast as an act of '*reflecting*', a visual action that resonates with the visionary aspect of 'Circe''s technic, particularly in the notion of memory as a 'seeing again' of an image: a re-imagining. The notion of reflection also evokes the corrupting effect of mirrors that has been a concern throughout 'Circe', suggesting that, in his act of memory, Bloom is not simply going to recall his memories of Virag's cures, but rather creatively re-member them. This is exactly what he does, rendering Virag's mention of 'honey and nutmeg' as 'lycopodium and syllabax'. The textuality inherent in this act of memory resonates strongly with Dantean forms; Bloom effectively engages in his own act of 'assemprare', of transformative 'copying', harvesting the elements of 'lycopodium' (U 15. 2366) and 'syllabax' (U 15. 2335) from their earlier appearances in the conversation, and translating them into a new context.

This act of transformative re-membering demonstrates, on a micro level, the processes of Dantean creative memory that underpin many of the transfigurations and transformations that stud the text of 'Circe'. For instance, from the position of a rearranging, creative form of memory, the moment in which the lemon soap purchased in 'Lotus Eaters' bursts into an advertising jingle ('We're a capital couple are Bloom and I./He brightens the earth. I polish the sky', U 15. 338–9) is revealed not as a subjective fantasy on the part of Bloom, but as an act of textual re-membering. In this respect, an effective recuperative strategy for encountering the strange transfigured recurrences and recapitulations of earlier episodes of *Ulysses* on the streets of nighttown is to conceive of them, not as fantasies,

---

[79] Mercanton, 'The Hours of James Joyce', 207.

hallucinations or even conventional recollections, but as re-memberings of the earlier text. In other words, the memorial textuality of 'Circe' would seem to rearrange and creatively re-member *Ulysses*.

Given the presence of Dantean mechanisms of creative memory within the textual operation of 'Circe', does the chapter also demonstrate the concepts of textual generation and origination inherent in the self-authorising discourse of Dante's memorial writing? One way in which 'Circe' enacts a connection between ideas of origination, textual generation and memory is discernible in the two opposed notions of memory it expresses through the language of familial and hereditary relations. 'Circe' can be seen to embody a discourse between, on one side, the sisters and the daughters, and, on the other, the mothers of memory.[80] In the course of his defence during the 'street-trial' scene, Bloom evokes this first form of memory:

> *(Bloom, pleading not guilty and holding a fullblown waterlily, begins a long unintelligible speech. They would hear what counsel had to say in his stirring address to the grand jury. He was down and out but, though branded as a black sheep, if he might say so, he meant to reform, to retrieve the memory of the past in a purely sisterly way and return to nature as a purely domestic animal [...])*
> (*U* 15. 898–903)

This notion of retrieving 'the memory of the past in a purely sisterly way' would seem to present the possibility of recalling the fixed sense of the past in a generatively neutral manner. In other words, by evoking sisterhood as the model for the action of his memory, Bloom's defence denies the possibility of procreation through recollection, of creatively re-membering the past; a process circumscribed by incestuous taboo. The verity of Bloom's defence rests in the isomorphism of his account with the historical reality of the events under question, and this isomorphism is guaranteed by his evocation of the non-sexual identity of the sister as model for the mechanism of memory: his memory will act in a '*purely sisterly way*'. Furthermore, the static conception of a retrievable 'past' is aligned with the gendered – and non-generative – identity of memory: the role of the 'sister' within a family, attained through shared heredity, is thus an inflicted form of identity and not dependent upon generative intercourse. The notion that the supposedly stable 'sisterly' relation can offer a model for an objective, non-transformative process of recollection, is of course somewhat ironised by Joyce's later exploration of the sexual potential of fraternal incest in *Finnegans Wake*; a form of familial interaction

---

[80] In connecting textual generation with sexual and familial models of genesis, I am drawing on Vicki Mahaffey's account of Joyce's textuality, see *Reauthorizing Joyce*, 195–202.

that resonates strongly with Dante's exploration of sexualised sisterhood in the *Inferno*.[81]

The association between non-generative, de-sexualised gendered identities and the notion of recollective, neutral memory is further strengthened by the presence of the 'Daughters of Erin'. In their sole appearance within nighttown, these ladies offer an aphoristic rehearsal of the progress of the second part of *Ulysses*:

> THE DAUGHTERS OF ERIN
>
> Kidney of Bloom, pray for us
> Flower of the Bath, pray for us
> Mentor of Menton, pray for us
> Canvasser of the Freeman, pray for us
> Charitable Mason, pray for us
> Wandering Soap, pray for us
> Sweets of Sin, pray for us
> Music without Words, pray for us
> Reprover of the Citizen, pray for us
> Friend of all Frillies, pray for us
> Midwife Most Merciful, pray for us
> Potato Preservative against Plague and Pestilence, pray for us.
> (*U* 15. 1940–52)

Whilst selective and condensed, these evocations of each chapter from 'Calypso' to 'Circe', recall key events in those episodes rather than creatively re-membering them. Thus, a connection is again drawn between sexually neutral – or at least sexually circumscribed – identity and a form of memory that lays claim to both an objective and, ironically, an isomorphically reproductive nature.

In contrast to the 'sisterly' or 'daughterly' model, the creative, generative notion of memory is emphasised at the end of 'Circe' when Stephen, confronting the malevolent presences of Privates Carr and Compton declares:

> You are my guests. Uninvited. By virtue of the fifth of George and seventh of Edward. History to blame. Fabled by mothers of memory. (*U* 15. 4370–1)

In this moment, as Vicki Mahaffey has pointed out, 'Circe' enters into a clearly discernible – and hermeneutically important – dialogue with the earlier 'Nestor' chapter.[82] In Stephen's Circean statement there is a paraphrasing appropriation both of Haines's moronic claim in 'Telemachus'

---

[81] See below, pp. 200–03.
[82] Mahaffey, 'Joyce and Gender', 122.

that 'it seems history is to blame' for poor Anglo-Irish relations (*U* 1. 649), and a re-membering of Stephen's thoughts on history in 'Nestor':

> Fabled by the daughters of memory. And yet it was in some way if not as memory fabled it. (*U* 2. 7–8)

In her discussion of the contrasting formulations of memory in these two passages, Mahaffey raises the possibility that, if history is 'fabled by the daughters of memory' – if the past is only accessible through fiction – then in 'Circe' Joyce is exploring hopes for the future, 'fabled by the mothers of desire'.[83] Mahaffey's reading is astute and intriguing, yet if we resist the alteration of the object of Stephen's thought ('memory' turning to 'desire') we can look instead at the changing character of the action of memory: the shift between the daughters and the mothers of memory.

So what might be at stake in the distinction between the mothering and the daughtering of memory, between the position of 'Circe' and 'Nestor'? As the Daughters of Erin have shown, the identity of a daughter is static, a given state inflicted by a process of unitary authority in the form of a heredity over which the subject has no control. Stephen's initial formulation of his reflection on the nature of memory posits an equally fixed position, with the narrative of history deriving from the fabling of the nevertheless static, extant reality of the past: 'And yet it *was* in some way if not as memory fabled it.' However, in contrast to the daughter (or the sister), the figure of the mother derives its identity both from intercourse in the terms of genetic intermingling and generation through parturition and creation. Thus, the view of memory as a 'mothering' is one that embraces the creative, generative aspect of medieval formulations of the process, the formulations that underpinned Dante's acts of textual re-membering.

If history is seen to be fabled by the mothering action of memory, then we acknowledge a fundamental assonance between history, memory and the past, as all are acknowledged as shaped, rearranged narratives. Mahaffey's reading of this discourse is persuasive: 'except through its irreversible consequences, the past in all its complexity is unknowable; however, we have limited access to the past through memory, which fictively rearranges or re-members it'.[84] However, in the idea of an 'unknowable', consequential past lying behind history there arguably persists the notion of an ontologically substantive past, untouched by the fabling process. The

---

[83] Mahaffey, 'Joyce and Gender', 122–3.
[84] Mahaffey, 'Joyce and Gender', 122.

view that arises from a Dantean poetics, rooted in the mothering action of memory, thus emphasises the shared contingency of any conception of temporality or history on essentially fluid narrative forms. In the Circean version of Stephen's thought, the significance of the 'realness' of the past is denied, there is no 'true' history behind the fable to be recovered, no way in which something *was* other than the way it has been fabled.

In this respect, the Circean notion of the mothering of memory, and the view of fundamentally contingent, narrativised history that arises from it, are predicated on the same conceptions of textuality, originality and authorisation as in the work of Dante. Just as Dantean textuality resisted the notion of a fixed originary point, and unsettled this concept through its continual subjection to 'memorative composition' and re-membering, so too does 'Circe' embrace this textual relativism. Hans Walter Gabler explored the issue of the nature of reference and relation in 'Circe' through 'narrative rereading', a process that 'engenders narrative analogous to, and at the same time significantly different from, a pre-existing narrative that stands revealed as its pre-narrative by the referential links'.[85] Thus, 'Circe' – which Joyce wrote concomitantly with a period of substantial revisions to the earlier episodes – is seen to be composed through a process of rereading that generated the Circean versions of the reread portions of *Ulysses*.[86] Medieval notions of the interconnection of rhetoric and hermeneutics can significantly expand and condition Gabler's argument, and offer a fuller explication of his intriguing observation that, in 'Circe', Joyce enacts the 'lowering of empiric reality to the state of relativity of fiction'.[87]

Inherent in the notion of 'narrative rereading' is a relatively simple hereditary model of textual generation: 'Circe' is posited as the fabled daughter of the earlier parts of *Ulysses*, the copy to their original. However, when we consider Joyce's continual revision of *Ulysses* from the perspective of the kind of textuality he observed in his reading of Dante, a non-originary, reciprocal model for the interrelation of 'Circe' with the rest of the novel emerges. I would argue that 'Circe' can be understood both as a hermeneutical act that, in a Dantean sense, authorises *Ulysses* – making the earlier parts of the book an *auctoritas*, a source for textual generation – and as a rhetorical act that destabilises the originary claims of these earlier parts by pointing up their shared method of composition and nature as memoratively fabled rearrangements, re-visions and re-memberings. If the reading

---

[85] Gabler, 'Narrative Rereadings', 58.
[86] See Gabler, 'Narrative Rereadings', 57, 65; and Brown, '"Everything" in "Circe"', 229–32.
[87] Gabler, 'Narrative Rereadings', 66.

of the previous episodes stimulated the writing of 'Circe', and the writing of 'Circe' stimulated both the reading and the rewriting of the previous episodes, then the hereditary 'original-copy' model of textual generation fails to account for the chapter's reciprocal textuality.

This levelling of hierarchical, hereditary textual models, and the rejection of originary claims that the Dantean poetics of Joyce's compositional technique reveals, holds a range of implications for the experience of reading the oddity and 'otherness' of 'Circe'.[88] For one thing, a Dantean poetics of re-membering can clarify the way in which, in a manner fundamentally analogous both to the medieval theory, and to the poetic practice of Dante that Joyce encountered in the *Vita Nuova* and the *Commedia*, 'Circe' has encoded within it its own hermeneutical position in the form of recognisable, transfigured re-memberings of earlier features of the text. Furthermore, the creative associations that the Dantean textuality of 'Circe' elicits between unstable and yet familiar textual elements would seem to have great relevance to any reading of *Finnegans Wake*, where the recognition and appreciation of recurring figures provides one of the best hermeneutics for anyone beginning on the journey of Joyce's last work.

However, perhaps the strongest influence of a Dantean conception of textuality is on the ways in which we might read the multiplicity of narratives encountered both in 'Circe' itself and the whole of *Ulysses*, and the form of the hermeneutical relations that we construct between them. Does Dante's poetics of memory pattern the form of the relation between repeated narratives throughout the book? The figure of the Citizen addresses this question. The narrative of the conversation between Bloom and the Citizen is encountered three times in *Ulysses*: firstly in its most extended form in 'Cyclops', where the meeting is presented as being (on the Citizen's part at least) nasty, vitriolic and hate-filled. Next the narrative appears in its Circean re-membering whereby the Citizen first enters as part of the praising crowd signalling the advent of the 'new Bloomusalem' (*U* 15. 1617–18), and subsequently takes up a more familiarly antagonistic position, crying out, 'Thank heaven!' (*U* 15. 1933) as '*the Dublin Fire Brigade by general request sets fire to Bloom*' (*U* 15. 1930–1). Finally, in 'Eumaeus' we find Bloom's narrative of the encounter, as delivered to the sleepy and entirely uninterested Stephen:

---

[88] For another account of Joyce's textuality as rejecting originary claims see Mahaffey, *Reauthorizing Joyce*, 197–8.

—He took umbrage at something or other, that muchinjured but on the whole eventempered person declared, I let slip. He called me a jew and in a heated fashion offensively. So I without deviating from plain facts in the least told him his God, I mean Christ, was a jew too and all his family like me though in reality I'm not. That was one for him. A soft answer turns away wrath. He hadn't a word to say for himself as everyone saw. Am I not right? (*U* 16. 1081–7)

One hermeneutic through which we can discern the narrative relation between these three apparently competing versions of the Citizen narrative, based on the authoritarian model of the 'original' and the 'copy', would offer the reading that the 'Cyclops' narrative represents the reality of the encounter, and thus the 'Eumaeus' narrative represents a touchingly pathetic attempt on Bloom's part to redeem his memory of the episode. In which case the easiest recuperative strategy for fitting the Circean version into this hermeneutical narrative is to see it as Bloom's unsustainable fantasy in which he tries to imagine how the Citizen *could* have related to him, a fantasy that is quickly supplanted by the recognition of the hostile 'reality' of the 'Cyclops' narrative. In effect, the 'Circe' narrative appears as the act of psychological 'imagination' that leads to the 'Eumaeus' narrative. However, from the perspective arising from a Dantean poetics, we realise that if 'Cyclops' is the 'real version' of the story – the originary point of the subsequent versions – then it is only made so through its hermeneutical authorising by the re-membering action of the 'Circe' narrative. It is the reworking into the 'copies' of 'Circe' and subsequently 'Eumaeus' that establishes the 'Cyclops' narrative as the 'original'; yet, this re-membering in 'Circe' points up the shared memorial processes that underpin all three versions of the narrative, and thus deconstructs the claim of any one narrative to generative primacy.

With a hermeneutic thus rooted in the creative, mothering action of Dantean memory, we are freed from the necessity of taking an authoritatively dictated, and somewhat reductive, approach to the 'Eumaeus' narrative. There is no necessity to see it as the product of 'Cyclops' – as Bloom struggling to escape an unpleasant and ultimately intractable memory – and instead we can choose to view it as an independent, epistemologically equal re-membering, whose significance washes onto the 'Cyclops' version, just as much as it is coloured by it. In this way, the 'retelling' of the story of the Citizen in 'Eumaeus' – and the fundamentally re-membered nature of all narratives that Circean textuality reveals – emphasises for us the way in which, through the nameless narrator of 'Cyclops', Joyce previously foregrounded the shaping, fictionalising action of the 'original' narrative, and recalls the rhetorical deconstruction of the interpolated parodic passages that undercut the various rhetorics of the characters in Barney Kiernan's pub.

The effect seen in the Circean re-membering of the Citizen is not limited to this instance of what we might call narrative recursion, indeed the model that is discerned through this particular repeated narrative can be extended to all the other characters, objects and narratives that are re-encountered in nighttown. For instance, consider the figure of Gerty MacDowell in her Circean manifestation:

> *(Leering, Gerty MacDowell limps forward. She draws from behind, ogling, and shows coyly her bloodied clout.)*
>
> GERTY
>
> With all my worldly goods I thee and thou. *(she murmurs)* You did that. I hate you. (*U* 15. 372–6)

In order to make sense of Gerty's striking, somewhat grotesque appearance in this moment, we don't have to conceive of her as an aberration of her 'original' form in 'Nausicaa'; rather we can think of her as a fable encountered three times in the book: on the beach in 'Nausicaa' where she is 'fabled' by Bloom's mis-perception ('See her as she is spoil all', *U* 13. 855), on the streets of nighttown in her Circean re-membering, and in Molly's 'misread' narrative of the source of Bloom's sexual satisfaction ('yes he came somewhere [...] it was one of those night women', *U* 18. 34–6). Each of these textual encounters with Gerty's narrative has equal and opposing claims to being 'real' or fictional. Indeed, as is clarified by the echo of the 'Nausicaa' narrative in 'Penelope' – or the connection between 'Cyclops' and 'Eumaeus' – such is the alchemy of the Circean form of narrative re-membering that it need not even be exclusively comported towards the past. Whilst less common than the recurrent elements, there are numerous examples of events and narratives in 'Circe' that prefigure those encountered in the final three chapters of the book; for instance, the echo of 'Mary Shortall that was in the lock with the pox she got from Jimmy Pidgeon' (*U* 15. 2578–9) heard in Bloom's later discussion of 'a wretched creature like that from the Lock hospital reeking with disease' (*U* 16. 729). In this way, the Circean re-membering process even manages to offer a 'memory' of the future, and in doing so it challenges the primacy of sequential reading as the normative hermeneutic for *Ulysses*, a challenge and an alternative mode of reading encapsulated in Bloom's beautiful final encounter in 'Circe'. When Rudy, Bloom's dead son, appears, leaning against a wall, we are presented with a visual image of an heterodox reading strategy: '*holding a book in his hand. He reads from right to left inaudibly, smiling, kissing the page*' (*U* 15. 4958–60).[89]

The levelling of narrative reference that takes place within 'Circe' also has a substantial impact on the wider trajectory of Joyce's Dantean engagements, and can be related back to our earlier discussions of 'Proteus' and 'Scylla and Charybdis'. Through its unique form of medieval textuality, underpinned by a Dantean poetics that negates the notion of a fixed authority sustaining originary claims, 'Circe' enacts a transformation on *Ulysses* that dislodges the book from a range of stifling narrative stringencies. These stringencies, as we have seen, include the hereditary model of textual generation underpinning the relations of variant narratives within the book itself (and within the hermeneutical approach of its reader); however, they also extend to the literary and historical metanarratives with which Joyce's book is in discourse. Thus, by revealing the equally re-membered character of the narratives of and within such episodes as 'Cyclops', 'Circe' and 'Eumaeus', Joyce's poetics emphasise the potential for us to see all narratives – both within and without *Ulysses* – as equally fluid.

On one hand, this view presents a form of narrative relativity that holds the potential for staggering authoritarian abuse. In emphasising the essential fictiveness of all narratives, especially historical ones, and thus denying the 'common-sense' view of an originary past, Joyce illuminates the darker recesses of the mechanisms of power and control that writers like Kafka and Orwell would fully explore. Yet in denying the fixity of historical narratives and revealing them as the only ontologically substantive aspect of the past, Joyce's practice in 'Circe' explodes their position as stringencies. Earlier in *Ulysses*, the personal-historic narrative of Stephen Dedalus's 'exile' had ceased to be a mechanism of Dantean self-fashioning and individuation, and become another net that bound him. Stephen's exile had failed and degenerated into a narrative of failure trapping him in a no longer productive, alienated relation to the community of the city. This narrative was underpinned by a form of memory predicated on recollection: recollection of his failure in Paris and recollection of his narrative in *A Portrait of the Artist as a Young Man*. This form of memory served to reaffirm the circumstances of Stephen's failed exile as an inevitable,

---

[89] On Rudy and reading see Brown, ' "Everything" in "Circe" ', 239–40. Derek Attridge has proposed non-sequential reading of episodes as a rewarding approach for the opening of *Ulysses* and for *Finnegans Wake* in general; see *How to Read Joyce*, 43–4; and 'Reading Joyce', 11–12.

inescapable fixity, a narrative influence on his life from which he could not escape. In contrast, the Dantean poetics of 'Circe' offer a way to enact a liberation from this narrative stringency: the possibility of re-membering his narrative of exile and alienation into a less restrictive and destructive shape. Thus, when, for instance, Stephen strikes the lampshade in Bella Cohen's brothel and cries '*Nothung!*' (*U* 15. 4242), he both evokes and punningly illustrates his resistance to the kind of narrative mechanisms that bind the characters of Wagner's *Ring* cycle into their 'needful', unchangeable fates.[90]

In this respect, the forms of transfiguration encountered through the recurrent, re-membered elements within 'Circe' offer a view of change that draws a stark contrast with the kind of semiotic transformations that underpinned Stephen's 'Infernal metamorphosis'. The Circean position emphasises instead the potential for all of the narratives that we encounter as fracturing the communities of Dublin in *Ulysses* – narratives of history, religion, politics, nation, love and hate – to be recalled differently, to be rewritten, to be re-membered. In essence, the resonance of Dante's poetics and medieval forms of textuality within 'Circe' presents us with a view of memory that, when necessary, allows us to 'forget'.

This form of forgetting and creative re-membering, of embracing the narrativity of the past – whilst ethically problematic – has been seen to underpin many of the political attempts to resolve sectarian, racial and nationalist conflict and effect the reconciliation of communities in the latter-half of the twentieth century. For instance, in post-apartheid South Africa the Truth and Reconciliation Commission was charged with hearing testimony from alleged victims and alleged perpetrators of crimes during the apartheid era, with the ultimate purpose being 'to put an end to potentially endless confessions, to decide in each case whether the truth had been attained'.[91] In this determination of the 'truth', we can see the action of Joyce's fabling: re-membering the flux of competing pasts into a coherent narrative from which a subsidiary narrative of reconciliation can spring. Within an Irish context, Seamus Heaney noted that, whilst Joyce's work contributed to the necessary process of denying 'the normative authority of the dominant language or literary tradition' inherent in any struggle for political liberation, it is also the role of poetry and literature to provide a 'working model of inclusive consciousness' on which the

---

[90] See Brown, '"Everything in "Circe"'', 238. On Wagner's influence see Vicki Mahaffey, 'Wagner, Joyce, and Revolution', 237–47; and Timothy Martin, *Joyce and Wagner: A Study of Influence*.
[91] Derek Attridge, *J. M. Coetzee and the Ethics of Reading: Literature in the Event*, 142–3.

redress of conflict can be built.[92] This model, as *Ulysses* shows, can only be constructed through the ability to transcend and re-member the narratives that bind us.

Dante's conception of creative memory and his poetics of re-membering thus provide a stimulating hermeneutic position from which to read 'Circe', one that provides a robust recuperative strategy for engaging with the 'otherness' of the chapter without 'explaining away' its oddity, and one that also clarifies the progression of the wider trajectory in Joyce's reading of Dante. Furthermore, through its Dantean poetics, 'Circe' effectively 're-members' the initial path of Joyce's reading. We have already seen a sense of inherent implication and strengthening tension between the poles of exile and community throughout *Ulysses* and, in its poetic re-membering of narrative and historical stringencies, 'Circe' redresses the dominance of alienation and exile in the mode of Joyce's Dantean reading, emphasising instead the other term of Dante's uneasy orthodoxy and the growing importance of interconnection and involvement in community.

---

[92] Seamus Heaney, *The Redress of Poetry: Oxford Lectures*, 7–8.

CHAPTER 5

'The Flower that Stars the Day'
Issy, Dantean Femininity and the Family as Community in Finnegans Wake

Family as Community: Finding the Dantean Daughter in the *Wake*

In *Finnegans Wake,* it is not the city that makes up the archetypal community but the family. Joyce had explored separation from the family within *A Portrait of the Artist, Exiles* and *Ulysses,* yet in these earlier books familial alienation was circumscribed by 'exile' from the range of other communities that made up the city. But in *Finnegans Wake* the idea of the 'family as unity' emerges, and through the interactions of the patriarch HCE, his wife ALP, and their children Shem, Shaun and Issy, an archetypal community is located at the heart of Joyce's most ambitious, challenging work; as Patrick McCarthy has put it, in the *Wake* 'the family is the central unit of all action in myth and history'.[1] Whilst Joyce moved from an initial sense of the artistic and spiritual potential of exile in *A Portrait of the Artist* to explore the dangers and shortcomings, and the eventual possibility of surmounting such a 'heroic' approach within *Ulysses,* in *Finnegans Wake* the polarities of his initial trajectory – polarities constantly in tension through their latent implication – were firmly reversed. In thus positioning the family and not the city as the central form of community, Joyce might be seen as breaking with Dante, who, after all, clung to Florence to such an extent that his lost city patterned the streets of the Infernal 'community'.[2] However, Joyce's reconceptualisation of the importance of familial community reveals a deepening of his reading of Dante, for the concept of family was integral to the poet's understanding of both social and spiritual community.[3]

---

[1] Patrick McCarthy, *Joyce, Family, 'Finnegans Wake',* 4. On 'family as unity' see Cixous, *Exile of James Joyce,* 9–18.
[2] See above, p. 89.
[3] See Keen, *Dante and the City,* 58–60, 208–22.

Following Aristotle's lead (*Politics* 1. 2. 1253a, section 9), Dante's political philosophy saw the 'compagnia domestica di famiglia' ['domestic company of the family'] (*Convivio* 4. 4. 2) as the fundamental unit of any society; the microcosm underpinning such political superstructures as the city and the empire. In the *Commedia* (*Par.* 15–17) Dante developed this Aristotelian position, not only through its inclusion within an otherworldly, eschatological context but through a new-found emphasis on the centrality of women to the proper functioning of the family, the household and, through this, the wider community of the city.[4] The view of femininity that thus arises from such works as the *Commedia* and the *Vita Nuova* is complex and dual-sided, embracing the spirituality of such figures as the Virgin Mary, St Lucia and Beatrice – the 'tre donne benedette' (*Inf.* 2. 124) who dispatch Virgil to rescue Dante-pilgrim from the dark wood – as well as the heightened eroticism of *stilnovisti* love poetry.[5]

This final chapter will thus explore the duality of Dantean femininity and investigate the resonance between these ideas and Joyce's own exploration of the interconnection of femininity and community within *Finnegans Wake*. In doing so, it will return to the issue of Dante's mediation by a range of nineteenth-century voices, locating Joyce's reading of the poet within the context of the work of such writers as Dante Gabriel Rossetti and Leigh Hunt. The chapter's focus will be a series of intertextual moments in the *Wake*, moments that resonate strongly both with the *Commedia* and with Dante's lyric poetry, a source that has not yet entered the critical conversation around Joyce's Dantean engagements.[6] Through a careful exploration of these intersections between *Finnegans Wake* and a number of Dantean texts, we will follow the trajectory of exile and community into its final stage, and see how the disparities and contradictions already observed within Joyce's reading ultimately sharpened into fundamental and creative dissonance with Dante.

When critics discuss the feminine in *Finnegans Wake*, Anna Livia Plurabelle tends to get the most attention. She is the most dominant, demanding, and persistent of the book's many manifestations of the

---

[4] For more on Dante's thought on the importance of women to society see Keen, *Dante and the City*, 208–10.
[5] On aspects of the feminine in Dante's works see Marianne Shapiro, *Woman, Earthly and Divine, in the 'Comedy' of Dante*; Jaroslav Pelikan, *Eternal Feminines: Three Theological Allegories in Dante's 'Paradiso'*; Joan Ferrante, *Woman as Image in Medieval Literature: From the Twelfth Century to Dante*; and Marina Warner, *Alone of All Her Sex: The Myth and Cult of the Virgin Mary*, 162–76.
[6] For the questionable claim that 'Joyce's Dante was not the "lyric Dante"' and that Joyce had no interest in Dante's lyric poetry or such figures as Guido Cavalcanti and Petrarch see Dasenbrock, *Imitating the Italians*, 126.

Family as Community: Finding the Dantean Daughter 163

feminine, the 'total ... female presence' as David Hayman put it, the maternal archetype whose existence is felt in 'the noncoherence of every page of the *Wake*'.[7] Given this centrality, and the close connections that have been drawn between her and other feminine figures within Joyce's work (such as Molly Bloom), it is not surprising that most studies of femininity within the *Wake* have tended to focus their attention upon ALP, to the detriment of her daughter Issy.[8] This is not to claim, of course, that Issy has been overlooked or ignored by scholars, far from it. However, as Bonnie Kime Scott noted, 'in the rare times when we encounter her, [Issy] is usually oriented toward her father and brother figures [...] [and] it is her mother who tells the only tales of the mother–daughter relationship'.[9] Indeed, whether addressing her orientation towards the male figures of the family through the narrative and textual dynamics of incest, or examining her relationship with ALP through the narrow lens of Freudian maternal anxiety, critical fascination with Issy's relation to her parents has led to her being seen primarily as a daughter.[10] Such a view risks missing the complex and troubling portrait of femininity that Joyce drew independently in the youngest member of the *Wake*'s family.[11]

Given Issy's doubled presentation as both child and sexual temptation, both innocence and experience, dual-natured Dantean femininity seems a uniquely appropriate concept through which to encounter the daughter of the *Wake*.[12] This Dantean resonance has the potential to offer a new language for talking about Issy's character, one that, through its rooting in demonstrable intertextuality, resists the reductive reading of her duality through such archetypes as the 'madonna–whore' structure.[13] However, Issy, as one of the book's central figures, appears in the form of one or more of her avatars on nearly every page of the text, and so, just as much as with her riverine mother, if we seek to address her presence throughout

---

[7] David Hayman, *The 'Wake' in Transit*, 165; Sheldon Brivic, *Joyce's Waking Women: An Introduction to 'Finnegans Wake'*, 5.
[8] For some examples of an ALP-centric approach, see Bonnie Kime Scott, *James Joyce: Feminist Readings*, 77–106; Hayman, *The 'Wake' in Transit*, 95; Brivic, *Joyce's Waking Women*, 5–6.
[9] Scott, *James Joyce*, 95.
[10] On Issy, HCE and incest see John Nash, 'The Logic of Incest: Issy, Princes and Professors', 435–56; and Jen Shelton, *Joyce and the Narrative Structure of Incest*. For a largely Freudian reading of Issy and ALP see Scott, *James Joyce*, 77–106.
[11] See, for instance, Laurent Milesi's nuanced linguistic reading of Issy in *Finnegans Wake* II. 2, which nevertheless relies on her relation to HCE: 'Toward a Female Grammar of Sexuality: The De/ Recomposition of "Storiella As She is Syung"', 570, 578.
[12] On Issy's innocence and sexual attraction see Attridge, *How to Read Joyce*, 99.
[13] For the origin of this archetype in the nineteenth-century 'science' of Otto Weininger see his *Sex and Character: An Investigation of Fundamental Principles*, 188–210.

Finnegans Wake we run the risk of drowning under a flow of occurrences.[14] Instead, our focus will be on two places in the book where Issy steps into the limelight, and where her Dantean resonances can be most clearly felt.

As Lucia Boldrini has noted, 'allusions to the *Divine Comedy* are scattered throughout the *Wake*', and whilst the greatest concentrations of these allusions occur within the first and second chapters of Book II, there are numerous other passages, such as Shaun's lecture to Issy (*FW* 440), in which Dante makes a significant appearance.[15] One of the most prominent of these Dantean episodes occurs at the end of the story of the Mookse and the Gripes, when Issy manifests as an avatar who seems strikingly reminiscent of such celestial women as the 'tre donne benedette':

> Nuvoletta in her lightdress, spunn of sisteen shimmers, was looking down on them, leaning over the bannistars and listening all she childishly could. (*FW* 157. 8–10)

Mary Reynolds's reading of the 'Nuvoletta' passage has explored a little of the Dantean heritage of this nebulous avatar's name, but the wider influence of the poet on the presentation of Issy as Nuvoletta seems ripe for further elaboration.[16] However, as Boldrini showed, it is in the second book of the *Wake* that Dante comes most clearly into focus. Whilst previous discussion has tended to focus on the children's geometry lesson of Book II. 2, there are equally substantial Dantean resonances in Book II. 1, 'The Mime of Mick, Nick and the Maggies', with its extended references to *Inferno* 5 (*FW* 251. 21–32), that would reward fuller discussion.[17]

If these two passages of *Finnegans Wake*, 'Nuvoletta' and the 'Mime', offer potentially strong Dantean resonances in Joyce's text, they present an equally unique perspective on Issy herself. As noted earlier, despite her continual presence throughout the *Wake*, Issy rarely features as a focus of the text; yet in both the 'Mime' and 'Nuvoletta' passages we find her in just such an unusually central role. Within the text of the 'Nuvoletta' episode, as she drifts above the arguing Mookse and Gripes, Issy for once ventures out of the shadow of her parents, as her mother is 'off in the Fuerst quarter scrubbing the backsteps of Number 28' (*FW* 157. 15–16)

[14] Adaline Glasheen has argued that 'every "is" indicates Issy and it is out of the question to list them all', see *Third Census of 'Finnegans Wake': An Index of the Characters and Their Roles*, 138.
[15] Boldrini, *Joyce, Dante*, 141.
[16] Reynolds, *Joyce and Dante*, 133–4. Lucia Boldrini has also briefly discussed Issy as Nuvoletta, most particularly in her sharing of watery characteristics with her mother ALP; see *Joyce, Dante*, 176–7.
[17] On Dante's presence within *Finnegans Wake* II. 1 and II. 2 see Boldrini, *Joyce, Dante*, 141–2, 207 n. 8; Reynolds, *Joyce and Dante*, 212–13, 216; and James Atherton, *The Books at the Wake: A Study of the Literary Allusions in James Joyce's 'Finnegans Wake'*, 79–81.

and her father is 'up in Norwood's sokaparlour, eating oceans of Voking's Blemish' (*FW* 157. 16–17). Thus, for the majority of the 'Nuvoletta' passage, Issy appears as the singular representation of the feminine. Similarly, in the 'Mime', with its depiction of the children in the street, playing the game 'Angels and Devils or colours' (*SL* 355), Issy appears once again as the feminine focus, and the figure around whom the children's voyeuristic game revolves. In these passages we can thus explore the Dantean formulation of the feminine within the daughter of the *Wake*, a femininity that Joyce constructed through a number of intertextual resonances, both with Dante's own works and those of other, mediating figures, and which underpins her complex and compromised involvement within the community of her family.

'She Reflected Herself': Multiple Nuvolettas and the Dantean Lyric Lady

'Nuvoletta', the Italian word meaning 'little cloud', has long been acknowledged as a potentially Dantean crux within Joyce's work. Robert Spoo has linked the word to the title of the *Dubliners* story 'A Little Cloud' through a reference to the historian and sociologist Guglielmo Ferrero, in whose 1897 work *L'Europa giovane* the ephemeracy of idealism is compared to 'una piccola nuvoletta'.[18] Other critics have interpreted the title of the story as an allusion to Byron or the Bible, or even an expression of the linguistic patterning of Joyce's text; however, undoubtedly the most convincing argument mounted to explain the relation of 'nuvoletta' to 'A Little Cloud' was that made by Mary Reynolds, who argued that Joyce's title is a reference to a passage of *Inferno* 26.[19] In this canto Dante describes the counsellors of fraud burning in the eighth *bolgia* through a striking simile:

> E qual colui che si vengiò con gli orsi,
> Vide il carro d'Elia al dipartire,
> Quando i cavalli al cielo erti levorsi;
> Chè nol potea sì con gli occhi seguire,
> Ch'ei vedesse altro che la fiamma sola,
> Sì come nuvoletta, in sù salire:

---

[18] Robert E. Spoo, '"Una Piccola Nuvoletta": Ferrero's *Young Europe* and Joyce's Mature *Dubliners* Stories', 401–10; see also Manganiello, *Joyce's Politics*, 46–53; McCourt, *The Years of Bloom*, 67–70.
[19] Reynolds, *Joyce and Dante*, 160–1. On 'A Little Cloud' and Byron see Clarice Short, 'Joyce's "A Little Cloud"', 277; on the biblical association see William Tindall, *A Reader's Guide to James Joyce*, 163–4; and on the nebulous patterning of the story see David Weir, '"A Little Cloud": New Light on the Title', 301–2.

> [And as he who avenged himself with the bears saw Elijah's chariot departing, when the horses rose so steeply to Heaven that he could not follow them with his eyes so as to see more than the flame alone, like a little cloud, rising up.] (*Inf.* 26. 34–9)

However, whilst Reynolds's argument may convince that an allusion to *Inferno* 26 and the counsellors of fraud is appropriate to a story in which Ignatius Gallaher's 'fraudulent' advice leads Little Chandler to wreck his domestic life, this allusion to *Inferno* 26 in the title of the *Dubliners* story doesn't seem to help very much in explaining why an avatar of Issy should be named Nuvoletta in *Finnegans Wake*. We can note that, prior to Nuvoletta's appearance, the Mookse does seem to refer to Elijah ('for par the unicum of Elelijiacks', *FW* 156. 25–6), and the following Nuvoletta passage is littered with ascension imagery, most obviously in the closing section when the Mookse and the Gripes are both 'taken up' from the riverbank by two older, maternal figures, leaving 'an only elmtree and but a stone' (*FW* 159. 4). Whilst these references do perhaps correspond with the appearance of Nuvoletta, the 'little cloud', at the end of 'The Mookse and the Gripes' episode, there is nothing particularly female about the 'nuvoletta' of *Inferno* 26 and its association with the biblical figures of Elijah and Elishah. Thus, the reading of Dante's presence in the 'Nuvoletta' passage that would result from seeing her as an allusion to *Inferno* 26 doesn't tell us anything further about the presentation of the feminine in this incarnation of Issy.

However, in discussing the similarity between the presentation of Beatrice Justice in *Exiles* and Beatrice in *Purgatorio* 30, Reynolds pointed to a further usage of the word 'nuvoletta' in *Vita Nuova* 23, an appearance that is more securely situated within a feminine context.[20] In a passage that Joyce drew on in his correspondence with Marthe Fleischmann (and that was the only episode in de Rubris's edition to feature two Rossetti illustrations), the Dante-protagonist, having been told in a vision that 'tua mirabile donna è partita di questo secolo' ['your miraculous lady has departed from this life'] (*VN* 23. 6), watches the soul of Beatrice ascend towards heaven in a dream:

> Io imaginava di guardare verso il cielo, e pareami vedere moltitudine di angeli, i quali tornassero in suso ed avessero dinanzi da loro una nebuletta bianchissima.

---

[20] Reynolds, *Joyce and Dante*, 166.

> [I imagined I was looking up at the sky, and I seemed to see a multitude of angels whom were returning heavenwards, and in front of them was a little pure-white cloud.] (*VN* 23. 7; translation modified)

The 'nebuletta bianchissima' of this vision is then transformed, in the chapter's *canzone*, 'Donna pietosa e di novella etate':

> *Levava gli occhi miei bagnati in pianti,*
> *E vedea, che parean pioggia di manna,*
> *Gli angeli che tornavan suso in cielo:*
> *Ed una nuvoletta avean davanti,*
> *Dopo la qual cantavan tutti: Osanna;*
>
> [I raised my tear-bathed eyes to look above
> and saw, what seemed to be a rain of manna,
> the angels that ascended to the heavens;
> in front of them they had a little cloud;
> they sang; 'Hosanna' as they rose with it.] (VN 23. 25)

This is a 'nuvoletta' that seems far more resonant with the Nuvoletta of the *Wake*. First, it is an aspect of a female character, for while the association with heaven and ascension present in the 'nuvoletta' of *Inferno* 26 is also felt strongly here, a crucial change has taken place in the subject of the imagery: this is not Elijah but the soul of Beatrice rising up to heaven, transformed into a little white cloud. Furthermore, the imagery of vision and celestial witness seems far more in keeping with the appearance of Nuvoletta within the *Wake*:

> Nuvoletta in her lightdress, spunn of sisteen shimmers, was looking down on them, leaning over the bannistars and listening all she childishly could. (*FW* 157. 8–10)

Whilst the version of 'nuvoletta' that appears in *Vita Nuova* 23 does undoubtedly bear more relevance to the character in *Finnegans Wake* than *Inferno* 26, the strongest Dantean resonance of Nuvoletta is with neither of these passages but with a short lyric poem that hasn't yet entered the conversation around Joyce's engagement with Dante, the ballata 'Deh, Vïoletta':

> *Deh, Vïoletta, che in ombra d'Amore*
> *ne gli occhi miei sí subito apparisti,*
> *aggi pietà del cor che tu feristi,*
> *che spera in te e disïando more.*[21]

---

[21] Dante Alighieri, *Rime*, 43.

[Ah, Violetta, you who so suddenly appeared to my eyes in Love's shadow, pity the heart that you have wounded and which puts its trust in you and is dying of desire.] (*Rime* 12. 1–4; translation modified)

This poem, part of Dante's lyric poetry usually collected as the *Rime*, may at first appear to bear only a slight relation to the Nuvoletta of the *Wake*, namely the shared feminine diminutive ending '-etta', which, whilst characteristic of Cavalcanti, is relatively unusual within the corpus of Dante's Italian.[22] However, a far more significant association exists between 'Deh, Violetta' and Issy's incarnation as Nuvoletta, a resonance that has become buried by a heavy weight of textual scholarship.

The reading of the first line of the poem as 'Deh, Violetta, che in ombra d'Amore' is a relatively new development within Dante Studies, being the result of the work of Tommaso Casini first published in 1895.[23] Casini discovered a manuscript copy of the lyric in the Biblioteca Nazionale Vittorio Emanuele di Roma that appeared to pre-date the existing tradition for the poem, established by Segni's 1527 edition, *Sonetti e canzoni d' antichi autori toscani*. In this manuscript, the reading of the first line was given as: 'Deh uioletta che 'n ombra di Amore', which Casini standardised as Violetta, a reading that has since appeared in all modern editions of the *Rime*.[24] However, 'in tutte le stampe antichi', from Segni's edition to that of Edward Moore in 1894, the poem's first line read: 'Deh, nuvoletta, che in ombra d'Amore' ['Ah, little cloud that in the shadow of Love'].[25]

Whilst we have no firm way of knowing the edition of Dante's *opere minori* in which Joyce would have first encountered the poem, the persistence of the reading 'Deh, nuvoletta' was constant for over two centuries up to 1895, reinforced, in Casini's opinion, by the relation to Beatrice's 'nuvoletta' in *Vita Nuova* 23 and the tendency to interpret 'Deh, nuvoletta' along similarly allegorical lines.[26] The first edition of the *Rime* to instate Casini's revised reading is, as far as I can ascertain, that of Barbi in 1921 and, given the early date of Joyce's first reading of Dante, it therefore seems likely that the reading Joyce would have known was 'Deh, nuvoletta'.[27] The likelihood of Joyce's being aware of this earlier form also

---

[22] See Kenelm Foster and Patrick Boyde, *Dante's Lyric Poetry*, vol. 2, 62.
[23] Tommaso Casini, *Aneddoti e Studi Danteschi*, 23–8.
[24] Casini, *Aneddoti*, 23–4.
[25] Casini, *Aneddoti*, 26–7.
[26] Casini, *Aneddoti*, 24–5.
[27] I am very grateful to Nick Havely for his help in tracing the textual history of 'Deh, Violetta'.

increases when we consider that Ezra Pound translated the ballata as 'La Nuvoletta', in his *Canzoni* of 1911.[28] Therefore, whether he ever encountered the revised reading 'Deh, Vïoletta' or not, Joyce would have known Dante's ballata as part of the poet's small array of *nuvolette*. The poem is sufficiently important to the ongoing discussion of Nuvoletta to merit giving it here in full, returning to the original variant in Moore's 1894 edition:

> Deh nuvoletta, che in ombra d' Amore
> Negli occhi miei di subito apparisti,
> Abbi pietà del cor che tu feristi,
> Che spera in te, e desiando muore.
> Tu, nuvoletta, in forma più che umana,
> Foco mettesti dentro alla mia mente
> Col tuo parlar ch'ancide,
> Poi con atto di spirito cocente
> Creasti speme, che 'n parte m' è sana:
> Laddove tu mi ride,
> Deh non guardare perchè a lei mi fide,
> Ma drizza gli occhi al gran disio che m'arde;
> Chè mille donne già, per esser tarde,
> Sentito han pena dell'altrui dolore.

[Ah, little cloud, you who so suddenly appeared to my eyes in Love's shadow, pity the heart that you have wounded and which puts its trust in you and is dying of desire. You, little cloud, in a more than human form, you kindled a fire in my mind through your speech that strikes me down; and then, by the action of a fiery spirit, you quickened a hope that partly heals me when you smile at me. Ah, do not heed my trusting in this hope, but consider rather the great desire that burns me: for countless ladies, through their slowness to respond, have themselves been tormented because of their lover's anguish.] ('Ballata II' ll. 1–14; translation modified)

That the 'nuvoletta' of this lyric was the foremost influence on the Nuvoletta of the *Wake* can be clarified by considering the long-established connection between Issy and Joyce's daughter, Lucia. Whilst resisting the urge to read Lucia Joyce and Issy as identical, that she served as the central model for the daughter of the *Wake* is beyond doubt.[29] Indeed, Jen Shelton has shown that there is a remarkable similarity between the

---

[28] Pound's reference to Dante's poem as 'Ballata II' in his epigraph certainly derives from Moore's numbering of the *Rime*; see Ezra Pound, 'La Nuvoletta', *Collected Early Poems of Ezra Pound*, 151. On Joyce's interest in Pound's early poetry see *JJ* 661.
[29] See Glasheen, *Third Census of 'Finnegans Wake'*, 149; Carol L. Shloss, *Lucia Joyce: To Dance in the Wake*, 10.

'Nuvoletta' passage of the *Wake* and a letter (BL Add MS 57351, f. 114) that Lucia wrote to her friend Mathilde Wönecke in 1932, following her mental breakdown.[30] This letter would seem to suggest that the association of Lucia and Issy is thus particularly strong when Issy is present in the form of Nuvoletta or, as she becomes later in the passage, 'Nuvoluccia' (*FW* 157. 24). If, then, we were to follow Reynolds in viewing Nuvoletta as a reference to *Inferno* 26 (or even *Vita Nuova* 23), we would miss an important resonance between Dante's lyric 'Deh, nuvoletta', Issy and Lucia Joyce.

One of the most widely quoted of Joyce's statements about his troubled daughter is his rejection of the prevailing view of her as being mentally ill, and his defiant association of her apparent 'insanity' with his own artistic powers: 'whatever spark of gift I possess has been transmitted to Lucia and has kindled a fire in her brain'.[31] Having unearthed the earlier reading of Dante's poem as 'Deh, nuvoletta', we can see that this statement of Joyce's strongly echoes the sixth line of Dante's ballata: 'Foco mettesti dentro alla mia mente' ['You have set a fire in my mind/brain'], demonstrating an association between Dante's lyric, Joyce's thoughts on his troubled daughter and Issy's presentation as Nuvoletta.[32] That Joyce may well have made this association unconsciously, blending his memories of 'Deh, nuvoletta' with his present worries about Lucia, only strengthens the significance of this hitherto unnoticed allusion to Dante's ballata; indeed, it indicates that Dante's poem was of sufficient importance to Joyce as to colour his most painful concerns about his family.

The association that Joyce's statement draws between Lucia and Dante's lyric no doubt arose out of, and went someway towards strengthening, the ongoing connection between Lucia and Dante that had started in 1907 with her naming for St Lucia, the patron saint of sight and one of the 'tre donne benedette'.[33] This connection persisted throughout Lucia's youth, most notably through two gifts given to her, first by Samuel Beckett and then by her father. Around 1929, whilst she was besotted with him, Beckett presented Lucia with his own copy of the *Commedia*, only for her to leave it behind in a Parisian cafe (a loss that was re-enacted by the Syra-Cusa

---

[30] See Shelton, *Joyce and the Narrative Structure of Incest*, 50–51.
[31] Joyce, quoted in a letter from Paul Léon to Harriet Shaw Weaver, 19 July 1935 (*JJ* 650); see also Shloss, *Lucia Joyce*, 7; Glasheen, *Third Census of 'Finnegans Wake'*, 149.
[32] Note, however, the interesting disparities in the relationship that Joyce's statement constructs: in Dante's poem it is the woman, the 'nuvoletta' who has burnt the poet, whereas in Joyce's formulation it is the poet who kindles the little cloud, Joyce's genius that 'damages' Lucia.
[33] On Lucia's naming for St Lucia see Glasheen, *Third Census of 'Finnegans Wake'*, 149; on Lucia's name as inspired by *Inferno* 2 see Shloss, *Lucia Joyce*, 38.

'She Reflected Herself': Nuvoletta and the Lyric Lady 171

in *Dream of Fair to Middling Women*); later, as part of an effort to help her 'spiritual' rehabilitation whilst recovering from her breakdown in 1935, Joyce gave Lucia his own 'meaningful gift' of a copy of the *Vita Nuova*.[34] Given the association Joyce's statement forms between 'Deh, nuvoletta' and Issy's primary model, Lucia Joyce, it seems that Dante's lyric, rather than *Inferno* 26 or even *Vita Nuova* 23, was the foremost influence on the Nuvoletta of the *Wake*, the girl who is also a 'little cloud'. However, before examining how Nuvoletta's new 'lyric identity' might condition the form of her femininity, we can strengthen our sense of the influence of 'Deh, nuvoletta' by unravelling a further intertextual strand in this passage of *Finnegans Wake*.

Following Nuvoletta's first appearance in the text, her observation of the ongoing dispute between the Mookse and the Gripes, and her wonderful summation of its origins ('— I see, she sighed. There are menner', *FW* 158. 5), Joyce presents a lyrical description of the wind on which Nuvoletta floats:

> The siss of the whisp of the sigh of the softzing at the stir of the ver grose O arundo of a long one in midias reeds: (*FW* 158. 6–7)

In amongst the numerous references to grass and reeds, to King Midas and '*in medias res*' that figure in these lines, there is a clear allusion to Yeats's 1899 collection *The Wind Among the Reeds*. The line in 'Deh, nuvoletta' that established the connection between Nuvoletta, Joyce's daughter Lucia and Dante was, 'Foco mettesti dentro alla mia mente', and in Yeats's poem 'The Song of Wandering Aengus', which was included in *The Wind Among the Reeds*, there is an equally clear allusion to Dante's poem:

> I went out to the hazel wood,
> Because a fire was in my head.[35]
> ('The Song of Wandering Aengus', ll. 1–2)

From this intertextual shadow of the 'Deh, nuvoletta' lyric, the allusive chain extends even further, as the title of 'The Song of Wandering Aengus' cannot help but bring to mind the most famous example of wandering in English poetry:

---

[34] On Beckett's gift of the *Commedia* see James Knowlson, *Damned to Fame: The Life of Samuel Beckett*, 150–51; Shloss, *Lucia Joyce*, 190; on Joyce's gift of the *Vita Nuova* see *JJ* 681, and Shloss, *Lucia Joyce*, 336.
[35] W. B. Yeats, *The Poems of W. B. Yeats*, 59. Note also the similarity between Dante's 'nuvoletta', Joyce's Nuvoletta and Yeats's 'glimmering girl' who, later in the poem, fades 'through the brightening air' (ll. 13, 16).

> I wandered lonely as a Cloud
> That floats on high o'er Vales and Hills.[36]
> ('I Wandered Lonely as a Cloud', ll. 1–2)

In Wordsworth's poem we are brought back once again to the image of a lonely cloud, to Nuvoletta ('She was alone. All her nubied companions were asleeping with the squirrels', *FW* 157. 13–14) drifting over 'Vallee Maraia to Grasyaplaina' (*FW* 158. 19). However, quite apart from making us wonder whether Wordsworth's 'vales' might lie beneath Nuvoletta's flight-path, this link with the Romantic poet's most famous lines lets us extend the reach of Joyce's intertextual web one final step, to embrace what must surely be one of the best-known and unjustly underappreciated examples of a cloud in English lyric poetry:

> How sweet to be a Cloud
>   Floating in the Blue!
> Every little cloud
> *Always* sings aloud.
> 'How sweet to be a Cloud
>   Floating in the Blue!'
> It makes him very proud
> To be a little cloud.[37]
> ('Cloud Song', ll. 1–8)

Pooh's 'little Cloud Song', from A. A. Milne's *Winnie-the-Pooh*, brings us full circle, back to a personified 'little cloud', and thus we find waiting, at the end of the unravelled intertextual thread, the figure of Dante's – and now Joyce's – Nuvoletta.

Perhaps this chain of intertextual reference is a little frivolous, but there is a serious point to be made through its suggestion of an allusive link between the two passages of *Finnegans Wake* with which we are concerned, as during the 'Mime of Mick, Nick and the Maggies', one of the Rainbow Girls (the playmates and fractured aspects of Issy's avatar, Izod) is named 'Beatrice' and another is named 'Winnie' (*FW* 227. 14).[38] It may not, then, be too far-fetched to speculate that, during his extensive research into children's games, songs and rhymes whilst writing the 'Mime', Joyce might have come across Milne's recently published classic (1926) and noticed its connection with Dante's 'nuvoletta'.

---

[36] William Wordsworth, *The Major Works including 'The Prelude'*, 303.
[37] A. A. Milne, *Winnie-the-Pooh & The House at Pooh Corner*, 15.
[38] It is also a possibility that the nomenclature of 'Rue', the last of the Rainbow Girls named in this passage, might owe a debt to Milne's Baby Roo.

Nuvoletta's 'Feignt Reflection, Nuvoluccia': Reconciling the Dantean Feminine

In the implicit association that Joyce drew between 'Deh, nuvoletta', Lucia Joyce and the Nuvoletta of the *Wake*, both aspects of the Dantean feminine seem to be at play. On the one hand, the lady of 'Deh, nuvoletta' is clearly a typical figure of *trecento* love poetry: the lady whose pity the poet beseeches and whom he claims has 'wounded' him ('Abbi pietà del cor che tu feristi' ['Have pity on the heart you have wounded'], l. 3); yet on the other hand, the lady is also a cloud who might be allegorically associated with Beatrice, and thus a heavenly, interceding lady in the mode of the 'tre donne benedette' of *Inferno* 2. In the Nuvoletta passage of the *Wake* a range of Dantean resonances thus reveal themselves; for instance, from her first appearance, Nuvoletta (as we might expect from a 'little cloud') is a figure associated with skies and light:

> Nuvoletta in her lightdress, spunn of sisteen shimmers, was looking down on them, leaning over the bannistars and listening all she childishly could. (*FW* 157. 8–10)

Her celestial character develops throughout the passage, with Joyce repeatedly employing the language of light and astronomy; the banisters through which Nuvoletta watches her arguing brothers, the Mookse and the Gripes, are transformed into stars by the switch of a vowel, and this association of stellar witness also evokes Beatrice in *Inferno* 2, of whom Virgil observes that 'Lucevan gli occhi suoi più che la stella' ['Her eyes were shining brighter than the morning star'] (*Inf*. 2. 55). This interplay of light and vision also leads us, ineluctably, back through the 'bannistars' to the mediation of Joyce's Dantean reading by the figure of Dante Gabriel Rossetti, who exerted a strong influence on Joyce's reception of Dantean conceptions of exile, and significantly shaped his reading of the *Vita Nuova* in the edition of Marcus de Rubris.[39] Rossetti also provides another newly discernible intertext for the 'Nuvoletta' passage:

> The blessed damozel leaned out
>   From the gold bar of Heaven;
> Her eyes were deeper than the depth
>   Of waters stilled at even;
> She had three lilies in her hand,
>   And the stars in her hair were seven.
>   ('The Blessed Damozel', ll. 1–6)

---

[39] See above, pp. 47–50.

Thus, in drawing the figure of Dante's 'nuvoletta' into *Finnegans Wake* – even at the far end of the trajectory of his Dantean engagement – Joyce was still 'reading through' the nineteenth-century literary contexts of his initial encounter with the poet.

Dante's interconnection of celestial femininity and light is most fully explored by Joyce in the recurring image of Nuvoletta 'reflecting' herself. This variant of Issy and the mirror, one of the *Wake*'s more common leitmotifs, here carries clear connotations of both self-revelation and the literal refraction of light as it passes through a cloud, a process that seems to lie behind the splintering of Nuvoletta (in a suggestion of the Rainbow Girls in the 'Mime') into 'her feignt reflection, Nuvoluccia' (*FW* 157. 24). Indeed, it is the reversal of this process that triggers the end of Nuvoletta's passage through *Finnegans Wake*:

> Then Nuvoletta reflected for the last time in her little long life and she made up all her myriads of drifting minds in one. She cancelled all her engauzements. She climbed over the bannistars; she gave a childy cloudy cry: *Nuée! Nuée!* A lightdress fluttered. She was gone. (*FW* 159. 6–10)

Conditions of light even seem to influence the expression of Nuvoletta's volatile emotions: we are told that 'she was brightened' (*FW* 157. 10) when the Mookse raises his walking stick towards her, and that 'she was overclused' when the Gripes voices his doubts (*FW* 157. 11–12). In this respect, we find another way in which Nuvoletta is closely related to Joyce's daughter, with her whole existence seemingly determined by changes in light or *luce*.

However, whilst a character who is both a young girl and a cloud might naturally be associated with images of light and the skies (as a literally 'heavenly' lady), it is through the role she attempts to perform within the narrative of the ongoing dispute between the Mookse and the Gripes that Nuvoletta stakes her clearest claim to be a truly Dantean celestial figure. Hovering above their dispute and watching them argue, Nuvoletta tries to intercede between the warring Mookse and Gripes, with the aim of distracting them from their cycle of conflict:

> she tried all she tried to make the Mookse look up at her (but *he* was fore too adiaptotously farseeing) and to make the Gripes hear how coy she could be (though he was much too schystimatically auricular about *his ens* to heed her). (*FW* 157. 19–23)

This image of a lady looking down from a celestial vantage point and seeing male figures in distress most obviously recalls the 'tre donne benedette'

'Nuvoluccia': Reconciling the Dantean Feminine 175

and their intercession on behalf of Dante-pilgrim when lost in the dark wood. Whilst this image could be to a certain extent generic, Joyce may be deliberately evoking *Inferno* 2 in this scene through the way in which he subverts and frustrates the expectation of the Dantean narrative. The 'tre donne benedette' manage to dispatch Virgil to aid Dante-pilgrim, whereas Nuvoletta ultimately fails in her attempt to intercede with the Mookse and the Gripes when she cannot even manage to make them realise that she is there.[40]

However, Nuvoletta's failure to intercede with her brothers, and the contrast it makes with the success of Mary, Lucia and Beatrice, also indicates a resonant Dantean aspect of her femininity: she too is reliant for the success of her role as intercessor on the validation of a male figure. Just as Beatrice (although ultimately dispatched by the feminine figure of Mary) cannot save Dante-pilgrim without relying on Virgil and his 'parlare onesto' (*Inf.* 2. 113), his 'honest speech', to convince Dante-pilgrim of the veracity of her intercession; so Nuvoletta cannot get the Mookse and the Gripes to hear her, not only because she lacks her own Virgil to act as mediator but because the male figure of HCE, 'the heavenly one with his constellatria and his emanations' (*FW* 157. 18–19) stands as a definite obstacle between them. This sense that the female, would-be intercessory figure of Nuvoletta is obscured from her siblings, the Mookse and the Gripes (and her attempted intervention in her community negated), by the influence of a male, paternal figure is further compounded when they fail to be distracted by Nuvoletta's refraction into a form even more immediately reminiscent of one of Dante's 'tre donne benedette':

> Not even her feignt reflection, Nuvoluccia, could they toke their gnoses off for their minds with intrepifide fate and bungless curiasity, were conclaved with Heliogobbleus and Commodus and Enobarbarus and whatever the coordinal dickens they did as their damprauch of papyrs and buchstubs said. (*FW* 157. 23–8)

Here, the 'heavenly one', HCE, takes the form of two Roman emperors and a character from Shakespeare, but the effect is the same as with his previous incarnation, leaving the Mookse and the Gripes trapped in the male-dominated sphere of Catholic church ritual (note the 'bungless

---

[40] On narrativity and narrative expectation in *Finnegans Wake* see Attridge, *Joyce Effects*, 126–32.

curia-sity') and entirely unaware of the female figure attempting their celestial rescue.[41]

Within the medieval tradition of intercession, from which Dante drew his 'tre donne benedette', there was a strong connection between the spiritual work of such heavenly ladies and the earthly reality of the queenly role as political intercessor. Just as Mary, the Queen of Heaven, was understood to intercede with God on behalf of sinners 'sì che duro giudicio lassù frange' ['so that she vanquishes harsh judgement there on high'] (*Inf.* 2. 96), so too did later medieval queens become important figures within their communities as mediators and moderators of kingly power, wielding 'a particular kind of power [...] premised on exceptional vulnerability'; a power that 'credited women with special spiritual faculties but conditioned these faculties on an exclusion from the centres of mundane authority'.[42] This liminal, queenly form of intervention in the community is clearly of crucial importance in understanding the intercession of Dante's 'tre donne', and it is possible to detect this element of the Dantean feminine within the presentation of Joyce's Nuvoletta as well:

> she smiled over herself like the beauty of the image of the pose of the daughter of the queen of the Emperour of Irelande. (*FW* 157. 34–6)

In this brief flirtation with the role of royal figure, Nuvoletta appears to register the reality of feminine intercession in an era of dynastic marriage alliance; as the Tristan and Isolde myth briefly reasserts itself in the surface of the text, Nuvoletta (in an echo of one of Issy's most important and most frequently recurring avatars, Iseult) is described as having 'sighed after herself as were she born to bride with Tristis Tristior Tristissimus' (*FW* 157. 36–158. 1). However, Nuvoletta's attempt to act as a queenly intercessor is no more successful than her celestial efforts:

> But, sweet madonine, she might fair as well have carried her daisy's worth to Florida. For the Mookse, a dogmad Accanite, were not amoosed and the Gripes, a dubliboused Catalick, wis pinefully obliviscent.
> — I see, she sighed. There are menner. (*FW* 158. 1–5)

In this defeated act of intercession, Nuvoletta finds the tables turned on her by the Mookse's assumption of a royal lexis and his appropriation

---

[41] On the Mookse and the Gripes as attending a papal conclave see R. J. Schork, 'Genetic Primer: *Chapter I.6*', 136–7. Note also the resonance between Nuvoletta, Dante's 'nebuletta bianchissima' (*VN* 23. 7) and the white smoke used to signal the conclave's election of a new pontiff.

[42] See Paul Strohm, *Hochon's Arrow: The Social Imagination of Fourteenth-Century Texts*, 95–9. On Dante and Marian intercession see Warner, *Alone of All Her Sex*, 160–74.

of the 'queenly' role through a paraphrasing of Queen Victoria: 'We are not amused.' Arguably, Nuvoletta's equal-parts despairing and withering summation of her brothers' shortcomings, 'There are menner', indicates a degree of resignation to the failure of her attempt to intercede in the conflict between her brothers.

However, whilst these intercessory elements of the Dantean feminine within Nuvoletta are striking, they do not take full account of the importance of the 'Deh, nuvoletta' lyric; after all, the role of celestial lady could just as easily derive from the 'nuvoletta' of *Vita Nuova* 23. What is arguably unique in the 'Deh, nuvoletta' lyric is the way in which both sides of Dante's female equation are held in tension: the celestial idea of the lady as 'nuvoletta' with her role in the process of *trasumanazione*, and the sense of erotic menace detectable in the closing warning that a thousand previous ladies who failed to recognise their effect on a man, have felt the 'pena dell' altrui dolore' ['the pain of another's sorrow'] (l. 14).[43] When he translated 'Deh, nuvoletta' in his *Canzoni*, Ezra Pound included a note explaining the poem as being from 'Dante to an unknown lady, beseeching her not to interrupt his cult of the dead Beatrice'.[44] Perhaps instinctively agreeing with Casini that the association of the lyrical 'nuvoletta' with the Beatrice of *Vita Nuova* 23 was the kind of allegory 'non pur di Dante, ma anche degli altri minori poeti dello *stil novo*, sono alienissime' ['not only most averse to Dante but also to the other, minor poets of the *stil novo*'], Pound effectively introduced a second feminine presence to Dante's lyric. This reading postulated both the post-mortem persistence of Beatrice through Dante's 'cult' and placed her alongside a more conventional lyric lady, to whom the poem is addressed (and whom Casini renamed 'Violetta'). In this respect, Pound's reading of 'Deh, nuvoletta' is symptomatic of the dual aspects of Dante's presentation of the female figure as a whole.

If Joyce followed Pound's reading of the poem, we might then expect to find the second side of the Dantean feminine within his Nuvoletta as well, the spurned lady of 'Deh, nuvoletta' and an aspect deriving more directly from Dante's erotic poetry. Indeed, given the 'Cavalcantian' strangeness of Dante's use of the diminutive feminine ending '-etta', 'nuvoletta' has relatively few parallels within Dante's other writings, one example of which is the ballata, 'Io mi son pargoletta bella e nuova'.[45] This poem shares

---

[43] Contini draws attention to the stilnovistic reading of Dante's line 'in forma piú che umana' in his edition, see Alighieri, *Rime*, 43 n. 5.
[44] Pound, *Collected Early Poems*, 151.
[45] See Foster and Boyde, *Dante's Lyric Poetry*, vol. 2, 62.

something of the simultaneity of the dual aspects of the feminine in 'Deh, nuvoletta', presenting the figure of a young, celestial girl who

> [...] son venuta per mostrarmi a vui
> Dalle bellezze e loco, dond' io fui.

[has come to show men something of the beauty and the place whence I came.] ('Ballata VI' ll. 2–3; translation modified)

However, the girl does not seem to fit the template of Dante's later celestial ladies as, whilst she boldly declares that 'Io fui del cielo, e tornerovvi ancora' ['I came from heaven and shall return there once more'] (l. 4) and is described (with another unusual diminutive) as 'angioletta' (l. 19), she is also brazen in her eroticism:

> E chi mi vede, e non se n' innamora,
> D'amor non averà mai intelletto;

[and anyone who sees me and does not fall in love with me will never have understanding of love;] ('Ballata VI' ll. 6–7)

While the eroticism of the 'pargoletta' could be interpreted within an allegorical framework, her claim that nobody with any experience of love can resist her, together with the same emphasis on 'piacer' ['beauty'] as in 'Deh, nuvoletta' (l. 7) (and that also appears in Francesca's speech in *Inferno* 5. 104), presents an unabashedly sexual element on the literal level of the text.

What then is the significance of this 'other lady' in 'Deh, nuvoletta' or her parallel in the figure of the 'pargoletta' for reading Nuvoletta in the *Wake*? For a start, there seems a clear resonance between 'Nuvoletta in her lightdress ... leaning over the bannistars' (*FW* 157. 8–9) and the 'pargoletta"s claim that,

> Ciascuna stella negli occhi mi piove
> Della sua luce e della sua virtute.

[Every star showers its light and power into my eyes.]
('Ballata VI' ll. 11–12)

However, reading the erotic side of the Dantean feminine within Nuvoletta helps to reorientate perception of her away from a stark unitary mode in which she appears as 'a picture of pure, childish narcissism, full of naïve ideals that tend towards self-love', and in which the other aspect of her femininity is ignored or repressed.[46] When considering the

---

[46] cf. Christy Burns, 'An Erotics of the Word: Female "Assaucyetiams"' in *Finnegans Wake*, 323.

side of Nuvoletta that seeks to embrace the intercessory character of the Dantean feminine, there is a similar cross-fertilisation with the erotic as in 'Deh, nuvoletta' or 'Io mi son pargoletta'; as Nuvoletta watches the Mookse and the Gripes 'conclaved' and unresponsive to her attempts to call to them, she seems to both simultaneously reject her brothers and desire their erotic attention:

> As if that was their spiration! As if theirs could duiparate her queendim! As if she would be third perty to search on search proceedings! She tried all the winsome wonsome ways her four winds had taught her. (*FW* 157. 28–32)

With its echo of nineteenth-century slang for vagina ('quim'), and the blending of 'duo' and 'separate', Nuvoletta's rhetorical declaration, 'As if theirs could duiparate her queendim!' introduces a decidedly earthier element into her fantasy of being the Dantean queenly intercessor than the surrounding celestial imagery might suggest.[47] Indeed, this sense of erotic interest in the Mookse and the Gripes, maintained by her use of her 'winsome wonsome ways', appears to be at the heart of Nuvoletta's perception of them, as when she dismisses their apparent interest in the male-dominated Church she does so by ridiculing the notion that it could be 'their spiration', an expression that seems to carry within it the triple idea of the sighing lover of traditional erotic poetry, the breath with which God created woman in Genesis and also the 'spera', the hope of the wounded lover of 'Deh, nuvoletta'.[48]

If this sexual desire on the part of a celestial lady seems surprising, then Nuvoletta equally frustrates expectations for the narrative progression of the Dantean feminine; instead of finding a Beatrice figure who progresses from the status of erotic, 'lyric' lady to an image of the spiritual, perfected female form, Nuvoletta presents us with a cloud-lady who is destined to return to the earthly realm. In another echo of Lucia Joyce – named by Joyce whilst he wondered 'what strange morose creature [Nora] will bring forth after all her tears' (*SL* 66) – Nuvoletta first comes into contact with the terrestrial plane through weeping:

> It was so duusk that the tears of night began to fall, first by ones and twos, then by threes and fours, at last by fives and sixes of sevens, for the tired

---

[47] This concomitance of Nuvoletta and slang for the female genitals recurs later in the *Wake*, when the mysterious figure viewing the Porter children as they sleep is introduced to Issy as 'a pussy, purr esimple' (*FW* 561. 9), and when asking 'Has your pussy a pessname?' is answered 'Yes, indeed, you will hear it passim in all the noveletta and she is named Buttercup' (*FW* 561. 10–12).
[48] For more on the Ru'ak, the generative breath of God see below, p. 196.

ones were wecking, as we weep now with them. *O! O! O! Par la pluie!* (*FW* 158. 20–3)

As well as starting the process of Nuvoletta's earthly reabsorption, this fall of rain in 'sevens' echoes strongly the year of Lucia's birth, 1907. Nuvoletta's path downwards concludes in her rapid descent and disappearance into the river:

> She climbed over the bannistars; she gave a childy cloudy cry: *Nuée! Nuée!* A lightdress fluttered. She was gone. And into the river that had been a stream (for a thousand of tears had gone eon her and come on her and she was stout and struck on dancing and her muddied name was Missisliffi) there fell a tear, a singult tear, the loveliest of all tears (I mean for those crylove fable fans who are 'keen' on the pretty-pretty commonface sort of thing you meet by hopeharrods) for it was a leaptear.[49] (*FW* 159. 6–16)

In his reference to 'crylove fable fans who are 'keen' on the pretty-pretty commonface sort of thing', Joyce appears to mock the reader who, having sensed Nuvoletta's Dantean overtones, is now expecting her to realign the two sides of her feminine nature in a similar way to Beatrice: by ascending from the earthly to the celestial. Instead, in a movement that is aligned with the fundamental thematic structure of *Finnegans Wake*, Nuvoletta plummets from the sky into the river, falling from the spiritual to the earthly. However, this 'death' of Nuvoletta does, despite the mockery thrown at the concept, undergo some level of transformation, for the tear that finally falls into ALP as river is a 'leaptear'. In its reference to a 'leap year', a 'leaptear' evokes Issy and her twenty-eight female companions who appear throughout *Finnegans Wake* – such as in the 'Mime' where they take the form of Izod and the 'Floras' (*FW* 220. 3) – suggesting that, whilst Nuvoletta may have disappeared for the present, she will reappear later as 'that little cloud [...] nibulissa' (*FW* 256. 33).

So, it would seem that in her celestial and earthly aspects, and in her failed attempts to combine these elements of her character by intervening in the conflict between her brothers, Nuvoletta manages to embrace both the erotic and intercessory traditions of the Dantean feminine. However, despite the absence of her parents, Nuvoletta's character remains

---

[49] Note a further resonance here with the ending of Rossetti's 'The Blessed Damozel':

> And then she cast her arms along
> The golden barriers,
> And laid her face between her hands,
> And wept. (I heard her tears.) (ll. 141–4)

fundamentally bounded by the sphere of her family. Whilst she sometimes appears to embrace the role of a spurned lover, and at other times that of a failed intercessor, she always remains, through her archetypal relation to Issy, 'spunn of sisteen shimmers' (*FW* 157. 8): a *sister*. In this respect, we can begin to see an interesting continuity in Nuvoletta's presentation, a continuity Joyce points up when he describes 'Nuvoluccia' (the image of Nuvoletta in a mirror) as a 'feignt reflection' (*FW* 157. 24) with the connotation that any desire to separate Nuvoletta (or any avatar of Issy) out into multiple, independent girls may be, from a certain perspective, 'feignt', or 'false'. In the 'Mime of Mick, Nick and the Maggies', Joyce found an even more creative and significant way to explore the possibility of reconciling the two halves of Dante's feminine equation.

Izod, the Floras and Dante's Floral Ladies

Although she does not share the same kind of evocative Dantean nomenclature, Izod, the avatar of Issy who appears in Book II. 1 of *Finnegans Wake*, presents no less an intertextually resonant manifestation of the feminine than Nuvoletta.[50] The 'Mime' consists of two central strands of narrative: in one it presents the family of *Finnegans Wake* consciously adopting the parts of their respective avatars and performing, 'every evening at lighting up o'clock sharp' (*FW* 219. 1), the '*Mime of Mick, Nick and the Maggies*' (*FW* 219. 18–19), the play that has lent its name to the episode. In the other, the children, Glugg, Chuff and Izod (or Shem, Shaun and Issy) play games and sing rhymes in the street whilst their father and mother remain indoors. That the avatar of Issy is to be the most resonantly Dantean element in the 'Mime' is clear from the start of the chapter where, in the programme notes for the imagined theatrical production, we find the listing for the part played by the Issy archetype, and the details of the actress who is filling the role:

> IZOD (Miss Butys Pott, ask the attendantess for a leaflet), a bewitching blonde who dimples delightfully and is approached in loveliness only by her grateful sister reflection in a mirror, the cloud of the opal. (*FW* 220. 7–10)

The similarities with Nuvoletta ('the cloud of the opal') and Nuvoluccia ('her grateful sister reflection') are striking, but, were we to miss them, then Joyce includes another playful textual hint: 'ask the atten*dante*ss for a leaflet'.[51]

---

[50] Although Dante does make reference to Tristan (*Inf.* 5. 67), he doesn't anywhere refer to Isolde.
[51] And it is just possible that in 'Miss Butys Pott' we can hear an abbreviation of 'Miss Beatrice Portinari'.

From the outset then, Joyce seems to be crafting an association between Izod and Issy's earlier incarnation as Nuvoletta, making us wonder whether we will find a similar exploration of the Dantean feminine within the 'Mime', as in that earlier passage of the *Wake*.

Certainly Izod's appearance, along with that of 'the Floras' – that 'month's bunch of pretty maidens' (*FW* 220. 4–5) representing Issy's twenty-eight companions and her own fractured self – within the context of the children's game seems to confirm that we are in familiar, angelic-feminine territory:

> So and so, toe by toe, to and fro they go round, for they are the ingelles, scattering nods as girls who may, for they are an angel's garland. (*FW* 226. 21–3)

This image of Izod and the dancing Floras in the 'Mime' echoes the appearance of Matelda in the Terrestrial Paradise:

> Come si volge, con le piante strette
> A terra ed intra sè, donna che balli,
> E piede innanzi piede a pena mette,
> Volsesi in su' vermigli ed in su' gialli
> Fioretti verso me, non altrimenti
> Che vergine, che gli occhi onesti avvalli:
>
> [As a lady turns who is dancing, with her feet pressed to the ground and together, scarcely placing one foot before the other: so she turned on the crimson and yellow flowers toward me, not otherwise than a virgin who lowers her modest eyes,] (*Purg.* 28. 52–7)

However, in the combination of 'the Floras' as both flowers and 'ingelles' and Izod as an angel wearing them as a garland, Joyce hints at a further resonance between Dante's lyric poetry and the feminine nature of Issy, a resonance that also holds important connotations for reading the eroticism repeatedly associated with flowers throughout the 'Mime'.

Apart perhaps from the Floras themselves, the most notable formulation of the flower in the 'Mime' is the heliotrope. Margot Norris has argued that the heliotrope, which recurs in various, often acrostic forms throughout the chapter, is 'an overdetermined figure', but it is in its aspect as 'any flower that assumes a desirous attitude, that turns towards the sun', or 'a specific flower, a fragrant purple annual', that the heliotrope comes to operate as a kind of presiding image in both the 'Mime' and *Finnegans Wake* as a whole.[52] Noting the recurrence of the heliotrope throughout

---

[52] Margot Norris, 'Joyce's Heliotrope', 3, 6–7.

Joyce's other works, most notably in 'Nausicaa' (*U* 13. 1007), Norris sees the name of the 'overdetermined' purple flower as 'a word that means many things at once and yet points to only one thing: desire'.[53] The influence of Dante's lyric poetry on the presentation of Izod and the Floras in the 'Mime' both strengthens this association between flowers and eroticism and complicates its interpretation as a primarily sensual form of desire.

Another example of the small group of 'Cavalcantian' lyric poems in which Dante employed the female diminutive ending '-etta', was the ballata 'Per una ghirlandetta'. Dante here crafts a typical scene of idealised erotic love, and places the lady of the ballata into an angelic context:

> Per una ghirlandetta
> Ch' io vidi, mi farà
> Sospirar ogni fiore.
> Vidi a voi, Donna, portar ghirlandetta
> A par di fior gentile.
> E sovra lei vidi volare in fretta
> Un angiolel d'amore tutto umile;
> E 'n suo cantar sottile
> Dicea: 'Chi mi vedrà
> Lauderà il mio signore.'

> [Because of a garland I saw, every flower will make me sigh. Lady, I saw you wearing a garland of sweet flowers, and over it a little angel swiftly fluttering, a modest angel of love, who said in his delicate song: 'Whoever sees me will praise my Lord.'] ('Ballata VIII', ll. 1–10)

The usual motifs of vision, witness and the celestial lady (this time attended by a personal guardian angel) all feature prominently in these opening lines. Indeed, in the concept of the 'angiolel d'amore tutto umile', we seem to find the same blending of spirituality and eroticism as in both the 'nuvoletta' and 'pargoletta' lyrics, an intertwining that Dante develops further with his image of the lady's coronal:

> Dirò: 'La bella gentil donna mia
> Porta in testa i fioretti del mio sire:
> Ma per crescer desire
> La mia donna verrà
> Coronata da Amore.'

---

[53] Norris, 'Joyce's Heliotrope', 9.

> [I will say that my beautiful, noble lady wears the little flowers of my lord around her head. But my lady will come crowned by Love, to increase desire.] ('Ballata VIII' ll. 13–17; translation modified)

However, whilst these elements of the poem appear to stress the familiar celestial associations of the idealised beloved in Dantean love lyrics, it is the floral imagery of Dante's poem that most concerns us. As well as the central image of the garland of flowers, the lady herself is given a floral name:

> S' io sarò là, dove un fioretta sia,
> Allor fia ch' io sospire.
>
> [When I am where my fair Fioretta is, then will I sigh.]
> ('Ballata VIII' ll. 11–12)

In the image Dante presents of Fioretta, the 'little flower', wearing a celestial garland, we have a scene that closely resembles the appearance of Izod and the Floras:

> for they are the ingelles, scattering nods as girls who may, for they are an angel's garland. (*FW* 226. 21–3)

However, the resonance between Dante's poem and the *Wake* extends beyond this shared image of the diminutive floral lady, surrounded by flowers; for, if we follow Norris in holding the flower to be an important textual element of the 'Mime' and of the *Wake* as a whole, then we find the same interest in the potential textuality of flowers in Dante's lyric:

> Di fior le parolette mie novelle
> Han fatto una ballata:
> Da lor per leggiadria s' hanno tolt' elle
> Una vesta, ch' altrui non fu mai data:
>
> [These new little verses of mine have made a ballata of flowers; they have taken, to adorn themselves, a garment that was never given to another.]
> ('Ballata VIII', ll. 18–21; translation modified)

The interconnection between Fioretta as the subject of Dante's poem, the 'ghirlandetta', and his intricate verse form, arguably anticipates the complex textuality of the *Wake*, where the central flower of the 'Mime', the heliotrope, is woven into the allusive levels of the text:

> My top it was brought Achill's low, my middle I ope before you, my bottom's a vulser if ever there valsed and my whole the flower that stars the day (*FW* 248. 11–13)

Izod's self-identification as 'the flower that stars the day' encodes within it a reference to the heliotrope (Achilles – heel; 'my middle' – stomach – eat; 'I ope' – itrope) and is just one of numerous examples throughout the 'Mime' where either Izod or the Floras, or all of them together, embrace their role as floral ladies:

> Here they come back, all the gay pack, for they are the florals, from foncey and pansey to papvere's blush, forsake-me-nought, while there's leaf there's hope, with primtim's ruse and marry-may's blossom, all the flowers of the ancelles' garden.[54] (*FW* 227. 14–18)

If this floral identity derives from Dante's erotic poetry, it would go some way to providing intertextual support for Norris's assertion that flowers within the *Wake* evoke a series of well-worn love stories, as well as deepening our reading of the floral imagery in the frequent sexual passages associated with Izod and the Floras:

> Just so styled with the nattes are their flowerheads now and each of all has a lovestalk onto herself and the tot of all the tits of their understamens is as open as he can posably she and is tournesoled straightcut or sidewaist, accourdant to the coursets of things feminite, towooerds him in heliolatry so they may catchcup in their calyzettes,[55] (*FW* 236. 33–237. 1)

So, it would seem that through their floral nature, Izod and her companions already embrace one aspect of the Dantean feminine: the erotic lady of the love lyric, a side of their presentation that can partially contribute to understanding the riot of eroticism throughout the text of the 'Mime'.

However, flowers can evoke a much more famous passage of Dante's work than 'Per una ghirlandetta'. This alternative passage brings us to the other term of his feminine equation and demonstrates the possibility of, if not joining both sides of the Dantean feminine together into a reconciled whole, then at least further complicating their division:

> Così dentro una nuvola di fiori,
> Che dalle mani angeliche saliva
> E ricadeva giù dentro e di fuori,
> Sovra candido vel cinta d'oliva
> Donna m'apparve, sotto verde manto,
> Vestita di color di fiamma viva.
>
> [So, within a cloud of flowers that from the hands of the angels was rising and falling back within and without, her white veil girt with olive, a lady

---

[54] On the encoded heliotrope see Roland McHugh, *Annotations to 'Finnegans Wake'*, 227.
[55] See Norris, 'Joyce's Heliotrope', 6–8.

appeared to me, clothed, beneath a green mantle, in the colour of living flame.] (*Purg.* 30. 28–33)

The appearance of Beatrice in the Earthly Paradise of *Purgatorio* 30 is present within various elements of the 'Mime', not simply the presentation of Issy. There is an obvious resonance with the importance of clothing and its symbolic colouring, not only in the central motif of Glugg's increasingly desperate attempts to guess the colour of Izod's underwear ('haps thee jaoneofergs?' *FW* 233. 21), but also in the contrast between Beatrice's vestments (whose colours would go on to form the tricolour of the unified Italy) and Chuff/Kevin's absurd nationalistic attire:

> Candidatus, viridosus, aurilucens, sinelab? Of all the green heroes everwore coton breiches, the whitemost, the goldenest! How he stud theirs with himselfs mookst kevinly. (*FW* 234. 8–10)

Whilst a discussion of Dante's influence on Joyce's attitude to nationalism and the creation of the Irish Republic (and its own tricolour) would be well worth pursuing, we should keep our focus on the issue at hand and note here how Beatrice's descent amongst a cloud of flowers, cast by her accompanying angels, represents a development and resolution of the feminine tension within the *stilnovista* position; in the *Purgatorio* the language of the love lyric has been firmly appropriated to spiritual, Christian purposes.

Yet this alternative example of the Dantean lady framed amongst both flowers and angels also has a strong resonance with the depiction of Izod and the Floras. In a letter to Harriet Weaver outlining the scheme of the game the children play in the 'Mime' as 'Angels and Devils, or colours', Joyce drew attention to his 'treatment of the double rainbow in which the iritic colours are first normal and then reversed' (*SL* 356). This appears to refer to the passage in the 'Mime' in which the Floras transmute into the seven Rainbow Girls:

> Say them all but tell them apart, cadenzando coloratura! R is Rubretta and A is Arancia, Y is for Yilla and N for greeneriN. B is Boyblue with odalisque O while W waters the fleurettes of novembrance. (*FW* 226. 30–33)

Even in the form of the Rainbow Girls, Izod's companions retain their floral character (note particularly 'Rubretta'), and in the image of W watering 'the fleurettes of novembrance', there is both an instance of the repeated motif of Issy weeping, and a marked echo of Nuvoletta crying herself into the river (*FW* 158. 20–4, 159. 10–18). When Joyce came to

Izod, the Floras and Dante's Floral Ladies

reverse the double 'RRAAYYNNBBOOWW' into an 'iritic' version, one name in particular stands out amongst the Rainbow Girls:

> And these ways wend they. And those ways went they. Winnie, Olive and Beatrice, Nelly and Ida, Amy and Rue.[56] (*FW* 227. 13–14)

In this passage we therefore have a floral rainbow, associated with Beatrice, and running both forwards and back; in this respect, Joyce's text resonates strongly with the Beatrice of *Purgatorio* 30, whose 'nuvola di fiori' are thrown both 'dentro e di fuori' (*Purg.* 30. 30). Thus, through Beatrice, we can find a reading of Izod and the Floras that truly combines both sides of the Dantean feminine: the earthy eroticism of flowers, with the celestial figure of the rainbow. Indeed, Izod herself is clearly presented as a celestial lady through a wonderful passage of the 'Mime' in which Joyce equates voyeurism and astronomy:

> So warred he from first to last, forebanned and betweenly, a smuggler for lifer. Lift the blank ve veered as heil! Split the hvide and aye seize heaven! He knows for he's seen it in black and white through his eyetrompit trained upon jenny's and all that sort of thing which is dandymount to a clearobscure. (*FW* 247. 29–34)

There is a lexis of optical physics and astronomical observation throughout this passage, as Glugg contemplates spying on Izod in an attempt to at last determine the colour of her knickers; indeed, despite his eventual failure, Glugg seems to have at least hit upon the correct method to accomplish his task, as his notion of splitting white light ('hvide' being Danish for 'whites'), would have revealed the heliotropic shade of his sister's underwear.[57] Furthermore, Glugg associates observation of Izod with observation of the heavens: he views her through a telescope (with the suggestion of other visual aids such as a camera obscura) and seems to see the division of her white light into the seven shades of the rainbow (and the division of Issy into the seven Rainbow Girls) as tantamount to seizing (or 'seeing') heaven. Whilst there is certainly an important lexis of Luciferian

---

[56] Note here the similarity of the seven Rainbow Girls to the handmaidens of the Blessed Damozel:

> With her five handmaidens, whose names
> Are five sweet symphonies,
> Cecily, Gertrude, Magdalen,
> Margaret and Rosalys.
>   (ll. 105–8)

[57] On the various multilingual references to white in the passage quoted see McHugh, *Annotations to 'Finnegans Wake'*, 247.

188   'The Flower that Stars the Day'

exile in this short passage, ultimately Glugg's treatment of Izod as if she were a celestial phenomenon – a lady of stars and not of flowers – serves to strengthen the 'heavenly' side of the dual-natured Dantean feminine.

'If You Sprig Poplar You're Bound to Twig This': Learning Issy's Dantean Lesson

One of Joyce's most famous references to Dante occurs within the 'Mime': 'turning up and fingering over the most dantellising peaches in the lingerous longerous book of the dark' (*FW* 251. 23–4). And so, before relating the Dantean resonance of Issy's dual-natured femininity to the wider trajectory of community and exile in Joyce's engagement with Dante, we need to deal with the 'dantellising peaches' in front of us. Indeed, Joyce's explicit engagement with *Inferno* 5 and the figure of Francesca da Rimini at this point in *Finnegans Wake* further compounds the Dantean nature of Issy's femininity which we've already seen throughout the lyric elements of 'Nuvoletta' and the 'Mime'.

One of the most famous characters in the whole of the *Commedia* – particularly for a nineteenth-century readership – Francesca da Rimini is also perhaps the foremost example of the erotically dangerous feminine in Dante's work.[58] When Dante-pilgrim and Virgil encounter Francesca and Paolo – her unfortunate brother-in-law and lover – in the circle of the lustful in *Inferno* 5, her heritage in the lyric poetry of Dante's youth is evident through her complaint against love:

> Amor, che al cor gentil ratto s'apprende,
>   Prese costui della bella persona
>   Che mi fu tolta, e il modo ancor m'offende.
> Amor, che a nullo amato amar perdona,
>   Mi prese del costui piacer sì forte
>   Che, come vedi, ancor non m'abbandona.
> Amor condusse noi ad una morte:

['Love, which is swiftly kindled in the noble heart, seized this one [Paolo] for the lovely person [flesh] that was taken from me; and the manner still injures me. Love, which pardons no one loved from loving in return, seized me for his beauty so strongly that, as you see, it still does not abandon me. Love led us on to one death.'] (*Inf.* 5. 100–6)

---

[58] For a discussion of nineteenth-century responses to Francesca see Havely, *Dante's British Public*, 154–8, 165–77, 182–5.

Learning Issy's Dantean Lesson 189

Francesca's fate seems on one hand the realisation of the threat implicit in 'Deh, nuvoletta' that the lover will feel the 'pena dell 'altrui dolore' ['the pain of another's sorrow'] (l. 14); and yet, on the other, the horror of the effects of her love far outstrip the realm of the stilnovistic, as now Paolo and Francesca do not simply share a death but also a place in the second circle of Hell.[59] Through her combination of the world of Dante's lyric poetry with the eschatological context of the *Commedia*, Francesca da Rimini contrasts strongly with Beatrice, and represents a feminine figure who significantly heightens the dangerous eroticism of Dante's feminine equation, and one whose heritage in love poetry is re-emphasised by the role which the reading of an Arthurian romance played in her inevitable downfall:

> Quando leggemmo il disiato riso
> Esser basciato da cotanto amante,
> Questi, che mai da me non fia diviso,
> La bocca mi baciò tutto tremante:
> Galeotto fu il libro e chi lo scrisse:
> Quel giorno più non vi leggemmo avante.

['When we read that the yearned-for smile was kissed by so great a lover, he, who will never be separated from me, kissed my mouth all trembling. Galeotto was the book, and he who wrote it: that day we read no further.'] (*Inf.* 5. 133–8)

These themes of reading, eroticism and incest, with its fracturing and fragmenting effect upon the family (Paolo and Francesca's indiscretion does, after all, result in an act of fratricide on the part of Giovanni Malatesta, Paolo's brother and Francesca's husband) were all key to Joyce's engagement with *Inferno* 5 in *Finnegans Wake*, both in the 'Mime' and later in Book II. 2, with its transmogrification of Francesca's famous lines on the pain of remembered happiness:

> Nessun maggior dolore,
> Che ricordarsi del tempo felice
> Nella miseria; e ciò sa il tuo Dottore.

['There is no greater pain than to remember the happy time in wretchedness; and this your teacher knows.'] (*Inf.* 5. 121–3)

Which, in the Wakean version becomes:

---

[59] On Francesca's 'beautiful language' and her relation to lyric poetry see Barolini, *The Undivine Comedy*, 41–2.

And the greater the patrarc the griefer the pinch. And that's what your doctor knows.⁶⁰ (*FW* 269. 24–6)

Nowhere in the *Wake*, however, is Joyce's engagement with the figure of Francesca more sustained or more important to his conception of Issy's femininity than in the 'dantellising peaches' of the 'Mime':

> As for she could shake him. An oaf, no more. Still he'd be good tutor two in his big armschair lerningstoel and she be waxen in his hands. Turning up and fingering over the most dantellising peaches in the lingerous longerous book of the dark. Look at this passage about Galilleotto! I know it is difficult but when your goche I go dead. Turn now to this patch upon Smachiavelluti! Soot allours, he's sure to spot it! 'Twas ever so in monitorology since Headmaster Adam became Eva Harte's toucher, *in omnibus moribus et temporibus*, with man's mischief in his mind whilst her pupils swimmed too heavenlies, let his be exasperated, letters be blowed! I is a femaline person. O, of provocative gender. U unisingular case. (*FW* 251. 21–32)

The 'peaches' of this passage have received both tentative and rough handling from Joycean critics. Mary Reynolds simply claimed that, in his allusions to *Inferno* 5, 'Joyce runs the risk of reducing the sublime to the merely facetious'; or as Lucia Boldrini puts it, 'Francesca's story is brought down to the level of a teacher seducing his pupil.'⁶¹ The pedagogical overtones of the passage that both Reynolds and Boldrini highlight are also crucial to Shari Benstock's reading of Dante's presence. However, Benstock wants to view the readers who turn up and finger over the 'dantellising peaches' as being in some way Dante Alighieri and Beatrice Portinari, an interpretation that rests on her unsubstantiated claim that, at this point in the text, Issy has assumed the character of Beatrice and is ' "waxen" in the hands of her tutor, Denti Alligator himself'. Benstock's reading thus appropriates the reference to 'Denti Alligator' from nearly two hundred pages later in the *Wake* (*FW* 440. 6), and transplants it to speculate whether 'Denti is nibbling away at [Beatrice's] firmly shaped and tantalizing breasts', and even wonder whether 'it is possible that young Beatrice/Issy is fingering old Dante's testicles'.⁶²

Quite apart from these methodological problems, Benstock's reading of the passage highlights two interconnected misapprehensions that have

---
⁶⁰ Along with the clear reference to Petrarch, note also that Shem's shouldernote for this section of the 'night lessons' chapter reads '*Undante umoroso*' (*FW* 269. 21–2). See Atherton, *Books at the Wake*, 79–81; Boldrini, *Joyce, Dante*, 142–3.
⁶¹ Reynolds, *Joyce and Dante*, 216; Boldrini, *Joyce, Dante*, 207 n. 8.
⁶² Shari Benstock, 'The Genuine Christine: Psychodynamics of Issy', 179–80.

come to dominate readings of the 'dantellising peaches'. First, arising out of an uncomplicated understanding of the pedagogical dynamic, there is a tendency to see Dante and Beatrice as conforming to what Robert Polhemus termed 'the Lot complex': a relationship between an older man and a younger girl. In this view of the passage, the thinking seems to run that, as Dante is clearly fulfilling the 'tutor' role, then Beatrice must be both his intellectual and chronological junior.[63] However, as even the most cursory engagement with the *Vita Nuova* reveals, Dante is quite explicit about his age in relation to Beatrice's:

> sì che quasi dal principio del suo anno nono apparve a me, ed io la vidi quasi dalla fine del mio.
>
> [that is, she appeared to me almost in the beginning of her ninth year, and I first saw her near to the end of my ninth year.] (*VN* 2. 2)

The second misapprehension was concisely repudiated by Corinna del Greco Lobner: 'if a tutor–pupil relationship must be established, it is Beatrice who is Dante's tutor, never Dante of Beatrice'.[64] Thus, whilst previous critics have somewhat struggled to get their teeth into the 'dantellising peaches', perhaps by abandoning the unsustainable desire to read the presence of Dante himself (after all, 'dantellising' is an adjectival form of the poet's name) and instead focusing attention upon the textual allusion to *Inferno* 5 and its connection with the figure of Issy, we can find a new reading of this element of the 'Mime'.

Initially, the pedagogical nature of the passage – its references to tutors and headmasters and pupils – might seem confusing; after all, this is the 'night games' chapter of the *Wake*, not the 'night lessons'. However, the interest in textual exegesis and interpretation within the passage ('Look at this passage about Galilleotto! I know it is difficult', *FW* 251. 25) forms part of Izod's wider concern with hermeneutic strategies. Earlier she raised the issue of textual exegesis: 'Underwoods spells bushment's business. So if you sprig poplar you're bound to twig this' (*FW* 248. 28–9), and this foregrounding of issues of understanding and interpretation resonates with the *Commedia*'s famous apostrophes:

> Aguzza qui, Lettor, ben gli occhi al vero,
> Chè il velo è ora ben tanto sottile,
> Certo, che il trapassar dentro è leggiero.

---

[63] See Robert M. Polhemus, 'Dantellising Peaches and Miching Daddy, the Gushy Old Goof: The Browning Case and *Finnegans Wake*', 81.
[64] Corinna del Greco Lobner, 'Letters to the Editor', 235.

[Sharpen here, reader, your eyes to the truth, for the veil is now surely so fine that passing within is easy.] (*Purg.* 8. 19–21)

However, whereas Dante's apostrophes are directed towards the reader, Issy's hermeneutic appeal, 'if you sprig poplar you're bound to twig this' (*FW* 248. 29), seems to be addressed to another character within the text of the 'Mime'. The arboreal lexis that surrounds Issy's statement hints at a possible identity for the person who is meant to 'twig' her meaning: in *Finnegans Wake* the tree is an emblem and sometime avatar of Shem, and so the repetition of treeish words in Izod's plea for interpretation suggests that her statement is directed to Glugg. If indeed it is Glugg who is implicated in her appeal, then he would also seem to be addressed by Izod's earlier statement, 'If my tutor here is cut out for an oldeborre I'm Flo, shy of peeps, you know' (*FW* 248. 16–17). While the presence within the 'Mime' of an older, professorial character (and a possible avatar of HCE) has been suggested, I think it's reasonable to assume that the associations in this earlier passage of the text between the tutor and Shem, and Issy, Shem and a Dantean exegetical apostrophe, might indicate that the 'tutor' with whom Izod imagines 'turning up and fingering over' the 'dantellising peaches' is also a form of her brother.[65]

The realisation that Izod has already shown an interest in hermeneutics, and that her exegetical process may be connected to her brother as 'tutor', holds an important implication for reading the sexually desirous connotations of the 'dantellising peaches' passage. If the 'tutor' imagined by the prospective form of Izod's musing that 'still he'd be good tutor two in his big armschair lerningstoel and she be waxen in his hands' (*FW* 251. 21–3) is seen to be Glugg, then an exclusively patriarchal approach to navigating the incestuous discourse of the *Wake* is unsustainable.[66] Instead, by reading the passage as an explicit engagement with both the text and hermeneutics of the Paolo and Francesca episode of *Inferno* 5, Issy's concern over interpretation and reading strategies, her presentation as a feminine figure of desire, and the incestuous formulation of this desire, can all be reconciled. After all, whilst Paolo and Francesca may live in the popular imagination as star-crossed lovers, they were – from a legal standpoint – also brother and sister.

---

[65] On the 'Professor' see Nash, 'The Logic of Incest', 435–56.
[66] Shelton, for instance, sees Issy's concern with being 'understood' as an attempt to reassert her own narrative in the face of its appropriation by an incestuous, paternal figure; see *Joyce and the Narrative Structure of Incest*, 3–34.

Although blown about by the 'bufera infernal' ['infernal whirlwind'] (*Inf.* 5. 31) that punishes the lustful, Paolo and Francesca's undoing was not primarily a matter of sex but rather, as Mary Carruthers has argued, one of reading.[67] In her long explanation and attempted justification of their sin (a possible analogue for the 'tantalizing speeches' that we can see within 'dantellising peaches'), Francesca makes it plain where the problem lies:

> Noi leggevamo un giorno per diletto
> Di Lancilotto, come amor lo strinse:
> Soli eravamo e sanza alcun sospetto.
> Per più fiate gli occhi ci sospinse
> Quella lettura, e scolorocci il viso;
> Ma solo un punto fu quel che ci vinse.
> Quando leggemmo il disiato riso
> Esser baciato da cotanto amante,
> Questi, che mai da me non fia diviso,
> La bocca mi baciò tutto tremante:
> Galeotto fu il libro e chi lo scrisse:
> Quel giorno più non vi leggemmo avante.

['We were reading one day, for pleasure, of Lancelot, how Love beset him; we were alone and without any suspicion. Many times that reading drove our eyes together and turned our faces pale; but one point alone was the one that overpowered us. When we read that the yearned-for smile was kissed by so great a lover, he, who will never be separated from me, kissed my mouth all trembling. Galeotto was the book and he who wrote it: that day we read there no further.'] (*Inf.* 5. 127–38)

Whilst it's often claimed that Francesca is here trying to defer her moral responsibility for the incestuous adultery onto the book itself, in reality she is entirely honest about where she went wrong: 'ma solo un punto fu quel che ci vinse'. This 'punto' that undid the lovers was, as Mary Carruthers has brilliantly observed, just that: a punctuation mark. Paolo and Francesca's guilt lay in an 'incomplete reading' of the Lancelot romance: they stopped reading at the kiss between Lancelot and Guinevere and so missed the twist in the tale in which the lovers are immediately discovered by the Lady of Malehault and brought to ruin, just as Paolo and Francesca are by their murderous brother/husband Giovanni.[68] By failing to read past the punctuation mark in the romance text and into the next clause, Paolo and

---

[67] See Carruthers, *The Book of Memory*, 230–3.
[68] Carruthers, *The Book of Memory*, 232–3.

Francesca adopted a reading strategy that cherry-picked the 'sexy' part of the romance narrative, and left behind the moral.

How, then, does Paolo and Francesca's flawed reading of the Lancelot romance impact on a reading of Joyce's 'dantellising peaches'? Well, already we have seen in the identity of the 'tutor' character with whom Izod imagines reading the 'lingerous longerous book of the dark', a parallel with Paolo and Francesca: just as Francesca read about Galeotto with her brother-in-law, so Izod reads Dante's rendition of Francesca's recounting of this original reading with her own brother, Glugg. Similarly, just as Francesca claims that it was their act of reading that transformed them from brother and sister to lovers, so too the 'dantellising peaches' passage represents an explicit statement of the latent eroticism surrounding Izod and Glugg in the 'Mime'. The 'dantellising peaches' passage of the *Wake* represents a reiteration of the Paolo and Francesca episode, in which elements of the earlier situation repeatedly recur.[69]

A further level of recursion within the *Wake* at this point reveals another intertext for the 'dantellising peaches' episode and returns us to the issue of the nineteenth-century mediation of Joyce's reading of Dante. The key lexis surrounding the reference to Dante and the 'book of the dark' ('peaches', 'lingerous', 'longerous') derives from the third canto of Leigh Hunt's *The Story of Rimini* (1816), which was itself a retelling of the Paolo and Francesca story:

> And Paulo, by degrees, gently embrac'd
> With one permitted arm her lovely waist;
> And both their cheeks, like peaches on a tree,
> Came with a touch together thrillingly,
> And o'er the book they hung, and nothing said,
> And every lingering page grew longer as they read.[70]
> (*The Story of Rimini*, Canto III, 442–7)

It seems quite apparent. then, given Hunt's use of the image of the lovers' cheeks as touching peaches, and the 'lingerous longerous' nature of their reading, that *The Story of Rimini* is actually the account of Paolo

---

[69] Recursion – a form of infinitely extending self-repetition – is a concept pertinent to optical physics and commonly associated with a house of mirrors and illusion. It thus seems a particularly appropriate device through which to explore Issy's role within both the passage at hand, and the *Wake* in general. For the earlier discussion of recursion in the poetics of Infernal metamorphosis, see above, p. 103.

[70] Leigh Hunt, *The Poetical Works of Leigh Hunt*, 28; I am grateful to Nick Havely for first suggesting this allusion. For more on the importance of Hunt's *The Story of Rimini* to the English reception of *Inferno* 5 see Milbank, *Dante and the Victorians*, 21–4; and Timothy Webb, 'Stories of Rimini: Leigh Hunt, Byron and the Fate of Francesca', 31–54.

and Francesca most immediate to the text of the 'Mime', and that Hunt's reworking of *Inferno* 5 is an important and unacknowledged element in the chain of recursion extending from Paolo and Francesca's first reading of the Lancelot romance to Izod and Glugg's adventure with the 'lingerous longerous book of the dark' (*FW* 251. 24).[71]

The recursion of the Paolo and Francesca story extends to the reading strategies employed by the Wakean characters as well. Izod's notion of 'turning up and fingering over the most dantellising peaches' perfectly mirrors Paolo and Francesca's flawed reading strategy, only this time it is *Inferno* 5 (or its recursion in *The Story of Rimini*) that is being incompletely read; just as Paolo and Francesca read about Lancelot and Guinevere 'per diletto' ['for pleasure'], so too are Izod and Glugg interested only in the 'peaches'. Indeed, Joyce seems to point us directly to the pitfalls of this approach when he shows Izod and Glugg failing to make the connections a perceptive reader like Carruthers has made, and skipping on through the Italian literary tradition in search of more such highlights:

> Look at this passage about Galilleotto! I know it is difficult but when your goche I go dead. Turn now to this patch upon Smacchiavelluti! Soot allours, he's sure to spot it! (*FW* 251. 25–7)

The notion that there are 'dantellising peaches' to be extracted from a book whose very description encourages taking a 'longerous' time to 'linger' over is obviously relevant to any impatient reader of *Finnegans Wake*. In this respect, the echoes between the Lancelot romance, Dante's *Inferno*, Hunt's *The Story of Rimini* and Joyce's own book extend to become a form of infinite recursion, in which the reader of the *Wake* itself is implicated in the nesting structure of reading strategies, and given a playful warning as to the dangers of skipping through Joyce's text and not acceding to his demand that '[they] should devote [their] whole life to reading my works' (*JJ* 703).

If Joyce thus presents Issy and Shem in the 'dantellising peaches' passage of the 'Mime' as a recursive reiteration of Paolo and Francesca, what significance does this hold for the presentation of Issy's dual femininity and

---

[71] No doubt Joyce's interest in using Hunt's poem at this point in the *Wake* was strengthened by the way in which Hunt actively 'corrupts' the Dantean original, recasting it in Arthurian terms. In Hunt's poem Francesca falls in love with Paolo when she mistakes him for his brother, with whom she already knows she is to be married. This motif of mistaken identity was to be central to Tennyson's rendition of the Lancelot and Guinevere story in *Idylls of the King*, and it is easy to see how Joyce would have delighted in the way that, through the pander of Hunt's poem, Tennyson's retelling of Francesca's Lancelot romance could cross-pollinate with Dante's original version within the textual thicket of *Finnegans Wake*.

her position within the community of the family in *Finnegans Wake*? On one hand, the link to Francesca and her legally incestuous relationship with Paolo presents another evocation of the erotic side of Dante's feminine equation, albeit within a more dangerous context than the ladies of the *Rime*; an intensification of eroticism and its perils that Joyce seems to point to through his appropriation of a phrase from Edith Thompson's letters, 'I know it is difficult but when your goche I go dead' (*FW* 251. 25–6).[72] Through her connection to Francesca, the potential for destructive eroticism latent in Dante's 'floral ladies' is brought more fully into focus within Issy's femininity. However, as seen earlier in the 'Mime' – and in the 'Nuvoletta' passage – one side of the feminine equation is usually balanced by the close proximity of the other. Thus, the presence of Issy's simultaneous spirituality and eroticism – her celestial and floral natures – at play in the 'dantellising peaches' passage, would seem to be indicated by the pedagogical image of Adam and Eve:

> 'Twas ever so in monitorology since Headmaster Adam became Eva Harte's toucher, *in omnibus moribus et temporibus*, with man's mischief in his mind whilst her pupils swimmed too heavenlies, let his be exaspirated, letters be blowed! I is a femaline person. O, of provocative gender. U is unisingular case.[73] (*FW* 251. 28–32)

Here, then, is both another example of recursion (Adam is Eve's teacher, who has her own 'pupils') and a Dantean image of celestial eyes and vision: 'her pupils swimmed too heavenlies'.[74]

Yet, if Issy, as 'Eva Harte', is a heavenly lady, she is equally the Eve of Genesis, iterated out of a man made from earth and dust, as indicated by the repeated references to breath ('exaspirated', 'blowed') and its association with the Ru'ak that first brought life to Adam (Genesis 2:7–25). Indeed, in this relation to Eve, there is an important development of the dual-natured femininity of Issy; she appears to define herself through her debt to Adam, her 'IOU' for the mingling of the heavenly and earthly that occurs in the biblical account of the creation of woman. This emergence of Eve within the femininity of Issy, with the possible reconciliation of the

---

[72] For the Thompson and Bywaters murder trial as an intertext for the 'dantellising peaches' passage of the 'Mime' see McHugh, *Annotations to 'Finnegans Wake'*, 251.
[73] We should also note that, in an echo of Glugg's astronomical observation of Izod, Dante's Galeotto is earlier transformed into 'Galilleotto', with its clear echo of the father of astronomy.
[74] If we were to follow Benstock and Polhemus in wanting to see a historical, age-differentiated pedagogical relationship at work within the 'dantellising peaches' passage (a desire that presumably originates in the reference to 'Headmaster Adam'), then 'Abel lord of all our haloease' (*FW* 237. 34–5), or Abelard and Heloise, might make a more profitable medieval example of a 'toucher'/teacher to investigate than Dante and Beatrice.

Issy and the End of Exile 197

heavenly and the earthly that she offers (and her heritage as one of the two original biblical exiles), suggests the way in which the dual-natured feminine and its position within the family might impact our reading of the trajectory of exile and community in Joyce's engagement with Dante. The two sides of Issy's Dantean feminine equation inform the previous Dantean dialogues within Joyce's work and continue to complicate Joyce's initial reading of Dantean exile, suggesting a form of reconciliation and the re-establishment of community that builds upon, but ultimately departs from, Dante's conceptions of *peregrinatio* and *communitas*.

'Can That Sobstuff Whingeywilly!': Issy and the End of Exile

In the figure of Beatrice as encountered in *Purgatorio* 30, Dante seemed to reconcile the two elements of her feminine heritage, elements that were held in tension in the other examples of women in Dante's work, most particularly in the case of his diminutive lyric ladies. To a large extent, this reconciliation takes place through Beatrice's death; in a process begun in *Vita Nuova* 23, when she transformed into 'una nuvoletta', and completed by her descent in the 'nuvola di fiori' (*Purg.* 30. 28), Beatrice seems to have unified her nature, embracing both her spiritual and erotic aspects. That this transformation cannot be considered a simple purging of the earthly and a transition into a purely spiritual figure is clear from Dante-pilgrim's reaction to her advent:

> E lo spirito mio, che già cotanto
> Tempo era stato ch'alla sua presenza
> Non era di stupor tremando, affranto,
> Senza degli occhi aver più conoscenza,
> Per occulta virtù, che da lei mosse,
> D'antico amor sentì la gran potenza.

[And my spirit, which already for so long a time had not known in her presence the awe that overcame it with trembling, without having more knowledge through the eyes, because of hidden power that moved from her, felt the great force of ancient love.] (*Purg.* 30. 34–9)

The Earthly Paradise where Dante-pilgrim is reunited with his beloved is a realm underwritten by Cavalcantian love poetry, and his earlier meeting with the figure of Matelda (whom he encounters almost as an avatar of Beatrice, anticipating the narrative climax of the reunion) derives in large part from Cavalcanti's poem 'In un boschetto trova' pastorella'.[75] Therefore, despite

---

[75] On Cavalcanti's influence on Matelda and the Earthly Paradise see Teodolinda Barolini, *Dante's*

her otherworldly nature, in the moment of her appearance in *Purgatorio* 30 Beatrice balances the eroticism of her stilnovistic presentation in the *Rime* and the *Vita Nuova*, with her role as a celestial lady, one of the 'tre donne benedette' who rescue Dante from the dark wood. Only as the pilgrim and his lady ascend into the *Paradiso* does Beatrice begin to lose this equilibrium, becoming more and more the purely spiritual figure. This simultaneity of feminine identity – the attempt to hold the halves of the Dantean equation in balance – is characteristic of Izod's presentation within the 'Mime', where she strives to embody both her role as a celestial lady of stars and the floral heritage of her eroticism, a task made all the more difficult by her pervading familial identity as sister to Glugg and Chuff.

However, whilst Izod lacks the transcendent spirituality of Dante's Christian context, and thus has a harder time than Beatrice in achieving equilibrium, she shares a further aspect with Dante's 'leading lady' by assuming a dual role as both a locus of exile and alienation, and a locus of reconciliation and community. It would be tempting to try to simply map this further dichotomy in Issy and Beatrice's characters onto the already-established duality of the Dantean feminine, seeing the exilic aspects of the characters as deriving from their eroticism, and the reconciliatory side from their celestial natures. However, as with Beatrice in the Terrestrial Paradise, postulating a firm dichotomy between the different aspects of femininity would be reductive and textually unjustifiable; as here in the 'Mime', unlike in the earlier discussions of *Portrait* and *Ulysses*, there is no dominant Stephen Dedalus engaged in a process of reductive self-fashioning and poetically compromised re-presentation. Instead, by examining how Joyce followed Dante in creating a female figure who holds both division and reconciliation in tension within herself, and attempts to find a way to balance both elements of her character, we can find a wider significance to Issy's portrayal within the 'Mime', revealing her as a Dantean figure who holds important implications for the reading of *Finnegans Wake* as a whole.

That Izod acts as a locus of exile is immediately apparent from the form that the children's games take; as Glugg fails each time to guess the colour of Izod and the Flora's underwear, he flees, feeling rejected by the female figures: 'He was feeling so funny and floored for the cue, all over which girls as he don't know whose hue' (*FW* 227. 23–5). Glugg then transforms

---

Poets, 135, 149–53; for a contrasting argument that interestingly opens with a quotation of the 'Nausicaa' chapter of *Ulysses* see Patrizia Grimaldi Pizzorno, 'Matelda's Dance and the Smile of the Poets', 115–32.

Issy and the End of Exile 199

Izod's playful rejection into a form of exile modelled upon the mass Irish emigrations of the late nineteenth and early twentieth centuries, as well as on the biography of St Patrick:

> Cross of a coppersmith bishop! He would split. He do big squeal like holy Trichepatte. Seek hells where from yank islanders the petriote's absolation. Mocknitza! Genik! He take skiff come first dagrene day overwide tumbler, rough and dark, till when bow of the shower show of the bower with three shirts and a wind. (*FW* 228. 5–10)

Amongst the complex polyvalent allusions of the phrase 'seek hells where from yank islanders', there may be a reference to Dante's quest to 'seek hell', scattered among the shadows of Nazism ('sieg heil') and nineteenth-century Irish nationalism ('young Irelanders'). Further evidence of the Dantean influence on the supposed 'exile' of Glugg can be seen in Joyce's reference to his own, self-fashioning exile in the 'unredeemed' lands of Austrian Italy, 'catch the Paname-Turricum and regain that absendee tarry easty, his città immediata' (*FW* 228. 22–3).

Izod's role as a potential generator of exile and alienation continues throughout the 'Mime', most notably in the passage in which she seeks to call Glugg back from his exile, only to reject him once again:

> When (pip!) a message interfering intermitting interskips from them (pet!) on herzian waves, (call her venicey names! call her a stell!) a butterfly from her zipclasped handbag, a wounded dove astarted from, escaping out her forecotes. Isle wail for yews, O doherlynt! The poetesser. And around its scorced cap she has twilled a twine of flame to let the laitiest know she's marrid. (*FW* 232. 9–15)

Here, in a passage full of words with a Dantean resonance (particularly the instruction to 'call her a stell', to call her a star), Izod assumes the role of the lover calling Glugg back from the exile into which she herself has sent him. This positioning of the female figure as both lover and 'exiler' seems on one hand to embrace a classically Dantean trope of erotic, subjective exile, recalling not only the equal-parts alluring and distressing ladies of the *Rime* and the *Vita Nuova*, but also the strong eroticism of several of Dante's *canzoni* of exile such as 'Tre donne intorno al cor mi son venute' and the *canzone montanina*.[76] However, in his ongoing presentation of Izod within the 'Mime' (and Issy within the *Wake* in general) Joyce

---

[76] On the role of love poetry in the rhetoric and experience of exile by Dante and his contemporaries see Catherine Keen, 'Images of Exile: Distance and Memory in the Poetry of Cino da Pistoia', 21–36.

blurs any such neat associations between his concept of the feminine and this aspect of Dantean femininity. This blurring is achieved in the 'Mime' through two striking techniques; firstly, whilst presenting Izod within the Dantean frame of the erotic lady, he also positions her in the role usually assumed by the male lover in Dante's poetry:

> Poor Isa sits a glooming so gleaming in the gloaming; the tincelles a touch tarnished wind no lovelinoise awound her swan's. Hey, lass! Woefear gleam she so glooming, this pooripathete I solde? Her beauman's gone of a cool. (*FW* 226. 4–7)

This view of Issy as a moping, spurned lover represents a fundamental inversion of the Dantean gender roles of erotic exile; Izod is, in the 'Mime', both lover and rejecter, both banisher and exiled. Furthermore, in what represents the *Wake*'s starkest challenge to Dantean self-fashioning, Izod is also portrayed as fatally puncturing the exilic rhetoric that Glugg spins around himself, asking him:

> Is you zealous of mes, brother? Did you boo moiety lowd? You suppoted to be the on conditiously rejected? Satanly, lade! Can that sobstuff, whingeywilly! Stop up, mavrone, and sit in my lap, Pepette, though I'd much rather not. (*FW* 232. 21–5)

This ridiculing of Glugg's posture as 'exile' (a sentiment from which you can't help but feel that Stephen Dedalus, that other 'Satanly lad', might have benefited) occurs in the text of the 'Mime' some six lines after Izod's own act of posturing as the lover welcoming home the exiled Glugg with a 'wounded dove' (*FW* 232. 12). In this respect, then, we can again see the duality of Issy's presentation as the lady of flowers and the lady of stars, but we also find an increasingly explicit statement of the compromised rhetorical nature of exile as a mode of alienation that Joyce had started to explore within the poetics of *Ulysses*. Izod seems straining to escape the double-bind of her dual nature, to 'can that sobstuff' and move beyond the pattern of exile and return into a more meaningful form of reconciliation and community.

Indeed, elsewhere in the 'Mime' Izod attempts to find a way to balance the two sides of her nature more directly; however, whereas Beatrice finds brief equilibrium during the ascendancy of her spiritual nature between the end of the *Purgatorio* and the start of the *Paradiso*, Izod's attempts are decidedly more earthy:

> My bellyswain's a twalf whulerusspower though he knows as much how to man a wife as Dunckle Dalton of matching wools. Shake hands through

Issy and the End of Exile

the thicketloch! Sweet swanwater! My other is mouthfilled. This kissing wold's full of killing fellows kneeling voyantly to the cope of heaven. And somebody's coming, I feel for a fect. (*FW* 248. 21–6)

The key to Issy's thinking here is the line 'shake hands through the thicketloch!', a reference to the events in 1492 when the warring earls of Ormond and Kildare, 'ceased their quarrel when they shook hands through the hole in [the] Chapter House door of St Patrick's Cathedral'.[77] This image of the reconciliation of warring male factions 'through the thicketloch' has its (already substantial) sexual connotations strengthened by Izod's later revelation that:

> 'Twas my lord of Glendalough benedixed the gape for me that time at Long Entry, commanding the approaches to my intimast innermost. Look how they're browthered! (*FW* 248. 30–32)

The lord of Glendalough was the abbot of St Kevin's Monastery (and Kevin is an avatar of Shaun), suggesting that Izod is conceiving of her own body, and most specifically her genitals (her 'gape'), as a locus of reconciliation for the warring brothers of Glugg and Chuff, Shem and Shaun. Just as Beatrice finds reconciliation of her femininity through the tension of her erotic heritage in the Terrestrial Paradise and her assumption of a spiritual, guiding role in the *Paradiso*, so Issy attempts to reconcile her own character by becoming both sister and lover to her brothers. Were reconciliation between these two figures to be achieved through Izod's sexual favours then, on all levels of the text, from the archetypal interactions across the whole landscape of the *Wake*, to the more immediate dynamics of the children's game, a healing solidification of the community of the family could take place. If the angel and the devil were not opposed, the ongoing, cyclical process of exile and return created by the rules of the game of 'colours' would be ended.

Izod's desire to reconcile her own erotic and spiritual natures, and at the same time resolve the disputes of her two brothers and thus heal her community, posits a physical act of 'coming together' that resonates with the Circean poetics of re-membering in its potential to 'rewrite' the narrative of their conflict into one of peace and wholeness.[78] However, it is difficult to see this apparent final shift away from exile and withdrawal and towards an expression of participation and community, in an entirely Dantean light. In *Paradiso* 15–17, Dante's ancestor Cacciaguida sets out a

---

[77] McHugh, *Annotations to 'Finnegans Wake'*, 248.
[78] See above, pp. 159–60.

social prescription for the problems of Florence, a view of the ideal civic society in which 'women play an important part [...] as indicators of the moral wellbeing of the whole social order'.[79] This positioning of women at the heart of both the family and the commune of Florence is clearly expressed by the contrast Cacciaguida draws between the life of women in the city of his era and those of Dante's day:

> L'uno vegghiava a studio della culla,
> E consolando usava l'idioma
> Che pria li padri e le madri trastulla;
> L'altra, traendo alla rocca la chioma,
> Favoleggiava con la sua famiglia
> De' Troiani, di Fiesole, e di Roma.

['This one watched late in her care of the cradle, and, comforting, used the idiom that first delights fathers and mothers; this other, drawing the strands from the distaff, told with her household tales of the Trojans, of Fiesole, and of Rome.'] (*Par.* 15. 121–6)

Whilst certainly not envisioning a scene of such domestic harmony as this, Izod's desire to act as a place of healing for her fractious family does recall Cacciaguida's views in the way that it resituates the female figure at the heart of the family unit, and thus by extension at the heart of the social community. However, it is difficult to conceive of Issy's femininity as a route through which the characters of *Finnegans Wake* might enter into the kind of transcendent social equilibrium that was essential to Dante's teleological project in the *Commedia*; Issy's prospective reconciliation of her dual feminine nature through her bodily and sexual peacemaking doesn't seem to offer anything approaching the medieval idea of radically egalitarian *communitas* that lay at the heart of Dante's understanding of the ideal community.[80]

This divergence from the Dantean conception of reconciliation and wholeness is immediately obvious when we consider that, in her positioning of Shaun as 'commanding the approaches to my intimast innermost' (*FW* 248. 31–2), Issy's plan more closely resembles the attitude towards the feminine displayed by Venedico Caccianemico in *Inferno* 18 than Cacciaguida's. Caccianemico (whose name – 'Caccia-nemico' – with its strong echoes of nemesis and enmity, signals his adversity with Cacciaguida), a Bolognese politician whom Dante-pilgrim encounters in

---

[79] Keen, *Dante and the City*, 207–13.
[80] See Mazzotta, *Dante, Poet of the Desert*, 107–46.

An Irreconcilable Resolution 203

the first *bolgia*, was willing to go to such lengths to please his factional patron that he pimped his own sister:

> Io fui colui, che la Ghisola bella
> Condussi a far la voglia del Marchese
> Come che suoni la sconcia novella.
>
> [It was I who induced the beautiful Ghisola to do the marchese's will, however they tell the shameful tale.] (*Inf.* 18. 55–7; translation modified)

This episode of the sexual exploitation of a sister, with its obviously destructive and infernal repercussions for Caccianemico (not to mention poor Ghisola), is particularly apposite to Izod's scheme to reconcile Shem and Shaun through her pimping by the latter, the 'lord of Glendalough' who controls access to her 'intimast innermost', and indeed Izod's hopes that they will 'shake hands through the thicketloch' (*FW* 248. 23) is indicative of the wider problem with Issy's attempts to act as a healer of her community.

'Loud, Heap Miseries Upon Us Yet Entwine Our Arts With Laughters Low': An Irreconcilable Resolution

At the end of the 'Mime', as the children are called inside by their parents, Joyce provides a description of their return that resonates with the trajectory this study has been tracing:

> For they are now tearing, that is, teartoretorning. Too soon are coming tasbooks and goody, hominy bread and bible bee, with jaggery-yo to juju-jaw, Fine's French phrases from the Grandmère des Grammaires and bothered parsenaps from the Four Massores, Mattatias, Marusias, Lucanias, Jokinias. (*FW* 256. 17–21)

In *Finnegans Wake*, there is no Christian telos as in the *Commedia*, no 'hominy bread and bible bee' to guarantee a happy conclusion, and hence there can be no lasting reconciliation of the discourse of exile and return that lies behind the fragmentation of the *Wake*'s family. As Joyce indicates in this passage, whilst Issy might long to provide a resolution to her brother's disputes and thus heal her community, she can never achieve this desire, as every return is also simultaneously a 'tearing' and a source of returning tears ('teartoretorning'). Indeed, as if to underscore this point, as the boys are gathered back into the house, and the framing play of 'The Mime of Mick, Nick and the Maggies' comes to a close, Joyce gives us a final view of a familiar character:

> That little cloud, a nibulissa, still hangs isky. Singabed sulks before slumber.
> Light at night has an alps on his druckhouse. (*FW* 256. 33–5)

Despite her best efforts, Issy still remains 'a little cloud', Nuvoletta trapped between the celestial and the earthly, unable to truly reconcile the two halves of her Dantean femininity. In the futility of Issy's attempts to achieve an equilibrium between the two aspects of the dual femininity so clearly foregrounded in the text of the chapter, it seems as if Joyce is expressing a fundamental suspicion of the totalising conception of Dantean *communitas*. Perhaps influenced by the horrifying positions of inter-war political movements, Joyce reminds the reader of the *Wake* that a homogeneous, 'holistic' society cannot be achieved without the damaging or destruction of some of its members. Issy's complex femininity cannot be reconciled into the structure of her family, nor her community's discord healed, without the prospect of her further wounding through an incestuous association with her brothers.

In various ways, then, Issy's feminine identity is intertextually determined, constructed through her inclusion within a textual community that, whilst most strongly resonant with the poetry of Dante, was mediated by such nineteenth-century Dantean figures as Rossetti, Yeats and Leigh Hunt. The view of Issy that emerges from these poetic intertexts has offered a new language through which to discuss her, one that, in its grounding in demonstrable and complex intertextuality, resists the urge to reduce her to the level of an archetype, or to encounter her through notions of psychosis and fragmentation. Given the inherent tension of the duality of the Dantean feminine, there is no need to speculate existentially distinct identities for Issy's various avatars; rather, we can accept her as a complex, contradictory whole, and allow her identity to coalesce in its very irreconcilability. This perspective on Issy also puts her back into the community of the *Wake* in her own right, not simply through her determination by her parents, and in the compromised form of this involvement we are returned to the issues of liminality and uneasiness with which this study began.

Issy's dual-natured femininity and her position within the family of *Finnegans Wake* represents the final stage of the trajectory of exile and community in Joyce's engagement with Dante. The tensions inherent in Dante's position of liminality and 'uneasy orthodoxy' that triggered this trajectory in Joyce's reading have increasingly disrupted and unsettled his initial choice of an exilic path. The scepticism towards both subjective alienation and 'heroic' exile that emerged towards the end of *A Portrait of the Artist as a Young Man* grew and strengthened in *Ulysses* through its Dantean poetics of Infernal metamorphosis and re-membering. Issy's self-destructive attempt to intervene in, and so 'heal', her community, and the criticism of totalising notions of stability and wholeness that this suggests, would also seem to unsettle the other pole of the trajectory. Through the figure of Stephen Dedalus and his Dantean poetics, Joyce explored the naivety of simply absenting oneself from the difficulties and compromises of life within a community through the notion of 'exile'. Equally, in his representation of Issy he highlighted the danger of subsuming identity within a communal structure, a process that would seem to simply engender further destruction and rupture.

Yet to see a scepticism towards both exile and community as the endpoint of Joyce's Dantean reading, and thus an implicit rejection of the teleological wholeness of the *Paradiso* and the 'poema sacro' that ultimately allowed Dante to poetically surmount his exile, is not to suggest a simple form of nihilism; this is not the exchanging of religious certitude for directionless secular fragmentation and despair – far from it. Rather than simply eschewing the prospect of *communitas*, Joyce's Dantean path through the *Wake* emphasises instead the importance of embracing the *peregrinatio*, the difficult, compromised process of life and living, and of finding through life's continuing irreconcilability its purpose and enjoyment; or, as the final invocation of the 'Mime' puts it, 'Loud, heap miseries upon us yet entwine our arts with laughters low!' (*FW* 259. 7–8).

Joyce's first encounter with Dante was coloured by the competing demands of opposing orthodoxies and the poet's uneasy position between them. His lifelong engagement with Dante did not arise from simply 'picking a side' and shutting down the contradictions and complications in his reading, but rather through embracing the creative possibilities of such a compromised presentation. Similarly, Issy's tangled position in her community urges the living-through of the often painful but necessary – and potentially joyous – contradictions and complications of life. Issy's Dantean femininity clarifies the celebration of difference, dissonance and discord within *Finnegans Wake*, a dissonant resonance that challenges the satisfying, holistic conclusion of a *Paradiso*, finding in the ongoing – and very un-Dantean – brokenness of its central family, the key to the continuing power and vitality that moves the world.

Epilogue

Joyce inherited a number of versions of Dante. These mediations, shaped by nineteenth-century writers like Rossetti and movements such as the Risorgimento, led to his view of Dante as uneasily orthodox: able to move between contrasting and competing discourses, and to negotiate poetic space within otherwise stifling stringencies. In this way, Dante became Joyce's 'inside man', a collaborator to work alongside and a figure deeply implicated in the poetics of his work; in contrast to the monumental constructions and authoritative invocations of such other modernists as T. S. Eliot or Ezra Pound. But did 'Joyce's Dante' have a life after Joyce? Was his version of the poet inherited and transformed by later writers as he had inherited and transformed the 'Dantes' of the nineteenth century? Whilst this isn't the right place to answer such questions in full, we can perhaps sketch some directions in which future enquiries might proceed, and suggest a few likely suspects as the inheritors of Joyce's 'Dante with a difference'.

Although innumerable writers since Joyce have drawn on Dante, interestingly many of those who have tackled him in forms that resonate with the Joycean approach have been English-language poets.[1] For instance, the notion of exile as a formative mode of alienation shaped Ted Hughes's reading of both authors; writing to his friend Lucas Myers in 1958, Hughes observed that 'the way to really develop [*sic*] as a writer is to make yourself a political outcast [...] this is how Dante developed into Dante, & Joyce into Joyce.'[2] Whilst this formulation of the effect of exile on poetic development was based on Hughes's encounter with Herbert Gorman's biography (of which he observed, 'I never read a more stupid book'), his remark certainly indicates an

---

[1] On twentieth- and twenty-first-century English prose responses see Havely, *Dante's British Public*, 274–8.
[2] Ted Hughes, *Letters of Ted Hughes*, 120.

Epilogue 207

awareness of the same kind of dynamics traced through the trajectory of this study.[3]

However, whilst Hughes drew on Dante in such works as *Birthday Letters*, a more likely poetic candidate as the inheritor of Joyce's Dante would be Derek Walcott. Dante has been a recurrent concern in Walcott's work ever since his second collection, *Epitaph for the Young: XII Cantos*, was published in 1949 and, whilst Dante's presence can be detected throughout many of Walcott's subsequent works, its most obviously Joycean formulation is his long poem *Omeros*.[4] Telling the story of the Caribbean fishermen Achille and Philoctete, *Omeros* employs a structure of Homeric parallel that is clearly in dialogue with T. S. Eliot's famous formulation of the 'mythical method' of *Ulysses*.[5] However, Walcott's Joycean myth is framed within a tercet form that derives from the *terza rima* of the *Commedia*, and the poem is studded with Dantean encounters and intertextual resonances.[6] Thus, in Walcott's interrogation of literary canonicity through the exploration of life on the colonial margins, Joyce and Dante are drawn into productive, poetic alignment.

Nevertheless, the leading inheritor of Joyce's Dante, and a figure whose engagement with the poet was perhaps the most sustained and reflective of all modern poets, was Seamus Heaney.[7] There is a long tradition of Dantean engagement in modern Irish poetry, in which poets such as Thomas Kinsella, Ciaran Carson and Bernard O'Donoghue (not to mention the looming shade of W.B. Yeats) all figure prominently. Yet Dante was even more crucial to Heaney's poetic project, and no other engagement so clearly reveals the shaping influence of Joyce, most particularly in his sense of Dante as a collaborator and negotiator between the competing orthodoxies and stringencies of Irish life.[8] Despite his arguably harsher experience of liminality and marginality as a Catholic growing up in mid-twentieth-century Ulster, Heaney himself pointed out the resonance

---

[3] Hughes, *Letters of Ted Hughes*, 36.
[4] Mark Balfour, 'The Place of the Poet: Dante in Walcott's Narrative Poetry', 223, 233; see also Havely, *Dante's British Public*, 295–6.
[5] T. S. Eliot, *Selected Prose of T. S. Eliot*, 178.
[6] See Balfour, 'The Place of the Poet', 233–6. Indeed, Joyce himself, the 'undimmed Master', appears in one of these encounters, see Derek Walcott, *Omeros*, 200–1.
[7] For discussions of Heaney's engagement with Dante see Bernard O'Donoghue, *Seamus Heaney and the Language of Poetry*, 94–100, 135–52; Bernard O'Donoghue, 'Dante's Versatility and Seamus Heaney's Modernism', 242–57; Maria C. Fumagalli, '"What Dante Means to Me": Seamus Heaney's Translation of the First Three Cantos of Dante's *Inferno*', 204–34.
[8] For one 'antagonistic' formulation of the relationship between Joyce, Dante and Heaney see Carla de Petris, 'Heaney's Use of Dante Against Joyce', 79–90.

between his and Joyce's childhood and education. Asked whether a parallel could be drawn between his time at St Columb's College in Derry, and Joyce's depiction of the education of Stephen Dedalus in *A Portrait of the Artist as a Young Man*, Heaney memorably replied: 'It certainly could. When it comes to Catholic boarding schools of the late nineteenth and early to mid-twentieth century, it's very much a one-story-fits-all situation.'[9] During this 'Joycean' education, Heaney experienced the same sense of contestation over issues of interpretation and canonicity in his classroom reading, only this time it was not the medieval figure of Dante but modernism itself that was undergoing 'orthodox' appropriation. Remembering his teacher's approach to Eliot's 'The Hollow Men', Heaney observed that: 'the modernist canon was to be co-opted by the ideology that rang the college bell, and indeed [...] the rhetoric of the poem's distress connived with the complacencies of the college's orthodoxies'.[10]

Dante emerged within Heaney's poetic work in 1979 in the collection *Field Work*, and was a substantial presence in all of his subsequent books until his final collection, *Human Chain*, in 2010. From the outset, Heaney set Dante to the Joycean work of negotiating his place within the threatening political climate of a fractured community. 'Ugolino', the final poem in *Field Work*, figures a translation of *Inferno* 32. 124–39 and *Inferno* 33. 1–90 as a response to the bloody stalemate of the internecine strife in Northern Ireland.[11] Earlier in the collection, in 'The Strand at Lough Beg', Heaney meditated on and mediated the sectarian murder of his second cousin Colum McCartney through the frame of the opening canto of the *Purgatorio*.[12] This Joycean sense of Dante as a figure who could not only live up to the demands of sorrow and conflict within a community, but also clear some breathing room for the writer between the claims of contesting 'orthodoxies' was later clarified in the 'The Flight Path' from *The Spirit Level*. In this poem, Heaney is angrily confronted by a Sinn Féin spokesman: 'When, for fuck's sake, are you going to write/Something for us?' The poet's response is a typically Joycean resistance – 'If I do write something,/Whatever it is, I'll be writing for myself' – and he then withdraws into bitter meditation

---

[9] Dennis O'Driscoll, *Stepping Stones: Interviews with Seamus Heaney*, 184.
[10] Seamus Heaney, *Finders Keepers: Selected Prose 1971–2001*, 32.
[11] See Maria C. Fumagalli, 'Seamus Heaney's Northern Irish "Ugolino": An "Original Reproduction" of the Dantean Episode', 124–43.
[12] See O'Driscoll, *Stepping Stones*, 220–2.

on lines from 'Ugolino', and an implicit reconsideration of the political fashioning of that earlier poem.[13]

However, whilst the focus of continued poetic engagement, Dante was also central to Heaney's critical writing, most influentially in 'Envies and Identifications: Dante and the Modern Poet', where he discussed the differing approaches of T.S. Eliot and Osip Mandelstam.[14] Bernard O'Donoghue has observed that Heaney's reading of Mandelstam's Dante in this essay 'is so selective that it might be more accurate to call it "Heaney's Dante" instead'.[15] In which case, the view of Dante that emerges – emphasising his poetic usefulness, his status as a fellow craftsman and ultimately seeking to 'bring him from the pantheon back to the palate' – although framed in a discussion of Mandelstam, would seem to have an equally Joycean origin.[16] In the essay Heaney deploys an unmistakably Joycean lexis to describe Dante's influence on his own 'Station Island':

> The way in which Dante could place himself in an historical world yet submit that world to scrutiny from a perspective beyond history, the way he could accommodate the political and the transcendent, this too encouraged my attempt at a sequence of poems which would explore the typical strains which the consciousness labours under in this country. The main tension is between two often contradictory commands: to be faithful to the collective historical experience and to be true to the recognitions of the emerging self.[17]

Thus, Heaney's Dante – like Joyce's – was positioned as a figure negotiating between the 'contradictory commands' of individuality and community, between the stringencies of history and the self. 'Station Island' presents a Dantean exploration of literary, religious, political and personal history through the form of a visionary journey round Lough Derg, and famously the sequence culminates in the appearance of the guiding shade of James Joyce, who counsels the poet that:

> You lose more of yourself than you redeem
> doing the decent thing. Keep at a tangent.
> When they make the circle wide, it's time to swim

---

[13] Seamus Heaney, *The Spirit Level*, 25. On Heaney's original intention to dedicate 'Ugolino' to imprisoned members of the IRA, and for the background to 'The Flight Path' encounter, see O'Driscoll, *Stepping Stones*, 257–8.
[14] Heaney, 'Envies and Identifications', 7–18.
[15] O'Donoghue, *Seamus Heaney and the Language of Poetry*, 139.
[16] Heaney, 'Envies and Identifications', 16.
[17] Heaney, 'Envies and Identifications', 18–19.

> out on your own and fill the element
> with signatures on your own frequency[18]

In discussing the necessity of thus drawing Joyce and this passage of 'exilic' advice into his Dantean poem, Heaney once again revealed an unmistakable resonance with the character of Joyce's Dante:

> Yet the choice of Lough Derg as a locus for the poem did, in fact, represent a solidarity with orthodox ways and obedient attitudes, and that very solidarity and obedience were what had to be challenged. And who better to offer the challenge than the shade of Joyce himself? [...] yet the obvious shaping influence is the *Commedia*.[19]

Joyce and Dante were thus brought together by Heaney to both challenge and obey an orthodoxy over which he felt a distinct uneasiness. The wider conversation over 'Heaney's Dante' is well under way and, as Heaney's stature in modern poetry continues to grow, it shows no sign of abating. Having seen throughout this book how Joyce's engagement with Dante was framed in just such terms of orthodoxy and poetic collaboration as Heaney would later follow, it would seem that this conversation is one in which Joyce's voice – and that of Joyce's Dante – will in future be heard more clearly.

---

[18] Seamus Heaney, *Station Island*, 93–4.
[19] Heaney, 'Envies and Identifications', 19.

Bibliography

Works by Joyce and Dante

Alighieri, Dante. *The Convivio*. Trans. Richard Lansing. http://dante.ilt.columbia.edu/books/convivi/ July 2014.
Dante's Lyric Poetry. Ed. and trans. Kenelm Foster and Patrick Boyde. 2 vols. Oxford: Oxford University Press, 1967.
Dantis Alagherii Epistolae: The Letters of Dante. Ed. and trans. Paget Toynbee. Oxford: Oxford University Press, 1920.
La Divina Commedia di Dante Alighieri con note tratte dai migliori commenti. Ed. Eugenio Camerini. Milan: Società Editrice Sonzogno, 1904.
The Divine Comedy of Dante Alighieri. Ed. and trans. Robert M. Durling. 3 vols. Oxford: Oxford University Press, 1996–2011.
Rime. Ed. Gianfranco Contini. Turin: Einaudi, 1965.
Tutte le opere di Dante Alighieri. Ed. Edward Moore. Oxford: Oxford University Press, 1894.
La Vita Nova di Dante Alighieri illustrata dei quadri di Dante Gabriele Rossetti. Ed. Marco de Rubris. Turin: Società Tipografica-Editrice Nazionale, 1911.
Vita Nuova. Trans. Mark Musa. Oxford: Oxford University Press, 1999.
Joyce, James. *Dubliners*. Ed. Hans Walter Gabler with Walter Hetche. New York: Vintage, 1993.
Exiles. Harmondsworth: Penguin Books, 1973.
Finnegans Wake. London: Faber and Faber, 1968.
Letters. Ed. Stuart Gilbert and Richard Ellmann. 3 vols. New York: Viking, 1957–1966.
Occasional, Critical, and Political Writing. Ed. Kevin Barry. Oxford: Oxford University Press, 2000.
Poems and Shorter Writings. Ed. Richard Ellmann, A. Walton Litz and John Whittier-Ferguson. London: Faber and Faber, 1991.
A Portrait of the Artist as a Young Man. Ed. Hans Walter Gabler with Walter Hetche. New York: Garland/Viking, 1993.
Selected Letters. Ed. Richard Ellmann. London: Faber and Faber, 1975.
Stephen Hero. Ed. Theodore Spencer, John J. Slocum and Herbert Cahoon. London: Granada, 1977.

Ulysses: The Corrected Text. Ed. Hans Walter Gabler with Wolfhard Steppe and Claus Melchior. London: Penguin Books, 1986.
Ulysses: A Critical and Synoptic Edition. Ed. Hans Walter Gabler with Wolfhard Steppe and Claus Melchior. 3 vols. New York: Garland, 1984.

Unpublished Primary Material

'Transcriptions from and Related Annotations to "The Inferno" of Dante's *Divina Commedia*; also, Notes on Italian Words and Phrases'. Joyce Papers 2002. MS 36,639/1, f. 1r–28v. National Library of Ireland, Dublin.

Other Primary Texts Cited

Agresti, Antonio. 'Dell'arte di Dante Gabriele Rossetti'. *La Vita Nova di Dante Alighieri illustrata dei quadri di Dante Gabriele Rossetti*. Ed. Marco de Rubris. Turin: Società Tipografica-Editrice Nazionale, 1911. vii–xxiv.
Aquinas, Thomas. *Selected Philosophical Writings*. Ed. and trans. Timothy McDermott. Oxford: Oxford University Press, 1998.
Augustine. *Confessions*. Trans. Henry Chadwick. Oxford: Oxford University Press, 2008.
Beckett, Samuel. *The Letters of Samuel Beckett*, vol. 2, *1941–1956*. Ed. George Craig, Martha Dow Fehsenfeld, Dan Gunn and Lois More Overbeck. Cambridge: Cambridge University Press, 2011.
Benedict XV. '*In praeclara summorum*: Encyclical of Pope Benedict XV on Dante, to Professors and Students of Literature and Learning in the Catholic World'. *Papal Archive*. www.vatican.va/holy_father/benedict_xv/encyclicals/documents/hf_ben-xv_enc_30041921_in-praeclara-summorum_en.html. July 2015.
Bennassuti, Luigi. *La Divina Commedia di Dante Alighieri col Commento Cattolico di Luigi Bennassuti*. 3 vols. Verona: Civelli, 1864.
  La Divina Commedia di Dante Alighieri col Commento Medio tra il Grande ed il Piccolo di Bennassuti Luigi. 3 vols. Verona: Stereo-Tipografica. Vescovile in Seminario, 1878.
Bettinelli, Saverio. *Lettere Virgiliane e inglesi e altri scritti critici*. Ed. Vittorio Enzo Alfieri. Bari: G. Laterza, 1930.
Boccaccio, Giovanni. *Il comento di Giovanni Boccacci sopra La Commedia con le annotazioni di A. M. Salvini; preceduto dalla Vita di Dante Allighieri scritta dal medesimo*. Ed. Gaetano Milanesi. 2 vols. Florence: Le Monnier, 1863.
  Decameron. Ed. Vittore Branca. 2 vols. Milan: Oscar Classici Mondadori, 1989.
  The Decameron. Trans. G. H. McWilliam. London: Penguin, 1972.
  La vita di Dante: Testo critico, con introduzione, note e appendice di Francesco Marcrì-Leone; Raccolta di opere inedite o rare di ogni secolo della letteratura italiana. Ed. Francesco Macrì-Leone. Florence: G.G. Sansoni, 1888.
Byron, George Gordon. *Poetical Works*. Ed. Frederick Page. Oxford: Oxford University Press, 1970.

Camerini, Eugenio. *La Divina Commedia di Dante Alighieri con note tratte dai migliori commenti*. Milan: Società Editrice Sonzogno, 1904.
'Vita di Dante'. *La Divina Commedia di Dante Alighieri con note tratte dai migliori commenti*. Ed. Eugenio Camerini. Milan: Società Editrice Sonzogno, 1904. 7–13.
Eliot, T. S. *Dante*. London: Faber and Faber, 1965.
Eliot, T. S. *The Letters of T. S. Eliot*, vol. 1, *1898–1922*. 2nd ed. Ed. Valerie Eliot and Hugh Haughton. London: Faber and Faber, 2009.
Selected Prose of T. S. Eliot. Ed. Frank Kermode. London: Faber and Faber, 1975.
Foscolo, Ugo. 'Article IX – Dante: With a New Italian Commentary'. *Edinburgh Review* 29 (1818). 453–74.
Heaney, Seamus. 'Envies and Identifications: Dante and the Modern Poet'. *Irish University Review* 15 (1985). 5–19.
The Redress of Poetry: Oxford Lectures. London: Faber and Faber, 1995.
The Spirit Level. London: Faber and Faber, 1996.
Station Island. London: Faber and Faber, 1984.
Hughes, Ted. *Letters of Ted Hughes*. Ed. Christopher Reid. London: Faber and Faber, 2007.
Hunt, Leigh. *The Poetical Works of Leigh Hunt*. London: Moxon, 1860.
Latini, Brunetto. *Il Tesoro di Brunetto Latini volgarizzato da Bono Giamboni*. Ed. Luigi Gaiter. 4 vols. Bologna: Gaetano Romagnoli, 1878–83.
Leo XIII. '*Auspicato Concessum*: Encyclical of Pope Leo XIII on St Francis of Assisi'. *Papal Archive*. www.vatican.va/holy_father/leo_xiii/encyclicals/documents/hf_l-xiii_enc_17091882_auspicato-concessum_en.html. July 2015.
Milne, A. A. *Winnie-the-Pooh & the House at Pooh Corner*. London: The Reprint Society, 1957.
O'Driscoll, Dennis. *Stepping Stones: Interviews with Seamus Heaney*. London: Faber and Faber, 2008.
Pisacane, Carlo. *Saggio su la rivoluzione*. Ed. Giaime Pintor. Turin: Einaudi, 1956.
Polidori, Gaetano. *Dello Spirito Cattolico di Dante Alighieri: Opera di Carlo Lyell tradotta dall'originale Inglese*. London: C. F. Molini, 1844.
Pound, Ezra. *Collected Early Poems of Ezra Pound*. Ed. Michael J. King. London: Faber and Faber, 1977.
Literary Essays of Ezra Pound. Ed. T. S. Eliot. London: Faber and Faber, 1960.
Pound/Joyce: The Letters of Ezra Pound to James Joyce, with Pound's Essays on Joyce. Ed. Forrest Read. London: Faber and Faber, 1967.
Rossetti, Dante Gabriel. *Collected Poetry and Prose*. Ed. Jerome McGann. New Haven, CN and London: Yale University Press, 2003.
Ruskin, John. *The Works of John Ruskin*. Ed. E. T. Cook and Alexander Wedderburn. 39 vols. London: George Allen, 1903–12.
Sorio, Bartolomeo. *Lettere Dantesche dal P. Bart. Sorio P. D. O. di Verona scritte all' amico il Prof Francesco Longhena a Milano*. Rome: Tipografia Delle Belle Arti, 1863.
Svevo, Italo. *Scritti su Joyce*. Ed. Giancarlo Mazzacurati. Parma: Pratiche, 1986.

Virgil. *Eclogues, Georgics, Aeneid I–VI*. Ed. and trans. H. Rushton Fairclough and G. P. Goold. Cambridge, MA: Harvard University Press, 1999.
Walcott, Derek. *Omeros*. London: Faber and Faber, 1990.
Wordsworth, William. *The Major Works Including 'The Prelude'*. Ed. Stephen Gill. Oxford: Oxford University Press, 2000.
Yeats, W. B. *Essays and Introductions*. London: Macmillan & Co., 1961.
The Poems of W. B. Yeats. Ed. Richard J. Finneran. New York: Macmillan, 1983.

Secondary Texts

Amtower, Laurel. *Engaging Words: The Culture of Reading in the Later Middle Ages*. Basingstoke: Palgrave, 2000.
Ardizzone, Maria Luisa. *Guido Cavalcanti: The Other Middle Ages*. Toronto: University of Toronto Press, 2002.
Armour, Peter. 'Brunetto Latini'. *The Dante Encyclopedia*. Ed. Richard Lansing. New York: Garland Publishing, Inc., 2000. 127–9.
Armstrong, Guyda. 'Nineteenth-Century Translations and the Invention of Boccaccio-*Dantista*'. *Dante in the Nineteenth Century: Reception, Portrayal, Popularization*. Ed. Nick Havely. Oxford and Bern: Peter Lang, 2011. 201–20.
Ascoli, Albert Russell. *Dante and the Making of a Modern Author*. Cambridge: Cambridge University Press, 2010.
Atherton, James S. *The Books at the Wake: A Study of the Literary Allusions in James Joyce's 'Finnegans Wake'*. Carbondale: Southern Illinois University Press, 1974.
Attridge, Derek. *How to Read Joyce*. London: Granta Books, 2007.
J. M. Coetzee and the Ethics of Reading: Literature in the Event. Chicago: University of Chicago Press, 2004.
Joyce Effects: On Language, Theory, and History. Cambridge: Cambridge University Press, 2000.
'Pararealism in "Circe"'. *Joycean Unions: Post-Millennial Essays from East to West*. Ed. R. Brandon Kershner and Tekla Mecsnóber. European Joyce Studies 22. Amsterdam: Rodopi, 2013. 119–25.
'Reading Joyce'. *The Cambridge Companion to James Joyce*. 2nd ed. Ed. Derek Attridge. Cambridge: Cambridge University Press, 2004. 1–27.
Audeh, Aida and Havely, Nick, eds. *Dante in the Long Nineteenth Century: Nationality, Identity and Appropriation*. Oxford: Oxford University Press, 2012.
Baddeley, Alan. *Human Memory: Theory and Practice*. 2nd ed. Hove: Psychology Press, 1997.
Balfour, Mark. 'The Place of the Poet: Dante in Walcott's Narrative Poetry'. *Dante's Modern Afterlife: Reception and Response from Blake to Heaney*. Ed. Nick Havely. Basingstoke: Palgrave, 1998. 223–41.
Balsamo, Gian. *Joyce's Messianism: Dante, Negative Existence, and the Messianic Self*. Columbia: University of South Carolina Press, 2004.
Barolini, Teodolinda. *Dante and the Origins of Italian Literary Culture*. New York: Fordham University Press, 2006.

Bibliography

Dante's Poets: Textuality and Truth in the 'Comedy'. Princeton: Princeton University Press, 1984.
The Undivine Comedy: Detheologizing Dante. Princeton: Princeton University Press, 1992.
Bauerle, Ruth. 'Bertha's Role in *Exiles*'. *Women in Joyce*. Ed. Suzette Henke and Elaine Unkeless. Brighton: Harvester Press, 1982. 108–31.
Beckett, Samuel. 'Dante ... Bruno. Vico ... Joyce'. *Our Exagmination Round His Factification For Incamination of Work in Progress*. ED. Samuel Beckett et al. London: Faber and Faber, 1972. 3–22.
Benstock, Shari. 'The Genuine Christine: Psychodynamics of Issy'. *Women in Joyce*. Ed. Suzette Henke and Elaine Unkeless. Brighton: Harvester Press, 1982. 169–96.
Betti, Franco. 'Dante, the Jansenists and the Jesuits in XVII–XIX Century Italian Literary Criticism'. *Italian Quarterly* 15 (1971). 3–22.
Bisson, Lillian M. 'Brunetto Latini as a Failed Mentor'. *Medievalia et Humanistica* 18 (1992). 1–15.
Boldrini, Lucia. 'Introduction: Middayevil Joyce'. *Medieval Joyce*. European Joyce Studies 13. Ed. Lucia Boldrini. Amsterdam: Rodopi, 2002. 11–44.
Joyce, Dante, and the Poetics of Literary Relations: Language and Meaning in 'Finnegans Wake'. Cambridge: Cambridge University Press, 2001.
ed. *Medieval Joyce*. European Joyce Studies 13. Amsterdam: Rodopi, 2002.
'The Artist Paring His Quotations: Aesthetic and Ethical Implications of the Dantean Intertext in *Dubliners*'. *ReJoycing: New Readings of 'Dubliners'*. Ed. Rosa M. Bolletieri Bosinelli and Harold F. Mosher. Lexington: University Press of Kentucky, 1998. 228–48.
Booker, Keith M. 'From the Sublime to the Ridiculous: Dante's Beatrice and Joyce's Bella Cohen'. *James Joyce Quarterly* 29 (1992). 357–68.
Boyde, Patrick. *Perception and Passion in Dante's 'Comedy'*. Cambridge: Cambridge University Press, 1993.
Bradley, Bruce. *James Joyce's Schooldays*. New York: St Martin's Press, 1982.
Brivic, Sheldon R. *Joyce's Waking Women: An Introduction to 'Finnegans Wake'*. Madison: University of Wisconsin Press, 1995.
'Structure and Meaning in Joyce's *Exiles*'. *James Joyce Quarterly* 6 (1968). 29–52.
Brown, Richard. '"Everything" in "Circe"'. *Reading Joyce's 'Circe'*. Ed. Andrew Gibson. European Joyce Studies 3. Amsterdam: Rodopi, 1994. 222–40.
Budgen, Frank. *James Joyce and the Making of 'Ulysses' and Other Writings*. Oxford: Oxford University Press, 1989.
Myselves When Young. Oxford: Oxford University Press, 1970.
Burns, Christy. 'An Erotics of the Word: Female "Assaucyetiams" in *Finnegans Wake*'. *James Joyce Quarterly* 31 (1994). 315–35.
Byrne, John Francis. *Silent Years: An Autobiography with Memoirs of James Joyce and Our Ireland*. New York: Farrar, Staus and Young, 1975.
Caesar, Michael. *Dante: The Critical Heritage: 1314(?)-1870*. London: Routledge, 1989.

Capaci, Bruno. 'Attacco a Dante: Saverio Bettinelli'. *Dante oscuro e barbaro: commenti e dispute (secoli XVII e XVIII)*. Ed. Bruno Capaci. Rome: Carocci, 2008. 159–76.
Carducci, Nicola. 'Bennassuti, Luigi'. *Enciclopedia Dantesca*. vol. 1. Ed. Umberto Bosco. Rome: Istituto della Enciclopedia Italiana. 589–90 cols. 2–1.
Carruthers, Mary. *The Book of Memory: A Study of Memory in Medieval Culture*. Rev. ed. Cambridge: Cambridge University Press, 2008.
Casini, Tommaso. *Aneddoti e Studi Danteschi*. Città di Castello: S. Lapi Tipografo Editore, 1895.
Ceva, Bianca. *Brunetto Latini: l'uomo e l'opera*. Milan: Ricciardi, 1965.
Ciccarelli, Andrea. 'Dante and Italian Culture from the Risorgimento to World War I'. *Dante Studies* 119 (2001). 125–54.
'Dante and the Culture of Risorgimento: Literary, Political or Ideological Icon?' *Making and Remaking Italy: The Cultivation of National Identity around the Risorgimento*. Ed. Albert Ascoli and Krystyna von Henneberg. Oxford: Berg, 2001. 77–102.
Cixous, Hélène. 'At Circe's, or the Self-Opener'. *Boundary 2* 3. Trans. Carol Bové. (1975). 387–97.
The Exile of James Joyce. Trans. Sally A. J. Purcell. London: John Calder, 1976.
Conti, Aidan. 'Scribes as Authors, Transmission as Composition: Towards a Science of Copying'. *Modes of Authorship in the Middle Ages*. Ed. Slavica Rankovic. Toronto: Pontifical Institute of Medieval Studies, 2012. 267–88.
Contini, Gianfranco. *Varianti e Altra Linguistica: una raccolta di saggi (1938–1968)*. Turin: Einaudi, 1970.
Copeland, Rita. *Rhetoric, Hermeneutics, and Translation in the Middle Ages: Academic Traditions and Vernacular Texts*. Cambridge: Cambridge University Press, 1991.
Corrigan, Beatrice. 'Foscolo's Articles on Dante in the *Edinburgh Review*: A Study in Collaboration'. *Collected Essays on Italian Literature Presented to Kathleen Speight*. Ed. Stephen Cristea and Sheila Ralph. Manchester: Manchester University Press, 1971. 211–25.
Corti, Claudia. *'Esuli': Dramma, Psicodramma, Metadramma*. Ospedaletto: Pacini, 2007.
Crisafulli, Edoardo. *The Vision of Dante: Cary's Translation of 'The Divine Comedy'*. Market Harborough: Troubador Publishing, 2003.
Dasenbrock, Reed Way. *Imitating the Italians: Wyatt, Spenser, Synge, Pound, Joyce*. Baltimore: Johns Hopkins University Press, 1991.
Davis, Charles T. 'Brunetto Latini and Dante'. *Studi Medievali* 8 (1967). 421–50.
'Dante and Italian Nationalism'. *A Dante Symposium in Commemoration of the 700th Anniversary of the Poet's Birth (1265–1965)*. Ed. William De Sua and Gino Rizzo. Chapel Hill: *University of North Carolina Press*, 1965. 199–213.
De Robertis, Dino. *Il Libro Della 'Vita Nuova'*. 2nd ed. Florence: G.C. Sansoni, 1970.
Degl'Innocenti Pierini, Rita. 'Il Foscolo e la letteratura classica sull'esilio: appunti di lettura'. *Maia* 44 (1992). 147–55.

Derrida, Jacques. *Acts of Literature*. Ed. Derek Attridge. London: Routledge, 1992.
Margins of Philosophy. Trans. Alan Bass. Chicago: University of Chicago Press, 1984.
Of Grammatology. 2nd ed. Trans. Gayatri Chakravorty Spivak. Baltimore: Johns Hopkins University Press, 1997.
Downing, Gregory M. 'Richard Chenevix Trench and Joyce's Historical Study of Words'. *Joyce Studies Annual* 9 (1998). 37–68.
Duggan, Christopher. *The Force of Destiny: A History of Italy since 1796*. London: Penguin, 2008.
Dumol, Paul A. 'Imagination'. *The Dante Encyclopedia*. Ed. Richard Lansing. New York: Garland Publishing, 2000. 505–6.
Dumol. Paul A. 'Memory'. *The Dante Encyclopedia*. Ed. Richard Lansing. New York: Garland Publishing, 2000. 605–6.
Eco, Umberto. *The Middle Ages of James Joyce: The Aesthetics of Chaosmos*. London: Hutchison Radius, 1989.
Ellis, Steve. *Dante and English Poetry: Shelley to T. S. Eliot*. Cambridge: Cambridge University Press, 1983.
Ellmann, Richard. *James Joyce*. Rev. ed. Oxford: Oxford University Press, 1982.
Ulysses on the Liffey. London: Faber and Faber, 1972.
Ferrante, Joan M. *Woman as Image in Medieval Literature: From the Twelfth Century to Dante*. New York: Columbia University Press, 1975.
Ferrer, Daniel. 'Circe, Regret and Regression'. *Post-structuralist Joyce: Essays from the French*. Ed. Derek Attridge and Daniel Ferrer. Cambridge: Cambridge University Press, 1984. 127–44.
Fordham, Finn. *I Do I Undo I Redo: The Textual Genesis of Modernist Selves in Hopkins, Yeats, Conrad, Forster, Joyce, and Woolf*. Oxford: Oxford University Press, 2010.
Forster, E. M. *Aspects of the Novel*. London: Penguin, 1963.
Foster, Kenelm and Boyde, Patrick. *Dante's Lyric Poetry: Commentary*. vol. 2. Oxford: Oxford University Press, 1967.
Frank, Nino. 'The Shadow That Had Lost Its Man'. *Portraits of the Artist in Exile: Recollections of James Joyce by Europeans*. Ed. Willard Potts. Dublin: Wolfhound Press, 1979. 74–105.
Franke, William. *Dante's Interpretive Journey*. Chicago: University of Chicago Press, 1994.
Fraser, Jennifer Margaret. *Rite of Passage in the Narratives of Dante and Joyce*. Gainesville: University Press of Florida, 2002.
Freeman, Mark. *Rewriting the Self: History, Memory, Narrative*. London: Routledge, 1993.
Friedman, John Block. 'Antichrist and the Iconography of Dante's Geryon'. *Journal of the Warburg and Courtauld Institutes* 35 (1972). 108–22.
Fumagalli, Maria Cristina. 'Seamus Heaney's Northern Irish "Ugolino": An "Original Reproduction" of the Dantean Episode'. *Journal of Anglo-Irish Studies* 4 (1995). 124–43.

'"What Dante Means to Me": Seamus Heaney's Translation of the First Three Cantos of Dante's *Inferno*'. *Agenda* 34 (1997). 204–34.
Furlong, Justin. 'A Magnificent Pile! A Brief Architectural Tour of the Main Library Building'. *National Library of Ireland Blog*. www.nli.ie/blog/index.php/2014/08/29/a-magnificent-pile-a-brief-architectural-tour-of-the-main-library-building/. July 2015.
Gabler, Hans Walter. 'Narrative Rereadings: Some Remarks on "Proteus", "Circe" and "Penelope"'. *James Joyce 1: 'Scribble' 1, Genèse des Textes*. Ed. Claude Jacquet. Paris: Minard, 1988. 57–68.
Gardner, Edmund G. 'Dante'. *The Catholic Encyclopedia: An International Work of Reference on the Constitution, Doctrine, Discipline, and History of the Catholic Church*. vol. 4. Ed. Charles G. Herbermann et al. London: Encyclopedia Press, Inc., 1908. 628–33.
Gellrich, Jesse M. *The Idea of the Book in the Middle Ages: Language Theory, Mythology, and Fiction*. Ithaca: Cornell University Press, 1985.
Gibson, Andrew. 'Introduction'. *Reading Joyce's 'Circe'*. European Joyce Studies 3. Ed. Andrew Gibson. Amsterdam: Rodopi, 1994. 3–32.
Gifford, Don. *'Ulysses' Annotated: Notes for James Joyce's 'Ulysses'*. Berkeley: University of California Press, 2008.
Gilbert, Stuart. *James Joyce's 'Ulysses'*. New York: Vintage Books, 1955.
Glasheen, Adaline. *Third Census of 'Finnegans Wake': An Index of the Characters and Their Roles*. Berkeley: University of California Press, 1977.
Gorman, Herbert Sherman. *James Joyce: A Definitive Biography*. London: John Lane/The Bodley Head, 1941.
Gorni, Guglielmo. 'La Vita Nuova di Dante Alighieri'. *Letteratura italiana: Le Opere: volume primo: Dalle Origini al Cinquecento*. Ed. Alberto Asor Rosa. Turin: Einaudi, 1992. 153–86.
Gottfried, Roy. *Joyce's Misbelief*. Gainesville: University Press of Florida, 2008.
del Greco Lobner, Corinna. *James Joyce's Italian Connection: The Poetics of the Word*. Iowa City: University of Iowa Press, 1989.
'Letters to the Editor'. *James Joyce Quarterly* 24 (1987). 235–7.
Greenblatt, Stephen. *Renaissance Self-Fashioning: From More to Shakespeare*. Chicago: University of Chicago Press, 1980.
Groden, Michael. 'The National Library of Ireland's New Joyce Manuscripts: A Narrative and Document Summaries'. *Journal of Modern Literature* 26 (2002). 1–16.
Haidu, Peter. *The Subject Medieval/Modern: Text and Governance in the Middle Ages*. Stanford, CA: Stanford University Press, 2004.
Havely, Nick. 'Brunetto and Palinurus'. *Dante Studies* 108 (1990). 20–38.
Dante. Oxford: Blackwell Publishing, 2007.
ed. *Dante in the Nineteenth Century: Reception, Canonicity, Popularization*. Oxford and Bern: Peter Lang, 2011.
Dante's British Public: Readers and Texts from the Fourteenth Century to the Present. Oxford: Oxford University Press, 2014.

ed. *Dante's Modern Afterlife: Reception and Response from Blake to Heaney*. Basingstoke: Palgrave, 1998.
'*Francesca franciosa*: Exile, Language and History in Foscolo's Articles on Dante'. *Dante in the Nineteenth Century: Reception, Portrayal, Popularization*. Ed. Nick Havely. Oxford and Bern: Peter Lang, 2011. 55–74.
'"An Italian Writer Against the Pope"? Dante in Reformation England, c. 1560–c. 1640'. *Dante Metamorphoses: Episodes in a Literary Afterlife*. Ed. Eric G. Haywood. Dublin: Four Courts Press, 2003. 127–49.
'The Self-Consuming City: Florence as Body Politic in Dante's *Commedia*'. *Deutsches Dante Jahrbuch* 61 (1986). 99–113.
Hayman, David. *The 'Wake' in Transit*. Ithaca: Cornell University Press, 1990.
Hearder, Harry. *Italy in the Age of the Risorgimento 1790–1870*. London: Longman, 1983.
Heidegger, Martin. 'The Origin of the Work of Art'. *Basic Writings: From 'Being and Time' (1927) to 'The Task of Thinking' (1964)*. Rev. ed. Ed. David F. Krell. London: Routledge, 1993. 139–212.
Helsinger, Howard. 'Joyce and Dante'. *English Literary History* 35 (1968). 591–605.
Houston, Jason M. *Building a Monument to Dante: Boccaccio as 'Dantista'*. Toronto: University of Toronto Press, 2010.
van Hulle, Dirk. *Joyce & Beckett: Discovering Dante*. National Library of Ireland Joyce Studies 7. Dublin: National Library of Ireland, 2004.
Isabella, Maurizio. 'Exile and Nationalism: The Case of the *Risorgimento*'. *European History Quarterly* 36 (2006). 493–520.
Isba, Anne. *Gladstone and Dante: Victorian Statesman, Medieval Poet*. London: Royal Historical Society, 2006.
Javadi, Iman. 'The English Reception of Dante's *De Vulgari Eloquentia*'. *Forum for Modern Language Studies* 44 (2008). 295–306.
Jossa, Stefano. 'Politics vs. Literature: The Myth of Dante and the Italian National Identity'. *Dante in the Long Nineteenth Century: Nationality, Identity and Appropriation*. Ed. Aida Audeh and Nick Havely. Oxford: Oxford University Press, 2012. 30–50.
Joyce, Stanislaus. 'James Joyce: A Memoir'. *The Hudson Review* 2 (1950). 485–514.
My Brother's Keeper. London: Faber and Faber, 1958.
Keach, William. 'The Shelleys and Dante's Matilda'. *Dante's Modern Afterlife: Reception and Response from Blake to Heaney*. Ed. Nick Havely. Basingstoke: Palgrave, 1998. 60–70.
Keen, Catherine. *Dante and the City*. Stroud: Tempus, 2003.
'Images of Exile: Distance and Memory in the Poetry of Cino da Pistoia'. *Italian Studies* 55 (2000). 21–36.
Kelly, Joseph. 'Joyce's Exile: The Prodigal Son'. *James Joyce Quarterly* 48 (2011). 603–35.
Kenner, Hugh. 'Circe'. *James Joyce's 'Ulysses': Critical Essays*. Ed. Clive Hart and David Hayman. Berkeley: University of California Press, 1974. 341–62.
Dublin's Joyce. London: Chatto & Windus, 1955.

Kerby, Anthony Paul. *Narrative and the Self.* Bloomington: Indiana University Press, 1991.
Kiberd, Declan. *'Ulysses' and Us: The Art of Everyday Living.* London: Faber and Faber, 2009.
Knowlson, James. *Damned to Fame: The Life of Samuel Beckett.* London: Bloomsbury, 1996.
Kolve, V. A. *Chaucer and the Imagery of Narrative: The First Five Canterbury Tales.* London: Edward Arnold, 1984.
Koonce, B. G. 'Satan the Fowler'. *Mediaeval Studies* 21 (1959). 176–84
Kumar, Udaya. *The Joycean Labyrinth: Repetition, Time, and Tradition in 'Ulysses'.* Oxford: Oxford University Press, 1991.
Kuon, Peter. *'Lo mio maestro e 'l mio autore': die Produktive Rezeption der 'Divina Commedia' in der Erzählliteratur der Moderne.* Frankfurt: Vittorio Klostermann, 1993.
Ladner, Gerhart B. 'Homo Viator'. *Speculum* 42 (1967). 233–59.
Lanigan, Liam. '"A Necessary Evil": Anti-Spatial Behaviour in "Circe"'. *James Joyce Metamorphosis and Re-Writing.* Ed. Franca Ruggieri. Joyce Studies in Italy 11. Rome: Bulzoni Editore, 2010. 99–112.
Lanza, Antonio. 'L'allegoria della corda nel canto XVI dell'*Inferno*'. *Rassegna della letteratura italiana* 84 (1980). 97–100.
Laria, Vincenzo. 'Assembrare'. *Encilopedia Dantesca.* vol. 1. Ed. Umberto Bosca *et al.* Rome: Istituto della Enciclopedia Italiana, 1970. 419 col. 1.
   'Assemprare (ASSEMPLARE)'. *Encilopedia Dantesca.* vol. 1. Ed. Umberto Bosca *et al.* Rome: Istituto della Enciclopedia Italiana, 1970. 419 col. 1.
Lernout, Geert. *'Help My Unbelief': James Joyce & Religion.* London: Continuum, 2010.
Lewis, C. S. *The Allegory of Love.* Oxford: Oxford University Press, 1938.
Livorni, Ernesto. '"Ineluctable modality of the visible": Diaphane in the "Proteus" Episode'. *James Joyce Quarterly* 36 (1999). 127–69.
Luzzi, Joseph. ' "Founders of Italian Literature": Dante, Petrarch, and National Identity in Ugo Foscolo'. *Dante in the Long Nineteenth Century: Nationality, Identity, and Appropriation.* Ed. Aida Audeh and Nick Havely. Oxford: Oxford University Press, 13–29.
Lyttelton, Adrian. 'Creating a National Past: History, Myth and Image in the Risorgimento'. *Making and Remaking Italy: The Cultivation of National Identity around the Risorgimento.* Ed. Albert Ascoli and Krystyna von Henneberg. Oxford: Berg, 2001. 27–74.
MacCabe, Colin. *James Joyce and the Revolution of the Word.* London: Macmillan, 1978.
McCarthy, Patrick A. *Joyce, Family, 'Finnegans Wake'.* National Library of Ireland Joyce Studies 19. Dublin: National Library of Ireland, 2004.
McCourt, John. 'Trieste'. *James Joyce in Context.* Ed. John McCourt. Cambridge: Cambridge University Press, 2009. 228–38.
   The Years of Bloom: James Joyce in Trieste 1904–1920. Dublin: Lilliput Press, 2001.

McGreevy, Thomas. 'The Catholic Element in *Work in Progress*'. *Our Exagmination Round His Factification for Incamination of Work in Progress*. Ed. Samuel Beckett *et al*. London: Faber and Faber, 1972. 115–27.
McHugh, Roland. *Annotations to 'Finnegans Wake'*. 3rd ed. Baltimore: Johns Hopkins University Press, 2006.
Maddox, Brenda. *Nora: A Biography of Nora Joyce*. London: Minerva, 1989.
Magee, W. K. 'The Beginnings of Joyce'. *The Workshop of Daedalus: James Joyce and the Raw Material for 'A Portrait of the Artist as a Young Man'*. Ed. Robert Scholes and Richard M. Kain. Evanston: Northwestern University Press, 1965. 197–208.
Mahaffey, Vicki. 'James Joyce in Transition: A Study of *A Portrait of the Artist as a Young Man, Giacomo Joyce, Exiles* and *Ulysses*'. Ph.D. diss., Princeton University, 1980.
'Joyce and Gender'. *Palgrave Advances in James Joyce Studies*. Ed. Jean-Michel Rabaté. Basingstoke: Palgrave Macmillan, 2004. 121–43.
'Joyce's Shorter Works'. *The Cambridge Companion to James Joyce*. Ed. Derek Attridge. Cambridge: Cambridge University Press, 1996. 185–212.
Reauthorizing Joyce. Gainesville: University Press of Florida, 1995.
'Wagner, Joyce, and Revolution'. *James Joyce Quarterly* 25 (1988). 237–47.
Maierù, Alfonso. 'Memoria'. *Encilopedia Dantesca*. vol. 3. Ed. Umberto Bosca *et al*. Rome: Istituto della Enciclopedia Italiana, 1970. 888–92.
Manganiello, Dominic. *Joyce's Politics*. London: Routledge, 1980.
T. S. Eliot and Dante. New York: St Martin's Press, 1989.
Mango, Achille. 'Gli *Esuli* di Joyce'. *Oltre il romanzo: da Sterne a Joyce*. Ed. Franca Ruggieri. Sezione atti convegni miscellanee 48. Naples: Edizioni Scientifiche Italiane, 1995. 169–80.
Martin, Timothy. *Joyce and Wagner: A Study of Influence*. Cambridge: Cambridge University Press, 1991.
Martines, Lauro. *Power and Imagination: City-States in Renaissance Italy*. London: Allen Lane, 1979.
Martinez, Ronald L. and Durling, Robert M. 'Notes to Canto 24'. *The Divine Comedy of Dante Alighieri Volume 1: Inferno*. Ed. Robert M. Durling. Oxford: Oxford University Press, 1996. 372–9.
Matthews, Terence. 'A Significant Trieste Address: 1 via Giovanni Boccaccio.' *James Joyce Quarterly* 36 (1999). 18–20
Mazzotta, Giuseppe. *Dante, Poet of the Desert*. Princeton: Princeton University Press, 1979.
Mercanton, Jacques. 'The Hours of James Joyce'. *Portraits of the Artist in Exile: Recollections of James Joyce by Europeans*. Ed. Willard Potts. Dublin: Wolfhound Press, 1979. 206–52.
van Mierlo, Wim. 'The Greater Ireland Beyond the Sea: James Joyce, Exile, and Irish Emigration'. *Joyce, Ireland, Britain*. Ed. Andrew Gibson and Len Platt. Gainesville: University Press of Florida, 2007. 178–97.
Milbank, Alison. *Dante and the Victorians*. Manchester: Manchester University Press, 1998.

Milesi, Laurent. 'Toward a Female Grammar of Sexuality: The De/Recomposition of "Storiella As She is Syung"'. *Modern Fiction Studies* 35 (1989). 569–85.
Miller, Kerby. *Emigrants and Exiles: Ireland and the Irish Exodus to North America*. Oxford: Oxford University Press, 1985.
Minnis, Alastair J. 'Literary Imagination and Memory'. *The Cambridge History of Literary Criticism*, vol. 2, *The Middle Ages*. Ed. Alastair J. Minnis and Ian Johnson. Cambridge: Cambridge University Press, 2005. 239–74.
  Medieval Theory of Authorship: Scholastic Literary Attitudes in the Later Middle Ages. 2nd ed. Aldershot: Wildwood House, 1988.
Moody, A. David. *Ezra Pound: Poet*, vol. 1, *The Young Genius 1885–1920*. Oxford: Oxford University Press, 2007.
Morgan, Alison. *Dante and the Medieval Other World*. Cambridge: Cambridge University Press, 1990.
Mullin, Katherine. 'Don't Cry for Me, Argentina: "Eveline" and the Seductions of Emigration Propaganda'. *Semicolonial Joyce*. Ed. Derek Attridge and Marjorie Howes. Cambridge: Cambridge University Press, 2000. 172–200.
Mussetter, Sally. 'Fantasy'. *The Dante Encyclopedia*. Ed. Richard Lansing. New York: Garland Publishing, Inc., 2000. 370.
Nagel, Thomas. *The View from Nowhere*. Oxford: Oxford University Press, 1986.
Nash, John. 'The Logic of Incest: Issy, Princes and Professors'. *James Joyce Quarterly* 39 (2002). 435–56.
Norris, Margot. 'Joyce's Heliotrope'. *Coping with Joyce: Essays from the Copenhagen Symposium*. Ed. Morris Beja and Shari Benstock. Columbus: Ohio State University Press, 1989. 3–24.
  'The Stakes of Stephen's Gambit in "Scylla and Charybdis"'. *Joyce Studies Annual* (2009). 1–33.
O'Donoghue, Bernard. 'Dante's Versatility and Seamus Heaney's Modernism'. *Dante's Modern Afterlife: Reception and Response from Blake to Heaney*. Ed. Nick Havely. Basingstoke: Palgrave, 1998. 242–57.
  Seamus Heaney and the Language of Poetry. London: Harvester Wheatsheaf, 1994.
O'Neill, Michael. '"Admirable for Conciseness and Vigour": Dante and English Romantic Poetry's Dealings with Epic'. *Dante in the Nineteenth Century: Reception, Portrayal, Popularization*. Ed. Nick Havely. Oxford and Bern: Peter Lang, 2011. 11–29.
Okay, Cüneyd. 'The Reception of Dante in Turkey through the Long Nineteenth Century'. *Dante in the Long Nineteenth Century: Nationality, Identity and Appropriation*. Ed. Aida Audeh and Nick Havely. Oxford: Oxford University Press, 2012. 339–52.
Palermo, A. 'Camerini, Salomone (Eugenio)'. *Dizionario biografia degli italiani*. vol. 17. Ed. V. Cappelletti. Rome: Instituto della Enciclopedia italiana, 1974. 187–8.
Parandowski, Jan. 'Meeting with Joyce'. *Portraits of the Artist in Exile: Recollections of James Joyce by Europeans*. Ed. Willard Potts. Dublin: Wolfhound Press, 1979. 154–62.

Parkes, Malcolm B. 'The Influence of the Concepts of *Ordinatio* and *Compilatio* on the Development of the Book'. *Medieval Learning and Literature*. Ed. J. J. G. Alexander and M. T. Gibson. Oxford: Clarendon Press, 1976. 115–41.
Paschini, Pio, ed. *La Enciclopedia Cattolica*. 12 vols. Vatican City: Ente per l'Enciclopedia Cattolica e per il Libro Cattolico, 1948–54.
Peake, Charles H. *James Joyce: The Citizen and the Artist*. Stanford: Stanford University Press, 1977.
Pearce, Spencer. 'Dante and the Art of Memory'. *The Italianist* 16 (1996). 20–61.
Pelikan, Jaroslav. *Eternal Feminines: Three Theological Allegories in Dante's 'Paradiso'*. New Brunswick: Rutgers University Press, 1990.
de Petris, Carla. 'Exiles, or the Necessity of Theatre'. *Myriadminded Man: Jottings on Joyce*. Ed. Rosa Maria Bosinelli, Paola Pugliatti and Romana Zacchi. Testi e Discorsi: Strumenti Linguistici e Letterari 5. Bologna: CLUEB, 1986. 65–75.
'Heaney's Use of Dante Against Joyce'. *Fin de Siècle and Italy*. Ed. Franca Ruggieri. Joyce Studies in Italy 5. Rome: Bulzoni Editore, 1998. 79–90.
'Léon Blum's *Du Mariage* and James Joyce's *Exiles*: "Yet There Is Method in't"'. *Names and Disguises*. Ed. Carla de Petris. Joyce Studies in Italy 3. Rome: Bulzoni, 1991. 31–42.
Picone, Michelangelo. 'Songbook and Lyric Genres in the *Vita Nuova*'. *The Italianist* 15 supp. no. 2 (1995). 158–70.
'*Vita Nuova*'. *The Dante Encyclopedia*. Ed. Richard Lansing. New York: Garland Publishing, 2000. 874–8.
Pieri, Giuliana. 'Dante and the Pre-Raphaelites: British and Italian Responses'. *Dante on View: The Reception of Dante in the Visual and Performing Arts*. Ed. Antonella Braida and Luisa Calè. Aldershot: Ashgate Publishing, 2007. 109–40.
Pizzorno, Patrizia Grimaldi. 'Matelda's Dance and the Smile of the Poets'. *Dante Studies* 112 (1994). 115–32.
Polhemus, Robert M. 'Dantellising Peaches and Miching Daddy, the Gushy Old Goof: The Browning Case and *Finnegans Wake*'. *Joyce Studies Annual* 5 (1994). 75–103.
Pollard, G. 'The Pecia System in Medieval Universities'. *Medieval Scribes, Manuscripts and Libraries: Essays Presented to N.R. Ker*. Ed. N. R. Ker, Malcolm B. Parkes, Andrew G. Watson and Joan Gibbs. London: Scolar Press, 1978. 145–61
Pollen, J. H. 'Society of Jesus (Company of Jesus, Jesuits)'. *The Catholic Encyclopedia: An International Work of Reference on the Constitution, Doctrine, Discipline, and History of the Catholic Church*. vol. 14. Ed. Charles G. Herbermann *et al*. London: Encyclopedia Press, Inc., 1912. 81–110.
Pugliatti, Paola. 'Isotopia e monologo interiore'. *Terribilia Meditans: La coerenza del monologo interiore in 'Ulysses'*. Ed. Paola Pugliatti and Romana Zacchi. Bologna: Società editrice il Mulino, 1983. 15–63.
'The Ulyssean Challenge: Time, Monologue, Discourse, "Arranger"'. *Myriadminded Man: Jottings on Joyce*. Ed. Rosa Maria Bosinelli, Paola

Pugliatti and Romana Zacchi. *Testi e Discorsi: Strumenti Linguistici e Letterari* 5. Bologna: CLUEB, 1986. 167–71.
Rabaté, Jean-Michel. *James Joyce and the Politics of Egoism*. Cambridge: Cambridge University Press, 2001.
James Joyce, Authorized Reader. Baltimore: Johns Hopkins University Press, 1991.
Rainey, Lawrence. 'The Cultural Economy of Modernism'. *The Cambridge Companion to Modernism*. Ed. Michael Levenson. Cambridge: Cambridge University Press, 2011. 33–68.
Rak, Michele. 'Fantasia'. *Enciclopedia Dantesca*. vol. 3. Ed. Umberto Bosca et al. Rome: Istituto della Enciclopedia Italiana, 1970. 792–3.
Read, Forrest., ed. *Pound/Joyce: The Letters of Ezra Pound to James Joyce*. London: Faber and Faber, 1968.
Reichert, Klaus. 'The European Background of Joyce's Writing'. *The Cambridge Companion to James Joyce*. Ed. Derek Attridge. Cambridge: Cambridge University Press, 1996. 55–82.
Restivo, Giuseppina. 'L'*Otello* di James Joyce: nota sulla vicenda di *Esuli*'. *Inscenare/interpretare Otello*. Ed. Giuseppina Restivo and Renzo S. Teatro Crivelli. Bologna: CLUEB, 2006. 101–20.
Reynolds, Mary T. 'Dante in Joyce's *Exiles*'. *James Joyce Quarterly* 18 (1980). 35–44.
Joyce and Dante: The Shaping Imagination. Princeton: Princeton University Press, 1981.
'Joyce's Editions of Dante'. *James Joyce Quarterly* 15 (1978). 380–4.
Riall, Lucy. *Garibaldi: Invention of a Hero*. New Haven: Yale University Press, 2007.
Rickard, John S. *Joyce's Book of Memory: The Mnemotechnic of 'Ulysses'*. Durham, NC: Duke University Press, 1999.
Riquelme, John Paul. *Teller and Tale in Joyce's Fiction: Oscillating Perspectives*. Baltimore: Johns Hopkins University Press, 1983.
Robinson, James. '*Purgatorio* in the *Portrait*: Dante, Heterodoxy, and the Education of James Joyce'. *Dante in the Nineteenth Century: Reception, Portrayal, Popularization*. Ed. Nick Havely. Oxford and Bern: Peter Lang, 2011. 261–79.
Ruggieri, Franca. 'Foreword'. *James Joyce Metamorphosis and Re-writing*. Ed. Franca Ruggieri. Joyce Studies in Italy 11. Rome: Bulzoni Editore, 2010. 9–11.
Saturni, Alessandra. 'La Parola al Femminile: Molly vs. Cassandra'. *Fin de Siècle and Italy*. Ed. Franca Ruggieri. Joyce Studies in Italy 5. Rome: Bluzoni Editore, 1998. 107–32.
Schechner, Mark. *Joyce in Nighttown: A Psychoanalytic Inquiry into 'Ulysses'*. Berkeley: University of California Press, 1974.
Schmitt, Jean-Claude. *Ghosts in the Middle Ages: The Living and the Dead in Medieval Society*. Chicago: University of Chicago Press, 1998.
Scholes, Robert E. *The Cornell Joyce Collection: A Catalogue*. Ithaca: Cornell University Press, 1961.

Scholes, Robert E. and Kain, Richard M., eds. *The Workshop of Daedalus: James Joyce and the Raw Materials for 'A Portrait of the Artist as a Young Man'*. Evanston: Northwestern University Press, 1965.
Schork, R. J. 'Genetic Primer: Chapter I.6'. *How Joyce Wrote 'Finnegans Wake': A Chapter-by-Chapter Genetic Guide*. Ed. Luca Crispi and Sam Slote. Madison: University of Wisconsin Press, 2007. 124–41.
Scott, Bonnie Kime. 'James Joyce: A Subversive Geography of Gender'. *Irish Writing: Exile and Subversion*. Ed. Paul Hyland and Neil Sammells. Basingstoke: Macmillan, 1991. 159–72.
  James Joyce: Feminist Readings. Atlantic Highlands: Humanities Press International, 1987.
Seigel, Jerrold. *The Idea of the Self: Thought and Experience in Western Europe Since the Seventeenth Century*. Cambridge: Cambridge University Press, 2005.
Shapiro, Marianne. *Woman, Earthly and Divine, in the 'Comedy' of Dante*. Lexington: University Press of Kentucky, 1975.
Sheehy, Eugene. 'My School Friend, James Joyce'. *James Joyce: Interviews and Recollections*. Ed. E. H. Mikhail. Basingstoke: Macmillan, 1990. 9–15.
Shelton, Jen. *Joyce and the Narrative Structure of Incest*. Gainesville: University Press of Florida, 2006.
Shloss, Carol Loeb. *Lucia Joyce: To Dance in the Wake*. London: Bloomsbury, 2004.
Short, Clarice. 'Joyce's "A Little Cloud"'. *Modern Language Notes* 72 (1957). 275–8.
Sicari, Stephen. *Pound's Epic Ambition: Dante and the Modern World*. Albany: State University of New York Press, 1991.
Slote, Sam. *The Silence in Progress of Dante, Mallarmé, and Joyce*. Currents in Comparative Romance Language and Literatures 82. New York: Peter Lang, 1999.
Spoo, Robert E. '"Una Piccola Nuvoletta": Ferrero's *Young Europe* and Joyce's Mature *Dubliners* Stories'. *James Joyce Quarterly* 24 (1987). 401–10.
Squarotti, Giorgio B., et al., eds. *Grande Dizionario Della Lingua Italiana*. 21 vols., 2 supp. Turin: Unione tipografica-editrice torinese, 1961–2009.
Starn, Randolph. *Contrary Commonwealth: The Theme of Exile in Medieval and Renaissance Italy*. Berkeley: University of California Press, 1982.
Straub, Julia. *A Victorian Muse: The Afterlife of Dante's Beatrice in Nineteenth-Century Literature*. London: Continuum, 2009.
Straumann, Heinrich. 'Four Letters to Martha Fleischmann'. *Letters of James Joyce*. vol. 2. Ed. Richard Ellmann. New York: Viking Press, 1966. 426–31.
Strohm, Paul. *Hochon's Arrow: The Social Imagination of Fourteenth-Century Texts*. Princeton: Princeton University Press, 1992.
Sullivan, Kevin. *Joyce Among the Jesuits*. New York: Columbia University Press, 1958.
Surette, Leon and Tryphonopoulos, Demtres, eds. *'I Cease Not to Yowl': Ezra Pound's Letters to Olivia Rossetti Agresti*. Urbana: University of Illinois Press, 1998.
Terrinoni, Enrico. *Leggere, tradurre, interpretare: percorsi letterari possibili d'Inghilterra e Irlanda*. Latina: Yorick Libri, 2006.

Tindall, William York. *A Reader's Guide to James Joyce*. London: Thames and Hudson, 1959.
Tinker-Villani, Valeria. *Visions of Dante in English Poetry*. Amsterdam: Rodopi, 1989.
Trone, George Andrew. 'Exile'. *The Dante Encyclopedia*. Ed. Richard Lansing. New York: Garland Publishing, Inc., 2000. 362–5.
Vaglio, Carla Marengo. '*Giacomo Joyce* or the *Vita Nuova*'. *Fin de Siècle and Italy*. Ed. Franca Ruggieri. Joyce Studies in Italy 5. Rome: Bluzoni Editore, 1998. 91–106.
Vance, Eugene. *Mervelous Signals: Poetics and Sign Theory in the Middle Ages*. Lincoln: University of Nebraska Press, 1986.
Vitoux, Pierre. 'Aristotle, Berkeley, and Newman in "Proteus" and *Finnegans Wake*'. *James Joyce Quarterly* 18 (1981). 161–75.
Warner, Marina. *Alone of All Her Sex: The Myth and Cult of the Virgin Mary*. 2nd ed. Oxford: Oxford University Press, 2013.
Webb, Timothy. 'Stories of Rimini: Leigh Hunt, Byron and the Fate of Francesca'. *Dante in the Nineteenth Century: Reception, Portrayal, Popularization*. Ed. Nick Havely. Oxford and Bern: Peter Lang, 2011. 31–54.
Weininger, Otto. *Sex and Character: An Investigation of Fundamental Principles*. Ed. Daniel Steuer and Laura Marcus. Bloomington: Indiana University Press, 2005.
Weir, David. '"A Little Cloud": New Light on the Title'. *James Joyce Quarterly* 17 (1980). 301–2.
Wilhelm, James J. *Dante and Pound: The Epic of Judgement*. Orono: University of Maine Press, 1974.
Worthington, Kim. *Self as Narrative: Subjectivity and Community in Contemporary Fiction*. Oxford: Clarendon Press, 1996.
Yates, Frances A. *The Art of Memory*. Chicago: Chicago University Press, 1966.
Zacchetti, Corrado. *Shelley e Dante*. Milan: Sandron, 1922.

Index

Abelard, Peter, 196 n. 73
Agresti, Antonio, 48 n. 36, 48–50, 54, 76
Agresti, Olivia Rossetti, 48 n. 36
ALP. (Anna Livia Plurabelle) 161–63, 180
Aquinas, Thomas, Saint, 29, 95, 97, 107 n. 56, 134, 142, 148
Arezzo, 44
Aristotle, 54, 87, 95–98, 101, 107, 111, 121, 133–34, 148, 162
Armstrong, Guyda, 118 n. 76
Artifoni, Almidano, 27–28, 27 n. 63, 30, 91
Ascoli, Albert, 2 n. 2, 145 n. 69, 147
Asiatic Society of Mumbai, 19
Attridge, Derek, 78, 93 n. 27, 121 n. 78, 123, 128, 138, 138 n. 46, 158 n. 89
Augustine of Hippo, Saint, 134, 134 n. 39, 142, 148, 148 n. 77
Avicenna (Ibn Sina), 142

Barbi, Michele, 168
Barolini, Teodolinda, 22 n. 44, 106 n. 54
Beckett, Samuel, 4, 57 n. 61, 170–71
Bellarmine, Roberto, Cardinal, 17, 19
Belvedere College, 11–12, 19, 24–27, 33
Benjamin, Walter, 139
Bennassuti, Luigi, 20–21, 23, 32
Benstock, Shari, 190
Bergamo, 27, 29
Berkeley, George, 95, 97
Bertha, 70, 71–73
Betti, Franco, 14, 16–17
Bettinelli, Saverio, 15
 references to works
  Lettere Virgiliane, 14–15, 18, 47 n. 32
Blake, William, 35
Bloom, Leopold, 91, 119, 125, 128
 and family, 130–31, 157–58
 and Stephen Dedalus, 121
 and the Citizen, 131–32, 155–57
 memory of, 129–31, 149–51

Bloom, Molly, 46 n. 27, 119, 157, 163
Bloom, Rudy, 157–58
Boccaccio, Giovanni, 104–105 n. 49, 105 n. 51, 106 n. 55, 112, 115, 117–18, 118 n. 76, 122
 references to works
  Decameron, 104–07, 105 n. 50, 119–20
  Vita di Dante, 118
Boldrini, Lucia, 5, 7, 99, 101, 164, 190
Boyd, Henry, 24
Bradley, Bruce, 24
Brown, Richard, 127
Bruno, Giordano, 33
Budgen, Frank, 81 n. 1, 82 n. 6, 98, 102
Burnet, John, 96 n. 35
Byrne, John Francis, 25–26
Byron, George Gordon, Lord, 23, 43, 46–47, 47 n. 32, 50–51, 54, 165
 references to works
  'Age of Bronze', 47, 50
  'Prophecy of Dante, The', 47

Camerini, Eugenio, 30–33, 49, 54, 91 n. 23, 100 n. 44, 113, 118, 126, 148
 references to works
  'Vita di Dante', 50–51, 67–68, 71, 114, 118 n. 77
Carlucci, Rocco, 48
Carlyle, Thomas, 23
Carruthers, Mary, 133–34 n. 37, 142 n. 60, 143–45, 145 n. 69, 193
Carson, Ciaran, 207
Cary, Henry Francis, 23–24
Casini, Tommaso, 140, 168, 177
Catholic Encyclopedia, 21
Cavalcanti, Guido, 3, 3 n. 8, 43, 104–07, 105 n. 51, 107 n. 56, 112, 115, 118, 122, 162 n. 6, 168, 197
Christian Brothers, 12
Ciccarelli, Andrea, 53 n. 50

227

Index

Cicero, Marcus Tullius, 45
Cixous, Hélène, 7, 30 n. 74, 37, 64, 72 n. 79, 74, 78–9, 82 n. 7, 86, 112, 112 n. 66, 124
Clongowes Wood College, 12, 24, 61, 102
community
    city as, 158–59, 161–62, 201–02
    communitas, 197, 202, 204–05
    family as, 161–62, 165, 201–02, 204
    textual forms of, 80, 88, 109, 122, 204
Compagni, Dino, 105 n. 51
Contini, Gianfranco, 145, 177 n. 43
Copeland, Rita, 145 n. 72
Corti, Claudia, 70

d'Azeglio, Massimo, 32
Daedalus, Stephen, 26–28, 34–35, 34 n. 85, 46, 114
Dante
    and anti-papalism, 17–19, 21–22, 35
    and Beatrice, 58, 60–62, 64, 83–84, 166–67, 197
    and community, 64, 161–62, 201–02, 204
    and eroticism, 177–78, 183–85, 189, 195–96, 197–99
    and exile, 7, 9, 41, 42–47, 49–51, 54–56, 67–68, 74–75, 77, 112 n. 66, 205
    and femininity, 162, 173, 176, 177–79, 183–86, 189, 195–97, 201–02
    and Florence, 43–44, 50, 67–69, 89–90
    and imagination, 134–36
    and memory, 9, 134–36, 142, 146
    and return from exile, 67–69, 73
    as heterodox author, 33–36, 39
    Catholic commentaries on, 19–21
    Catholic interpretations of, 13, 13 n. 7, 17, 18–23, 32–35, 54, 57
    cosmology of, 125
    metamorphosis, writings on, 87, 99–102, 116, 120
    narratives of the life of, 32, 43–44, 50–51, 67–68, 118
    political readings of, 17–18, 20, 22–23, 36, 43, 45–47, 49–53, 56–57
    references to works
        Commedia
            (generally), 2, 5, 12, 17, 20–21, 34, 41, 44, 56–57, 64, 85, 130, 162, 203, 205
            fiction in, 117–18, 136, 142, 146–47
            hermeneutics in, 89–91, 94
            textuality of, 145–47
            visionary mode of, 136–37
        Convivio, xi, 34, 44, 54–55, 57, 68, 93 n. 28, 97, 134, 141 n. 54, 145 n. 69, 162, 211
        De Vulgari Eloquentia, 4 n. 13, 17, 34, 44, 57
        Epistolae, 67–68

Inferno (generally), 47, 90, 125
    1, 31, 32–33 n. 82, 78, 84–85, 91, 116–17; **2**, 135–36, 148, 162, 170, 173, 175–76, 198; **3**, 8, 90, 94; **4**, 96–98 n. 35; **5**, 164, 178, 181 n. 50, 188–89, 191–95; **9**, 89; **10**, 106, 136–37; **15**, 91, 91 n. 23, 114–15, 131 n. 29; **17**, 136–37; **18**, 202–03; **21**, 110; **24**, 99–101, 108 n. 57, 116, 120; **25**, 116; **26**, 165–67; **32**, 208; **33**, 208
Monarchia, 13 n. 8, 17–19, 21–22, 32, 34, 44, 57
Paradiso (canto numbers in bold)
    (generally), 84, 125, 198, 201, 205
    1, 90, 135; **2**, 90; **9**, 101–02; **15**, 131 n. 29, 162, 201–02; **16**, 131 n. 29, 162, 201; **17**, 44, 50, 73, 131 n. 29, 162, 201; **25**, 50, 56, 68–69, 79; **26**, 55 n. 57; **29**, 13 n. 8; **30**, 64; **33**, 90, 135
Purgatorio (canto numbers in bold)
    (generally), 84, 125
    1, 76; **8**, 191–92; **9**, 90; **17**, 135; **25**, 32; **28**, 1–2, 84, 182, 197, 197 n. 74, 223; **30**, 146–47, 166, 185–86, 197–98; **31**, 70, 75–76, 88, 146–47
Rime (lyric poetry), 69, 162, 177–78, 183–84, 196, 198–99
'Deh, Vïoletta'/'Deh, nuvoletta', 167–71, 173, 177, 189
'Tre donne intorno', 56
Vita Nuova, 5, 9, 41, 47 n. 33, 47–48, 57 n. 61, 56–66, 82–83, 85, 141, 149, 168, 176 n. 41, 176–77, 191, 198–99
    'screen lady', 59–60
    death of Beatrice, 166–67, 177, 197
    silence in, 58–59, 62, 66, 71, 92
    subjectivity and alienation in, 58–60, 69, 79
    textuality of, 139–46
secular interpretations of, 13, 13 n. 7, 16–18, 20, 23, 32, 34–35, 46, 54
De Amicis, Edmondo, 25
de Petris, Carla, 70
de Rubris, Marco, 48, 126, 139, 147, 166, 173
Dedalus, Stephen, 1, 9, 28, 74, 82, 152, 208
    alienation of, 28, 41, 60–62, 64–66, 74–75, 86, 88–89, 91–92
    and family, 64, 128
    and Leopold Bloom, 121
    intellect of, 95–98, 102, 107–09, 111 n. 62
    representation of, 78–80, 87 n. 17, 85–89, 91, 96–98, 102–04, 107–09, 110–22, 198, 205

Index

self-fashioning of, 39–40, 57, 60–62, 64–66, 73–74, 85, 88–89, 92, 102–07, 114–17, 122, 198
silence of, 62, 64, 66, 74, 78, 92–95
del Greco Lobner, Corinna, 191
Del Poggetto, Pietro, 19
della Scala, Cangrande, 44, 50
Derrida, Jacques, 40 n. 9, 86–87 n. 15, 145 n. 72
di Canossa, Luigi, Cardinal, 20–21
Dublin, 4, 37, 69, 125
  compared to Trieste, 53–54
Duggan, Christopher, 18

Eco, Umberto, 3–4, 42, 96, 99
Edinburgh Review, 14–16
Eliot, Thomas Stearns, 3, 125, 147 n. 74, 206, 208–09
Ellis, Steve, 6 n. 19, 46
Ellmann, Richard, 2, 29, 82 n. 6, 85
Elphinstone, Mountstuart, 19
exile
  exile of, 38–39, 41, 74–76, 78–80, 86, 88–89, 91–92, 102–04, 112, 112 n. 66, 158–59, 200
  and identity, 39–41, 56, 58, 67–69, 71, 73–74, 80, 92
  and Italian nationalism, 44–45, 47, 49, 51–52
  and memory, 158–59
  and rhetoric, 38–40, 42, 49, 52, 56, 69–70, 74–75, 78–79, 92, 200
  as hermeneutic, 37
  as mode of alienation, 37, 39, 41, 55–56, 58–60, 62–64, 67, 69, 74–75, 77–79, 88–89, 200
  Irish tradition of, 42
  literary tradition of, 42–43, 45–47
  medieval forms of, 54
  political forms of, 42–45, 49, 56, 67, 77
  spiritual forms of, 55–58, 60, 63–64, 67, 77

Felicetti, Lorenzo, 19
Ferrer, Daniel, 124, 129
Ferrero, Guglielmo, 165
Fleischmann, Marthe, 84 n. 11, 85 n. 13, 81–87, 87 n. 16, 116, 122, 166
Florence, 13 n. 7, 32, 43–44, 66, 89–90, 202
Forster, Edward Morgan, 127, 129 n. 25, 132
Foscolo, Ugo, 14–16, 18, 18 n. 30, 20, 22, 44–45, 46 n. 27, 51
Francis, Saint, 21
Franke, William, 89 n. 21
Futurism, 53

Gabbrielli, Cante de', 51
Gabler, Hans Walter, 88, 102, 130, 132, 147, 149, 154

Galileo, Galilei, 196 n. 72
Gardner, Edmund, 21, 21 n. 42, 218
Garibaldi, Giuseppe, 32
Genesis, 179, 196
Ghezzi, Charles, 27–30, 33–34, 107 n. 56
Giamboni, Bono, 113, 113 n. 68
Gilbert, Stuart, 127
Giotto di Bondone, 48
Glasheen, Adaline, 164 n. 14
Gogarty, Oliver St John, 2
Gorman, Herbert, 24, 29, 206
Gorni, Guglielmo, 141
Gottfried, Roy, 33
Greenblatt, Stephen, 41 n. 12
Gregory, Isabella Augusta, Lady, 38–39, 78
Guelpa, Luigi, 52
Gültekin, Cevad, 52 n. 49

Haidu, Peter, 40 n. 7
Hand, Robert, 71–73
Havely, Nick, 2 n. 2, 6 n. 19, 13 n. 8, 19 n. 33, 43 n. 20, 75 n. 81, 91 n. 26, 194 n. 69
Hayman, David, 163
HCE. (H. C. Earwicker), 161, 175, 192
Heaney, Seamus, 3, 159–60, 207–10, 213, 222
  references to works
  'Envies and Identifications: Dante and the Modern Poet', 3, 209–10
  Field Work, 208
  'Strand at Lough Beg, The', 208
  'Ugolino', 208–09
  Human Chain, 208
  Spirit Level, The
  'Flight Path, The', 208–09
  Station Island
  'Station Island', 210
Heidegger, Martin, 145 n. 72
Heloise d'Argenteuil, 196 n. 73
Homer
  references to works
  Odyssey, The, 98, 98 n. 40, 100–01
homo viator, 55–56, 60, 63, 77, 90
Hughes, Ted, 206–07
Hunt, Leigh, 162, 204
  references to works
  Story of Rimini, The, 194–95, 195 n. 70

Ibsen, Henrik, 23, 34, 43, 43 n. 19
India, 19, 29
irridentism, 52–53, 53 n. 51
Issy, 9–10, 161, 163–64
  and her parents, 163–65, 180–81, 192
  and light, 174
  and Shaun, 164, 174–75, 178–79, 200–03
  and Shem, 174–75, 178–79, 192, 194–95, 200–01, 203

Issy (*cont.*)
  as intercessor, 174–79
  as Izod, 172, 180–82, 184–85, 187–88,
    191–92, 195–96, 198–201
  as locus of community, 198, 200–03, 205
  as locus of exile, 198–200, 203
  as Nuvoletta, 164–68, 171, 173, 178–82,
    179 n. 47, 186, 203–04
  as textual focus, 164–65
  eroticism of, 178–79, 184–85, 192, 194–96, 199,
    201, 203
  intertextual identity of, 204
  reading, 191–92, 194–96

Jansenism, 14–16, 18
Jesuits, 9, 11–13, 32
  and the Jansenists, 14–16
  attitudes to Dante, 13–16, 18–22, 25, 33
  Ratio Studiorum, 26–27
  suppression of, 16–17
Johnson, Samuel, 96
Jossa, Stefano, 20 n. 35, 51
Joyce, James
  and 'exile', 7, 9, 37–40, 42, 54, 69–70, 73,
    78–80, 122, 199
  and Italian language, 11, 24–25, 29
  and Jesuits, 9, 11–13, 24–25, 57
  and Lucia Joyce, 170, 170 n. 32, 179
  and return from 'exile', 69–70
  editions of Dante used by, 5–6, 30–32, 30 n. 73,
    47–51, 60, 67–68, 71, 82–83, 91 n. 23,
    100 n. 44, 113, 113 n. 68, 117–18, 126,
    139, 147–48, 166, 168, 173
  education of, 2, 4, 9, 11–13, 24–27, 29, 33,
    107 n. 56
  in Trieste, 23, 30, 52–53, 53 n. 51, 54
  manuscripts, 5, 11, 24, 31
  modelling self on Dante, 81–87, 87 n. 16, 122
  notes on Dante, 11, 24, 26 n. 61, 31, 32–33 n. 82,
    57 n. 61, 106–07, 117
  reading Dante, 2, 4, 5, 7, 9, 11, 27, 30, 31–32,
    33–35, 48, 57 n. 61, 122, 126, 147,
    148, 162
  reading Guido Cavalcanti, 107 n. 56
  references to works
    'Aristotle on Education', 96–97 n. 35
    Brilliant Career, A, 39 n. 5
    '*Catilina*', 23, 46
    Dream Stuff, 39 n. 5
    Dubliners, 7–8, 25, 106 n. 55, 165–66
    Exiles, 7, 37, 41, 57, 70–74, 91, 161, 166
      and narrative, 71–72, 72 n. 79
      discourse of identity in, 71–73 *see also*
        Bertha; Hand, Robert; Justice,
        Beatrice; Rowan, Richard

Finnegans Wake, 5, 7, 155, 180, 203, 205
  chapters
    I.6 ('Nuvoletta'), 164–65, 166, 167,
      169–70, 171–80, 186
    I.6 ('The Mookse and The Gripes'),
      164, 166
    II.1 ('dantellising peaches'), 188,
      190–92, 194–96
    II.1 ('The Mime of Mick, Nick and
      the Maggies'), 164, 172, 181–82,
      184–88, 198–204
    II.2, 164, 189–90, 190 n. 59
    III.2, 164, 190
    III.4, 179 n. 47
  family as community in, 161, 165,
    180–81, 201, 203–04
  Floras, the, 182, 184–87
  heliotrope, 182–85, 187
  hermeneutics in, 191–92, 195
  incest in, 151, 163, 192, 200–01, 203–04
  Rainbow Girls, the, 172, 174, 186–87
  recursion in, 194 n. 68, 194–96
Giacomo Joyce, 57, 148 n. 76
Letters, 29, 38–40, 69, 78–79, 81–87,
  87 n. 16, 107 n. 56, 165, 179, 186
'L'Irlanda isola dei santi e dei
  savi', 23–24
'Portrait of the Artist, A' (essay), 37–38,
  46, 79
Portrait of the Artist as a Young Man, A, 7,
  37–38, 41, 46, 49 n. 40, 57, 60–62,
  61 n. 63, 75–76, 77 n. 83, 77–79,
  88–89, 95, 103–04, 108, 129, 158,
  161, 198, 205, 208
  'bird-girl', 1–2, 61, 84
  silence in, 61–62, 66, 92
  Stephen's diary, 28, 38, 76–79, 85, 88
  villanelle scene, 62–66 *see also* Dedalus,
    Stephen
Stephen Hero, 5, 11, 15 n. 17, 26–28, 30,
  34 n. 85, 46, 61 n. 63, 114
  encounter with the President, 34–35 *see
    also* Daedalus, Stephen
Ulysses, 5, 7, 9, 57, 85–86, 119, 155–61,
  198
  and history, 9, 127, 132, 153–54, 158–60
  and memory, 129–33, 137–38, 149–53
  and origination, 151–57
  and realism, 128, 136–38
  chapters
    'Aeolus', 109
    'Circe', 9, 87 n. 16, 119, 123–25,
      127–33, 137–38, 148–59
    'Cyclops', 123, 129, 131, 155–57
    'Eumaeus', 128, 155–57

Index

'Ithaca', 121
'Lotus Eaters', 150
'Nausicaa', 129, 157, 183, 198 n. 74
'Nestor', 132, 152–53
'Oxen of the Sun', 100 n. 44, 123–24, 129
'Penelope', 157
'Proteus', 9, 87–89, 92, 94–99, 102–04, 108–09, 111, 115, 118, 120, 126, 158–59
'Scylla and Charybdis', 9, 81, 87, 109–13, 115–21, 141 n. 54
'Sirens', 81 n. 1, 123
'Telemachus', 88, 91–94, 102, 104, 120, 152–53
'Wandering Rocks', 28
  fantasy in, 127–28, 131–32, 137–38, 150–51
  hallucination in, 127–29, 132, 150–51
  hermeneutics in, 89, 93–95, 102–04, 110
  interior monologue in, 93–95, 93 n. 27
  metamorphosis in, 98–99, 107–09, 111–12
  poetics of, 74, 87, 97–98, 107–08, 111–16, 118–22, 125–26, 138, 159, 200, 205
  schemas, 98, 127, 131, 133
  silence in, 92–95
  technics, 126–33, 137–38, 150
  textuality of, 124, 126–30, 132–33, 138, 148–60
  writing of, 81, 81 n. 1, 85, 147, 147 n. 75, 154 *see also* Artifoni, Almidano; Bloom, Leopold; Bloom, Molly; Bloom, Rudy; Dedalus, Stephen; Kelly, Bridie; MacDowell, Gerty; Mulligan, Buck
Joyce, Lucia, 169–71, 174, 179–80
Joyce, Nora, 37, 179
Joyce, Stanislaus, 8, 29–30, 30 n. 70, 35, 39
Justice, Beatrice, 70–73, 166

Kafka, Franz, 158
Kelly, Bridie, 129–30, 137
Kenner, Hugh, 95, 128
Kiberd, Declan, 95–96
Kinsella, Thomas, 207
Kumar, Udaya, 128, 132

Lami, Giovanni, 15–16, 18
Laria, Vincenzo, 140
Latini, Brunetto, 87, 114–16, 114 n. 71, 122
  references to works
  Livres dou Tresor, Les, 112–13, 113 n. 70, 115
  Tesoro, 113, 113 n. 68, 113 n. 70, 115–16
Lernout, Geert, 36

Livorni, Ernesto, 95, 97
London, 49
Loup, Mr (Joyce's teacher), 24
Loyola, Ignatius, Saint, 21
Lucia, Saint, 162, 170, 175
Lucifer, 55, 65

MacCabe, Colin, 130
MacDowell, Gerty, 129, 157
Macrì-Leone, Francesco, 118
Maddox, Brenda, 81 n. 2, 82 n. 6
Maeterlinck, Maurice, 34
Mahaffey, Vicki, 47 n. 33, 70–71, 132–33, 142 n. 59, 148, 152–53
Mandelstam, Osip, 209
Manganiello, Dominic, 30 n. 72, 42, 53
Manzoni, Alessandro, 45 n. 25
Marsh's Library, Dublin, 34, 34 n. 85
Mary, the Virgin, 162, 175–76
Mazzini, Giuseppe, 18, 18 n. 30, 32, 44–45, 52
Mazzotta, Giuseppe, 89 n. 21, 93 n. 28, 141 n. 55
memory
  and exile, 126
  and imagination, 131–34, 136, 142, 146–47
  and rhetoric, 142–43
  creative forms of, 136, 139, 142–55, 148 n. 77, 149–55, 157–60
  medieval theories of, 133–134, 133–134 n. 37, 148
  recollective forms of, 126, 133, 151–52, 158–59
  textual forms of, 130, 132–33, 142, 145–47, 149–51, 154–55, 157–58
Metastasio, Pietro, 25
Milan, 70
Milanesi, Gaetano, 118
Milbank, Alison, 6 n. 19
Milne, Alan Alexander, 172, 172 n. 38
Milton, John, 109–10
Minnis, Alistair, 142 n. 58
Moore, Edward, 12, 168–69, 169 n. 28
Mulligan, Buck, 91–94, 104, 107, 119
Mullin, Katherine, 8 n. 23
Mumbai, 19
Musa, Mark, 139
Myers, Lucas, 206

Nagel, Thomas, 40–41
National Library of Ireland, 11, 11 n. 1, 34, 61, 64, 109–10, 118, 212, 218–20
Nationalism
  Irish, 30 n. 72, 53, 186, 199
  Italian, 15–18, 30, 30 n. 72, 32, 44–45, 47, 51–53
Newman, John Henry, Cardinal, 19, 95
Norris, Margot, 111 n. 62, 182, 184

Index

O'Donoghue, Bernard, 207, 209
Orwell, George, 158
Ovid, 99
Oxford Dante Society, 12

Papacy
  and the Risorgimento, 17
  condemnation of Dante's *Monarchia* by,
    18–19, 32
  encyclicals on Dante, 21–22
  Popes
    Benedict XV, 22
    Boniface VIII, 32, 43, 51
    Clement XIV, 16
    John XXII, 32
    Leo XIII, 20–22
Parandowski, Jan, 148 n. 77
Paris, 38
Parsons, Robert, 13, 22
peregrinatio, 55, 63, 197, 205
Petrarch, Francesco, 14, 162 n. 6, 190 n. 59
Picone, Michelangelo, 141–42
Piedmont, 32
pilgrimage, 55
Pisacane, Carlo, 53–54, 76
Plato, 111, 121
Pola, 39
Polhemus, Robert, 191
Polidori, Gaetano, 19–20
Pound, Ezra, 3, 48 n. 36, 107 n. 56, 125, 169,
    169 n. 28, 177, 206
Pre-Raphaelite Brotherhood, 48, 49 n. 40
Prezioso, Roberto, 53
Pugliatti, Paola, 94–95, 95 n. 30, 110

Quintilian, Marcus Fabus, 142

Rabaté, Jean-Michel, 37 n. 1, 79
Ravenna, 17, 44
Reichert, Klaus, 23
Reynolds, Mary, 5, 7, 12, 26, 30, 32, 47, 62, 64,
    70, 75, 106, 113 n. 70, 164–66, 190
Risorgimento, Italian, 13, 15–18, 20, 22, 30,
    30 n. 72, 32, 36, 50–54, 206
  in Trieste, 52–53, 53 n. 50
  myth of exile, 44–47, 49, 51–52, 56–57, 73–78
Ritelli, Luigi, 19
Rossetti, Dante Gabriel, 20, 47 n. 33, 47–51, 54,
    84 n. 9, 84–85, 162, 204, 206
  Dante paintings of, 48, 60, 82–83, 166
  references to works
    'Blessed Damozel, The', 173, 180 n. 49,
      187 n. 55
    'Dante at Verona', 49–50
Rossetti, Gabriele, 49–50

Rossetti, William Michael, 49 n. 40
Rowan, Richard, 41, 70–71, 80, 91–92, 126
  self-fashioning of, 71–74
Royal University of Ireland, 27
Ruskin, John, 2, 36
Ryan, Francis, 24–25

Salvini, A.M., 118
Scott, Bonnie Kime, 163
Scott, Walter, Sir
  references to works
    Ivanhoe, 25
Segni, Bardo, 168
Seigel, Jerrold, 40 n. 6
Shakespeare, William, 81–82, 87, 111, 117–20
Shaun, 161
  as Chuff, 181
  as The Mookse, 174–75
Sheehy, Eugene, 27, 29
Shelley, Percy Bysshe, 23, 43, 46, 47 n. 32
Shelton, Jen, 169
Shem, 161, 190 n. 59
  as 'exile', 198–200
  as Glugg, 181, 187–88, 192, 198–99
  as The Gripes, 174–75
Siena, 44
Slataper, Scipio, 52, 53 n. 51
Società Dante Alighieri, 52–53, 52 n. 49
Sorio, Bartolomeo, 19
Spoo, Robert, 165
Straumann, Heinrich, 84, 84 n. 11
subjectivity, 40–41, 58–59, 64–67, 71, 73–74
  and metamorphosis, 101
Svevo, Italo, 70–71

Tennyson, Alfred, Lord, 195 n. 70
textuality
  and authority, 144–46, 151–55
  and hermeneutics, 143, 147
  and memory, 130, 132–33, 146–47, 149–51
  and rhetoric, 143, 147
  medieval forms of, 126–27, 139–45
Thompson, Edith, 196
Toynbee, Paget, 12
Trieste, 23, 30, 199
  compared to Dublin, 53–54
  Italian nationalism in, 52–53, 53 n. 50
  Società Dante Alighieri in, 52–53, 52 n. 49
Truth and Reconciliation Commission (South
    Africa), 159
Turin, 32, 48

University College Dublin, 2, 11 n. 3, 11–12, 27,
    29–30, 33–35

van Hulle, Dirk, 11, 26, 31
Vasto, 49
Venice, 29
Verona, 20, 44, 47, 50
Virgil, 14, 98 n. 40, 109
  references to works
  Aeneid, 136 n. 43
  Georgics, 100, 100 n. 44
Voce, La, 52
vociani, 52, 53 n. 51, 53–54

Wagner, Richard, 159

Walcott, Derek, 207
Weaver, Harriet Shaw, 186
Wönecke, Mathilde, 170
Wordsworth, William, 172

Yeats, William Butler, 35–36, 110, 171, 171 n. 35, 204, 207

Zaccheti, Corrado, 47 n. 32
Zola, Émile, 26 n. 56
Zurich, 81